Joyce and Hagiography

⚜

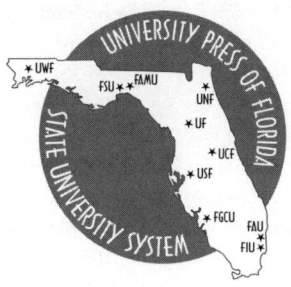

Florida A&M University, Tallahassee
Florida Atlantic University, Boca Raton
Florida Gulf Coast University, Fort Myers
Florida International University, Miami
Florida State University, Tallahassee
University of Central Florida, Orlando
University of Florida, Gainesville
University of North Florida, Jacksonville
University of South Florida, Tampa
University of West Florida, Pensacola

The Florida James Joyce Series
Edited by Zack Bowen

The Autobiographical Novel of Co-Consciousness: Goncharov, Woolf, and Joyce, by Galya Diment (1994)

Bloom's Old Sweet Song: Essays on Joyce and Music, by Zack Bowen (1995)

Joyce's Iritis and the Irritated Text: The Dis-lexic Ulysses, by Roy Gottfried (1995)

Joyce, Milton, and the Theory of Influence, by Patrick Colm Hogan (1995)

Reauthorizing Joyce, by Vicki Mahaffey (paperback edition, 1995)

Shaw and Joyce: "The Last Word in Stolentelling," by Martha Fodaski Black (1995)

Bely, Joyce, Döblin: Peripatetics in the City Novel, by Peter I. Barta (1996)

Jocoserious Joyce: The Fate of Folly in Ulysses, by Robert H. Bell (paperback edition, 1996)

Joyce and Popular Culture, edited by R. B. Kershner (1996)

Joyce and the Jews: Culture and Texts, by Ira B. Nadel (paperback edition, 1996)

Narrative Design in Finnegans Wake: *The Wake Lock Picked,* by Harry Burrell (1996)

Gender in Joyce, edited by Jolanta W. Wawrzycka and Marlena G. Corcoran (1997)

Latin and Roman Culture in Joyce, by R. J. Schork (1997)

Reading Joyce Politically, by Trevor L. Williams (1997)

Advertising and Commodity Culture in Joyce, by Garry Leonard (1998)

Greek and Hellenic Culture in Joyce, by R. J. Schork (1998)

Joyce, Joyceans, and the Rhetoric of Citation, by Eloise Knowlton (1998)

Joyce's Music and Noise: Theme and Variation in His Writings, by Jack W. Weaver (1998)

Reading Derrida Reading Joyce, by Alan Roughley (1999)

Joyce through the Ages: A Nonlinear View, edited by Michael Patrick Gillespie (1999)

Chaos Theory and James Joyce's Everyman, by Peter Francis Mackey (1999)

Joyce's Comic Portrait, by Roy Gottfried (2000)

Joyce and Hagiography: Saints Above!, by R. J. Schork (2000)

Joyce and Hagiography

Saints Above!

R. J. Schork

University Press of Florida

GAINESVILLE   TALLAHASSEE   TAMPA
BOCA RATON   PENSACOLA   ORLANDO
MIAMI   JACKSONVILLE   FT. MYERS

Copyright 2000 by the Board of Regents of the State of Florida
Printed in the United States of America on acid-free paper
All rights reserved

05 04 03 02 01 00 6 5 4 3 2 1

Library of Congress Cataloging-in-Publication Data
Schork, R. J., 1933-
Joyce and hagiography: saints above! / R. J. Schork.
p. cm.
—(The Florida James Joyce series)
Includes bibliographical references (p.) and index.
ISBN 0-8130-1780-7 (alk. paper)
1. Joyce, James, 1882-1941—Religion. 2. Christianity and literature—Ireland—
History—20th century. 3. Christian saints in literature. I. Title. II. Series.
PR6019.09 Z87 2000
823'.912—dc21 00-009248

The University Press of Florida is the scholarly publishing agency for the State University System of Florida, comprising Florida A&M University, Florida Atlantic University, Florida Gulf Coast University Florida International University, Florida State University, University of Central Florida, University of Florida, University of North Florida, University of South Florida, and University of West Florida.

University Press of Florida
15 Northwest 15th Street
Gainesville, FL 32611-2079
http://www.upf.com

Sophiae Helenae Clarke
delectatio sponsionibus ollisque

CONTENTS

Foreword by Zack Bowen   ix

Preface   xi

Abbreviations   xv

1. Introduction   1
2. Archangels; Saints in the Gospels   17
3. The Apostolic Age   30
4. The Early Church   50
5. The Hairy Hermit   73
6. Irish and Other Celtic Saints   86
7. Medieval to Modern Times   108
8. Founders and Religious Orders   134
9. Relics, Symbols, Pilgrimages, and Feasts   153
10. Fictitious Saints   180
11. Sources and Parallels   188

Notes   197

Bibliography   221

Index   231

Foreword

Like R. J. Schork's previous compendia on Joyce and the Greek and Latin language, literature, and culture, his new volume is encyclopedic in treating Joyce's use of the literature of sainthood, beginning with the apostles and proceeding chronologically through the centuries of Roman Catholicism. His chapters encompass both periods and types. Containing much of his previously published material (from a score of previously published articles) and a great deal more, it is an indispensable tool to any reader interested in the hundreds of allusions to the saints (and would-be saints) and the way their own stories are all woven into the comic fabric of Joyce's work.

Schork never claims to supply any sort of skeleton key to the total understanding of Joyce's work, even as he meticulously documents the author's indebtedness to his Irish Jesuit training and his mining of ecclesiastical history and legend in each of his works. Schork focuses not only on well-known biblical and historical figures, but also on the relevant data on relics, pilgrimages, feasts, and fictitious saints.

Zack Bowen
SERIES EDITOR

Preface

I would not want to place serious money on a claim that James Joyce himself ever uttered my subtitular phrase, "Saints above!" On the other hand, all sorts of saints—genuine and bogus, famous and obscure, from the first martyrs in Jerusalem to a newly canonized Passionist priest—hover over his fiction and peek in from the margins of his correspondence. This book deals with the diverse manifestations of these religious heroes and heroines in Joyce's life and works. I plan another study that will focus on Joycean misappropriation of scripture and Catholic ritual. Naturally the division between these two topics has not been infallibly defined, and there is bound to be some overlap. Old Testament "saints" (holy men and women of the Mosaic covenant whose presence is deeply felt in Christian culture and ceremony) will be discussed in the later work, as are most of the angels. A major chapter in the volume on scripture will deal with the paramount New Testament saint, the Virgin Mary, in her manifold appearances and titles. With the exception, then, of two well-known archangels and several heroes and heroines of the gospels and apostolic era, the emphasis in this hagiographical volume falls primarily on those saints traditionally or formally canonized by the Roman Catholic Church. If all of this sounds a bit too sectarian, readers should rest assured that my project is rarely—and then only to give necessary background—concerned with theology, dogma, or matters of deep devotion. Rather, responding to its fictional and biographical sources, it is meant to be a monument to ecumenical irreverence.

Most of the textual citation comes from *Ulysses* and *Finnegans Wake*, precisely because most Joycean hagiography is deployed for humorous purposes, in distinctly surrealistic settings, and the final two works are where the zany comic action is. Since the literary techniques and narrative thrust of these fictional enterprises are frequently perplexing to many readers, I attempt to provide explanatory background for the obviously obscure passages. Many of the citations from *Finnegans Wake* involve purely verbal humor, which a discreet philological prod or two can help to explicate. Evidence from archival data (especially the *Wake* notebooks) is an important component of my presentation, because Joyce used not only the occasional scholarly study, but more frequently popular books about saints, their feasts, and symbols and the pan-European allusive force of hagiography. The connection between a source document and the *Wake's* text can often be detected only when its original pre-textual form is revealed. Moreover, in addition to Joyce's natural predilection for seeing an earthy aspect in supernatural phenomena, these sources provided congenial material for inclusion, with a latitudinarian chuckle, into his last "work-in-progress." In Joyce's fiction apostolic zealots, mutilated virgins, Celtic wanderers, stigmatic friars, Counter Reformation founders, ecstatic mystic-poets, and edifying figments of pious imagination earn their praise and take their lumps.

Documentary references in several ancient and modern languages have been fully translated. Careful attention has also been given to supplying a narrative setting for biblical citations and a chronological-cultural orientation for unfamiliar historical events. The only prerequisite definitions involve the official certification process for saints in the Roman Catholic Church. Simply put, there are three steps in the sometimes long path to formal sainthood: first, a papally appointed committee names a candidate "Venerable" (as, for example, the early English monk-chronicler Bede); next, more evidence of a holy and doctrinally sound life leads to the title of "Blessed" (as for the seventeenth-century Native American Kateri Tekakwitha, known as the "Lily of the Mohawks"); finally, authentication of patronal miracles and other proofs of supernatural distinction culminate in a pontifical proclamation that the applicant deserves to be called a "Saint." (A concise explanation of this process is included in the introduction to Attwater and John's *Penguin Dictionary of Saints;* more details and contemporary examples are found in Woodward's *Making Saints.*)

I take for granted that readers can refer to Gifford and Seidman's *"Ulysses" Annotated,* McHugh's *Annotations to "Finnegans Wake,"* and Glasheen's *Third Census of "Finnegans Wake."* None of these guides is complete or without occasional error, but each is a necessary resource and a source of useful information of every kind. It is also necessary to repeat a critical caveat: my hagiographical slant is never meant to foreclose other interpretations of the text. There is no grand, unified theory—even one hallowed by *"the puffpuff and pompom of Powther and Pall"* (FW 349.22–23)—to explain Joyce's fiction.

Versions of several sections of this book have appeared as articles or chapters in *Éire-Ireland* (copyright 1989: Irish American Cultural Institute, 1 Lackawanna Place, Morristown, NJ 07960), *A Collideorscape of Joyce: Festschrift for Fritz Senn,* edited by R. Frehner and U. Zeller (Dublin: Lilliput Press, 1998), *James Joyce Quarterly, Journal of Modern Greek Studies, Joyce Studies Annual,* Volume 5, Summer 1994 (copyright 1994 by the University of Texas Press, P.O. Box 7819, Austin, Texas 78713-7819), and *Writing Its Own Wrunes for Ever* (Du Lérot, 16140 Tusson, France). I thank the editors of these journals and collections for permission to adapt this material. Collegial (mostly archival) help came from Vincent Deane, John O'Hanlon, Christine and Tim O'Neill, and Danis Rose (Dublin); Inge Landuyt, Geert Lernout, and Dirk Van Hulle (Antwerp); Erika Rosiers and Wim Van Mierlo (Miami); and Ruth Frehner, Fritz Senn, and Ursula Zeller (Zürich). I enjoyed a brief visit to the present-day headquarters of the Société of Bollandists in Brussels, but there is no possibility that these superscholarly Jesuits would endorse my wild excesses. Once again Ellynn Packard provided patient and accurate word-processing assistance. As always Betsy Boehne contributed to my spiritual delinquency by putting up with gory accounts of assorted martyrdoms, creating hanging indents, and compiling the bibliography. Special thanks to freelance copy editor Sharon Damoff and to Gillian Hillis and Amy Gorelick of the editorial staff of the University Press of Florida. My dedication acknowledges a nova in the constellation of those who think that reading squirrelly books is fun; her patron saints predict a rewarding career as wise treasure-digger, in her backyard and in archival libraries.

Abbreviations

For almost all of the following abbreviations (cited parenthetically in the text) I have followed the standard conventions of the *James Joyce Quarterly*. I add several other items that are frequently cited.

CP   Joyce, James. *Collected Poems.* New York: Viking, 1957.
CW   Joyce, James. *The Critical Writings of James Joyce.* Edited by Ellsworth Mason and Richard Ellmann. New York: Viking, 1959.
D   Joyce, James. *Dubliners.* Edited by Robert Scholes with Richard Ellmann. New York: Viking, 1967.
E   Joyce, James. *Exiles.* New York: Penguin, 1973.
FW   Joyce, James. *Finnegans Wake.* New York: Viking, 1939.
GJ   Joyce, James. *Giacomo Joyce.* Edited by Richard Ellmann. New York: Viking, 1968.
JJII   Ellmann, Richard. *James Joyce.* New York: Oxford University Press, 1982.
JJA   *The James Joyce Archive.* Edited by Michael Groden et al. New York and London: Garland, 1977–78. I follow the *JJQ* guide for citing volumes and pages.
Letters   Joyce, James. *Letters of James Joyce.* Volume I, edited by Stuart Gilbert. New York: Viking, 1966. Volumes II and III, edited by Richard Ellmann. New York: Viking, 1964.
P   Joyce, James. *A Portrait of the Artist as a Young Man.* Corrected text by Chester G. Anderson and edited by Richard Ellmann. New York: Viking, 1968.
Scribbledehobble   *James Joyce's "Scribbledehobble": The Ur- Workbook for "Finnegans Wake."* Edited by Thomas E. Connolly. Evanston: Northwestern University Press, 1961. Citations refer to Connolly's page, followed by the original workbook page in brackets, e.g., 95 [511].
SH   Joyce, James. *Stephen Hero.* Edited by John J. Slocum and Herbert Cahoon. New York: New Directions, 1963.

SL   Joyce, James. *Selected Letters of James Joyce.* Edited by Richard Ellmann. New York: Viking, 1975.
U   Joyce, James. *Ulysses.* Edited by Hans Walter Gabler et al. New York: Random House, 1986.
UNBM *Joyce's "Ulysses" Notesheets in the British Museum.* Edited by Phillip F. Herring. Charlottesville: University of Virginia Press, 1972. Citations refer to page and line number, e.g., 142:94.

In the bibliography (and occasionally in the endnotes) the following abbreviations are used for frequently cited journals and other sources:

AFWC *A "Finnegans Wake" Circular*
AWN   *A Wake Newslitter*
EB   *Encylopaedia Britannica*
EJS   *European Joyce Studies*
JJLS *James Joyce Literary Supplement*
JJQ   *James Joyce Quarterly*
JSA   *Joyce Studies Annual*

Introduction

When F. Scott Fitzgerald was invited to meet James Joyce in Paris in the summer of 1928, the American writer's admiration seems to have veered to just this side of idolatry. To demonstrate his devotion to the author of *Ulysses*, Fitzgerald offered to jump out a window.[1] Joyce, an understandably "pusillanimous guest" at that gathering, declined the homage, but later sent a thank-you note with a photograph, and returned a book suitably autographed.[2] On his part, Fitzgerald showed his appreciation to Sylvia Beach, who had arranged the introductory dinner party, in a more conventional manner: he inscribed a copy of *The Great Gatsby* for her. Just beneath the words "Paris, July 1928," he drew an oval table at which three people are seated normally (Lucie and André Chamson and Zelda Fitzgerald); at each end Adrienne Monnier and Sylvia Beach are in chairs, but their bodies terminate with mermaids' tails. Even more bizarrely, Fitzgerald depicted himself kneeling in front of an enlarged, disembodied face of Joyce. This specter is crowned with a radiant halo. Below the caricature are two handwritten lines: "1 Rue D'Odeon" and "Festival of St. James."[3]

That festive gathering was probably the first occasion on which Joyce was unofficially canonized, but it was not the last. Richard Ellmann, a far more sober admirer than Fitzgerald, has written, "Without saying so to Gorman directly, he [Joyce] made clear that he was to be treated as a saint with an unusually protracted martyrdom" (*JJII* 631). Ellmann and others have accordingly seen the phrase *"the Martyrology of Gorman"* (FW 349.24) as a humorous reference to Herbert Gorman's semisanctioned biography, first published in 1940.[4] Joyce's fictional deployment of the name "Gorman" and, indeed, his choice of Herbert Gorman to write his life perpetuate a remarkable coincidence. There was an actual twelfth-century martyrology (calendar of saints' feast days) composed by Mael-Maire hua Gormain (Marianus Gorman), abbot of the monastery of the Hill of the Apostles at Knock, near Louth in east-central Ireland. Several oblique references to this and similar medieval documents appear in the *Wake*; but before I comment on their contextual relevance, it is necessary to present more general evidence about Joyce's awareness of the many ways and means of recording the marvelous feats of "all the sinkts in the colander" (*FW* 432.36).

In the introductory section of a 1907 lecture in Trieste on the cultural and political history of Ireland, Joyce said that "it would take the learning and patience of a leisurely *Bollandist* to relate the acts of these [Irish] saints and sages" (*CW* 154; my emphasis). Later in the same presentation he praised the missionary docility and doctrinal fidelity of his native land: "And, in fact, the ecclesiastical history of Ireland completely lacks a *martyrology*" (*CW* 169; my emphasis). Five years after this lecture Joyce wrote a newspaper article recounting a brief visit to the Aran Islands. Among the early inhabitants of that remote outpost was "the visionary Saint Fursa, described in the *hagiographic calendar* of Ireland as the precursor of Dante Alighieri" (*CW* 236; my emphasis).

The words that I have emphasized in those three quotations are external evidence that, while he was completing *Portrait*, Joyce was more than casually acquainted with the study of the lives of the saints, especially those connected with Ireland. Each of the italicized terms is derived from the technical vocabulary of hagiography, the compilation of legends and facts relating to the lives and cults of the saints of the Christian Church. The Bollandists are a select group of priest-scholars of the Belgian Province of the Society of Jesus. Since the early seventeenth century, these elite Jesuits, taking their title from their founder, Johannus Bollandus (d. 1665), have worked at scientifically establishing and publishing hagiographic texts.[5] Their primary publications are the massive—now about seventy-five folio volumes—*Acta Sanctorum* (The Deeds of the Saints) and the periodical *Analecta Bollandiana* (Bollandist Selections). Their mission, poised between pruning the inanities of pious tradition and applying the rigors of historical and textual criticism, proceeds slowly—hence Joyce's adverb "leisurely."

A martyrology is an official calendar not only of Christians executed for adherence to the new monotheistic creed, but of all the canonically recognized heroes and heroines of the Church. Thus, in his Triestine lecture when Joyce contrasts the prolonged brutality of the imposition of British rule in Ireland and that island's alleged lack of a martyrology, he is both right and wrong. The introduction of Christianity into Ireland was in fact remarkably bloodless. There were confrontations (such as the legendary dispute between Patrick and the Archdruid, which is so effectively recreated in the *Wake*), but none of the torture and wholesale executions that accompanied the advent of the new faith in so many pagan regions.[6] At the same time, there certainly were Irish martyrologies in the technical sense of an official calendar of the feasts of saints celebrated by the church. An entry on one of these medieval compilations, the "Martyrology of Tallaght," was recorded in a *Wake* notebook (VI.B.14.188); another, perhaps the most famous, was the calendar composed by Abbot Marianus Gorman. Thus, Joyce's point in citing the absence of an Irish "martyrology" in the lecture is to stress an enduring Christian and Catholic consensus in Ireland, a land not otherwise noted for its fraternal and filial unanimity. The final reference to a hagiographic calendar is an indication that Joyce could consult some sort of collection of the feast days and capsule biographies of the saints, arranged in order throughout the ecclesiastical or calendar year and sanctioned by church officials for use in the liturgy or private veneration.[7]

The three citations from Joyce's early writings are explicit indications that he was fully aware of the significant role of hagiography in the history of European culture. In the face of his national and religious background, Jesuit education, and literary inclinations, that emphasis is not surprising. The given names of Irish Catholic children reflected their parents' choice of a patron saint to protect and inspire their offspring. At the baptism of an infant that patronage is initially invoked; at their confirmation adolescent Catholics select another saintly name to mark their entrance into a more demanding phase of religious obligation. Both of these sacraments are administered (the former by a priest, the latter by a bishop) at a church, which is officially called by the name of a saint to whom the parish has been dedicated. In some traditions, the annual feast of a patron saint is celebrated with more gusto than a person's birthday. Some saints' days are local or national holidays; others mark seasonal changes or salient points in the year, as would be noted even on secular calendars. It is impossible to comprehend the history of Western art or to grasp the symbolic function of the statues and stained-glass windows in a Catholic church without some knowledge of the hagiographic themes and scenes that they so frequently portray. At parochial schools, during Sunday sermons, and in inspirational publications, the lives of the saints were scanned to provide edifying examples of sectarian loyalty, moral rectitude, and pious devotion.

A brief passage borrowed from *Finnegans Wake* neatly summarizes the point of the previous paragraphs. In the Ireland from which the young Joyce fled and the Trieste-Zürich-Paris to which the mature Joyce moved—as well as for the fictional world that he created—the author's "holyhagionous lips [were] continuously poised upon the rubicated annuals of [the] saint[s]" (*FW* 520.33–34). That sanctimonious claim is couched in the hyperbolic rhetoric used by Yawn to deflect the probes of the interrogators into the crimes of HCE. Nevertheless, in its application to the cultural milieu in which Joyce lived and wrote and to the imagined lives of the characters whom he produced, the exaggeration is not outlandish: saints are alive everywhere.

The rest of this initial chapter is a series of concrete examples, drawn from the entire range of Joyce's work and life, that illustrate and justify my claim for hagiographic universality. In subsequent chapters I concentrate on specific topics from different historical periods, places, perspectives, and sources to bolster the case. Throughout the presentation of textual evidence, I pay special attention to the detection of any documentary sources that Joyce used, and to the traces that this material may have left in archival notes. This method permits a thorough display of the evidence, from its inspirational genesis to its literary revelation.

Patron Saints

Joyce was intensely interested in names. Carola Giedion-Welcker, a close friend of his during the 1930s, reports that he applied the Latin adage "Nomen est omen [a name is a sign of future events] to his own [family] name too . . . [deriving it] genealogically from the old French name 'de Joyeuse'."[8] Fiction, in which the author is the literal and literary sponsor at his character's christening, facilitates this predictive function. In real life, since given (or Christian) names usually involve some element of parental or familial aspiration, they can serve a similar purpose. The primary hero of *Portrait* and the surrogate son of *Ulysses*, Stephen Dedalus, for example, has been given two ominous names. His surname is borrowed from the master craftsman of Greek mythology, Daedalus, the cunning architect-builder of the Cretan labyrinth. His first name comes from that of the heroic disciple of the infant Christian Church who was condemned to death before the high priest of the Jews and stoned to death in Jerusalem. The Jesuit director of vocations at Belvedere College alludes to this connection in a conference with the school's "prefect of Our Blessed Lady's sodality": "—I will offer up my mass tomorrow morning . . . that Almighty God may reveal to you His holy will. And let you, Stephen, make a novena to your holy patron saint, the first martyr . . . that God may enlighten your mind. But you must be quite sure, Stephen, that you have a vocation. . . . Once a priest always a priest, remember" (*P* 160–61). According to ecclesiastical legislation and custom during Joyce's lifetime, all patrons (individual or corporate) were taken from the ranks of canonized saints.[9] Subsequent discussion of the various categories of saints will take into account the historical and symbolic aspects of hagiographic patronage, such as St. Peter's keys of the kingdom, the cultural contributions of the Dominicans and the Franciscans, and St. Apollonia's dental pincers.

Two examples summarize Joyce's fictional exploitation of these pious customs. "The Sisters," the first of the *Dubliners* stories to be published, appeared in the August 13, 1904, issue of the *Irish Homestead*. Its plot involves a young boy's reaction to the death of a troubled priest who had acted as his informal tutor-mentor about some of the arcane aspects of Catholic tradition and practice. Father Flynn's death notice parenthetically identified him as "(formerly of S. Catherine's Church, Meath Street)" (*D* 12). That place and title are Joyce's original—and restored—indication of the deceased priest's church. When the story was accepted by the *Irish Homestead*'s editor, however, he wrote to Joyce that he was altering the name of the parish simply to "St. Ita's Church." Although St. Ita was widely venerated as an early Irish holy woman, there were in fact no churches in the Archdiocese of Dublin under her titular patronage. Joyce's original choice of "S. Catherine's" may have symbolic force: St. Catherine of Siena—like Father Flynn—experienced periods of great spiritual aridity and died of a paralytic stroke. I also suggest that Joyce found a later opportunity to mock the newspaper's editorial scrupulosity in demanding a substitute "saint to make the details of the story more remote." In the carnivalesque procession of saints in the "Cyclops" chapter of *Ulysses*, St. Ita is slyly paired with "S. Dympna" (*U* 12.1710); the latter is the patroness of insane asylums (note VI.B.8.68: "S. Dympna (mad)").[10]

When the rector of Belvedere College announces the start of the retreat in *Portrait*, he informs the students that the annual spiritual exercise is "in honour of saint Francis Xavier whose feast day is Saturday." He also reminds them that the famous early Jesuit is the patron of the college, and stresses the missionary efforts of the saint, who went "from Africa to India to Japan, baptising the people. He is said to have baptised as many as ten thousand idolators in one month." As a consequence, he is a "saint who has great power in heaven, remember: power to intercede for us . . . , power above all to obtain for us the grace to repent if we be in sin. A great saint" (*P* 108–9). Those citations nicely underscore Francis Xavier's functions as an institutional patron, fervent apostle, and personal intercessor. In appreciation of these attributes—and in gentle mockery of overextended claims to potent celestial protection—Joyce concludes his catalogue of the recipients of ALP's souvenir gifts in the *Wake* with this Irish mouthful of hallowed baptismal names: "Marie Xavier Agnes Daisy Frances de Sales

Macleavy" (*FW* 212.14–15). The patrons who supplied each of those elements of nomenclature (including "Daisy," which is one of the plain English forms for the hagiographically certifiable "Marguerite") will be discussed in greater detail later.

A final example in this category of saintly patronage moves from fiction to biography. When he was a young boarding student at Clongowes Wood College, James Augustine Joyce was presented for confirmation (*JJII* 30). For the reception of this sacrament, he (not his parents or baptismal sponsors) chose an additional name to mark his transition into the ranks of the Church militant. As a matter of fact, however, St. Aloysius Gonzaga, the patron whom Joyce selected, was hardly noted for his martial contributions to the Christian heritage. He was one of "the three patrons of holy youth" (*P* 55–56 and *U* 12.1703–5). The young Florentine nobleman was so disgusted with the violence and indulgence of a courtier's life that he cut himself off from his family to enter the Society of Jesus at age sixteen. He died, after seven years of humility, withdrawal, and abnegation, from effects of the plague in 1591. A modern compendium of Jesuit saints reports that he wished an even more severe regimen of penance than was permitted in the novitiate; he told the director, "I am a piece of twisted iron. I entered religion to get twisted straight."[11]

Aloysius Gonzaga is a conspicuous example of the self-effacing spiritual athletes who were once held up as models of perfection to Catholic youth. At one stage of his life, Joyce was impressionable enough to select him as a personal patron, although there is clear evidence that the appeal later wore thin and became an object of self-mockery.[12] Stanislaus Joyce (himself named after another, even more cloying, patron of holy youth, St. Stanislaus Kostka) seems never to have fallen under the penitential sway of his brother's confirmation patron. In one of his frequent introspective asides in *The Complete Dublin Diary*, Stanislaus writes: "We find something fanatical or foolish always in those who are eternally virginal, something invigourous, unvirile, sentimental. Compare, for instance, a St. Augustine with a St. Aloysius."[13]

Hagiographic Calendar

Throughout his career Joyce was acutely concerned with the symbolic force of certain days and their anniversaries. The French printers of *Ulysses* dispatched the first two copies of the book by the evening Dijon-Paris express so that they would arrive in the capital on the morning of Joyce's fortieth birthday, February 2, 1922 (*JJII* 524).[14] The raft of last-minute additions delayed the official publication of *Finnegans Wake* until May 4,

1939, but Joyce had an advance copy in his hands for his fifty-seventh birthday party three months prior to that day.

The element common to the calculation of all calendars is the date when the first cycle began. The current worldwide standard is January 1 of the putative year of Christ's birth. That day marks the start of the initial twelve-month period A.D. (*anno Domini* [year of the Lord]). The prior period is B.C. (before Christ), although the sectarianly neutral abbreviations B.C.E. (before the common era) and C.E. (common era) have some academic currency. In his anthropological disquisition in the *Wake*, Professor Jones displays his multicultural awareness: "(Feigenbaumblatt and Father, Judapest, 5688, A.M.)" (*FW* 150.27–28). The date *anno mundi* (year of the world) is 1927. That is the precisely correct time, by the Jewish calendar, for the composition of this passage (if the difference between the lunar and solar cycles is ignored), since the year of the creation of the world for the ancient Hebrews was 3761 B.C.[15] The ancient Greeks began their calendar with the first Olympic games in honor of Zeus (776 B.C. in our system). The Roman cycle is traditionally calculated *ab urbe condita* (from the founding of the city), 753 B.C. The Islamic lunar calendar commences in 722 A.D.—or, in Muslim terms, 1 A.H. (*anno Hegirae*); the Hegira is Muhammad's departure from Mecca to Medina to begin preaching the word of Allah. The primary feast for Joyceans—now celebrated almost over the globe—is June 16, 1904 A.D./1 A.B. (*anno Bloomensis* [year of Bloom]).

In chapter 9 a section on feast days discusses this enormously rich source of commemoration—and comic appropriation—in the works of Joyce. Here a few typical examples demonstrate the significance of saints' days and other solemn holidays in Joyce's life and fiction. Even the essential distinction between fixed and movable feasts in the Christian liturgical calendar is cleverly elided in a phrase from the third page of the *Wake:* "the feast is a flyday" (*FW* 5.24).[16] The difference in the dates ("July 1st" or "July 2nd") assigned to Father Flynn's death in the three versions of "The Sisters" is not a minor and merely inconsistent detail in the textual history of that work. The explanation for Joyce's alteration of dates lies in the fact that the feast of the Most Precious Blood of Jesus was once a movable feast (first Sunday in July) and became fixed (July 1) only in 1917, during the pontificate of Pope Pius IX. Here, adherence to the realistic minutiae of the liturgical calendar is a distinct element in the thematic irony of that initial story about the demise of a priest who had once broken a chalice during Mass.

The opening clause of a parodic paragraph in the "Cyclops" chapter of *Ulysses* conflates dates from the secular and religious systems: "on the sixteenth day of the month of the oxeyed goddess and in the third week after the feastday of the Holy and Undivided Trinity" (*U* 12.1111–12). The epic patron-goddess of the month is Hera/Juno; hence the date so ponderously specified is June 16. Although the precise reference to the ecclesiastical calendar was probably not appreciated by the group at Kiernan's bar—including the day's soon-to-be-titular patron, Leopold Bloom—Trinity Sunday is celebrated on the first Sunday after Pentecost. In 1904, then, the appointed date on which to honor the Trinity fell on May 29, and Bloomsday did indeed occur in the third week after that movable feast.

A similarly formulaic reference to the Christian belief in three divine persons in one God reappears in the *Wake:* "the proverbial bishop of our holy and undivided with this me keen or no me ken Zot is the Quiztune" (*FW* 110.12–14; note VI.B.2.22). In that citation Joyce's comic intellectualization and distortion of Hamlet's existential query is designed to highlight the numerous attempts by theologians to explain and express this central mystery of divine unity and diversity. A final martyrological reference from the *Wake* involves the two most prominent Jesuit saints. At Clongowes Wood and Belvedere Colleges as well as at University College, Joyce was surely familiar with the feast days of the society's founder, St. Ignatius Loyola, and of its most famous missionary, St. Francis Xavier. Textual proof is supplied by the following excerpt from a passage loaded with calendric references: "ignitious Purpalume . . . Francisco Ultramare, last of scorchers, third of snows" (*FW* 433.1–2). The soldier *Ignatius* was severely wounded in a battle at *Pampeluma,* Spain, and while recuperating saw the light; his feast day is *July 31. Francis* is the Apostle of the East Indies, far *across the sea;* his feast day is *December 3.*

Hagiographical Frontiers

Apart from St. Stephen the Protomartyr (see *U* 12.1691–92), the first Christians to have merited universal recognition are the twelve apostles. Most of them died as martyrs in lands to which they had traveled to preach the new faith. St. Peter was crucified—upside down, according to tradition—probably during the reign of Nero. Although James the Greater was beheaded by King Herod Agrippa (Acts 12:1–2), Spanish legend claims that he visited that western peninsula and that his body was brought there after his execution. At any rate, James was the patron of the long Spanish crusade against the Moors, and his cathedral at Compostela was an enormously popular pilgrimage site during the medieval era. Another apostle, St. Thomas, is reputed to have taken the gospel through Parthia and Mesopotamia to south India. Especially in the *Wake* there are numerous references to these early followers of Christ and to the traditions associated with them. In a very late notebook Joyce includes a list of each of these apostles and their symbols: "Peter—a key / Andrew—cross / James G—staff / ... / Simon—saw / Matthias—halberd" (VI.B.43.63).[17]

The Roman historian Tacitus records that Nero ordered a large group of Christians to be executed as responsible for the great fire that destroyed large parts of the imperial capital. Nero hoped a public spectacle would deflect the anger of citizens away from himself; thus, the victims "were covered with the skins of wild animals and torn apart by hunting dogs, or fixed to crosses and set afire, so that when the light faded they served as evening torches." Tacitus concludes his report of this incident with a stinging indictment: "Thus, although the Christians were guilty and deserved the ultimate punishment, the Romans felt pity for them, since they were being dispatched not for the common good, but for the blood-lust of one man" (*Annals* 15.44). In the "Night Lessons" section of the *Wake*, the marginal "*Nero*" is linked to the essay topic "the Great Fire in the South City Markets" (*FW* 306 L.2 and 15–16). An uncrossed notebook entry indicates that Joyce knew something of imperial Roman topography: "Vatican Nero's garden" (VI.B.1.119).[18] It is suitably ironic, in urban and cosmic terms, that the traditional site of the burial of the crucified St. Peter is in a crypt beneath his titular church in the Vatican.

Stephen of Jerusalem and the scattered apostles are examples of Joyce's deployment in his fiction of first-century Christian heroes, the earliest saints of the new era. There are also at least two indications that Joyce kept abreast of more contemporary canonizations. His initial evocation of "the three patrons of holy youth" in *Portrait* is placed in Stephen Dedalus's first year at Clongowes Wood College, prior to at least 1888. That dramatic *terminus ante quem* is required by Joyce's style of citation for the last of the venerable trio, "*blessed* John Berchmans" (*P* 56; my emphasis). The Jesuit novice, originally from Flanders, died in Rome in 1621, but he was not officially named a saint until January 15, 1888.[19] Before that date his proper title would be "blessed," as used by Joyce. By the time John Berchmans reappears in the parade of holy men and women in *Ulysses*, he had been canonized for almost sixteen and a half years. Thus, on the second occasion, he is rightfully styled "*S*. John Berchmans" (*U* 12.1704–5; my emphasis).

A notebook entry, dated to late February–April 1924,[20] records up-to-the-minute evidence for Joyce's abiding interest in new additions to the official calendar of Roman Catholic saints: "S. Gabriel of Our Lady / of Sorrows" (VI.B.1.27). The reference is to Gabriel Possenti, who joined the

Passionist Order in 1856 and took the name Brother Gabriel of Our Lady of Sorrows. He died, after a brief but exemplarily penitential life in religion, at the age of twenty-four and was canonized by Pope Benedict XV in 1920. The entry is uncrossed, and there appear to be no references to Gabriel (or his Marian title) in the *Wake*. Perhaps this contemporary saint merited archival attention because his feast day is February 27, a month that repeatedly supplied hagiographical material for recycling in Joyce's works.

In between the first and the twentieth centuries Joyce found all sorts of saints to exploit in his fiction: biblical heroes and heroines, martyrs, virgins, virgin martyrs, doctors of the church, missionaries, and founders of religious orders. As would be expected, almost all the later examples are western European, Roman Catholic holy men and women. The Celtic lands (Ireland, with occasional recruits from Scotland, Britain, Wales, and Brittany) supply most of the flock, but there are a significant number of Anglo-Saxon saints. The four great Doctors of the Eastern Church (St. Basil of Caesarea [Cappadocia, Turkey], St. Gregory of Nazianzus [Cappadocia, Turkey], St. John Chrysostom [Antioch, Syria, and Constantinople], and St. Athanasius of Alexandria [Egypt]) were, of course, known to him; but there is slim evidence that Joyce had much interest in later, exclusively Orthodox, saints, Greek or Russian.[21]

In late antiquity, North Africa and Egypt were firmly Christian, with several important centers of theological study. St. Athanasius of Alexandria was the primary opponent of the contentious priest Arius, who denied the true divinity of Christ and was condemned at the Council of Nicaea (A.D. 325). The Egyptian heresiarch is phonetically paired with the orthodox champion in *"Bet you fippence, anythesious* [Athanasius], *there's no puggatory, are yous* [Arius] *game?"* (*FW* 266.L). That apparently farfetched identification, featuring an extraneous point of doctrinal contention, is supported by a crossed archival entry, "°Arian v Athan, w miracles" (VI.C.2.109), and another item in an index of several pages of Eastern Christian material, "Arius Athanasius" (VI.B.27.36).

Another illustrious theologian of ancient African origin is St. Augustine, the author of *Confessions, The City of God,* and numerous doctrinal, moral, and exegetical works. He was born in Tagaste and later became bishop of Hippo, both near ancient Carthage in what is today eastern Algeria/western Tunisia. In addition to his selection by John Stanislaus and Mary Jane Murray Joyce as one of their infant son's baptismal patrons, St. Augustine is referred to in several of the mature author's works. His famous dictum for theological consensus, *securus iudicat orbis terrarum* (free from interference, the entire Christian commonwealth makes its judgment), is first invoked in Joyce's 1900 essay "Drama and Life" (*CW* 42) and is repeated in various perverted forms throughout the *Wake*, as, for example, "*sigarius* (sic!) *vindicat urbes terrorum* (sicker!)" (*FW* 76.7–8). Father Arnall cites the reformed sinner St. Augustine as one of his authorities on the manifold stings of hellish conscience in the opening exercise of the retreat at Belvedere College (*P* 129). Finally, the North African origins of the theologian are viewed from a sub-Saharan perspective in a late, uncrossed (and unused) notebook item: "S. Augustine / negro spiritual" (VI.B.35.77). That multicultural presumption is nullified by the fact that Augustine's early life as a recalcitrant and reluctant Christian and his later prodigious literary contributions to western theology are fully and canonically situated in the late classical tradition.

Allusions to two other saints can more justifiably claim to push beyond the limits of normal geographical reference in Joyce. In Jaun's lecture to Issy he declares that he is "under the invocation of Saint Jamas Hanway, servant of Gamp, *lapidated*, and Jacobus a Pershawn, *intercissous*" (*FW* 449.14–15; my emphases). The former is a conflation of the apostle St. James the Less (stoned to death in Jerusalem for daring to preach the new faith) and Jonas Hanway (stoned by the crowd for daring to carry an umbrella in mid-eighteenth-century London). In correct martyrological terms, the audacious James and Jonas were both "lapidated" (*lapis, lapidis* is Latin for "stone"). St. James (*Jacobus* in Latin) the Persian was taunted for his Christian beliefs by the pagan King Varahran V in the fifth century. When James refused to recant, the Shah ordered him to be cut to pieces, bit by bit. The martyr is reported to have watched his arms being severed, then telling his tormentor: "You have done the boughs, now the trunk." His droll attitude and that grotesque method of execution earned the saint an appropriate epithet, "The Cut Up" (*intercisus* in Latin).[22]

Relics

In various branches of Christianity, relics of the saints were frequently seen as a means of bridging gaps in time (now/then) and space (here/there). Relics are pieces of a saint's body, clothes, books, tools, or material that has been touched to the death site or burial place of a biblical or Christian hero. When the church was being persecuted, the tombs of martyrs were of great symbolic importance. The faithful would gather to pray at these hallowed sites, especially on the anniversary of a saint's death. They hoped, of course, that such localized prayers would find ardent advocates in heaven for their appeals. Christians who lived at a distance from the holy places would seek to take mementos back to their home churches.

Two secular movements accelerated the process of seeking relics: the broadening of trade in the growing towns of trans-Alpine Europe and the conquest of the Holy Land, Egypt, and North Africa by the forces of Islam. During the Middle Ages, especially after the initial Crusades, there was lucrative commerce in all sorts of relics, genuine and fake. Scarcity of product and appreciation of value soon created a black market in and organized theft of relics.[23] Joyce was well acquainted with the historical and cultic significance of relics in western Christianity and was not squeamish about deploying them for comic purposes, primarily in the *Wake*.

The most memorable passage featuring readily recognizable—but evidently ersatz—relics is the following catalogue of the *"seals"* of *"Popey O'Donoshough, the jesuneral of the russuates. . . . the starre of the Son of Heaven, the girtel of Izodella the Calottica, the cross of Michelides Apaleogos, the lachet of Jan of Nepomuk . . . the great belt, band and bucklings of the Martyrology of Gorman* (FW 349.19–24). A few of those items require some comment. Behind "Izodella" lurks Queen Isabella of Castile; she and her husband, Ferdinand of Aragon, were known as the "Catholic" monarchs. "Michelides Apaleogos" is a thinly disguised "Michael Paleologos," the name of several members of a powerful Byzantine family, two of whom (Michael VIII and Michael IX) ascended to the imperial throne in the thirteenth century. St. John of Nepomuk was a canon in the cathedral of Prague; according to tradition, he was martyred by King Wenceslaus IV in 1393 for refusing to reveal the content of the Queen's confessions. The carefully enumerated accessories of the binding of the Martyrology of Gorman would have personal and patriotic claims to Joyce's devotion.

Another reference to sacred souvenirs is revealed only with a hint from a notebook item. The pious exclamation, "The relics of pharrer and livite!" (*FW* 578.5–6), is not a jumbled evocation of an ancient Egyptian king (Pharaoh) and a Hebrew temple-attendant (Levite); rather the two terms are directed at the *father* of the *Wake*'s family, HCE, and his consort, ALP, Anna *Livia* Plurabelle. That identification is based on the following archival entry: "[b]relics of ⊔⊔ /& △" (VI.B.27.44).

Bogus Hagiography

The most obviously phony saints in Joyce are interspersed with the real thing in the hagiographic catalogue in "Cyclops": "S. Anonymous and S. Eponymous and S. Pseudonymous," and so on (*U* 12.1696–98). They and their "blessed symbols of their efficacies" (*U* 12.1714–15), chanting monks, "and friars, brown and grey . . . capuchins, cordeliers, minimes and observants" (*U* 12.1684–85) will be discussed in detail in a later chapter. Before

I cite some other "saints" whose canonization is a function of Joyce's fiction, it must be noted that all of the varieties and colors of the friars just mentioned are certifiable members of the extended community of St. Francis of Assisi.

An indubitable example of an imaginary saint is found in a Joycean reference to the high holyday of English bird-shooting. The season opens on August 12, and in High-Church country circles that date is variously known as "St. Grouse's Day" or "St. Partridge's Day."[24] In the *Wake* the occasion is couched in an avian context and Latinized: "till the bark of Saint Grouseus for hoopoe's hours" (*FW* 449.27). The association with bird-shooting is confirmed by a note in *Scribbledehobble*, "gS. Grouse 12/8" (158 [805]). Earlier in the *Wake* Chuff/Shaun and Glugg/Shem exchange greetings and call down the blessings of "Saint Mowy of the Pleasant Grin" and "Saint Jerome of the Harlot's Curse" (*FW* 252.7 and 11). While there is a genuine and distinguished St. Jerome, Joyce concocted this pair of saints and the meaningful epithets from the nouns "moue" (with a typical reverse twist) and "jeremiad."[25]

The name of my last instance of a sham saint also involves apt etymology: "S. Peregrinus of footsore" (VI.B.26.64). In Latin *peregrinus* is the word for a pilgrim, whose feet undoubtedly become sore as he trudges from one relic-shrine to another. Joyce did not move this entry from notebook to text, but there are several instances of the same Latin root afoot in the *Wake:* "My ruridecanal [of a rural dean] caste is a cut above you peregrines" (*FW* 484.28–29) and, a bit earlier, the Four Old Men (two of whom are named "Peregrine") pray in the original language of Western monasticism "for navigants et peregrinantibus" (*FW* 398.15–16).

Resources and Parallels

The bibliography of hagiographical material that Joyce might have consulted is immense. There were literally hundreds of books on saints, ranging from scholarly compendia to inspirational tracts. Some works attempted to cover every date in the martyrology; others dealt with the saints of one region or even with an individual Christian heroine. Within this mass of documentation, the works on St. Patrick constitute a separate and challenging category. Vincent Deane (a Dublin genetic scholar and the editor of *A "Finnegans Wake" Circular*) and Roland McHugh (compiler of the *Annotations*) have for some time been investigating Joyce's written sources for his multiple references to St. Patrick. Readers are advised to wait for these long-anticipated publications, since it would be rash to attempt to cover the same ground as these experts; their lists of sources for and presentation of Patrick-indexes in the notebooks will be the definitive statements. My treatment of Patrician matters in this book, then, will be brief and marginal, with occasional references to several specialized articles already published.[26]

Deane has also shown the importance of J. M. Flood's compact study *Ireland: Its Saints and Scholars* (1917)[27] for the initial stages of the *Wake*. Among the earliest episodes that were later incorporated in the text is the St. Kevin–Glendalough sketch that was expanded to become the armature of *FW* 604.27–606.12. Years later, in 1938, Joyce added some of the saint's childhood miracles to this passage. His documentary source, supported by an equally late notebook reference (VI.B.47.57), was several pages from Canon John O'Hanlon's massive (and quite rare) collection, *Lives of the Irish Saints* (1890–1897).[28] During his university years Joyce certainly read the highly autobiographical novels of Joris Karl Huysmans. Parts of *La Cathédrale* (1898), with their catalogues of obliquely sexual martyrdoms, relics, and feasts, make the "Cyclopean" procession of saints in *Ulysses* seem positively puritanical by comparison.

I cite details about these three texts—the first short and popular, the second voluminous and scholarly, the third a work of bizarrely parochial French fiction—to illustrate the range of resources used by Joyce in his quest for hagiographical authenticity. For this topic, as for so many seemingly inconsequential others, the identification of the medium and the form of the author's original gobbet of information is an important prelude to an interpretation of the material after it has been digested into the text. Documentary resources and intertextual models matter for literary criticism.

Scope and Perspective

The foregoing general remarks present an overview of the topics and methods that are the core of this book. Although subsequent chapters generally follow a historical scheme from apostolic to modern times, incidental identification of sources and notebook entries are part of the background in all sections. As mentioned in the preface, the many saintly manifestations (in Catholic lore and in Joyce's fiction) of the Virgin Mary will be treated in another study. Here I survey the presence of a pair of archangels, and then the evangelists, St. Joseph, several other New Testament characters—including St. Peter, St. Paul, and the encrypted St. Onesimus—are the subjects of two scripturally based sections. The martyrs and missionaries, doctors and heretics of the growing church (second to seventh centuries A.D.) merit a chapter. Because he is the patron of *Wake's* patriarch, HCE, a chapter is devoted to the hairy Egyptian hermit St. Humphrey/

Onuphrius. Insular zeal and the desire to go into "exile for Christ" are the organizing principles for my treatment of Celtic saints—except for their master, St. Patrick. Medieval and modern holy men and women have their own chapter, as do the founders of various religious orders. A review of relics, symbols, and other paraphernalia associated with the veneration of saints precedes a calendar of feast days as commemorated in Joyce's letters, fiction, and notebooks. Joyce also extended his comic martyrology to embrace a number of purely imaginary saints. I discuss the deployment of these phantom patrons in a compact chapter. Following the identification of his significant documentary sources and brief notice of some parallels from fiction, the book concludes with a summary discussion of Joyce's rhetorical techniques and literary purposes in his presentation of hagiographical material.

As I hope has been made clear in my choice and treatment of the examples in this introduction, I have no ulterior motive—and certainly no theological design—in examining Joycean hagiography. I am also firmly convinced that Joyce's inclusion of saintly matters is not intended, even in his earliest fiction, to be an emblem of nostalgically rejected fervor or an overture to bitter anathemata. His mention of a "coloured print of the promises made to Blessed Margaret Mary Alacoque" in "Eveline" (D 37) and citation of "A holy saint (one of our own fathers I believe it was)" during the retreat in *Portrait* (P 132) are not prima facie irreverent or parodic; but they do perfectly capture the parochial outlook and diction of their time and place. This technique is typical of realistic fiction, designed to evoke a smile of sympathetic recognition, not a shudder of emancipated rebellion. Throughout *Ulysses* and *Finnegans Wake* most of the increasingly dense hagiographical references are overtly funny and often genially blasphemous. In the real world, humor and hagiography are not automatically linked. Nevertheless, even the early-fifth-century poems of Prudentius in praise of Christian martyrs contain several flashes of grotesque humor, as noted by Ernst Robert Curtius in the excursus, "Jest in Hagiography," appended to his magisterial study of medieval European literature.[29]

At his mother's knee—and on his own knees—James Joyce absorbed a great deal of essential information about the rituals, teachings, and heroes of the Irish brand of Roman Catholicism. Weird saints and bloody martyrdoms are part of that heritage. A more mature and demonstrably more skeptical Joyce enjoyed remembering feast days and gently skewing saintly symbols: "soupladles, stars, snakes, anvils, boxes of vaseline, bells, crutches, forceps, stags' horns, watertight boots" (U 12.1717–18). There is also concrete evidence that he picked up such bits of information from various books dealing with that perennial topic of interest, the lives of the saints. The imaginative adaptation of those data—like his utilization of classical tag-lines, operatic snippets, or cryptic allusions to the *suras* of the Koran—is not designed as a slashing critique of traditional belief or orthodox theology and practice. Again, Joyce does not engage in sectarian polemic.[30] Hagiography is a factor and function of the pervasive comic mode in his fiction. That perspective is stated quite nicely by one of the barmaids at the Ormond Hotel in *Ulysses:* "—O saints above! miss Douce said, sighed above her jumping rose. I wished I hadn't laughed so much. I feel all wet" (*U* 11.181–82).

2

Archangels; Saints in the Gospels

A number of God's holy people from the old and new covenants have traditionally been honored with feasts or inclusion in the rituals of the Christian church. Despite their harrowing fidelity, none of these "saints" (such as the relocated Jonah or the revivified Lazarus) has ever been officially canonized; nevertheless many are commemorated in prayers and religious art and music. Throughout both testaments angels ("messengers" in Greek) have also been frequent participants in the action; their service has also been traditionally honored in Christian liturgy and lore.

In my discussion of saints in the gospels, I do not include comment on the central role of Jesus; his teachings and miracles are more appropriately discussed in a projected study of Joyce's use of scripture. The life of the Virgin Mary, both canonical and apocryphal, and the wide range of devotions and art in her honor are of paramount importance to the culture of the Roman Catholic Church. That topic, too, is reserved for another work. The current chapter concentrates on a pair of archangels whose roles are analogous to those of Christian saints and on several other participants in the narratives, whose mission or patronage adds an occasional evangelical patina to Joyce's works.

Strictly speaking, Joyce was by no stretch of the imagination a scholar of the Bible. He did not know Greek, the language of the New Testament, and only in a single case is there evidence that he consulted a basic commentary. His rigorously Catholic formal education under Jesuit auspices included no specific courses preparing him to cite chapter and verse of scripture.[1] On the other hand, the primary texts that accompany the liturgy of the Catholic Church are derived from both the testaments; citations from the psalms, prophets, and parables accentuate sacramental rituals and daily prayers. Every mass in the pre–Vatican II era included assigned readings, in Latin, from the gospels, and selections from either the epistles or Old Testament "lessons." Merely by going to church on Sunday, Joyce would have heard, year after year, the cycle of these texts. Moreover, the sermons and devotional exercises of the Jesuits at Clongowes Wood and Belvedere Colleges not only would have explicated these passages, but also would have cited parallels and supporting material from other books of both testaments. Even the stained-glass windows of parish churches or school chapels, with their inevitably biblical or hagiographical subjects, contributed to the young author's awareness of the major events and characters in what is called "sacred history." This background, supplemented by later reference to readily available texts,[2] quite naturally left its allusive mark on Joyce's fiction.

Archangels

At one time, not so long ago, a prayer to their guardian angels was the customary prelude to more academic activities by pupils at parochial schools. The prayer is brief, a pair of rhymed couplets:

> Angel of God, my guardian dear,
> To whom God's love commits me here,
> Ever this day be at my side,
> To keep and save, to rule and guide.
>
> Amen

These incorporeal and anonymous nannies are not the same celestial creatures as patron saints, but they perform a similar function and were once an accepted part of the extended spiritual family of Catholic children. As he works up courage to confess his many sins, especially those of the flesh, the sixteen-year-old Stephen Dedalus "prayed mutely to his angel guardian to drive away with his sword the demon that was whispering to his brain" (*P* 140). My own vestigial image of these protectors does not include the fact that they were armed with swords—in those days it was my impression that only archangels had divine authorization to carry. Nor was I aware that "Tuesday [was dedicated] to the Guardian Angels" (*P* 147), but I accept Joyce's word for these two items of arcane information on the subject.

There is far more to be said about angels in the Judeo-Christian tradition than was dreamed of in Stephen Dedalus's adolescent autobiography. An expanded discussion of these fascinating details, however, must be reserved for a later study. Only a few angels, and usually from the elite rank (*arch-* is the Greek word-root for "primary," "beginning"), are endowed by the Church and Joyce with full hagiographical qualities.

A number of apocryphal supplements to the Old Testament, as well as Milton's epic account, deal with the primordial revolt by a portion of the angelic host. The traditional commander of the heavenly legions that rose up against God is the angel Lucifer. In Joycean terms his emblematic "*non serviam: I will not serve"* (*P* 117) is featured as the cardinal sin of pride in the *Portrait*'s retreat scene. In the "Circe" chapter of *Ulysses*, the same words are put into Stephen's mouth during a hallucinatory confrontation with his dying mother, who has just warned him, "Beware God's hand!" Stephen's "Shite!" is followed by *"Ah non, par exemple!* The intellectual imagination! With me all or not at all. *Non serviam!"* (*U* 15.4219–28). As Lucifer fell ("once a shining angel, a son of the morning, now a foul fiend" [*P* 118]), so the punishment for his rebellion awaits all subsequent sinners: *"Depart from me, ye cursed, into the everlasting fire which was prepared for the devil and his angels!"* (*P* 124, from Matthew 25:41).[3]

The role of victorious commander of the loyal angels who defeated Lucifer and his rebels is traditionally assigned to the archangel Michael. In *Portrait* that mission and another, more familiar, task are recalled: "and Michael, prince of the heavenly host, with a sword of flame in his hand appeared before the guilty pair [Adam and Eve] and drove them forth from Eden" (*P* 118). In "Wandering Rocks" Leopold Bloom peeks into the Jesuit church on Gardiner Street and hears, among other things, the prayer to the archangel recited at the end of mass; in it Michael is invoked as a "safeguard against the wickedness and snares of the devil" and is requested "by the power of God [to] thrust Satan down to hell and with him those other wicked spirits who wander through the world for the ruin of souls" (*U* 5.442–47). In accord with Michael's role as a foe of Satan, an abbreviated form of his name is given to Shaun in "Mime"; there the archangel is conflated with the ostensibly saintly Mick (a.k.a. Chuff), the rival of the devilish Nick (a.k.a. Glugg), who is that episode's manifestation of Shem. A prefatory "argument" of the mime's plot ends with a Wakean parody of the prayer cited just above: "Chuffy was a nangel then and his soard fleshed light like likening. Fools top! Singty, sangty, meekly loose, defendy nous from prowlabouts. Make a shine on the curst. Emen" (*FW* 222.21–24).

Following the traditional script sketched out in Revelation 12:7–9, the "princesome handsome angeline chiuff" triumphs, and "with a belchybubhub and a hellabelow [he] bedemmed and bediabbled the arimaining lucisphere. Helldsdend, whelldelse!" (*FW* 239.29–34). Earlier in the text the angelic duel is graphically described: "Mickmichael's soords shrieking shrecks through the wilkinses and neckanicholas' toastingforks prinking prongs up the tunnybladders. Let there be fight?" (*FW* 90.10–12). In the Earwicker's bedroom "[o]ver the mantlepiece [hangs a] picture of Michael, lance, slaying Satan, dragon with smoke" (*FW* 559.11–12). Finally, the results of that celestial combat are expressed in an appropriate (and Oxfordian) sports metaphor: "All Saints beat Belial! Mickil Goals to Nichil!" (*FW* 175.5; also note "ᵍangels" [VI.B.30.18]).

A reference in a contemporary dictionary of saints may help to explain an entry in one of Joyce's notebooks. The modern guide mentions a "very old tradition of Michael as the receiver of the souls of the dead."[4] In this role the archangel would be performing a duty similar to that of Hermes/Mercury, the *psychopomp* (soul-guide) of classical mythology, or of Anubis, the jackal-headed god of the ancient Egyptians. The latter divinity, frequently pictured in tomb paintings, presided over the ceremonies of mummification and the infernal trial of mortals. Given Joyce's interest in pharaonic texts and rituals of death and resurrection,[5] he certainly knew that Anubis was not merely involved in the embalming process, but that he also placed the deceased's heart in the scales in the underworld. This test was necessary so that Osiris could render a judgment (almost always favorable) on the person's entry into eternal life. As is depicted on countless papyrus *Books of the Dead* and tomb carvings or paintings, the god's scales are twin pans hanging from the ends of a balance-beam.[6]

The relevant *Wake* notebook entry is "S. Michael defender of souls / ⚖ Amiens" (VI.B.14.109). The sculpture in the pediment of the middle portal of the west facade of the cathedral at Amiens, in north-central France, is an elaborate scene of the Last Judgment. A figure of St. Michael the Archangel, holding the scales of divine justice, surmounts the gable over this panel. Joyce either saw or, more likely, read about this masterpiece of Gothic sculpture and recorded the observation in his notebook.[7] The entry, with its neatly drawn balance-scales, is not crossed and seems to have left no trace in the text of the *Wake*. On the other hand, speculation about the archival entry stimulated a congenially Joycean cross-cultural, multidisciplinary run through Christian hagiography, Egyptian mythology, and Gothic iconography.[8]

A difficult-to-read archival note suggests that Michael also served as the royal cup-bearer in the heavenly court: "Michael = grail" (VI.B.32.214). I am not aware of any legends that assign him that task, but the apocryphal scriptures and related documents are filled with descriptions of the celestial host and their various duties.

Michael was readily granted the title of saint, and many churches and monasteries took him as their patron. Perhaps the most famous is the abbey of Le Mont St.-Michel, which caps the granite cone of a tidal island that rises from the sea between Normandy and Brittany. His feast is celebrated on September 29, Michaelmas, a day of some importance in England and Ireland, as is noted in chapter 10. One final detail concerning the Joycean St. Michael needs to be addressed before I move on to a consideration of a second archangel. In his description of Doomsday in the retreat section, Father Arnall states that it will be Michael who will blow "from the archangelical trumpet the brazen death of time" (P 113). I had always taken it for granted that the mission of sounding the "last trump" had been assigned to the archangel Gabriel. The New Testament (1 Corinthians 15:52, Revelation 10:7) does not give a proper name to the angel. Since I am reluctant to question the scriptural knowledge of Joyce's eloquent Jesuit—and since there are a number of other significant missions that can be positively identified as Gabriel's—I move on to examine Joyce's deployment of that trusted messenger of God.

Because they are by far the most prominent archangels in scripture and Christian prayer, it is natural that Joyce would associate Michael (God's likeness) and Gabriel (God's strength). In "The Dead" their names are assigned to the two men in Gretta Conroy's life: her husband, Gabriel, and her youthful suitor, Michael Furey.[9] In the *Wake* notebooks the pair appear once as comrades ("S Michael & Gabriel / Eve & Mary" [VI.B.15.5]) and once as rivals ("SG v S Michael" [VI.B.14.20]). Gabriel's primary angelic function is to act as an intermediary between God and humans. In the Old Testament, for example, he interprets the vision of the ram for the Hebrew prophet Daniel in the third year of the reign of King Belshazzar of Babylon (Daniel 8:15–27). In the New Testament Gabriel announces the impending birth of John the Baptist to his father, the temple priest Zechariah (Luke 1:5–20). Shortly afterward, the same angel reveals to the Virgin Mary that she has been chosen to bear the "Son of the Most High" (Luke 1:26–38).

Late in *Portrait*, during "a dream or vision," Stephen Dedalus is momentarily enraptured by "the ecstasy of seraphic life." The youth compares this aesthetic experience to the Annunciation: "O! In the virgin womb of the imagination the word was made flesh. Gabriel the seraph had come to the virgin's chamber."[10] The aftereffect is also expressed in angelic terms:

Are you not weary of ardent ways,
Lure of the fallen seraphim?
Tell no more of enchanted days. (P 217)

A second allusion to the Annunciation occurs during one of Gerty MacDowell's reveries in "Nausicaa." The prayers at Our Lady Star of the Sea Church evoke the time she revealed a crush on a handsome young priest in his confession box—if, indeed, that is the ambiguous "that" that she told him. At any rate, Gerty reports the advice of a sympathetic confessor: "[She is] not to be troubled because that was only the voice of nature and we were all subject to nature's laws, he said, in this life and that that was no sin because that came from the nature of woman instituted by God, he said, and that Our Blessed Lady herself said to the archangel Gabriel be it done unto me according to Thy Word" (*U* 13.454–59). I am not entirely sure that the priest's Dominican professor of moral theology would approve of that interpretation of Luke 1:38,[11] but Joyce's reproduction of Gerty's adolescent psychology is right on the mark.

As for the *Wake*, it would be stretching allusive probability to claim that the phrase "oewfs à la Madame Gabrielle de l'Eglise" (*FW* 184.27) has anything to do with the archangel's message of conception to the Virgin, but there is a bizarre notebook entry that links the steadfast heavenly messenger with Issy: " ⊣ angel Gabielle" (VI.B.36.9). That wildly improbable association would seem to have nothing to do with Issy's character or actions in the book—or, for that matter, with Isolde/Yseult in the medieval romance. Yet it is a Wakean fact that a cluster of apocryphal Marian allusions is buried in the Joycean version of Issy's infancy tale (*FW* 561.32–562.11).[12]

The Evangelists

In *Ulysses* the authors of the four gospels appear only in one of the long catalogues in "Cyclops." Among the items on which the Citizen is asked to swear is an "intricately embroidered ancient Irish facecloth," decorated with figures that rivaled the "legendary beauty of the cornerpieces [of the Book of Ballymore] . . . wherein one can distinctly discern each of the evangelists in turn presenting to the four masters his evangelical symbol" (*U* 12.1438–44). In *Finnegans Wake* the evangelists—the etymology is significant: *eu aggelia* means "good message" or "good news" in Greek, "godspell" (good story) in Anglo-Saxon—are one of the several manifestations of the Four Old Men. In the narrative the quartet is most prominent as the Peeping Toms in section II.4, where they are identified with the Four Masters (sixteenth-century) of early Irish history. Joyce's usual form of collective address for this prurient gang is some variant of "mamalujo" (*FW* 398.4), a syllabic acronym for the evangelists Matthew, Mark, Luke, and John.

The gospel writers appear in lightly disguised form on a page that also includes the Greek term "evangelion": "matthued . . . mark . . . luked . . . johntily" (*FW* 223.19, 30–33). They are more or less out in the Irish open as "old Matt Gregory," "old Marcus Lyons," "old Luke Tarpey," and "old Johnny MacDougall" (*FW* 384.7–14). Once, they are metamorphosed into feminine form as "Magda, Marthe with Luz and Joan" (*FW* 528.12–13; note VI.B.4.15). When excited, they are jumbled together, "mummurrlubejubes!" (*FW* 396.34). A final example—which does not exhaust the catalogue of similar wordplay—brings onstage a semi-hysterical quartet of comic gospelers: "Kick! Playup! Mattahah! Marahah! Luchah! Joahanahanahana!" (*FW* 554.9–10).

In Christian tradition each of the four evangelists is, of course, granted the title of saint, and they have lent their names to churches and other places, such as "Saint Joan's Wood" (*FW* 223.20), which is a Wakean gender reversal for St. John's Wood, a fashionable residential area in northwestern London. "Mount Saint John's"(*FW* 359.34) is the Anglicization of Mont St.-Jean, a village near Waterloo, where Napoleon's forces were defeated on June 18, 1815. An archival note records the tradition that St. Luke, who is often thought to have been a physician, was also an artist and is known as the patron of painters: "S Luke—painter" (VI.B.10.56).

St. Joseph

At the start of the Christmas dinner scene in *Portrait*, Mr. Casey tells a rambling anecdote about the reaction of "a drunken old harridan" to a cruel surprise: she screams, "*O Jesus, Mary and Joseph!*" (*P* 37). That trio (who can be invoked piously or blasphemously) is the Holy Family. St. Joseph is the spouse-protector of the Virgin Mary and the foster father of Jesus (*U* 5.423). The day of the week that is specially dedicated to St. Joseph is Wednesday (*P* 147).

Several of the scriptural details of Joseph's life involve his reaction to the Annunciation by the archangel Gabriel. One gospel reports the apparition of an angel to calm his natural concern about the source of the Virgin Mary's supernatural pregnancy (Matthew 1.19–25). His traditional occupation as a carpenter (Matthew 13:55) lies behind the alliterative jingle "Joseph the Joiner" in the infamous ballad.[13] Catholic teaching presumes that the union of Mary and the older widower Joseph (see *FW* 243.35–36) was entirely chaste.[14] Because it is also assumed that Jesus and Mary were present at his final bedside, Joseph is the saint to whom Catholics appeal for a happy death. Joyce slyly links these two traditions by proclaiming Joseph the "patron of the happy demise of all unhappy marriages" (*U* 14.305–6; also note *UNBM* 191:38).

At the end of the Lesson in the mass celebrated in honor of Our Lady, Queen of the Apostles (Saturday after the Ascension), a short "Alleluia" is chanted. A verse of this prayer is based on a well-known Old Testament theme involving the special fertility of one branch of the sons of Israel (see Numbers 17:20–26): "The rod of Jesse has blossomed; a virgin has conceived him who is both God and Man." A variation on this motif also appears in the version of Mary's early life recounted in a medieval compendium of marvelous hagiographic tales, *The Golden Legend*. There it is told that the high priest sought a suitable mate for the Virgin, who had been placed in his care. He ordered all eligible men of Israel to bring a branch to the altar of the temple. Mary's spouse would be the man whose branch flowered. Joseph's branch blossomed immediately, and a dove came from heaven and perched on it.[15] In the light of Joyce's Ulyssean delight in Taxil's *sacre pigeon* (see *U* 3.161–68 and 15.2583–85)—and the prominence of Joseph's blooming branch in Christian art—it is difficult to explain the absence of this detail from his fiction. There is, however, archival evidence for Joyce's awareness of another instance of the motif: "Joseph of Arimathea / brought holy graal to / Glastonbury . . . / but staff flowered (VI.B.6.167). In this case it seems obvious that Joyce's mastery of concrete detail has precipitated a minor example of hagiographic identity-glide.

After that tantalizing bit of Joseph-apocrypha, my final references are downright prosaic. On his way to Dlugacz's porkbutcher shop for a breakfast kidney, Leopold Bloom passes "Saint Joseph's National school. Brats' clamour" (*U* 4.136). In Edwardian Dublin a "National" school emphasized vocational training in a practical trade. Perhaps the noisy students whom Bloom hears are taking a break from an early morning lesson in joinery, a subject given titular place of honor in the school's schedule. Early in "Wandering Rocks" Father John Conmee, S.J., passes by "Saint Joseph's church, Portland row. For aged and virtuous females" (*U* 10.79–80). This second reference is to an institution adjacent to one of Dublin's parish churches, St. Joseph's Asylum for Aged and Virtuous Females. The worthy women could not have a more suitable saintly patron.

In the *Wake* Joseph appears in two distorted versions of an ejaculation (a short, pithy prayer) that was meant to honor the Holy Family: "Luis-Marios Josephs" (*FW* 243.35) and its nearby mirror image, "Josephinus and Mario-Louis" (*FW* 246.17). Another invocation, "Holy Joe in lay Eden" (*FW* 282.17), may be meant to be addressed to the Virgin's spouse, but I know of no connection between St. Joseph and the primeval paradise or Leiden, the academic city in the southern part of the Netherlands.

St. John the Baptist

The priest Zechariah (also spelled "Zachary") was on duty at the temple in Jerusalem when the archangel Gabriel announced to him that his barren wife, Elizabeth, would bear a son. Because Zechariah did not believe this divine message, he was struck dumb, and did not speak until he insisted that the son be named "John," as the angel had commanded. When the Virgin Mary visited her cousin Elizabeth, John leaped for joy in his mother's womb at the presence of the still-to-be-born Son of God (Luke 1). A mature John preached repentance in the wilderness of Judea, where he ate locusts and wild honey; he baptized Jesus in the Jordan River (Matthew 3:1–7, Mark 1:1–12, Luke 3:1–22, John 1:19–34). Herod Antipas, the tetrarch of Galilee, arrested John for preaching against his crimes and debaucheries, especially his lust for his brother's wife. At a banquet, Salome, the daughter of Herod's beloved, danced and asked for John the Baptist's head as the reward for her performance. The preacher was executed, and his head was brought to the table on a platter (Matthew 14:1–12).[16]

That information from the New Testament summarizes the life and career of John the Baptist. As has been noted by several critics, Joyce uses the traditional story of the saint as a type (mold, die-impression) of the life of Stephen Dedalus's comrade Cranly. The hero of *Portrait*, with scandalous presumption, casts Cranly as *his* "precursor" (*P* 248). That noun is a term employed by the Western Church to denote John's mission as the one who "will prepare the way before [Christ]" (Matthew 11:10), "the one who has been sent in front of him" (John 3:28). It is derived from the Latin verb *precurro, precurrere, precursi* (to run in front of, to precede); its Greek equivalent, also applied to John the Baptist, is *prodromos* (the forerunner). In the *Wake* Joyce plays with the saint's name in what appears to be a baby-talk version: "done bapka" (*FW* 481.25); he also displays an understanding of the purpose of the parallel Eastern Orthodox term: it is an "occupational *agnomen* [nickname] (we are back in the presurnames *prodrom*arith period)" (*FW* 30.3–4; my emphases).

In the passage from *Portrait* mentioned in the previous paragraph, Stephen draws additional parallels between Cranly and John the Baptist. The young Irish man is a son of old parents, "the child of exhausted loins . . . [like] those of Elizabeth and Zachary."[17] Cranly "eats chiefly belly bacon and dried figs. Read locusts and wild honey" (*P* 248). The latter are the staples of the Baptist's diet in the Judean desert. When he thought of his friend, Stephen "saw always a stern severed head. . . . Decollation they call it in the fold" (*P* 248). This is the correct term, from the Latin *decollo, decollare* (to sever at the neck, to decapitate, to behead). In an earlier version of *Portrait*, Joyce depicts Cranly as inventing various schemes to flummox his college examiners in Latin composition (*SH* 127–28). That scene from the aborted novel is the clue to the final element in the elaborate equation between Cranly and John the Baptist in the text of *Portrait*:

"Puzzled for the moment by saint John at the Latin gate. What do I see? A decollated precursor trying to pick the lock" (*P* 248). The "saint John" is Cranly, but the "Latin gate" is not the famous church in Rome, St. John at the Latin Gate.[18] Rather, it is Dublin collegiate slang for Cranly's plan to outfox the examiners in his impending encounter with the intricacies of the language of ancient Romans. To compensate for a semester of sporadic study, Cranly hopes somehow "to pick" the "lock" of the closed academic door. That last bit of Joyce's elaborate intertextual typology between Cranly and St. John the Baptist is, even by microscopically intertextual standards, outrageously recherché.

In the desert John wore a garment made of camel hair, with a leather belt around his waist, and ate locusts and wild honey (Matthew 3:4). In the *Wake* the Norwegian sea-captain curses the tailor who has been fitting a suit for him: "blastfumed the nowraging scamptail, in flating furies outs threws his *cammelskins*" (*FW* 320.25–26; my emphasis). Close-fitting Scottish tartan trousers (trews) do not normally come with a made-to-measure suit in Dublin, but the material is biblically eccentric enough to be part of the tailor's store. Not much later in the *Wake*, the inebriated Four Old Men try to piece together a report of their interrogation of HCE. They describe the perpetrator: "Ruddy stackle hair besides a strawcamel belt" (*FW* 368.32). Shaun's list of Shem's suspect behavior includes his culinary skill in preparing fried eggs; he garnished them "with cinnamon and locusts and wildbeeswax" (*FW* 184.20–21).

All that is left in my discussion of the role of St. John in Joyce's fiction is his theatrical decollation. The most memorable modern reenactment of the Baptist's death is Oscar Wilde's *Salomé*. In the spring of 1909, Strauss's opera, with Wilde's text as the *libretto*, was performed in Trieste. Joyce wrote an article on the author and his persecution by the English public for *Il Piccolo della Sera*. Except for the title, "Oscar Wilde: The Poet of 'Salome,'" that piece does not deal with any aspect of the Baptist's death or the display of his decapitated head at Herod's banquet. The *Wake* mentions "two salaameds" (*FW* 497.33), but (as McHugh suggests) they could just as well be a brace of salamis as doubled daughters of Herodias. On the other hand, there were indeed several medieval cathedrals that pushed conflicting claims for possessing *the* genuine head of St. John.[19] Those multiple assertions about disputed relics might seem to justify Joyce's use of the plural, "*the heads of the baptist*," in the list of exhibits carried in "Circe" during the procession honoring Bloom's election as chief magistrate of Dublin. Such an assumption, however, would be unfair, since the full version of the phrase just cited makes it clear that Joyce is playing with sectarian titles, not multiple relics: "*the heads of the baptist, anabaptist, methodist, and Moravian chapels and the honorary secretary of the society of friends*" (*U* 15.1424–26).

Martha, Mary, Lazarus

The New Testament roles of Martha, Mary, and Lazarus are well known. They frequently welcomed Jesus into their house in Bethany. Once, when Lazarus was very ill, the sisters notified Jesus, but he delayed coming to Judea until Lazarus had been dead for four days. When he arrived, Jesus told the grieving family to remove the stone from the tomb, and he ordered Lazarus to come forth. He did, and all of Judea buzzed with the report of this miracle (John 11:1–54). In an unrelated episode, Martha complained to Jesus that Mary never helped with the serving when he was there, but sat at his feet listening to his teaching (Luke 10:38–42). The fourth gospel seems to incorporate that scene into Mary's anointing of Jesus' feet on the day before his last entry into Jerusalem (John 12:1–8).

Another layer of possible confusion results from the identification of Mary of Bethany with the sinful woman whose tears fell on Jesus' feet at the Pharisee's house; she dried them with her hair and anointed them with perfumed oil (Luke 7:36–50). Immediately after this incident, the gospel mentions "Mary surnamed the Magdalene, from whom seven demons had gone out" (Luke 8:2). Thus, Western Christian tradition tends to conflate Mary of Bethany, the unnamed repentant sinner, and Mary Magdalene. In *Ulysses* Joyce goes one step further; in the procession of saints in "Cyclops," he places "S. Martha of Bethany" right beside "S. Mary of Egypt" (*U* 12.1708–9); the latter was a notorious prostitute who was brought back to a pure life and spent years in the desert doing penance for her sins. At any rate, Mary Magdalene with two other women went to the tomb on Easter morning and there was told by an angel that Christ had risen. Then, before he came to any of the apostles, the resurrected Lord appeared to her (Mark 16:1–11, John 20:11–18).

Joyce worked allusions to a number of these scriptural episodes into his fiction. The most blatant and intentionally parodic is his insertion of Lazarus into Bloom's stream of consciousness at the burial of Paddy Dignam: "That last day idea. Knocking them all up out of their graves. Come forth, Lazarus! And he came fifth and lost the job. Get up! Last day!" (*U* 6.677–79). With the innate sense of a comic genius, Joyce does not attempt to top that. There are no other references to Lazarus in his works.[20]

After Bloom picks up his letter from Martha Clifford in "Lotus Eaters," he recalls a ditty about "*Mairy [who] lost the pin of her drawers*" (*U*

5.281). That leads him to ponder, "Martha, Mary. I saw that picture somewhere I forget now old master or faked for money. He is sitting in their house, talking. Mysterious" (*U* 5.289–90). The reference is not so mysterious if one has read Luke 10:38–42: "he" is Jesus; the "house" is at Bethany.[21]

The sisters Martha and Mary are present just beneath the surface of "marathon merry" (*FW* 9.33) and "Misses Mirtha and Merry" (*FW* 529.11–12), as is the twisted name of a genuine saint (Margaret Mary Alacoque): "marthared mary allacook" (*FW* 214.23; note VI.B.31.5). Mary Magdalene (who is sometimes conflated with Mary of Bethany) also appears in numerous Wakean disguises. For example, she is present alongside Martha in a feminized list of the Four Evangelists: "Magda, Marthe with Luz and Joan" (*FW* 528.12–13). The most direct reference is "a miry lot of maggalenes!" (*FW* 453.19; note VI.B.33.115–16). Italian, Russian, and Spanish versions of Mary's place-name are lined up in "lust for Olona Lena Magdalena" (*FW* 211.7–8). Specific notice of her canonization is provided by "the feast [July 22] of Marie Maudlin" (*FW* 434.16).

During his walk on the tidal flats in "Proteus," Stephen Dedalus spots two figures "walking shoreward"; he identifies them with Mary Magdalene and the other Mary who visited Christ's tomb: "the two maries" (*U* 3.297). Later in *Ulysses*, some friends of the recently deceased Paddy Dignam discuss persons from whom they might solicit money to defray young Dignam's education. One man suggests approaching Mr. Boyd; Martin Cunningham replies shortly, "Touch me not" (*U* 10.967). The original of that sentence was spoken by Jesus to Mary Magdalene after the resurrection, when she recognized him near the tomb and approached to embrace him (John 20:17).[22]

The Good Felon

On Mount Calvary Jesus was crucified between two thieves. One—traditionally the one on the right side—proclaimed his own guilt, but Jesus' innocence. As a reward for this confession of faith, he was told, "Today you will be with me in paradise" (Luke 23:33–43). Christian legend has certified the divine promise of canonization by giving the crucified criminal a name and a title, Saint Dismas. He is the patron of prisoners. Joyce certainly knew this tradition, as is reflected in a pair of allusions to the Good Thief. During the discussion in the National Library in *Ulysses*, "Penitent thief" (*U* 9.101) appears in a brief paragraph of oblique excuses for England's depredation of Ireland. In the *Wake* during his smarmy sermon to Issy, Jaun (who is a master at twisting scripture) intones, "canalized love, you understand, does a felon good" (*FW* 436.18–19).

The preceding exposition featured a pair of archangels and four evangelists, one guardian of the Holy Family (St. Joseph), two other hallowed families (Zachary, Elizabeth, and John the Baptist; Martha, Mary, and Lazarus), and one Good Thief. That tally, so to speak, makes the chapter sound like an exercise in literary-spiritual accountancy. For such a figurative thrust there exists a graceful Joycean precedent in Father Purdom's sermon (*D* 174)—and it is useful to recall that the writer of the first gospel, Matthew, is the patron saint of bookkeepers.

3

The Apostolic Age

After the narrative of Jesus' activity on earth concludes with his ascension into heaven (Acts 1:6–11), the most important figures in the history of the infant church are the apostles. These are traditionally the twelve men first selected by the Lord to be sent out (*apostellein* in Greek) to preach the new faith. Others who shared this mission are usually called the disciples (from the Latin for "pupils"), to whom the original eyewitness message was taught to prepare them for the evangelization of the Mediterranean world. Saints Peter and Paul are the foremost representatives of each group. This chapter discusses Joyce's literary appropriation of the careers of these well-known saints and patrons, as well as the contributions of various other early emissaries of the gospel, including a pair of renegades.

Peter and Paul

Jesus designated the Galilean fisherman Peter as the "rock" on which the church was to be built; he was accordingly given the symbolic "keys of the kingdom" (Matthew 16:18–19, and *U* 14.250–52). Following the thunderbolt of his call on the road to Damascus, Saul—renamed Paul—became a tireless itinerant preacher and earned the honorific title "Apostle to the Gentiles" (Acts 9:3–22 and *U* 12.1489). According to tradition, Peter and Paul were both martyred in Rome, on the same day, during Nero's brutal persecution of Christians in A.D. 64. For these reasons the names of these two first-generation saints are frequently linked in Joyce's fiction. An undistorted Ulyssean example comes from a somewhat muddled outline of Catholic teaching in which Leopold Bloom remembers to include "Peter and Paul" (*U* 5.423); in the *Wake* Shaun backs up one of his indictments of Shem with a mild oath, stated in distinctly French undertones: "so whelp you Sinner Pitre and Sinner Poule" (*FW* 192.12–13). In his debate with Taff, Butt supports an argument by calling on a compounded holy witness, "S. Pivorandbowl" (*FW* 351.14), but the underlying catch phrase (*pivo* is Slavic for "beer"; a form of nine-pin bowling is called "skittles" [see *FW* 341.12]) implies that the saints' mission was no big deal. A pseudo-Scandinavian gloss is intended in "admirable peadar poulsen" (*FW* 326.26); a Wakean list of saintly symbols and relics includes "*the puffpuff and pompom of Powther and Pall*" (*FW* 349.23). In "Cyclops" the apostolic connection is perpetuated by the baptismal name of the French delegate to the F.O.T.E.I. (Friends of the Emerald Isle), "Monsieur Pierrepaul Petitepatant" (*U* 12.558).

Throughout *Wake* there are more than a dozen similar examples of the juxtaposition of the names of Peter and Paul, most of them little more than clever instances of Joyce's penchant for onomastic wordplay. There is, of course, evangelical precedent for this sort of verbal finesse: Peter is so called by Jesus as a pun on *petra*, the Greek noun for "rock." At least one such example of the linked apostolic names in the *Wake*, however, has decided thematic purpose. At the end of the theological controversy between the Mookse and the Gripes, the disputants disperse: "And there were left now an only elmtree and but a stone. *Polled* with *pietrous, Sierre* but *saule*. O! Yes! And Nuvoletta, a *lass*" (*FW* 159.3–5; my emphases). The italicized words need etymological comment: "poll" is an archaic English verb meaning "to cut or trim the branches"; "pietrous" is derived from Pietro, Italian for Peter; "sierre" is close to *sierra* (Spanish for a "saw"), a range of mountains with jagged, rocky crags; "saule" is French both for a polled willow (a tree with its branches sawn off) and the name for Saul, Paul's pre-conversion title (note VI.B.4.328); "lass" refers to Issy, the sister of the twin debaters, and sounds like the ancient Greek *laas* (stone). In short, that passage with its repeated puns serves as a multilingual preface for the *Wake's* primary manifestation of "a tree and a stone."[1]

In a March 7, 1924, letter to Harriet Shaw Weaver, Joyce wrote that he had finished "the *Anna Livia* piece." He explains, "It is a chattering dialogue across the river by two washerwomen who as night falls become a tree and a stone" (*Letters* I.212–13). In that famous episode one woman says, "My branches lofty are taking root." Her companion on the opposite bank responds, "And my cold cher's gone ashley" (*FW* 213.13–14). The "root" and "branches" of the first sentence confirm a metamorphosis into a tree. I suggest that "ashley" in the contrariparian reply is meant to refer to an ashlar, a square-cut stone used in building. McHugh's *Annotations* refer to a suggestion that the transformation becomes clearer if "cher" is interpreted as "chair (seat)."[2] On his own, McHugh also—and with greater force and point, in my opinion—notes "F[rench] chair: flesh," an interpretation that is strengthened by the prior adjective "cold." Ovidian metamorphoses of women into trees (Daphne) and stone (Niobe) were well known to Joyce. As a matter of prefatory fact, Daphne (and the Latin/

English equivalent of her arboreal name) appears earlier in the same episode, with a bilingual Greek-English rock: "throw those laurels now on her daphdaph teasesong petrock" (*FW* 203.30–31).

The final paragraph of "Anna Livia Plurabelle" repeats the tree-stone motif: "I feel as old as yonder elm. A tale told of Shaun or Shem? . . . I feel as heavy as yonder stone. . . . Tell me, tell me, tell me, elm! Night night! Telmetale of stem or stone. Beside the rivering waters of, hitherandthithering waters of. Night" (*FW* 215.34–216.5). The interjection of Shaun and Shem into that twilight finale not only recalls the earlier description of the rival twins as a tree and a stone, but also prepares the reader for the major role that the boys will play in book II of the *Wake*. In that process, the paired Peter and Paul— in various languages, roles, and metamorphoses—make a significant hagiographical contribution.[3]

St. Peter

Joycean narrative casts Peter in several of his traditional New Testament roles. Before his selection as an apostle, Peter earned his living as a fisherman (Matthew 4:18–20). Thus, in the same Ulyssean sentence in which Jesus' foster-father is referred to as "Joseph the joiner," the leader of the twelve is called "Peter Piscator" (*U* 14.304–5), the Latin noun for "fisherman."[4] When Jesus was arrested and led away for interrogation, Peter fulfilled his Master's prophecy by denying him three times (Matthew 26:30–35, 69–75). Joyce refers to that lapse in loyalty on three different occasions, twice in *Ulysses* (*U* 14.304 and 14.373) and once, with proverbial exhortation, in the *Wake*: "To funk is only peternatural its daring feers divine. Bebold!" (*FW* 451.16–17). Tradition also assigns Peter the high position as Keeper of the Pearly Gates of Heaven. At Paddy Dignam's funeral, Leopold Bloom calls attention to the "Keys" (*U* 6.740) of the caretaker of Glasnevin Cemetery. He also recalls the official's good humor: "Cracking his jokes too. . . . The one about the bulletin. Spurgeon went to heaven 4 a.m. this morning. 11 p.m. (closing time). Not arrived yet. Peter" (*U* 6.786–789).

As the first bishop of Rome, Peter is also regarded by Catholics as the first pope.[5] In "Oxen of the Sun" one of the young medicals flippantly concludes an insular parody of the Homeric episode by reciting two lines of a "rollicking chanty: /—*Pope Peter's but a pissabed. / A man's a man for a' that*" (*U* 14.648–50). Surprisingly, the two washerwomen in the *Wake* are slightly more respectful in their allusive mockery of HCE. They claim he was seen reeling around town, "with oddfellow's tripple tiara busby rotundarinking round his scalp. Like Pate-by-the Neva or Pete-over-Meer" (*FW* 205.33–34). The "triple tiara" is an undoubted reference to the three-layered crown worn exclusively by the pope in ceremonial processions. The double mention of "Pate/Pete" appears to name two churches (the one by a Russian river, the other overlooking the German sea), both under the patronage of St. Peter. If that reference is meant to be local, I can cite only a single church in Dublin dedicated to Peter; it is located in Phibsborough/Cabra, briefly rechristened "S. Phibb" and "S. Phibia's" in the two catalogues of churches in the *Wake* (*FW* 568.8 and 601.21). St. Peter's in the Vatican is the mother church of Roman Catholicism; at its high altar only the pope, the successor of the fisherman-apostle, celebrates mass.[6] The bones of the martyred Peter are interred in the crypt beneath this altar.

Joyce admired Jesus' skill in the etymological pun for dubbing Peter the "rock" of the church. This foundation formula appears in English (*U* 14.251–52), in Latin, "Tu es Petrus" (*FW* 407.15), and with an Aramaic gloss (*Letters* I. 248).[7] Joyce himself reciprocated with several similar variations on that name in the *Wake*. An uncrossed notebook entry, "tu es pitre" (VI.C.14.34; also note VI.B.4.261), is repeated verbatim in the text: "*tu es pitre!*" (*FW* 291.25). The humor springs from inserting the French word for "clown," *pitre*, after the biblically correct Latin introduction, *tu es* (thou art). The same ploy is used in the distortion of the name of the London church St. Peter-le-Peor into "Pitre-le-Pore-in Petrin" (*FW* 135.10).[8] In the "Anna Livia Plurabelle" section of the *Wake*, ALP serves HCE his breakfast, an "ale of ferns in trueart pewter" (*FW* 199.19). In keeping with the episode's fluvial thrust, the Ale is a river in Scotland; Ferns is a town in County Wexford, noted for its Norman castle. It is not clear whether some sort of malt beverage is intended by "ale," or if it refers to a flagon once raised by a hypothetical "earl" who lived in the keep. At any rate, the archival precedent for the phrase is biblical, with a slightly medieval twist: "⁸Thou art pewter" (VI.C.13.280); a compact Celtic variation appears on the *Wake's* first page, "thuartpeatrick" (*FW* 3.10). An unused notebook entry brings to light another aspect of the saint's potential energy: "King Coal / Mrs Vapour / Thou are Petrol" (VI.B.8.187).

A clever misappropriation of Jesus' lapidary metaphor is attributed to Cranly in *Portrait*. In an argument with Stephen, he scores a neat, but unnoticed debater's point to deny any vestige of the institutional continuity of the apostolic commission: "The church is not the *stone building* nor even the clergy and their dogmas" (*P* 245; my emphasis). During his instruction to Issy in the *Wake*, Jaun transfers the gospel's grant of Petrine power to his catechumen: "What bondman ever you bind on earth I'll be bound 'twas combined in hemel [*Himmel* is German for "heaven"]" (*FW*

435.22–23). Those correlative spheres of authority also seem to be affirmed in "Twoways Peterborough" (*FW* 442.11) and "Twoedged Petard" (*FW* 497.8).

The Golden Legend records a brief account of the life of St. Peter's daughter, Petronilla. To avoid marriage to a pagan noble, she "began a regimen of fasting, prayer, and the reception of the Body of the Lord, [then] took to her bed, and after three days migrated to the Lord."[9] The chief apostle's virginal daughter does not appear in the *Wake*, but she does crop up in a notebook introduced by a paternally appropriate formula: "tu sei Petronilla" (VI.B.15.19).

One of the most important of papal prerogatives was the annual tax levied on the faithful. Its origin seems to have been in medieval England, but the obligation was soon extended over all Europe. Originally the amount sent to Rome each year was a penny from every family—hence its customary title, "Peter's pence." There are frequent allusions to this ecclesiastical tax in the *Wake:* "petery pence" (*FW* 13.2), "Penceless Peter" (*FW* 210.22), "Peter's pelf" (*FW* 520.14), and "potter's pance" (*FW* 618.33).[10] Another type of financial transaction conducted under the saint's patronage—this time reluctant—is "Robbing Peter to pay Paul" (*U* 12.1577). That proverbial practice is listed under the many civic flaws of Leopold Bloom by the astute experts in governmental fiscal policy who assemble at Barney Kiernan's pub in "Cyclops."

Just as contributions to Peter's pence came in from all over the Roman Catholic world, so too do popes customarily bestow a global blessing on the faithful. That solemn benediction is called *urbi et orbi* (to the city and to the world). Two archival entries indicate that Joyce knew the special pontifical form for that ceremony. The first, "rO.G. [Oliver Gogarty] imparts the pontifical blessing" (*UNBM* 202:47), is fictionally transferred to a Circean cardinal (*U* 15.2683–84). The second, "gpapel [*sic*] blessing / g2 fingers / gkey in hand" (VI.C.15.173), is reassigned to the hero of the *Wake*. Parts of the latter entry reappear in the text to describe the domestic cohesion (or the sexual compatibility) of the Earwickers/Porters: "A so united family *patermater* ["father-mother" in Latin] is not more existing on *papel* or off of it. As *keymaster* fits the lock it weds so this bally builder to his streamline secret" (*FW* 560.28–30; my emphases). This Wakean transfer of authority from universal church to Chapelizod home is justified by the fact that HCE is invested with the papal title of *pontifex maximus*, "maximost bridgesmaker" (*FW* 126.10–11).[11] It is also reported that HCE "raised but *two fingers* and yet smelt it would day" (*FW* 138.21–22). In the text there are also numerous distortions of the actual Latin words of the blessing; they range from "urbiandorbic bulges" (*FW* 96.36–97.1) through "Ruby and Roby" (*FW* 126.26–27) to "a blazing urbanorb" (*FW* 589.6).[12]

St. Paul

The life and works of St. Paul seem to have left very few traces on Joyce's works prior to the *Wake*.[13] The "apostle to the gentiles" (*U* 12.1489) is a formulaic title that he could have heard anywhere. A similar Old Testament phrase, "a light to the Gentiles" (Isaiah 49:6), reappears in the Ithacan catechism as a summary-answer to the question "What satisfied him [Bloom]?": "To have sustained no positive loss. To have brought a positive gain to others. Light to the gentiles" (*U* 17.351–53). The Pauline connection here is found in the epistle to the Romans, in which the apostle repeatedly stresses that his mission is to bring news of the new faith to the Gentiles (Romans 15:9–16).[14]

Logically, such conspicuously sparse citation from a text as readily available as the epistles of the New Testament would argue for an author's lack of interest in the subject. It is, therefore, surprising that Joyce's Trieste library held a massive two-volume, over-1300-page *The Life and Work of Saint Paul*.[15] Moreover, a sheet of notes in Joyce's handwriting was found in between the pages of the first volume. Although none of the entries was explicitly reused in *Ulysses*, two of the quite technical notes about Jewish and/or early Christian practices may have contributed to the process of its composition. The first of Joyce's incidental notes, "Jewish Gematria or Notarikin [with 'kon' written above]," refers to the rabbinical method of extracting hidden meaning from the numerical value of the letters in the Hebrew alphabet. A familiar example is "666: the number of this beast [Nero Caesar]" in Revelation 13:18. In the "Ithaca" chapter of *Ulysses*, there is an approximation of this hallowed practice, as "Bloom in turn wrote the Hebrew characters ghimel, aleph, daleth and (in the absence of mem) a substituted qoph, explaining their arithmetical values as ordinal and cardinal numbers, videlicet 3, 1, 4, and 100" (*U* 17.737–40). Those digits (the "100" indicates a decimal point) "spell" out Bloom's mnemotecnic for 3.14, *pi*, π—a formula useful to anyone hoping to square the circle.[16]

The second of Joyce's notes from the book on St. Paul reads "επιπασμος (1 Corinthians. vii, 18) after circumcision." The Greek term is derived from the apostle's instructions about a possible conflict with Jewish law by Gentile converts: "If any had already been circumcised at the time of his call [to Christianity], he need not disguise it and anyone who was uncircumcised at the time of his call need not be circumcised" (1 Corinthians 7:18).

The verb translated as "disguised" is *epispastho* in the original Greek of the epistle; its literal meaning is "draw [the skin] forward" as if not circumcised, a means of disguising one's original adherence to the Abrahamic-Mosaic covenant. Neither Bloom nor Stephen is noted for his competence in the exegesis of the Pauline epistles, but circumcision does crop up as a topic during their Ithacan discourse. Stephen is worried about "the problem of the sacerdotal integrity of Jesus circumcised" (*U* 17.1203); Bloom experiences "a sentiment of remorse" about his disregard of the Judaic practice of "the circumcision of male infants" (*U* 17.1893, 1899). And, although the context has nothing to do with Jewish religious law or its interpretation by early Christians, in her monologue Molly Bloom reveals that she "was dying to find out was he [Blazes Boylan] circumcised" (*U* 18.314–15).

A number of the Wakean allusions to the Apostle of the Gentiles have already been recorded in my initial section on correlative aspects of Peter and Paul; others, involving parodic excerpts from Paul's epistles, will appear later in this chapter in my discussion of St. Onesimus. During the verbose statement of the *Wake's* "First Question" (about the identity and character of HCE) Saul-Paul's miraculous conversion and subsequent change of name is reassigned to the novel's hero: "[he] was struck out of his sittem when he rowed *saulely* to *demask us* and to our ap*paul*ing predicament brought as plagues from Bud*da*pest" (*FW* 131.11–13; my emphases).

The Other Apostles

In the *Wake* the original dozen apostles selected by Jesus momentarily lend their names to an equal number of pub patrons. The occasion is the "Seventh Question" of book I.6, which seeks the identity of the twelve drinkers who frequent HCE's establishment. In that query they appear first as multilingual months of the year,[17] then as districts in Dublin, and finally as Irish versions of the apostles: "Matey [Matthias], Teddy [Thaddeus], Simon, Jorn [John], Pedher [Peter], Andy, Barty, Philly, Jamesy Mor [James the Greater] and Tom, Matt and Jakes MacCarty [James the Less]" (*FW* 142.27–28). In the introduction I briefly mentioned a notebook index (VI.B.43.63) listing the apostles and their (slightly askew) symbols. The order of the names in the notebook—ending with Matthias, who was selected to replace Judas Iscariot (Acts 1:25–26)—is more traditional than in the preceding list. In his apostolic catalogue in the text of the *Wake*, Joyce obviously wanted to conclude with a flourish of local color, "Jakes MacCarty," perhaps his own patron saint. In the New Testament book of Acts, there is no mention of how the Twelve were assigned their missionary territories.

Joyce, perhaps extrapolating from the method used to select Matthias, fills in that gap in early church history: "apostles cast lots for / preaching areas" (VI.B.14.91).

Several apostles are singled out for individual mention in the *Wake*. The "Seumas, thought little" (*FW* 211.4) who receives one of ALP's gifts in I.8 is an Irish stand-in for James the Less. "Barthalamou" (*FW* 314.22) is transformed into a place name, and a minor catalogue of London churches includes "Barth-the-Grete-by-the-Exchange" (*FW* 135.10–11; also note VI.B.24.144 and 147). In a brief but ingenious note, Kopper detects another allusion to Bartholomew. He interprets Jarl van Hooter's "*baretholo*-bruised heels" and his propensity for "shaking warm hands with himself" (*FW* 21.35–35; my emphasis) as covert allusions to the way the apostle was martyred: according to tradition, Bartholomew was flayed alive and crucified head down.[18] In the gospels James the Greater and his brother John are given a nickname by Jesus; he calls them "Boanerges," or "Sons of Thunder" (Mark 3:17). Joyce applies that epithet to three appropriate characters in the *Wake*. First, the same pseudo-Dutch lord who was just mentioned is also assigned the evangelical epithet of John and James: "like the campbells acoming with a fork lance of lightning, Jarl von Hooter Boanerges himself" (*FW* 22.30–32). Later, Shem is described as a "whirling dervish, Tumult, son of Thunder" (*FW* 184.6). Finally, the tailor realizes that he has hard-to-please customers in the Norwegian captain and the ship's chandler: "but give the devil his so long as those sohns of a blitzh [*Blitz* is German for "lightning"] call the tuone tuone [*tuono* is Italian for "thunder"] and thonder alout makes the thurd" (*FW* 314.27–29).

Because Thomas refused to accept the fact of the Resurrection until he could "see the holes that the nails made in [Christ's] hands ... and ... put [his] hand into His side" (John 20:25), he is justly known as the "doubting" apostle. In the *Wake* several references recall Thomas's demands for empirical proof; the most graphic is "Touchole Fitz Tuomush" (*FW* 8.26–27). An archival note calls attention to the fact that, according to the gospel (John 11:16, 20:24), Thomas was a twin (*didymos* in Greek): "S Thomas Didymus" (VI.B.10.18). In the text this bit of apostolic nomenclature is adapted to the conclusion of the Mime of Nick, Mick, and the Maggies, where a pair of guards is assigned to protect the twin boys as they drift off to sleep, "even Garda Didymus and Garda Domas" (*FW* 258.30–31).

Disciples

In addition to the twelve apostles (and the honorary member of that group, St. Paul), there are other early proponents of the new faith whose deeds merited mention in two canonical texts, Acts and the *Wake*. One of Paul's most faithful associates on his missionary journeys is Barnabas (Acts 11:30, 13:3), but they eventually go their own ways after a violent quarrel (Acts 15:39). Soon afterwards Timothy joins Paul (Acts 16:1, 1 Timothy 1:1). Those two disciples are linked together in a Joycean version of their service to the growing Christian community: "ministerbuilding up, as repreaches Timothy, in Saint Barmabrac's" (*FW* 274.11–12). Paul himself (apparently still at odds with Barnabas) is situated nearby: "as reproaches Paulus, on the Madderhorn" (*FW* 274.6–7).

Another disciple who accompanied Paul on his first trips to Macedonia and Corinth is Silas (Acts 15:40); in several of the epistles his name is given as Silvanus, and he is also associated with Timothy (1 Thessalonians 1:1, 1 Peter 5:12). A female disciple named Tabitha or Dorcas ("Gazelle" in Greek) was noted for her good works to the Christians in Jaffa. When St. Peter heard that she had died of a sudden illness, he rushed to her room, "where all the widows stood around him in tears"; then he restored Dorcas to life (Acts 9:36–42). This miracle is verbally reflected in the *Wake* as the "daughters of February . . . voiced approval . . . by dropping kneedeep in tears over . . . piopadey boy, their *solase in dorkaness*" (*FW* 470.4–7; my emphasis). Glasheen ingeniously sees both Silas and Dorcas in the murky confines of the italicized phrase of that citation. Be that as it may, there can be no doubt that St. Peter's raising of Dorcas from the dead was a great solace to her weeping companions. On the other hand, there is no thematic or narrative reason to connect the solitary "Titus" (*FW* 70.14) with St. Paul's disciple on several missionary journeys (2 Corinthians 8:6, Titus 1:5).

A number of critics have remarked that Stephen Dedalus's first name is that of the first Christian to be put to death for professing his beliefs. St. Stephen won his martyr's crown (*stephanos* in Greek) when he was stoned to death by an outraged mob after his testimony before the Sanhedrin in Jerusalem (Acts 6:8–8:2). In the *Wake* the ship's husband presses the Norwegian captain to convert to the true faith by promising (or threatening) to "first mardhyr you entirely" (*FW* 326.2–3).

The apocryphal *Acts of Paul and Thecla* is the tale of a beautiful young woman of Iconium who dedicated herself to a life of asceticism and chastity after hearing the apostle preach. Her pagan fiancé, Thamyris, protested to the officials and had Paul and Thecla hauled off to prison. After they repeatedly escaped death in a series of miraculous rescues, the virgin was commissioned to preach the word of God. This pious romance has left no traces in the *Wake*, but a notebook entry shows that Joyce had heard of the highly popular story: "Agnes & Thecla were with me" (VI.B.2.11).

Even in the genuine Acts of the Apostles there are some characters who are not fully dedicated to the greater glory of God. The most notorious villain was Simon the Magus, whose title indicates that he was regarded as a wonder-worker. Even after he had become a baptized believer, Simon tried to purchase the power of the Holy Spirit. When he was thoroughly chastised by St. Peter and ordered to pray for forgiveness, Simon told the apostle to do the praying himself (Acts 8:9–24). An English noun formed from the apostate magician's name denotes the act of trying to sell spiritual power and privilege: simony. That ecclesiastical term rings sharply in the opening paragraph of "The Sisters," Joyce's first published story (*D* 9). An adjectival form appears in the tangled canon-law marriage case in the *Wake:* "simoniac" (*FW* 573.31). Unlike his son's first name, I see no reason to push for allegorical or typological force in the Christian name of Simon Dedalus. His problems involve drink, hypocrisy, and lack of money—not profitable trade in miracles. Stephen Dedalus, on the other hand, when he contemplates a call to the priesthood, is well aware of the attraction of "secret knowledge and secret power" and the possibilities of its abuse (*P* 159).

Ananias and his wife, Sapphira, sell all their property to benefit the Christian community, but they hold some of the proceeds back for their own use. Peter berates them for trying to cheat the Holy Spirit, and causes Ananias to fall dead at the accusation. Three hours later his wife also lies about the sum, and instantly drops dead. Not surprisingly, "[t]his made a profound impression on the whole Church and on all who heard it" (Acts 5:1–11). The Wakean phrase "Ananias' cans" (*FW* 170.30) may appear to refer to the receptacles in which the deceitful couple hid their profit, but a nearby "junglegrown pineapple" signals that Joyce is playing with both the name of the biblical scoundrel and a common European word for pineapple, a tropical fruit that is frequently shipped in cans, "ananas" (French) or "Ananas" (German).

My final example of Joyce's manipulation of the history of the apostolic church involves one of his favorite techniques (wordplay with names), a recurring Wakean motif (allusion to Oscar Wilde), and borrowing from the form and content of sections of the biblical Acts and several Pauline epistles. The textual evidence is complex and subtle, but the results reveal how cleverly (and covertly) Joyce integrated even incidental hagiographical material into his fiction.

St. Onesimus

Joyce began his 1909 lecture on the poet of *Salomé* by reciting the names borne by the author: "Oscar Fingal O'Flahertie Wills Wilde" (*CW* 201). One element is picked out for special treatment: "O'Flahertie, a savage Irish tribe whose destiny it was to assail the gates of medieval cities: a name that incited terror in peaceful men, who still recite . . . in the ancient litany of the saints: 'from the wild O'Flaherties, libera nos Domine'" (*CW* 201).

In *Finnegans Wake* a similar string of names appears in the ninth stanza of Hosty's "The Ballad of Persse O'Reilly": "Fingal Mac Oscar Onesine Bargearse Boniface" (*FW* 46.20). The final element ("boniface" is a traditional title for an innkeeper) connects the convicted Wilde with the accused publican Humphrey Chimpden Earwicker. Wilde was broad in the beam, hence the moniker "Barge-arse." HCE has a "gross bild" (*FW* 559.25); in German the adjective *gross* means "large" or "great"; the noun *Bild* means "picture" or "form." The suggestion of a "large ass" conveyed by the name would apply appropriately to the build and image of both of the referents. "Fingal" and "Mac Oscar" obviously link HCE with Wilde's epic avatars: "Oscar, nephew of King Fingal . . . , who was treacherously killed by the hand of his host as he sat at table" (*CW* 201). What about "Onesine," which the *Wake* substitutes for "O'Flahertie"? The purpose of this section of my apostolic chapter is to demonstrate that that name is also part of Joyce's game. My methodological matrix is genetically onomastic hagiography—the name of a saint buried in the transmission of the text.

Before presenting the evidence to support the claim for an early Christian holy man as the mediator between Wilde and Earwicker, it would be instructive to examine other possibilities. For example, a philologically inclined interpreter might note that the two (linguistically unrelated) Latin nouns *os, oris* and *os, ossis* have relevant meanings: *os* = "mouth," "face"; *os* = "bone." The first syllable of Oscar's name, if repeated, yields "bony face," and thus prepares the way for the final term in the Wakean string: "Boniface." But neither Wilde nor HCE was slim, and it is unlikely that Joyce would have bothered to resort to Latin, twice, to come up with a skeletal visage that is gratuitous, even once.

How about a more complex division of words: M*ac Oscar One*sine"? The italicized section can be elided into a thematically on-target command in Spanish: *acos[c]a roña*, "attack the filth," "harass the scum." Both Oscar and Humphrey are the victims of unremitting accusation and condemnation. They are, *sin embargo,* a pair of scapegoats.[19] There is, however, no archival evidence that Joyce worked out that common bond in Spanish. A recent article, written with attention to initial draftings, suggests that Joyce's "Onesine" is a (negative?) echo of the Old English *onsene* ("appearance"), in as much as HCE "has neither one sign nor one sin . . . [nor] one visage."[20] This is a possibility, but one that is generated by an undocumented calque (archaic) and that in turn generates the excessive appearances of solecisms (contemporary).

Speculation aside, one should first examine the evidence of the evolving text. This is the genetic contribution to detecting the full force of the wild string of names. Two autograph drafts for this section of the *Wake* survive, both dated to November–December 1923; in them Joyce wrote, "Onesi*me*" (*JJA* 45:44, 53). That spelling is also found in the March–April 1927 typescript (*JJA* 45:83). The first appearance of "Onesi*ne*" comes in the April 1927 galley for *transition* 2 (*JJA* 45:100). There is no indication that this spelling, substituting an *n* for the *m*, is anything other than a simple typographical error. But the erroneous "Onesine," which entered the text at this point, was neither detected nor corrected. It stands in all subsequent versions of the episode and in the printed text of the entire *Wake*.

Next, it is useful to consider an explanation of the hagiography involved in these allusions to names. The Epistle to Philemon is the shortest piece in the New Testament: a single chapter of twenty-five brief verses. In it Paul, imprisoned at Rome, writes to Philemon in Asia Minor that he is returning, with the promise of any required compensation, his runaway slave. The apostle trusts that Philemon will make good use of him, now that he has become a Christian. In fact, most of St. Paul's letter is a play on the meaning of the freedman's name: "I mean Onesimus. He was of no *use* to you before, but he will be *useful* to you now, as he has been to me" (Philemon 10–11; my emphases). Philemon obviously followed Paul's advice, since Onesimus performed various services for the infant church (see Colossians 4:9), perhaps as a bishop. Tradition alleges that he died a martyr, stoned to death at Rome.

Now, onomastics comes into play as another factor in deciphering Joyce's distortion of Wilde's names. The Greek adjective *onesimos* means "useful" or "helpful," the point of Paul's wordplay with the italicized terms in the citation from his epistle. In French, the freed slave-saint's name is spelled "Onesime." Its substitution in the *Wake* for "O'Flahertie" is Joyce's extension of the Pauline pun: the name "Flaherty" (despite its savage historical reverberations) means "generous" or "hospitable" in Irish.[21] Latin also contributes to the name-game here. The final element in Joyce's pseudo-Wildean string is "Boniface," an entirely fitting title for HCE, the pub-keeper. The two Latin roots in that name are *bon-* ("good") and *fac-*

("to make," "to accomplish"): Boniface literally does well. The Greek, Irish, and Latin names are not precise synonyms, but I wager that their proximity in the *Wake* is not onomastic coincidence. The choice of the French form for the saint's name is also appropriate: Wilde fled to France after his prison term and died there in 1900. Moreover, like Onesimus the freed slave, he was a religious convert: the former left paganism for Christianity at Rome; the latter was formally received into the Church of Rome on his deathbed in Paris. Finally, Onesimus's feast day is February 16, and February was Joyce's favorite source for saints' feast days; he scoured that month's calendar to find allusive names for Issy's flower girls.

In addition to the primary trilingual aptness of the substitution of a Greco-Gallic name for an Irish name, there is a thematic link. Wilde, Paul, and Onesimus—sinner and saints—were tried and imprisoned by the authorities for their allegedly anti-social beliefs and practices. It would also be possible to call each of them a martyr. (On this point, Wilde's post-prison, exilic pseudonym is significant: the components of "Sebastian Melmoth" join an arrow-transfixed Christian saint to the hell-bound wanderer of Gothic romance.) In *Wake*, Humphrey Chimpden Earwicker is definitely accused of ineffable crimes and is subjected to repeated inquisitorial procedures.[22] He is, however, never brought before a civil court or imprisoned; nor (even allowing for Joyce's zany hagiography) is there any overt claim for his martyrdom, much less canonization.[23] On the other hand, it is possible to demonstrate a strong epistolary connection between St. Paul and Oscar Wilde inside and outside the text of the *Wake*. There are also a number of passages that make it clear that Joyce was familiar with both the form and content of the Pauline letters in the New Testament. This evidence reinforces my original suggestion that Paul's prison-mate lends his useful name, via Wilde, to HCE.

The most conspicuous Wakean bond between St. Paul and Wilde is the following passage: "gheol ghiornal, foull subustioned mullmud, his farced epistol to the hibruws" (*FW* 228.33–34). An analysis of each of these three phrases yields important and correlative results.

Tradition assigns a significant number of the Pauline epistles to the period when their author was in prison in Rome. These letters of encouragement and instruction to various sectors of the growing Christian community were not literally "jail journals," but there are in them occasional references to his status: "Remember the chains I wear" (Colossians 4:18); "From Paul, a prisoner of Christ Jesus" (Philemon 1). In Reading Gaol Wilde was allowed to write a long letter to his lover, Lord Alfred Douglas. This composition, usually called *De Profundis* (From the Depths),[24] is a long dramatic monologue of accusation of betrayal, self-recrimination, loss, pain, discovery, consolation, regeneration.[25] Wilde asked a friend to see that his letter was typed up for transmission to Douglas. In that request Wilde has some ironic comments on the personal importance of his passionate *apologia:* "for indeed it is an Encyclical Letter, and as the Bulls of the Holy Father are named from their opening words, it may be spoken of as the *Epistola: In Carcere et Vinculis* (A Letter: In Prison and in Chains).[26]

The name Wilde assumed to mask his identity after his release from jail, Sebastian Melmoth, is distorted in the *Wake's* second phrase, "foull subustioned mullmud" (*FW* 228.33). Joyce's "foull" combines the French *fou/fol* ("crazy/fool") with the English "foul"; a syllabification of "mullmud" reveals a curt estimate of Wilde's topics, a contemplation of filth. The relevance of "subustioned" involves an allusion to imputations of homosexuality and effeminacy against the Roman emperor Augustus. Mark Antony alleged that sodomy was the price of his adoption by Julius Caesar. Antony's brother Lucius claimed that Augustus was accustomed to singe his legs with red-hot nut shells, so that the new hairs would be softer.[27] The very rare Latin verb "to singe" is *suburo, suburere;* its perfect passive participle is *subustus.* In the weird morphology of the *Wake,* this form is remade into an English past participle (passive): "*subust*-ioned." I admit that this last link (a participle that connects Augustus to Wilde) pushes linguistic allusion to the limit. On the other hand, Joyce used other equally recherché material from Suetonius in the *Wake,* and the crosscultural mockery of conspicuous effeminacy is directly to the point.[28] The alternative would be to attribute Joyce's mutation of "Sebastian" into "subustion" to a random interchange of vowels—and to add an "-ed" to create the past tense of a verb unheard of in any language.

The final phrase, "his farced epistol to the hibruws" (*FW* 288.33–34), is quite a bit more straightforward. Although almost all modern scholars of the Bible seriously question its attribution to St. Paul, the Epistle to the Hebrews is firmly entrenched amid the apostolic letters in editions of the New Testament. Joyce interpolates a "farced" (Irish pronunciation of "first") before the title, but, unlike the epistles to the Corinthians or Thessalonians, there was only one letter to the Jewish Christians. In addition to its phonetic value, "farced" conveys the imputation that Wilde's letter from jail was a farce, and that it was "stuffed" with ludicrous material (*farcé* in French; *farcito* in Italian). That past participle (passive) also has an obscene meaning in many languages, as in the English phrase "Get stuffed!" The "hibruws" do double duty as the Hebrew converts to Christianity and the highbrows who condoned Wilde's behavior or praised his works.

Immediately following the three wildly Pauline phrases that have just been explicated, there is another line of allusion to the New Testament and the formula used in the salutations of its epistles: "From Cernilius slomtime prepositus of Toumaria to the clutch in Anteach. Salvo!" (*FW* 228.34–35). A significant moment in the Acts of the Apostles involves the miraculous conversion of Cornelius, a Roman centurion of the cohort stationed at Caesarea. Peter's concomitant vision and the celestial announcement that "What God made clean, you have not right to call profane" mark the opening of the nascent church to pagans who had received the Holy Spirit (Acts 10–11:18). The next episode in the apostolic history is the foundation of the church at Antioch. Barnabas was in charge of this mission, and he summoned the recently converted Saul (Paul) from Tarsus to work with him in Antioch. At this time a prophet named Agabus predicted a worldwide famine. The disciples from Antioch sent relief to their brethren in Judea (Acts 11:19–30).

That summary of two chapters of apostolic history was necessary because Joyce telescoped those events into the *Wake* passage cited at the start of the previous paragraph. The enlightened centurion Cornelius is converted into "Cernilius"; the church in Antioch becomes "the clutch in Anteach." The scope of the predicted famine will extend beyond all the seas, "Toumaria" (French *tout* ["all," "every"]; Latin *maria* ["the seas"]). The Latin perfect passive participle, *prepositus* ("appointed to command," "put in charge of"), agrees with Cornelius, an officer in the Roman contingent at Caesarea. Those are the correspondences between Acts and the *Wake*, in content.[29]

There is another aspect to the linkage. The form of Joyce's sentence is a fairly close imitation of the opening of a Pauline epistle: "From Paul . . . to the church of God at Corinth" (2 Corinthians 1:1); "From Paul to the churches of Galatia" (Galatians 1:1). The regular Latin greeting, in person or in a letter, is *salve* (singular) or *salvete* (plural). Immediately after his reproduction of the formulaic opening of a Pauline epistle, Joyce fires off a pseudo-Latin greeting, "Salvo!" (*FW* 228.35). This typical salutation-convention is not, in fact, followed by Paul, although similar forms: *salutant* ("they send greetings"), *salutatio* ("greetings"), *salutate* ("please greet") are used at the conclusion of many of the epistles.

The two adjacent passages that I have been discussing for the past several paragraphs are from the "Mime of Mick, Nick and Maggies" (*FW* II.1). There is no hint of an identification of Wilde or St. Paul with HCE here. Rather, the disgraced male in this instance is Glugg (Nick, Shem), who has failed to solve the first riddle. His words, written or spoken, are couched in the formal terms of a Latin epistle. The ensuing narrative presents the kaleidoscopic details of his reaction to his humiliation: he will go off into exile and write. But first, he will present his case in an incriminating document. (As McHugh points out, the writerly context is reinforced by the fact that the Russian word for ink is "chernila," which helps to form Glugg's pseudonym, "Cernilius." The self-production of ink by Shem is the point of an extended Latin passage at *FW* 185.14–26.)

In terms of the *Wake*, Glugg's Pauline epistle creates only a minor ripple on the surface of the plot. He is destined to be disgraced more than once. There is a document of far more significance, the letter from Boston that was uncovered by the hen. In its various manifestations throughout the book, the conclusion of this letter most frequently affixes four X's that are meant to be kisses.[30] The following is a representative example: "must now close it with fondest to the twoinns with four crosskisses . . ." (*FW* 111.16–17). Four New Testament epistles close with the formula "Greet one another with a holy kiss" (1 Corinthians 16:20, 2 Corinthians 13:12, 1 Thessalonians 5:26, 1 Peter 5:14). Joyce incorporated this apostolic flourish into the text of the Wakean letter just cited: "with four crosskisses for *holy paul* holey corner holi-poli whollyisland" (*FW* 111.17–18; my emphasis). The italicized reference intensifies the link to St. Paul that has already been suggested by the references to kisses.[31]

Another formula from the New Testament epistles has left its mark on the *Wake*: "Let Pauline be Irene" (*FW* 154.23). In Greek the word for "peace" is *eirēnē*, frequently converted into English as "irene." The epistolary form in the salutation is "Let the peace of God [be with you]" (1 Corinthians 1:3); in a conclusion the Apostle wished, "Peace to the brethren" (Ephesians 6:24). Thus, as far as the *Wake* citation goes, Joyce is not merely suggesting that someone change her name or that one woman play the role of another. Rather, he wants peace. Reference to the evolving text confirms this interpretation. The July–August 1927 first draft of this passage has "Let here be Irene" (*JJA* 47:129). The "here" was deleted and "Pauline" added in 1929 (*JJA* 47:203.) Naturally, I presume that the purpose of the substitution was to make the Pauline model (and the Apostle's original Greek) just slightly less cryptic.

The passages I have been discussing above involve Joyce's deployment of several *formal* elements of the Pauline epistles. There is at least one instance in the *Wake* in which the allusive emphasis is on the *content* of the Apostle's teaching. Early in the work, imputations and insinuations against HCE begin to surface. The alleged offense, it is countered, was, "at its wildest, a partial exposure with such attenuating circumstances" (*FW*

34.26–27). His supporters will rally as character witnesses: "We can't do without them. Wives, rush to the restyours!" (*FW* 34.30). Next, in the midst of jumbled song-titles, Volapük vocabulary, lilies and roses, there is a strange exclamation: "Pauline, allow!" (*FW* 34.33). These words could be interpreted as an appeal by the accused for some sympathy from a woman friend. Perhaps—but their primary purpose is to remind the readers of a unique loophole in early Christian teaching on the indissolubility of marriage.

In chapter 7 of his first epistle to the church at Corinth, St. Paul discusses marriage and virginity. His exhortations are about what one would expect, except for the following verse: "However, if the unbelieving partner [in a mixed pagan-Christian marriage] does not consent [to the partner's practice of her/his Christianity] they may separate; in these circumstances, the brother or sister is not tied: God has called you to a life of peace" (1 Corinthians 7:15). This verse is the scriptural authority for what is known as the "Pauline Privilege." That is, a couple may separate—and perhaps remarry—if one seriously and consistently prevents the other's practice of Christianity. Thus, in the *Wake's* "Pauline, allow!" I hear a muted fear. HCE is a Protestant; ALP is Catholic; their marriage is mixed. His alleged crimes may be judged to have put so much pressure on their domestic situation that his wife will invoke the apostolic privilege to free herself from this "redivivus of paganinism" (*FW* 50.15).

In the same section of the *Wake* as the appeal to Pauline, the Cad's wife repeats the calumnies against HCE to her sodality director. This ensures "that the gossiple so delivered in his epistolear" (*FW* 38.22–23) will rapidly spread all over town and eventually be immortalized in Hosty's "Ballad." The reference to the two primary New Testament forms, gospel and epistle, fits the tone of this passage in which the vilification is expressed in scriptural and ecclesiastical diction. Later in the work, just after the hen has unearthed the letter from Boston, that relic is curiously called an "old-world epistola" (*FW* 117.27).[32] These two explicit references to *epistolē/a*, the Greco-Latin word for "letter," are included here to complete the list of possible allusions to Pauline documents. Neither, however, seems to have any narrative or thematic connection with the roles of Oscar Wilde or St. Paul in the *Wake*.[33]

This section of my apostolic chapter began with an analysis of the source and significance of a string of Wildean names assigned to HCE. It is fitting that the discussion end with a look at a reprise of that onomastic exchange. In the section of the *Wake* that takes place in the barroom of Earwicker's pub, the bouncer threatens to sing Hosty's song if the customers do not leave. The owner is naturally eager to avoid the incriminating performance; he bows and scrapes to get the drinkers out the door. This obsequious behavior does not prevent the reintroduction of the publican's Wildesque title from the ballad, in altered form: "Fingool MacKishgmard Obesume Burgearse Benefice" (FW 371.22).[34]

McHugh glosses the key name, "Obesume," as a distortion of "obese" (French and English). That suggestion is reasonable. In the scene leading up to the first recitation of the names, HCE's detractors "apparently conceive of him as a great white caterpillar." Such a thought is preposterous to those "who knew and loved the christlikeness of the big cleanminded giant" (FW 33.23–29). It has long been recognized that the epithet "Great White Caterpillar" was originally attached to Wilde.[35] He was a large, pallid, puffy man. The rebuttal cited above also emphasizes the size of the alleged culprit, "big . . . giant."[36] In both versions of the name-string, the penultimate title ("Bargearse" [FW 46.22] and "Burgearse" [FW 371.22]) is a crude comment on the dimensions of the referent's rear end. In one case, it is as big as a barge; in the other case, it is the size of a German castle or a fortified Old English town. (The descriptions of Wellington, one of the many heroic prototypes of HCE, are also anatomically specific: "his big white harse" [FW 10.2, 11]; "his big wide harse" [FW 8.21, 10.21].)

In the reprise of names, the last title is "Benefice." Here the Latin roots of the name/occupation "Boniface" are made even more evident—as is the fact that the publican purports *to do well* by his customers. In the original string, the intended "Onesime" is a near-synonym for the terminal "Boniface." In the second version, the suggestion that "Obesume" means "obese" creates a more clinical, but less colorful match for "Burgearse."

What about "MacKishgmard," the substitution for "Oscar" in the revised name-list? First, an archival factor needs to be noted. In the first-draft autograph (1938) the form is clearly "MacKishguard" (JJA 55:448). The subsequent typescript repeats the *u*, but there is an inked-in correction to *m* (JJA 55:471). In the last-stage galley proofs (November 23, 1938) the series of commas between the names is removed; but the *m* in "MacKishgmard" remains untouched (JJA 55:534). The change in spelling could be significant, and it is worthwhile to speculate about the two forms, "-gu*ard*" and "-g*m*ard."

In Irish "kish" means "wicker" or "basket"; note "a wickered Kish" (FW 14.1). Two miles east of Kingstown (now Dun Laoghaire), lies the Kish Bank, a rock hazard (shaped like a basket, acting like a barrier?) at the southern entrance to Dublin Bay. A lightship was anchored nearby to warn approaching sea traffic (cf. *U* 2.267 and 13.1180–81). Perhaps the text's original "- Kishguard" was an allusion to this coast-guard ship. There is another possibility. In the argot of the English underworld, "kishlak" means "to spend the winter in jail."[37] If either of these two terms has any thematic bearing on the original form of the pseudo-Celtic patronymic "MacKishguard," the full import of that connection is obscure. Neither Wilde nor HCE nor St. Paul can by any stretch of the imagination be called a prison guard; none of them has any connection with a lightship.

There is another onomastic line of inquiry here. As the result of significant events in their lives, both Paul and Wilde changed their names—the former after his conversion, from "Saul" to "Paul"; the latter after his imprisonment, from "Oscar Wilde" to "Sebastian Melmoth." The apostle's Hebrew name, "Saul," was the same as that of the first king of Israel. In the Old Testament, after the judge Samuel anointed Saul, the Spirit of God came upon him, and he began to prophesy. The people were amazed and asked, "What is this that is come unto the son of Kish? Is Saul among the prophets?" (1 Samuel 10:11). King Saul's father was Kish. Joyce knew his ancient Hebrew history: "And so like the former *son of a kish* who went up and out to found his farmer's ashes we come down gently on our own turnedabout asses to meet Margareen" (*FW* 164.11–14; my emphasis). The allusion is to the occasion on which Saul first met Samuel: Kish had sent his son out into the country to search for some lost asses; there he was approached by the judge (1 Samuel 9:1–22). The Wakean context of the reference to the "son of a kish" is Shaun's muddled answer to the Eleventh Question in I.6.

The thematically relevant Old Testament–New Testament onomastics in the previous paragraph can, of course, be applied to both versions of "MacKishgu/mard." What Joyce intended by either of the two terminations ("-guard" or "-gmard") is not at all clear to me. I have no idea what the corrected and canonical form of the moniker, "MacKishgmard," means—or from what language its last component is derived.

The items discussed in this section have leapt from the detection of a typographical error in the final-draft stage of the *Wake* to Joyce's clever combination of an Old Testament and an apostolic name. In the analysis of intervening material, attention was called to the following points: the name-play that energizes the Epistle to Philemon, its Irish analogue in "Flahertie," and Oscar Wilde's letter from Reading Gaol. The bridge connecting these disparate elements is St. Paul, the early Christian missionary, and his letters to the primitive churches. Joyce knew the matter and form of those documents and applied that epistolary expertise to the composition of the *Wake*. In the interpretation of that monumental work, no detail of onomastics, hagiography, or comparative penology is irrelevant, but the initial step in the entire process is a careful investigation of the development of the text.

4

The Early Church

This chapter treats the saints who lived from the post-apostolic era through the first seven Christian centuries. Major events of this period include the destruction of the Jewish temple at Jerusalem (A.D. 70) and the great persecutions under Decius and Diocletian in the second half of the third century. Christianity was declared a legitimate religion by Constantine (313), and he founded an eastern capital at Constantinople (325); after the fall of the Roman Empire to the barbarians in the west (476), there was an early Byzantine revival of glory during the reign of Justinian the Great (527–565), but soon the hallowed city of Jerusalem was captured by the Muslims (638). Each event is a milestone in the history of the development of Western European civilization. From my perspective the primary consideration in this turbulent era was the growth of Christianity from an embryonic para-Jewish cell in Palestine into the official religion of the empire and the dominant social-cultural force in the Mediterranean basin.

In the early Church four primary categories of saints emerge, each having its distinct mission and memorable heroes: the martyrs who died as "witnesses" (that is the literal meaning of the term in Greek) to their faith; the popes whose authority laid the foundations of the Church's organization; the confessors by whom Christian teachings were refined and expressed; and the desert hermits and the founders of early monastic communities from whose example and rules the institution of cloistered religious life grew. These categories serve as the structural armature for this chapter, with special genetic emphasis on buried allusions to the miracles of St. Nicholas and to the career of the abbot-bishop St. Martin of Tours.

In the early third century the rigorist theologian Tertullian reminded the faithful that "the blood of Christian martyrs is the seed" of the Church.[1] In the early twentieth century James Joyce jotted down the following variation in one of his *Wake* notebooks: "martyrs' blood painted / wall of ⊓'s house (VI.B.6.109).[2] That entry is uncrossed, and no martyrs' blood appears anywhere in the text. In the absence of a broader archival context or Joycean application, I venture two guesses about the meaning of the entry. In as much as HCE is a Protestant, the money set down by customers for pints at his pub might be seen as blood wrung from a persecuted nation. A footnote in "Night Lessons" stresses the imperialistic aspect of England's emblematic color: "Porphyrious [*porphyreos* is "scarlet" or "purple" in Greek] Olbion, redcoatliar" (*FW* 264.F3). On a less sectarian domestic level, in the "Chamber scene," the bedroom of HCE and ALP is described as having "Salmon papered walls" (*FW* 559.1–2). In neither case am I prepared to argue for a direct allusion to Tertullian's well-known adage; at the same time that quite specific notebook entry is typical of the memorable phrases that attracted Joyce's pre-textual attention.

Virgin Martyrs

Among those whose blood earned them immediate enrollment in the canon of saints is a special class of virgin martyrs.[3] Three of these chaste early Christian heroines have namesakes among the twenty-nine handmaidens of Issy. When he encounters "that chorus of praise of goodwill girls," Jaun greets several of them individually: "(and where's *Agatha*'s lamb? and how are *Bernadetta*'s columbillas? And *Juliennaw*'s tubberbunnies? and *Eulalinas*'s tuggerfunnies?)" (*FW* 430.35–431.1; my emphases). Before she was martyred in Sicily, St. Agatha was tortured by having her breasts cut off. St. Juliana of Nicomedia was immersed in a tub of molten lead, then beheaded. As St. Eulalia of Barcelona (probably a doublet of the more popular St. Eulalia of Merida) was being burned to death, a white dove was seen to fly from her mouth. For Joyce, however, what unites these saints is not the horrible means of their martyrdom, but—at least from Jaun's perspective—their milky-white breasts. An archival index helps to illustrate and support that shared feature of both virginal purity and sexual provocation.

In a calendric cluster of February feasts and saints' days,[4] the following notebook entries occur:

ᵇAgatha /
ᵇScholastica /
ᵇ2 little white dovebirds / ᵇin her corsage / ᵇlamb /
ᵇSister of Benedict /
A/mazon/illa / her veil saves Catania / from Etna (VI.B.17.93)

The last three items in the citation are directly connected with St. Agatha and her cult—Joyce confirms the link by drawing an arc between these entries and the saint's name in the first line of the index. As mentioned in the previous paragraph, the breasts of this virgin martyr were cut off by the Roman official who tried to force her to renounce her faith. Many paintings show St. Agatha carrying her severed breasts on a tray.[5] Thus, in mythological and etymological terms, Agatha was an "a-mazon-illa": the prefix *a-* is a privative; *mazon* means "breast" (both in Greek); and *-illa* is a Latin diminutive suffix; this holy woman was literally a petite, presumably non-bellicose amazon. According to *The Golden Legend*, one year after the day of Agatha's martyrdom, Mount Aetna erupted, and a river of lava threatened to engulf the nearby Sicilian city of Catania. A crowd of pagans snatched the veil from the martyr's tomb and hung it in the path of the molten rock; the relic stopped the fiery flow and saved the city.[6]

The second saint cited in the notebook cluster is Scholastica, the sister of St. Benedict, the founder of western monasticism. She was not martyred, but there is a cogent reason for this virgin-nun's inclusion in the index. No relevant hagiographical incidents seem to involve "2 little white dovebirds in her corsage," but *The Golden Legend* reports that Benedict "saw his sister's soul in the form of a dove, penetrating the secret spaces of heaven."[7] Joyce's entry "lamb" also may be associated with St. Scholastica, but the traditional tales of her life do not contain any references to young sheep.

Although I do not pretend to grasp all the connections, I suggest that, in the opening section of Jaun's smarmy sermon to Issy and her handmaidens, Joyce (quite naturally) integrated virgin-martyrs, white breasts, beloved sisters, and male lust. First, Issy permits Jaun to approach "so tarnelly easy as all that since he was brotherbesides her benedict godfather" (FW 431.17–18). His greeting makes the relationship even more explicit: "—Sister dearest . . . as he began to take leave of his scolastica . . . yet we feel as a martyr to the dischurch of all duty" (FW 431.21–26). Then Jaun begins his moralizing, "I rise, O fair assemblage!" and reveals that he has been spiritually advised by Father Mike "in soandso many *nuncupiscent* words about how he had been *confarreating* teat-a-teat with two *viragos intactas*" (FW 432.4–11; my emphases). The italicized words are thinly disguised Latin, as befits an earnest young confessor. While *nuncupisco* is a genuine verb meaning "to begin to pronounce solemnly," Joyce's coinage can be distorted into a pseudo-English phrase meaning "eagerly desiring (*cupisco*) a nun." The most hallowed form of Roman marriage was *confarreatio*, which Joyce twists into a purely sexual, breast-to-breast form of communication. Finally, the addition of a single letter transforms the Latin *virgo* (virgin) into *virago* (a mannish woman), a pair of whom in either case remain appropriately "untouched" here.

In the middle of his fraternal instructions to Issy and her accomplices, Jaun warns them to beware falling into the hands of a rival, "inching up to you, disarranging your modesties and fumbling with his forte paws in your bodice after your billy doos twy . . . making much of you . . . about your glad neck and the round globe and the white milk and the red raspberries (O horrifier!)" (*FW* 438.3–10). It should horrify no reader of the Old Testament's Song of Songs to discover here the appropriation of another set of religiously decorous metaphors for breasts. The Hebrew poet addressed his beloved as "My dove, hiding in the clefts of the rock"; her "two breasts are two fawns, the twins of a gazelle, that feed among the lilies"; they are also "clusters of dates" and "clusters of grapes" (Song of Songs 2:14, 4:5, 7:8–9). Joyce's "raspberries" are a mere adjustment from semitropical to northern-temperate fruit.

In short, it seems to me that the fauna ("lamb," "columbillas [dovelets]," "tubberbunnies," and "tuggerfunnies") associated with the names of the three initial virgin-martyrs (Agatha, Juliana, Eulalia) are also Jaun's prefatory metaphors for the girl's breasts.[8] With a characteristic twist of source-energy, Joyce's series of notes on the mutilation of St. Agatha's breasts and the "2 little white dovebirds" in St. Scholastica's corsage serve as the hagiographic inspiration for Jaun's convoluted expressions and exhortations. The reaction of the young women to these homiletic improprieties is not recorded, but the randy sermonizer clearly makes his own feelings obvious with an appropriate scriptural flourish: "May my tunc fester if I ever see such a miry lot of maggalenes!" (*FW* 453.19; note VI.B.33.115–16).

Shortly after the consecration in the eucharistic portion of the Catholic mass, there is a commemoration of seven virgin-martyrs: Felicitas, Perpetua, Agatha, Lucy, Agnes, Cecilia, and Anastasia. Several of these heroines appear as subjects of typical Joycean name play in the *Wake*. The Greek noun *anastasis* (literally, "standing up") is the standard term for the Resurrection, and that is its primary force in "While flattering candles flare. Ana Stacy's" (*FW* 28.30–31) and "*Anna Stessa's Rise*" (*FW* 104.8).

St. Cecilia, another virgin-martyr, is the patroness of music, since she reportedly sang to God in her heart while instruments were being played at her unwanted wedding. (She convinced her pagan husband to respect her vow of chastity; he converted to Christianity, and both met their death for refusing to sacrifice to idols.) In a 1939 letter to Professor Rogers about his son Giorgio's allegedly poor performance at a singing audition for the BBC, Joyce invokes the heavenly uvula of the patroness of vocal music: "Per l'ugola [*sic*] celeste de Santa Cecilia" (*Letters* III.450). In the *Wake* "the parish of Saint Cecily" is associated with "Ceolmore," which McHugh glosses as "*I*[*rish*] ceól mór: great music." The School of Medicine in Dublin was located on Cecilia Street, which is loosely twisted into "Cecilia's treat" (*FW* 424.7; note VI.B.33.192).

Etymology (*lux, lucis* is Latin for "light") is most probably the reason why St. Lucy is invoked by people with eye problems. Hagiography, however, adds a few lurid details: either a pagan judge ordered her eyes torn out or she tore them out herself to avoid marrying a nonbeliever. In art St. Lucy is sometimes depicted carrying her two eyeballs on a plate. Joyce alludes to this grotesque detail by including "eyes on a dish" (*U* 12.1719) in his Cyclopean catalogue of saints' symbols. When their daughter was born, the Joyces decided that, in the light of her father's recurring and increasingly serious problems with his sight, she should be named "Lucia." The last line of a November 11, 1925, letter (with news of his latest ophthalmological condition) to Miss Weaver reaffirms that devotion: "*Santa Lucia* (Patron of eyes), *ora pro nobis*" (*Letters* I.237).

Another young woman whose father violently opposed her conversion to the new faith was Barbara. Indeed, her father was so enraged by her adherence to Christianity—and her refusal to marry a pagan suitor—that he personally beheaded his beautiful daughter. While walking back from the execution, he was struck, out of the blue, by a bolt of lightning. Thus, Barbara earned the honor of becoming the patron of bombardiers and artillerymen. The saint is perversely included among the historical dignitaries whom Joyce calls forth to witness the Black Mass in "Circe": "Heavy Gatling guns boom. Pandemonium. . . . Artillery. . . . On an eminence, the center of the earth, rises the fieldaltar of Saint Barbara. . . ." (*U* 15.4661-89).[9] In the "mamafesta" in the *Wake*, there appears the odd title, "*What Barbaras Done to a Barrel Organ Before the Rank, Tank and Bonnbtail*" (*FW* 105.15–16). During the interrogation of Shaun in III.1, the accused replies that he has "the gumpower and, by the benison of Barbe" (*FW* 410.26; note VI.B.36.4), is therefore able to do as he pleases.

Perhaps the weirdest virgin-martyr in the entire roster of holy women is Saint Wilgefortis. According to legend, she was a princess of Portugal whose father demanded that she marry the pagan king of Sicily. She prayed that her vow of virginity might be preserved, and God answered by causing a hideous beard to grow on her face. Her enraged father had Wilgefortis crucified. Under a variety of names (Liberata, Uncumber, Kümmernis), she is the patron saint of women who have troublesome husbands. Joyce may have had St. Wilgefortis in mind as his model for "*tout est sacré pour un sacreur, femme à barbe*" (everything is blessed [or cursed] for a blesser [or curser], a woman has a beard) (*FW* 81.28–29; also note "[b]femme colone, à barbe" [*UNBM* 299:8]).[10]

This section on virgin martyrs began with a discussion of Issy and her twenty-nine handmaidens, whose virtue and breasts were not in safe hands during their encounter with Jaun. Hagiography records a far larger entourage of Christian maidens who suffered even more tragic tribulation. Christian tradition—perhaps magnified by the mistaken reading of an inscription—honors St. Ursula and her 11,000 companions who were slaughtered by the Huns at Cologne. This chaste contingent marches in the procession of saints in "Cyclops" (*U* 12.1712). In the first chapter of *Ulysses*, Buck Mulligan typically acknowledges that some fates are worse than death, as he reveals the origin of the cracked mirror in the Martello tower: "—I pinched it out of the skivvy's room. . . . It does her all right. The aunt always keeps plainlooking servants for Malachi. Lead him not into temptation. And her name is Ursula" (*U* 1.138–40).

Finally, to return momentarily to Jaun and his designs on the breasts of every woman he meets, the following lament is spoken (apparently by Sigurdsen in female form) as the sanctimonious twin sails away after his sermon: "*hellyg Ursulinka*, full of woe (and how fitlier should goodboy's hand be shook than by the warmin of her besom that wrung his swaddles?)" (*FW* 471.31–33; my emphasis). The italicized invocation in that plaintive farewell is a brief linguistic nod to the place of Ursula's martyrdom and the center of her cult: "hellyg Ursulinka" is pseudo- (or perhaps proto-) German for "little saint Ursula." Jaun's lustful aspirations also impel him to substitute a "full of woe" for the conventional—and virginally more appropriate—"full of grace."

A brief tribute to another important virgin saint—even though she is not a martyr—concludes this section. In the fifth century, Genevieve, a nun in Paris, predicted that a crusade of prayers could turn Attila the Hun away from the city. For that and other benefactions, she remains a patroness of the capital of France. In the *Wake* Joyce refers to both the general and the saint who deflected the barbarian incursion into Frankish territory: "when Aetius check chokewill Atill's gambit, (that buxon bruzeup, give it a burl!) lead us seek, O june of eves the jenniest" (*FW* 266.25–27; also note VI.B.24.168, VI.B.28.87).[11]

Pontifical Saints

In the eucharistic portion of the mass, just before the consecration, five early popes are commemorated: Linus, Cletus, Clement, Sixtus, and Cornelius. All of them were martyred and all have official feast days as saints in the calendar of the Roman Catholic Church. Joyce managed to place most of those pontifical martyrs and many other papal names among the divisive factors in the theological controversy between the rival Roman Mookse and the Orthodox Gripes. The East-West schism is emphasized by the frequent use of Greek or Russian ecclesiastical terms, such as "babskissed nepogreasymost" (*FW* 156.17), which is phonetic Russian for "papal infallibility," and "what Ruby and Roby fall for, blissim" (*FW* 156.26–27), which scrambles the Latin spelling of the scope of a pontifical blessing, *urbi et orbi* (to the city and the world). Almost all of the early popes who appear in this episode do little more than lend their names in a frustrated attempt by the Mookse to add a solemn, antique tone to his bluster. The pontificate of Urban I, for example, was totally undistinguished, but he appears in a string of six popes (*FW* 154.20–21) and again as an inconsequential "Urban First" in a later list of regnal epithets (*FW* 539.32). Readers interested in detecting or deciphering the numerous examples of papal name play in the episode should consult McHugh's *Annotations* for pages 153–59 of the *Wake*.

Included in McHugh's glosses are references to the so-called prophecies of Saint Malachy (note "Malachy the Augurer" [*FW* 155.34]). This work, purporting to predict the identity of each pope until the end of the world, has nothing at all to do with the twelfth-century archbishop St. Malachi, the great reformer of the Irish church. On the other hand, the spurious text, with its ridiculously vague Latin predictions—for example, "*sus in cribro!*" (sow in a sieve) (*FW* 155.4) and "*Aquila Rapax*" (grasping eagle) (*FW* 158.29)—has attracted the frequent attention of those who seek the key to the future. Joyce obviously felt that the cryptic Latin phrases in which the pontiffs were predicted added a final layer of obscurantism to the debate between the Mookse and the Gripes.[12]

Almost all the popes mentioned by Joyce merit inclusion in the text for their zany names or ordinal irregularity, as, for example, the entirely fictional "Quintus the Sixth and Sixtus the Seventh" (*FW* 153.33). There are two exceptions. In the story "Grace" the current pope, Leo XIII (1878–1903), is praised for his intellect, his work to reunite the Latin and Greek churches, and his Latin poem on the invention of photography (*D* 168–69). Leo XIII, however, has not been canonized, so his inclusion in this chapter must be considered an honorary tribute to his many talents. Pope Gregory I (590–604), on the other hand, has been granted the title "the Great" and was declared a saint by acclamation immediately after his death. Tradition ascribes to Gregory a play on proper names that eventually led to the conversion of pagan England. He is reported to have seen some impressive-looking slaves for sale at a market in Rome. When he was told that they were Angles (*Angli*), he replied, "Good, they have the faces of Angels (*Angeli*), and should be coheirs with the angels in heaven."[13] Accordingly, in 596 Gregory dispatched St. Augustine and a band of monks as missionaries to convert the heathens in Britain.

During his interrogation in book III.3 of the *Wake*, Yawn is asked for additional information about the three British soldiers whom he has mentioned: "—Grenadiers. And tell me now. Were these anglers or angelers . . . ?" (FW 526.11–12). Although there is no overt narrative link with St. Gregory's ethnic pun, the extension of the wordplay to a third possibility (fishermen) is fully consistent with the context. Two brief notebook clusters also deal with Augustine's historic mission: "charms [??] of angels / Angli OSB / acute angles" (VI.B.27.45–46) and " ∧ Kevin and ⊏ Shem / defence of ⊓ / or ⊔ / S. Augustine / Angles ⊥ " (VI.B.19.92). In the first index the initials "OSB" stand for *Ordo Sancti Benedicti* (the Order of St. Benedict) and refer to the fact that St. Augustine and his fellow monks were members of a Benedictine community. I am a bit reluctant to suggest that "acute angles" means that the Angles were cute in the contemporary American sense of the term—but that connotation seems present in "whose say is soft but whose ee has a cute angle" (FW 254.29–30)—the two phonetic syllables of which could specify an Hispanic Issy ("e/cee").

The second index cited above suggests that the twin boys rallied to the side of their father (HCE as St. Augustine), who has been beset by Issy; here their sister seems to be equated with the pagan Angles, perhaps in contrast to the "angel-like" twins. The second index is also capable of another interpretation. In addition to his cathedral church, Augustine also built the monastery of Saints Peter and Paul at Canterbury. His greatest problem in Britain was convincing the indigenous Celtic church to accept the Roman date for Easter. Perhaps ∧ and ⊏ have something of Peter and Paul in them, missionaries united in Roman observance; whereas ⊥ is either an amenable Angle convert or a recalcitrant Celtic Christian. To go deeper or further in this sort of allegorical interpretation of the sigla would be folly. The essential evidence is a series of discrete, difficult-to-decipher, pre-textual notes, not a prophetic passage from scripture.

A final allusion to St. Gregory is straightforward: "[Kevin] collected gregorian water severfold and with ambrosian eucharistic joy of heart as many times receded" (FW 605.30–31). The narrative context is the highly hagiographical description of saintly Kevin in his element at Glendalough. The devotions of the holy, hydrophilous hermit mix elements from the Latin liturgical hymns of St. Ambrose and the plain monastic chants that Pope Gregory the Great fostered.

Male Martyrs

Their position as bishops of Rome caused a number of early popes to fall victim to imperial persecution and to win a martyr's crown. Many other male members of the growing Christian community also died giving witness to their faith and have been commemorated in the official martyrology. This section of the current chapter presents Joycean representatives of this important group of saints.

Each year in late January Catholics celebrate the feast of St. Polycarp, who was burned at the stake in Smyrna in the mid second century. The public commemoration of his martyrdom is the earliest to have been recorded, and the holy bishop's name is recorded in both the canon of the mass and the *Wake*. There is a clear reference to the liturgical citation (and its memorial purpose) in "for ancients link with presents as the human chain extends have done, do and will again as John, Polycarp and Irenews eye-to-eye ayewitnessed" (*FW* 254.8–10). The "John" and "Irenews" who flank Polycarp in that passage are, respectively, John the Evangelist, who knew Polycarp, and Ireneus, an early Christian theologian, also from Smyrna. The three saints are linked in the canon of the mass; the second may also be the namesake of the *Wake's* "Polycarp pool" (*FW* 600.5; VI.C.13.168).

In a 1915 letter to Michael Healy, Nora's uncle and generous benefactor, Joyce wrote, "Today is the feast of S. Justin Martyr, patron of Trieste" (*Letters* I.86). Justin was a pagan Greek, well trained in a number of systems of classical philosophy, who converted to Christianity sometime around A.D. 135. His writings vigorously explain and defend the new faith and its moral teachings. During a visit to Rome, Justin was denounced as a Christian. When he refused "to forsake truth for falsehood," he was beheaded. His epithet, "the Martyr," is thus justified on the double grounds of forceful witness and brave death. Joyce's identification of this famous apologist as the patron of Trieste is, however, incorrect. The similarly named saint whom the citizens of that Adriatic port venerate as their heavenly protector is an otherwise unknown local martyr of indeterminate date.

A far more exciting story about the fidelity and heroism of St. Tarsicius was once known by every Catholic schoolchild. It was most frequently told in classes that prepared seven-year-olds for their first Holy Communion. The climax of the tale emphasized the ultimate respect that must be shown for the eucharistic elements, which communicants believe to be the body and blood of the Lord. According to some versions of the legend, Tarsicius was an acolyte carrying a consecrated host to some imprisoned Christians. While on this mission through the streets of Rome, the young boy was apprehended by a mob and searched. Even as he was beaten to death, he protected the host in his cloak.[14] A recent article by George Hahn sees an allusion to these events in "Araby." In that story the narrator, a young boy, helps his aunt to carry some parcels "through the flaring streets, jostled by drunken men . . . amid the curses of labourers, the shrill litanies of shop-boys. . . . I imagined that I bore my chalice safely through a throng of foes" (*D* 31). Hahn is certainly correct to point out that Joyce could well have read a version of the saint's tale in Cardinal Wiseman's immensely popular historical novel *Fabiola: or, the Church of the Catacombs* (1854).[15] On the other hand, Tarsicius's heroism was just the sort of edifying story that would have been told to classes of younger pupils at Clongowes Wood College.

Despite the unspeakable atrocities that constituted the death of many martyrs, several of the traditional reports of those proceedings are noteworthy for their touches of black humor. The two-fold justification for St. James the Persian's hagiographical nickname, "the Cut-up," has already been mentioned in my introductory chapter. St. Laurence was executed in Rome by being roasted on an iron griddle. *The Golden Legend* reports that the dying martyr told Emperor Decius, "Look wretch, you have me well done on one side, turn me over and eat!"[16] Joyce worked an incomplete version of that bit of saintly wit into the *Wake*. During various man-in-the-street interviews to gauge the public's reaction to the allegations lodged against HCE, opinions are recorded from three Tommies, a dustman, and a railways barmaid; finally, a "wouldbe martyr . . . when grilled on the point, revealed . . ." (*FW* 60.16–18; my ellipses). I also suggest that Joyce discreetly positioned the anecdote's martyrological punchline a bit earlier on the same page of the text: "Well done, Drumcollakill!" (*FW* 60.8).

A tale that seemed too improbable even for *The Golden Legend* is recorded in other sources. During the reign of the emperor Diocletian, a Roman comic actor, Genesius, was assigned the role of a candidate for baptism in a farce mocking Christian ritual and belief. During the performance itself the pagan actor was infused with divine grace, converted on the stage, and was beheaded after his curtain call. At the opening of "the Mime of Mick, Nick and the Maggies," Joyce secures the success of the presentation "with the benediction of the Holy Genesius the Archimimus" (*FW* 219.8–9; note VI.B.42.71). Similar tales are told about other actor-martyrs, but St. Genesius entered the calendar as the patron of those who tread the stage.

Although the mode of death and the iconographic motif it inspired are most definitely not intended to be humorous, Christian cephalophors presented Joyce with an irresistible temptation. Cephalophors are a special class of martyrs who have been decapitated—"Decollation they call it in the fold" (*P* 248). They carry their severed heads in their hands. The most famous example of this bizarre group of saints is Dionysius (more commonly, Denis or Denys), the patron of France.[17] Probably the best-known artistic example of St. Denis as a cephalophor is his statue on the facade of Notre Dame in Paris, to the left of the main entrance. In a notebook entry Joyce jotted down an acute observation about this sort of representation of saints who have been beheaded: "aureole around neck / S. Dennis [sic]" (VI.B.2.47). With impeccable hagiographic logic, the saintly halo (*aureole* in French) encircles the bloody neck. In the *Wake* Joyce re-created that ingenious solution in two phrases: "our aureoles round our neckkandcropfs" (*FW* 306.1–2) and "necknoose aureal" (*FW* 568.20). Two generations of martyrologically challenged critics have seen merely a golden necklace in the latter citation. There is another textual reference to St. Denis in the *Wake*. It appears shortly before the recitation of "The Ballad of Persse O'Reilly," as the celebrants are feeling their drinks and asserting their authority, "—and he who *denays* it, may his hairs be rubbed in dirt!" (*FW* 43.30–31; my emphasis).[18]

In a footnote to Edward Gibbon's grisly narration of the garroting of the Christian philosopher St. Boethius is a reference to an anonymous cephalophor who toted his severed head a considerable way. Gibbon reports that, when she heard of a similar feat, a lady acquaintance of his observed, "The distance is nothing; it's only the first step that hurts."[19] Hagiographic archives do not record the longest distance covered by a cephalophoric saint, but *The Golden Legend* reports that the decapitated body of St. Denis "marched two miles" from Montmartre to its divinely ordained place of burial (II.240).

St. Blaise, a bishop/martyr of uncertain date, is remembered for miraculously removing a fishbone stuck in a child's throat and saving him from death by choking. Some Catholics still celebrate his feast day (February 3) by going to church to have their throats blessed by a priest to protect them from laryngeal obstruction and disease. Joyce must have remembered this experience, each year a day after his birthday, as is recorded in a notebook entry: "3/2 S. Blaize / °wool throat" (VI.C.5.68). In the note I take the word "wool" to refer to the scratchy discomfort of a sore throat; in the *Wake* the phrase is applied to a secular situation, the parched gullet of a dedicated boozer. Here the beneficiary is HCE in the guise of King Roderick O'Connor, who "finalised by lowering his wooly throat with the wonderful midnight thirst was on him" (*FW* 381.26–27).

Two martyrs named Valentine share a common feast on February 14. As Glasheen notes, it is difficult to distinguish this saintly patron of lovers from the matinee-idol of the 1920s, Rudolph Valentino. Joyce conflates them in the *Wake*: "—she laid her batsleeve for him two truevers tell love (on the Ides of Valentino's ...)" (*FW* 289.26–28; also see *FW* 458.2). (Calendric scrupulosity requires me to point out that the Ides fall on February 13, the eve or vigil of the feast.) St. Pancras is another early Roman martyr, but nothing is known of his life, beyond the legend that he was only fourteen when he died for his faith; thus he is one of several patrons of children. A church in Canterbury was dedicated in his honor by the apostle of the Anglo-Saxons, St. Augustine; a titular parish in London gave its name to the well-known railroad terminal. In a sentence in the *Wake* that includes several references to other London train stations, HCE claims to have offered his wife "subleties in jellywork, come the feast of Saint Pancreas" (*FW* 550.13).

One of the best-known saints in the martyrology is St. George. According to tradition (which is probably little more than a reworking of pagan legend), George was a heroic warrior-horseman from Cappadocia who rescued a virgin princess from a dragon.[20] After a prolonged series of fearful tortures, he was beheaded for refusing to renounce Christianity. St. George slaying the dragon is an immensely popular scene on Eastern icons and Western paintings. The mounted champion is the patron of Greece, Portugal, and England. A Dublin church, renowned for its steeple and bells (*U* 4.78, 4.544, 15.1184), is also under his patronage.[21] In "Circe," when the English soldiers threaten Stephen Dedalus, one of the bystanders backs the redcoats by asserting, "The gules doublet and merry saint George for me!" (*U* 15.4638–39). That same sentiment is expressed in the *Wake:* "And send Jarge for Mary Inklenders!" (*FW* 229.3–4).

Another saint—as pacific as George was bellicose—originating in Asia Minor is Phocas of Sinope. He was executed by soldiers to whom he had extended hospitality and a night's lodging, thereby giving him the opportunity of preparing his own grave in his beloved garden. For some inexplicable reason (perhaps his name, which means "seal" in Greek) Phocas is a patron of sailors. Joyce placed this fairly obscure Eastern martyr near the head of his procession of saints in "Cyclops," right next to one of his own patrons, "S. James the Less" (*U* 12.1690). It has been suggested that both the mention and the position are meant as a cryptic tribute to Paul Phocas, one of Joyce's closest friends—and his tutor in modern Greek—during his stay in Zürich during World War I.[22]

In the following example of Joyce's command of martyrological detail, a compact archival note and its sigla help, at least partially, to orient the thrust of my interpretation: " /⌐ Mamertius, Protase, Gervase / ⊣ Sophy" (VI.B.35.63). In the *Finnegans Wake* notebooks the siglum /⌐ stands for Shem-Shaun united; ⊣ is the siglum for Issy. Saints Protase and Gervase were twins and martyrs whose remains were discovered in Milan in the late fourth century; nothing is known of their lives. St. Madeleine Sophie Barat was the founder of the Sisters of the Sacred Heart (1815), one of the leading orders in Europe and America for the education of young women. Her own education, in secular and religious subjects, was under the strict discipline of her older brother, Louis, who was preparing to become a priest. The fact that Gervase and Protase are twins explains their choice as saintly substitutes for Shem and Shaun. Shaun's attempt (in *Wake* III.2) to direct his sister's cultural and moral formation in his "long absurd and rather incestuous Lenten lecture" (*Letters* I.216) explains the parallel between Issy and Sophy.

I cannot, however, explain how "Mamertius" fits into the picture. St. Mamertius was an early Romano-Gallic bishop best remembered for inaugurating the practice of "Rogation Days," a brief period of prayer, processions, and penance before the feast of the Ascension. There are no discernible associations with the *Wake's* twin boys in those venerable practices. Perhaps, then, Joyce intended a parallel in the fact that Mamertius was the elder brother of the late classical poet Caludian, who is said to have assisted his episcopal sibling in the administration of his diocese. If that is the intention, then Mamertius (and an unnoted Claudian) represents the practical Shaun and his literary twin, Shem—but I would not stake a plenary indulgence on that connection.

My final examples in this section on male martyrs involve two large groups of early Christians—like St. Ursula and her 11,000 virgins—who give witness to their faith with their lives. During a final wave of persecutions, a contingent of forty Roman soldiers, members of the Twelfth Legion (nicknamed *Fulminata*, "Thunder and Lightning") refused to offer sacrifice to the pagan gods; these men won their heavenly crowns by being left to freeze to death in a lake near Sebasteia in central Turkey. Their cult and icons depicting their heroic deaths were very popular in both the East and the West.[23] In a paragraph packed with allusions to ancient Rome, Joyce refers to an example of saintly treason by members of a fulminating military unit: "The thundering legion has stormed Olymp that it end" (*FW* 167.22–23). There is, however, no textual or archival evidence that Joyce knew about the fidelity of the Forty Martyrs of Sebasteia. On the other hand, the phrase just cited from the *Wake* can be easily understood as an allusion to a prior miracle that is ascribed to another contingent of Christian soldiers in the same legion. During his campaign in Dalmatia in A.D. 172, Emperor Marcus Aurelius and his troops were just about to be overwhelmed by the enemy when a sudden, violent thunderstorm relieved their thirst and terrified the barbarians. Legend attributes that unexpected victory to heavenly intervention sent in response to the prayers of the Christian members of the legion. The *Wake*'s specific mention of an assault on "Olymp" (Mount Olympus), the doomed bastion of the pagan gods, increases the likelihood that Joyce intends an allusion to this military miracle.[24]

Another similar legend involves an even larger group of Roman warriors who were adherents of the new—and still proscribed—faith. The Theban Legion, originally from Upper Egypt, mutinied at its encampment near the Rhone in Gaul: the soldiers refused orders to round up the believers in the area and to sacrifice to the pagan gods. Their punishment was double decimation. When neither the troopers nor Maurice, their leader, recanted their faith, most were executed on the spot. An archival note records this mass martyrdom: "S. Moritz buried / 6666 warriors" (VI.B.4.316).[25] The legion's commander (but demoted by Joyce to the status of "slave") may be the source of one of the masculine Latin names, "Mauritius," in the *Wake*'s tangled marriage case (*FW* 572.29, 32 and *FW* 573.31). St. Mortiz, of course, is the eponymous hero of the famous Swiss ski resort; some sources also report that the two patron saints of the city of Zürich, Felix and Regula, were members of an imperial delegation that traveled with the Theban Legion on its trek across the Alps. Both escaped the slaughter and fled (with St. Mauritius), only to be martyred later by another band of pagans. According to legend, they carried their severed heads to a knoll near the growing settlement at Zürich, where they were buried. Civic medallions clearly depict Saints Felix ("Prosperity") and Regula ("Order") as cephalophors.[26]

Confessors and Doctors

In hagiography the term "Confessor" is applied to those Christians whose witness to the new faith did not culminate in martyrdom, but in some significant contribution to the doctrinal, organizational, artistic, or spiritual life of the Church. Three centuries of sporadic persecution ended with Emperor Constantine's Edict of Toleration (313). Thereafter, the Christian community—at least in Mediterranean Europe—entered a new phase of growth and was guided by many men whose outstanding achievements merited their inclusion in the canon of saints. Eusebius of Caesarea's *Ecclesiastical History* is a principal source for the first two and a half centuries of Christianity, from the age of apostles and martyrs to the brief period of doctrinal harmony following the Council of Nicaea (325). Joyce alludes to the work of this "Father of Church History" in the reverse HCE-acrostic "Eusebian Concordant Homilies" (FW 409.36; note VI.C.2.217).[27]

A good example of the new-style churchman is St. Ambrose, who was mentioned several pages ago as a composer of hymns. He was also a most influential fourth-century lawyer, provincial governor, and eventually bishop of Milan. Justly famous for his wise judgment, firm leadership, moving sermons, and liturgical songs, St. Ambrose—with Augustine, Jerome, and Gregory the Great—is one of the four Latin Doctors of the Church.[28]

Perhaps the most significant purely religious act of Ambrose's life, however, was his baptism of the philosopher-theologian St. Augustine in 387. Although there is no record of Augustine (sinner that he was) being hauled before a court or refitted for sea duty, his *praenomen* (Aurelius) is combined in the *Wake* with the name of his mentor and advocate: "appeared in dry dock, appatently ambrosiaurealised" (FW 85.32).[29] This compound form appears in a paragraph packed with judicial terms, such as "Old Bailey" (FW 85.26), once the primary criminal court in London, and "mamertime" (FW 85.36), a slight corruption of the medieval term (Mamertine) for ancient Rome's prison.

The influence of St. Augustine of Hippo (to distinguish him from his later namesake of Canterbury) on Western civilization is immense. His *Confessions*, the narrative of his wild youth and late return to Christ, is included in the canon of most Great Books. Augustine's status as *the* spokesman for the nascent Latin church is demonstrated by one of the headlines in "Aeolus": "FROM THE FATHERS." This general acknowledgment of patriarchal authority is immediately followed by a citation from the *Confessions*, which merits specific attribution: "That's saint Augustine" (U 7.841–44). Stanislaus Joyce also clearly knew the philosopher-saint's reputation well, as the following passage from his memoir shows: "Augustine speaks of the cauldrons of lawless loves that seethed round him in Carthage. Talk, always slavering obscenity about sordid adventures, which Irish humor made as unappetizing as possible, frothed around me in the company of Jim's medical student friends."[30] Joyce's *Portrait* is purposefully confessional in many aspects, but its tone and form are not at all similar to those of Augustine's works.[31] Indeed, the title of the saint's book, *The Confessions*, has as much to do with "proclaiming the grace of God" as with a revelation of hidden sins.

Jan Parandowski met Joyce only once—over drinks after a PEN Congress in Paris in 1937—but he records a strange anecdote. During their discussion of the relationship of *Ulysses* to the *Odyssey*, Joyce "quoted a long passage out of Saint Augustine" (presumably in Latin) to bolster his contention that his work was "more an epic of the body than of the human spirit." Parandowski goes on to say that he could "neither remember this quotation nor find it in Augustine's writings."[32] Given the occasion, that difficulty is not surprising. But the problem of detecting allusions or citations and of determining documentary sources is daunting for any study of Joyce's use of the philosophy and theology of St. Augustine. Some critics have found much; others have concentrated on a single, controversial passage.[33]

My purpose in this chapter, however, is to investigate how Augustine *qua* saint (not rhetorician or metaphysician or Doctor of the Church) left a mark on Joyce's fiction. On that score—and that score alone—there is very little. At the end of his encounter with his Dilly in "Wandering Rocks," Simon Dedalus walks off murmuring about his daughter's plea for an extra shilling. He sarcastically equates her familial concern and insistence with the eleemosynary zeal of a nun: "—The little nuns! Nice little things! ... Is it little sister Monica!" (*U* 10.715–16). Although Mr. Dedalus probably pulled the name out of the Irish air, Monica was St. Augustine's devout mother, who never stopped praying for her son's return from a life of sin to the true faith. In the *Wake*, the frequent permutations of *O felix culpa* (O fortunate fall) and *securus iudicat orbis terrarum* (calmly and confidently the world renders its judgment) are primarily examples of Joyce's linguistic ingenuity—although it should be pointed out that the first key-phrase also appears, obscenely, in *Ulysses:* "We hereby nominate our faithful charger *Copula Felix* [Happy Fucking] hereditary Grand Vizier" (*U* 15.1504–5; my emphasis). From my fundamentally hagiographic perspective, then, I can come up with only a slim handful of even tangential references to the saint's life and cultic commemoration in all of Joyce's works.

In a 1912 lecture on William Blake, delivered at the Università Popolare in Trieste, Joyce said that eternity "appeared to the beloved disciple [St. John the Evangelist] and to St. Augustine as a heavenly city" (*CW* 221). This looks like an oblique reference to the title of Augustine's important book *De Civitate Dei* (About the City of God), which demonstrates that the gods of the Roman empire were powerless to prevent its fall to the barbarians. That work is a mine of information about the pagan cults and their function as props of the state, in opposition to God's heavenly city, which is the timeless home of Christians. After renouncing his life as a worldly intellectual in Rome and Milan, Augustine returned to the land of his birth in North Africa. In 396 he was chosen to be the bishop of Hippo, a city near the site of ancient Carthage.

In the *Wake* one reads that "the ruah of the Ecclectiastes of Hippos outpuffs the writress of Havvah-ban-Annah" (*FW* 38.28–29). In that citation "ruah" is the Hebrew word for "breath," "spirit," "wind"; it appears in the second verse of the Old Testament creation story: "and God's spirit hovered over the water" (Genesis 1:2). An additional allusion to biblical beginnings is "Havvah," which sounds something like "Hawah," the Hebrew spelling of "Eve." Book 13 of Augustine's *Confessions* is a detailed allegorical interpretation of the opening verses of Genesis. The saintly scholar himself appears in the quotation as the ecclesiastical leader of the diocese of Hippo.[34] There are, of course, other dimensions to the passage—including a truncated version of "Yes, We Have No Bananas"—but my only intent here is to suggest St. Augustine's presence.

In *The Books at the Wake*, James Atherton presents the case for a Shem-Shaun opposition in Joyce's use of St. Augustine and St. Jerome. Although several of his parallel passages from the *Wake* and Jerome's letters display intriguing correspondences, I am not convinced that Joyce had direct reference to the Loeb Library translation (1933) as his primary source.[35] At any rate, there are two undoubted references to Saint Jerome in the *Wake*. Joyce tumbles together the Latin forms of Jerome (*Hieronymus*) and Jerusalem (*Hierusalem*) in a list of the four cities that were the sees of the ancient bishop patriarchs: "old Jeromesolem, old Huffsnuff [Constantinople],[36] old Andycox [Antioch], old Olecasandrum [Alexandria]" (*FW* 124.35–36). That association is appropriate since Jerome spent more than thirty years in the Holy Land translating the Old Testament from the Hebrew into Latin.[37]

A second reference calls him "Saint Jerome of the Harlot's Curse" (*FW* 252.11). A common motif in hagiographical literature is the temptation of desert-hermits by the devil in the shape of an enticing woman. *The Golden Legend* cites a letter from Jerome to a friend about his life in the wilderness: "All the company I had was scorpions and wild beasts, yet at times I felt myself surrounded by clusters of pretty girls, and the fires of lust were lighted in my frozen body and moribund flesh."[38] Here I agree with Atherton's suggestion that that scene makes the scholarly saint sound remarkably like Jaun on the event of his sermon to Issy and her sodality of February girls. It also seems incontrovertible that Jerome's condemnation of "brothels [as] those cisterns of vice" is the model for Joyce's "Love through the usual channels, cisternbrothelly" (*FW* 436.14), one of Jaun's fraternal exhortations in his instruction.[39]

Archival Bishops: East and West

Neither of the following two saints was a great theologian or a participant in papal or imperial politics. The exemplary lives and memorable deeds of

St. Nicholas of Myra and St. Martin of Tours, however, have stamped them as two of the most enduringly popular Christian saints. Both of these holy bishops—one in the East, the other in the West—left minor but distinctly memorable traces in Joyce's fiction. What is significant about the episcopal pair is their presence in paradigmatic archival indices.

St. Nicholas of Myra

St. Nicholas was a fourth-century bishop of the once-thriving inland port of Myra in what is now southwest Turkey. The *Wake* commemorates the saint's episcopal see in the first catalogue of Dublin churches: "S. Nicholas Myre" (*FW* 569.6). He is most famous for his miracles (such as the provision of dowries to save three sisters from prostitution and the revivification of three murdered youths pickled in a barrel of brine), and he is a patron of children, those in need, pawnbrokers, and sailors.[40] Throughout Europe he is known as "Father Christmas"; in North America he is called "Santa Claus," from a Dutch form of his name, "Sinte Klaas." He appears in the procession of saints in *Ulysses* (*U* 12.1716) and, under his most familiar title, in the *Wake*: "Scenta Clauthes stiffstuffs your hose" (*FW* 434.23–24). In a 1912 article for a Trieste newspaper, "The City of the Tribes: Italian Echoes in an Irish Port," Joyce notes a legendary connection between St. Nicholas and Galway (*CW* 230).

In a *Wake* notebook the bishop and some of his deeds are recorded in a short index:

S. Niklaus
Rich Barham
naked / students arising / from tub of /
    pickled pork / blessed by S.N.
S. Gengulphus
S. Jingo . . .
3 Golden Balls / in stockings (VI.B.4.15–16; my ellipsis)

In *Joyce Studies Annual* (1994) I discussed these entries, with special emphasis on their immediate source (the *Encyclopaedia Britannica*) and their broader ramifications for a "theory" of genetic scholarship.[41] The point of that article pivoted around a hagiographical miracle attributed to both St. Gengulphus and to St. Nicholas: the resurrection and reassembly of dismembered corpses. A comic version involving an adulterous wife who kills and cuts apart her husband, Gengulphus ("Jingo," for short), was written in the mid nineteenth century, in verse, by Richard Harris Barham for his popular volume, *The Ingoldsby Legends*.

The miracle involving St. Nicholas and the three boys is known in many versions, all of which include the following details. Three children seek lodging at an inn. The host, who is also a butcher, cuts his young guests to pieces and places them in tubs of brine in which he usually pickled pork. Seven years after this hideous crime, St. Nicholas visits the inn and asks for supper; he refuses ham and veal, but demands a cut of whatever meat is curing in the barrels. The guilty butcher attempts to flee, then confesses and repents. After the saint blesses the tubs, the children rise, alive and whole, from the brine. A Victorian version by James Henry Dixon captures the joyous climax of the miracle:

> St. Nicholas the tub drew near,
> And lo! He placed three fingers there.
> The first one said, "I sweetly rest!"
> The second said, "I too blest!"
> The third replied, "'Tis well with me,
> In Paradise I seem to be!"[42]

I suspect that Joyce came across a very similar version of the tale in a French song, "La Légende de saint Nicholas," which was one of the pieces in a songbook that was in his Paris library.[43]

A phrase in the *Wake* might seem to echo Nicholas's spectacular miracle: "funfer all . . . in the porker barrel" (*FW* 304.12–14; my ellipsis). At the same time, McHugh calls attention to a notebook entry (crossed out in green crayon) as a far more likely contextual source: "sit in a barrel—funfair" (VI.B.36.180).

Another Wakean passage needs to be examined in the light of the original St. Nicholas cluster in the notebook: "benedicted be the barrel; kilderkins, lids off; a roache" (*FW* 596.17–18). Several aspects of archival evidence must be scrutinized to support a case for the possibility of a thematic hagiographical influence here. The passage appears in the first section of the *Wake*'s last book; in it a new day dawns, and the dormant HCE rises. I suggest that his awakening is, momentarily, seen in terms that resonate to St. Nicholas's restoration of the three clerks. Someone is invoked to bless (*benedicit* in Latin) some barrels. These containers are "kilderkins" (casks holding 16–18 gallons).[44] In this term I hear a metathesis of the original crime, in which children (*Kinder* in German) were *killed*. Saintly intervention caused the barrels' "lids" to come "off," and then the revivified youths arose ("a roache"). This section of the *Wake*'s narrative is a veritable resurrection episode. On the same page one reads the following phrases, which are, on the surface, applicable to the hero's return; just beneath the surface, they might also be applied to St. Nicholas's miracle: "he returns;

renascenent; fincarnate" (*FW* 596.4); "awike . . . risurging" (*FW* 596.6); "reconstitution; by the lord's order" (*FW* 596.9). Here it must emphatically be pointed out that the draft-stage at which the three phrases ("benedicted . . . roache") were added to the text is very late, mid-1938.

There are, then, in the allusively resonant passage discussed in the previous paragraph, two factors that might call seriously into question any claim for a connection between the original hagiographic cluster and the text. First, there is the crossed and apparently unrelated notebook entry ("ᵇkilderkin"); second, it and the draft-stage of this portion of the *Wake* were both written a decade later than the original VI.B.4 notebook. What prevents me from summarily dropping the case for a genetic link is the immediately preceding phrase in the text, "benedicted be the barrel" (*FW* 596.17). It is difficult to offer a reasonable explication for the intrusion into a resurrection-narrative of a Latinate appeal for a blessed barrel. (A vat of Benedictine liqueur is too farfetched.) Equally puzzling are the adjacent large tuns with their lids off. Thus, I suggest that, when Joyce extracted the entry "kilderkin" from the late notebook, he was reminded of the spectacular wonder by Nicholas, and recognized the possibility (strengthened by making the term plural) of wordplay with the brine casks and the slain children they contained. This verbal ploy triggered an inscription of the saint's ritual benediction before—and the miraculous result after—the central commemoration of the pickled kids. In this reading, the theoretical obstacle of a secondary notebook entry is transformed into a thematic catalyst through which tangential relevance to the narrative is bestowed on all three phrases. As exemplified by the late insertion of the childhood miracles of St. Kevin (see chapter 6), there is Joycean precedent for the compositional deferral (based on late notebook entries) of hagiographic motifs, especially when the material is thematically central to the plot.

St. Martin of Tours

The scope and depth of St. Nicholas's archival contribution to the *Wake* is minor, but working out the details provided some insight, by jingo, to Joyce's allusive mind at work. A second example involves a much longer notebook index, the direct source for which is a book that Joyce owned. Although its subject is St. Martin of Tours, the very important Romano-Gallic abbot and bishop, what is most significant about this index is, again, the light it sheds on Joyce's selection of material from a documentary source and on how he integrates those items into his text in progress.

Notebook VI.B.2 (August–September 1923) begins with a long index devoted to the life and works of St. Patrick.[45] Not much later follows a series of notes on St. Martin of Tours. Since this index has been thoroughly analyzed by Wim Van Mierlo, I will merely summarize the data and outline their significance.[46] The documentary source of the information is Margaret Maitland's *Life and Legends of St. Martin of Tours (317–397)*, a copy of which was in Joyce's Paris library.[47] The major moments of the saint's life are the following: Martin, the son of an officer in the Roman legions, was born in Sabaria, Pannonia. (That town, now called Szombathley in Hungary, would gain later fame as the ancestral home of the Virag/Bloom family [see *U* 17.532–36 and *U* 17.1906–10]). The traditional occasion of Martin's conversion to Christianity was his gift of half his military cloak to a naked beggar; he then left the army to become "a soldier of Christ." After a period of living as a hermit, he founded the first monastery in Gaul at Liguge, and another at Marmoutier. Although reluctant to serve, he was consecrated bishop of Tours about 370, and became extremely active as a missionary preacher and wonderworker, exerting firm ecclesiastical and civil authority throughout the area. His shrine at Tours (where the saint's half of the divided *capella* was kept) became one of the most popular pilgrimage sites in France.

From the pages of Maitland's pious biography of St. Martin, Joyce lifted over sixty words and phrases to be jotted down in his notebook. The following are several typical examples:

- VI.B.2.32: "ʳthe Adversary / devil in human form":

One day Martin was accosted by the devil in human form, who asked where he was going. When he answered, "Wherever God calls me," the Adversary said he would follow to oppose Martin (Maitland 22). In chapter I.4 of the *Wake*, HCE is attacked during an encounter with "the Adversary" (*FW* 81.19), who, however, does not have discernible satanic characteristics.

- VI.B.2.33–34: "ʳsoul of this particular / young boy dear / ʳto Martin . . . / S. Martin (Elias) lies on dead / youth (Kings II)":

These entries pertain to St. Martin's resurrection of a young candidate for baptism who had died while the abbot was away. That miracle is compared to Elijah's (Elias) revivification of the widow of Zarephath's son (1 Kings 17:17–24) (Maitland 33–34). Although crossed out, this seemingly thematic set of entries has not been located in the text.

- VI.B.2.33: "S. Martin kidnapped by / false sick call (hubby)":

When Martin at first refused to become bishop of Tours, a man lured him away from his hermitage by pretending that his dying wife needed a priest. The saint went with the man and was carried off to the city and consecrated (Maitland 38–40). These unmarked entries are not reused in the *Wake*.

- VI.B.2.37: "ʳa pious author":

Here Maitland, who generally does not indicate a source, reports some edifying detail of Martin's life as reported by an unnamed pious author (Maitland 73–74). Joyce inserts that notebook entry into his statement that slander never convicted "Earwicker, that homogenius man, as a pious author called him" (*FW* 34.14).

- VI.C.2.34: "ᵍextraord. clothes heretics"; this is Madame Raphael's transcription of the original entry, "extraord clothes = heretics" (VI.B.2.34):

St. Martin opposed the emperor's order of military action against Priscillian dissenters, since all persons who were pale or wore extraordinary attire were in danger of being slaughtered as heretics (Maitland 52–53). In the *Wake* this phrase is appropriately applied to the Protestant hero, HCE, in a footnote to "Night Lessons": "And he was a gay Lutharius anyway, Sinobiled. You can tell by their extraordinary clothes" (*FW* 263.F4).

In his careful study of these and similar entries from the St. Martin index, Van Mierlo has correctly stressed that the overriding rationale for Joyce's selection of material from Maitland's book is phraseology, not a role in the exposition of the source's argument or plot. Joyce was not collecting thematically pregnant items or autobiographically resonant details from his hagiographical source. Rather, he jotted down words or phrases that tickled his fancy because they were trite or odd, and because they supplied obscure information (the Seven Sleepers of Marmoutier) or even an opportunity to misquote Psalm 82 in an ad hoc translation from English into Latin. Finally, even the range of Joyce's use of these entries argues strongly against a premeditated, transcendent thematic purpose of their selection from the source. Several of the items crossed out in red crayon were placed in the text as early as the autumn of 1923; the seven VI.C.2 entries crossed out in green crayon did not become part of the *Wake* until late 1934, a gap of a dozen years. Finally, as Van Mierlo points out, none of the notebook items from Maitland's life of the saint are in any way connected with overt references to St. Martin in the *Wake*: "Sing Mattins in the Fields" (*FW* 328.24–25) is an allusion to the London church famous for its music; "Holy Saltmartin" (*FW* 419.8) is a conflation of two Elizabethan curses, one of them invoking the saint's name.[48]

In the wake of my statements in the previous paragraph about the rationale for the selection of genetic material, several general distinctions need to be drawn. First, my strictures about the thematic energy of notebook entries apply only to their status as *pre-textual* notes. I am convinced that at least the early notes were rarely selected from a documentary source with a specific Wakean motif or episode in mind. Just as infrequently were they originally bound to a single specific character—although here all those entries accompanied by sigla are to be excepted.[49] On the other hand, when the notebook entries were placed in the *text* of the developing *Wake*, the content of their source and/or their individual contributions to that source were sometimes—but not always or inevitably—of consequence. For example, at the notebook stage, the entry "the Adversary" was *not* originally extracted from the life of St. Martin so that it could be applied to HCE's opponent in the park; its use in that episode is, however, appropriate—although no reader of the *Wake* could be expected to be aware of its original devilish force in the saint's life. From the perspective of the *Wake*, the archival juxtaposition of St. Nicholas and St. Gengulphus (Jingo) makes some sense only in the light of Barham's *Ingoldsby Legends*, in which the latter's limbs are re-constituted; but to argue for a source-resonant resurrection motif in the phrase "and by jingo" (*FW* 67.2) would be foolhardy, since the Wakean passage is about deepnight burial—and since the passage was added to the text a year *before* the notebook index was compiled.

In short, at least for the *Wake*, there is an essential difference between an archival entry and a textual phrase: the former is pre-literary rumination; the latter is imaginative re-creation. Identification of the presence of archival material in the text is important, as is the detection of the documentary source for an index, but those exercises do not, generally speaking, respond to the same critical methods and perspectives that are readily applied to a finished literary text. In the foregoing chapter not just two bishops, but also several confessors, a couple of catalogued popes, a bevy of virgin martyrs with their lambkin breasts, and the bloody walls of HCE's house are meant to provide concrete illustrations of those interpretative principles.

5

The Hairy Hermit

There is no *Guinness Book of Records* for hagiographical categories. If there were, St. Simon (or Simeon) the Stylite would certainly be featured—perhaps with a photograph on the cover. Eyewitness accounts tell how the hermit Simon decided to flee the world more perfectly by living on top of a pillar (*stylos* in Greek). Over the years he increased its height to sixty feet; there on a twelve-foot-square platform he lived for thirty-six years. The usual explanation of this extraordinary feat is Simon's desire to avoid the crush of the faithful who came to hear his instructions or beseech his prayers. That plan, of course, did not work, and his pillar in the north Syrian desert became a major pilgrimage center. An American poet, Phyllis McGinley, captures modern reaction to his sort of ascetic extremism:

. . . .
Under the sun and desert sky
He sat on a pillar
Nine feet high.
When fool and his brother
Came round to admire,
He raised it another
Nine feet high'r.
. . . .
And why did Simeon sit like that,
Without a garment,
Without a hat,
In a holy rage
For the world to see?
It puzzles the age,
It puzzles me.
It puzzled many
A Desert Father.
And I think it puzzled the Good Lord, rather.[1]

Joyce, perhaps a bit more blasé about the eccentricities of Syrian holy men, inserts the saint into his Cyclopean procession without further comment: "S. Simon Stylites" (*U* 12.1691).

A paragraph on a stylite is an appropriate introduction to this chapter, which will present several other practitioners of extreme self-denial. With a single exception, the other saints to be discussed fled the cities of Egypt to fast and pray for years in the desert.[2] By far the most important of these hermits is the hairy anchorite, St. Onuphrius (Humphrey).

In a footnote in his *Decline and Fall of the Roman Empire,* Gibbon reports what is surely the world's record for poor hygiene in the service of a higher good. Sylvania, a virgin living in Jerusalem, devoted her life to studying commentaries on the bible, "to the amount of five millions of lines." Moreover, "[a]t the age of threescore she could boast that she had never washed her hands, face, or any part of her whole body, except the tips of her fingers, to receive communion."[3] Joyce cannot resist passing this information along to readers of the *Wake:* "We shall too downlook on that ford where Sylvanus Sanctus washed but hurdley those tips of his anointeds" (*FW* 570.31–33).[4] Perhaps Joyce altered the gender of the historical Sylvania to transfer her attributes in allusive honor of his fictional male "hydrophobe" (*U* 17.237); at any rate, his Sylvanus seems to be a priest (whose fingers would be anointed) rather than a communicant. There is a second, quite cryptic, Wakean allusion to this habit: "melanodactylism" (Greek for "state of having black fingers") occurs just ten lines before the phrase "appear periodically up your *sylvan* family tree" (*FW* 522.7 and 17; my emphasis). A final note on this odd anecdote: despite Joyce's "Sanctus" (Latin for "saint" or "holy") modifying his male Sylvanus, the long-term water-shy Sylvania was never canonized.

Mary of Egypt is one of several early saints known as "Sinners."[5] Her life in *The Golden Legend* states that she worked as a prostitute in Alexandria for seventeen years; when she decided to go to Jerusalem, she paid her fare with her body. In the Holy City she prayed to an image of the Blessed Virgin Mary for pardon. After that she went to the desert beyond the River Jordan and lived in complete solitude for forty-seven years. One day an old monk, Zozimus, came upon the penitent, heard her story, and gave her communion. A year later Father Zozimus found Mary's body at the spot where they had met before. He asked a desert lion to help him dig a grave in the sand for the holy sinner.[6] Joyce knows about St. Mary of Egypt and places her beside Mary of Bethany in his procession of saints in "Cyclops" (*U* 12.1709). Although she is mentioned in an archival note (VI.B.31.25), the sinner Mary does not appear in the *Wake;* that work's reference to "Zosimus, the crowder" (FW 567.30), records the nickname of a Dublin beggar-bard, not a monk in the decidedly uncrowded desert of Judea.

The "High Hilarion" who pops up in the midst of the "jocolarinas" and laughter, mirth, and merriment in the *Wake* (FW 361.28–31) is certainly so placed to contribute to the joyful mood of the passage. St. Jerome, however, wrote an actual life of St. Hilarion who lived as a hermit in the desert near Gaza for more than fifty years, until masses of monastic visitors impelled him to retreat into the wilderness of Egypt. Later, pagan persecution forced him to flee to Sicily, then Dalmatia, and finally to Cyprus, where he died.

The first of the desert hermits—and the mentor who originally directed St. Hilarion to the wilderness at Gaza—was St. Anthony of Egypt. He is regarded as the founder of Christian monasticism, because he gathered many of the anchorites around him into loosely defined communities. Even when he tortured his body by fasting, sleeplessness, and every conceivable form of austerity, Anthony was racked by violent sexual and culinary temptations. Hieronymus Bosch's allegorical depictions of those trials are masterpieces of fifteenth-century Flemish art. In those paintings and in others like them, there can be no doubt about the identity of the hermit's primary assailant. The devil is present in all sorts of grotesque and hideous forms as he seeks to lure the saint into sin. That hellish presence explains the following passage from an early version of Joyce's famous retreat-scene:

> The two [Stephen Daedalus and his brother Maurice] were standing together looking into the window of a stationer's shop and it was a picture of S. Anthony in the window which had led to the question [What kind of sermon was the priest giving?]. Maurice smiled broadly as he answered:
>
> —Hell today.
>
> —And what kind of sermon was it?
>
> —Usual kind of thing. Stink in the morning and pain of loss in the evening. (SH 57)

In *Portrait* itself, a reformed Stephen Dedalus reflects on this sort of spiritual assault:

> The very frequency and violence of temptations showed him at last the truth of what he had heard about the trials of the saints. Fre-

quent and violent temptations were a proof that the citadel of the soul had not fallen and that the devil raged to make it fall. (*P* 153)

One of the symbols associated with St. Anthony in hagiography and art is a pig, a conventional emblem of gluttony. The explanation for this apparently contradictory assignment may be the fact that Anthony was a patron saint of the Hospitallers, who held the right to forage the woods of France in search of truffles, an endeavor that required pigs to sniff out the succulent fungi. Whatever the connection between the anchorite and a pig, Joyce picks up on it twice. Included in a catalogue of "blessed symbols of their efficacies" that is part of the saints' procession in *Ulysses* are some "hogs." These mature animals are followed shortly by "bells" (for lepers) and "crutches" (for the crippled) (*U* 12.1717–18), which are also assigned to St. Anthony as the patron of Hospitallers. In the *Wake* "Anthony" is seen "ellegedly with a pedigree pig (unlicensed)" (*FW* 86.13–14), on a page of the text that swarms with swine of various sorts and in diverse languages.

All these spiritual athletes (Simon, Sylvania, Mary, Hilarion, and Anthony) sought to extend the limits of asceticism and solitude for the good of their souls and the glory of God. Apart from the eccentric Sylvania, who is a bad advertisement for an overly literal dedication to the Bible, each earned the right to the title of "saint" through heroic deeds in the wilderness. In the pages that follow, I present the evidence that some of the characteristics of another desert saint are transferred by Joyce to the hero of the *Wake:* St. Onuphrius was a model for HCE.

The Hairy Hermit

At the end of a previous chapter, St. Onesimus was introduced as a useful example of Joyce's penchant for onomastic wordplay.[7] A similar case can be made for the string of aliases under which the Christian name of the hero is inscribed in the *Wake:* "Humphrey Chimpden Earwicker" is a marvelously permutable moniker. Brendan O Hehir traces the various forms of "Humphrey" from the Old Norse (*Olafr*) to Irish (*Amhlaoibh*), and from there to Hamlet, Oliver Cromwell, Gruachan, and back again. He also acknowledges an independent derivation that is the actual source of the name. It comes from the Teutonic *Hunfrith* (Hun-peace), which was brought to Ireland by Anglo-Normans. There it became Gaelicized *Unfraidh* (pronounced "unfri") and *Unfradh* ("unfru").[8] O Hehir's native wit and deftness at beading these tangled threads of the name "Humphrey" in the *Wake* would seem to exhaust the topic. There is, however, room for a bit more onomastic sport—and for widening the field of play from mere comparative philology to thematic significance. My purpose, therefore, is to examine the Egyptian sources of one of HCE's more stately bynames and to chart the dimensions of its allusive expanse.

In an incredibly complex paragraph (*FW* 572.21–573.32) Joyce presents his version of an annotated legal case brought before an ecclesiastical court. The issues pivot around grotesque sexual irregularities in a marriage. The parties involved are Honuphrius (husband-father), Anita (wife-mother), Felicia (their daughter), Eugenius and Jeremias (their sons), and a large cast of retainers and associates, all of whom are party to the "depravities (*turpissimas!*)" (*FW* 573.30). The form of the names and the untranslated Latin adjective ("most squalid") signal Joyce's source for this burlesque document: a nineteenth-century manual of almost 500 test-cases of marital problems, written in Latin. Its author was a canon lawyer-priest, whose purpose was to train pastoral students in the matrimonial legislation and adjudication of the Roman Catholic Church. Joyce owned this seminary text, and sections of his copy are heavily underlined.[9]

Commentators have pointed out that the "Anita" in this case is ALP; the Latin root *an-* connects the name with an archetypal little old woman, a Romano-Irish "Annie." As far as the name "Honuphrius" goes, there is considerably more than just an initial "H" and an internal "-ph-" to link it with the "Humphrey" of HCE. St.Onuphrius (called "Abunafre" or "Benofer" in the Coptic versions of his life) is a familiar figure in the hallowed legends associated with the rise of Christianity in Egypt. In the Latin translations of these tales, the two forms of the saint's name add an *H* and become "Honuphrius" and "Honophraius." In hagiographic texts in English, the name is frequently translated as "Humphrey."[10]

The series of "Lives" (transmitted in Coptic, Ethiopic, Greek, and Latin versions) indicate that the desire to achieve ascetic perfection drove Onuphrius from his monastery. He abandoned his fellow monks and disciples in the Thebaid (the area around modern Luxor) to search for absolute solitude in the desert of far Upper Egypt near Aswan and Philae. Several record-breaking stretches of fasting and encounters with demons embroider these edifying legends, but by far the most memorable aspect of the life of St. Onuphrius is the circumstance of his death and burial. The monk-pilgrim Paphnutius discovers the aged holy man in his remote hut. The visitor is informed that he has been divinely guided to bury the hermit's body: "As Onuphrius' spirit leaves the flesh, Paphnutius hears the voices of angels praising and glorifying God. Paphnutius divides his own tunic, wraps the holy remains in one half of it, and deposits them in a rocky sepulcher. The hut of Onuphrius collapses and with it falls his date-palm."[11] This is the standard version. In several variants, two lions come out of the desert and assist Paphnutius by digging a grave in the sand for the dead saint.[12]

At the opening of the *Wake's* book I.4, HCE grandly imagines himself "[a]s the lion in our teargarten [who] remembers the nenuphars of his Nile" (*FW* 75.1–2). Here the habitat-nostalgia of a caged animal (*Tiergarten* is German for "zoo") is joined to a messianic agony in a Garden of Tears. But the primary emphasis in the simile just cited falls on an exotic memory by the captive beast of water lilies on the River Nile. Joyce's well-known use of the funeral texts from the Theban version of the *Book of the Dead* increased his Wakean vocabulary and supplied him with the key ancient Egyptian term, *nenuphar*, for "lily," in the text quoted above.[13] For Western Christians, lilies are symbolically associated with death, burial, and—in their Easter variety—resurrection.

In another, far more distinctly sepulchral, passage in the *Wake* there can be no doubt of H/Onuphrius's central presence. This time the saint has been transformed into a transparently nominal mausoleum: "any kind of inhumationary bric au brac for the adornment of his glasstone *honophreum*"(*FW* 77.33–34; my emphasis).[14] Among the aforementioned funereal knickknacks are some "lacrimal vases" (*FW* 77.30), which recall the lion's teary recollection of his lilies of the Nile valley. Elsewhere, a distinctive pharaonic name is introduced to associate HCE with a wonder-of-the-world builder from ancient Egypt: "Humpheres Cheops Exarchas" (*FW* 62.21; also note "chopes pyraimidous" [*FW* 553.10]). "Cheops" is the traditional Greek form of "Khufu," the fourth-dynasty Pharaoh (c. 2585–2560 B.C.) who constructed the Great Pyramid at Giza. In Byzantine Greek, an *exarchos* is a high government official in charge of a province (but not Egypt); as an ecclesiastical term it designates the chief bishop of an area, such as one of the many dioceses in heavily Christianized Egypt. The name "Humphrey Chimpden Earwicker" also lies just beneath what appears to be a phonetic transliteration of one of Joyce's original hieroglyphic cartouches: "Unfru-Chikda-Uru-Wukru" (*FW* 24.7). The Gaelic pronunciation of "Hunfrith"—"unfru," according to O Hehir—is undoubtedly meant to contribute to that multicultural melange of names.

Granted Joyce's passion for weird etymological connections and fortuitous phonetic similarities, he may also have connected the name "Onuphrius/Honuphrius" with one of the titles of the Egyptian resurrection-god, Osiris. Throughout the *Book of the Dead* a common epithet for Osiris, especially in the resurrection ceremonies at Abydos, is "Unnefer" or "Wenen-nefer."[15] The Greek form of this divine title is "Onnophris," meaning "The Good Being." It seems reasonable to me that the similarity in names might have contributed to a typically Joycean identity-glide here.

If so, then there is an incidental—and apparently coincidental—reason to suggest a link between the Coptic saint Onuphrius (whose most memorable act was his death and burial) and the ancient god Osiris-Onnophris (whose scattered limbs—including an erect, artificial phallus—were collected and revivified by his wife, Isis, and his son, Horus).

At any rate, there can be no doubt that Joyce played numerous changes on the basic tale of the reassembly of Osiris's body as a type of HCE's awakening: "healed, cured and embalsemate, pending a rouseruction of his bogey" (FW 498.36–499.1); "irise, Osirises!" (FW 493.28). Although the parallel is applied to Shaun, Joyce offered Harriet Shaw Weaver the following interpretation of an evolving chapter in the *Wake:* "[Shaun] departs like Osiris the body of the young god being pelted and incensed. He is seen as already a Yesterday (Gestern, Guesturing) [? turning] back his glance amid wails of 'Today!' from To Morrow (to-maronite's wail etc)" (*Letters* I.263). These plaintive phrases were translated from a divine dirge in the *Book of the Dead.* When placed into their final form of the *Wake,* they underwent another linguistic transformation. The English version of the ancient hieroglyphic text was reworked by Joyce into several European languages: "Eh jourd'weh! Oh jourd'woe! ["today" in French] . . . Guesturn's ["yesterday" in German] lothlied answring to-maronite's [English] wail" (FW 470.13–14). The significance of this litany of time-terms—and its link to St. Onuphrius—will become evident in the next two paragraphs, in which another typically Wakean language contributes to the fun.

Over and above the burial and the Osiris themes that make "Honuphrius" a particularly appropriate alias for HCE, there are other connections between the Egyptian hermit and the Chapelizod publican. In Coptic saint-lore and iconography St. Onuphrius is the prime example of "the hairy anchorite." That is, he is "a man of terrible appearance, shaggy like a beast; so great the profusion of hairs that they completely hid his body."[16] A recent investigator of hagiographic "romance" comments on this frequently recurring figure in early saint-tales: "in general wearing long hair is equivalent to being outside society. The use of clothing to cover the body instead of the natural hair distinguishes man from beast. The saint has here allied himself with the beasts, and with man before the Fall, who did not need artificial coverings for his body. But since he in fact lives after Adam's sin, the hermit may not go wholly uncovered."[17] Even though Joyce's hero does not retreat into the desert, HCE is a sinful outsider in the *Wake.* And readers are forcefully reminded that he does not always go about wholly covered and that he is indeed a hairy man: "He possessing from a child of highest valency for our privileged beholdings *ever complete hairy of chest, tramps,* and *eyebags* in pursuance to salesladies' affectionate company" (*FW* 616.12–15; my emphases).

Burial themes and ephemeral time are also combined in "Toborrow and toburrow and tobarrow! that's our *crass, hairy* and *everygrim* life until one finel *howdiedow*" (*FW* 455.12–14; my emphases). Here pseudo-Shakespeare is echoed in fake Latin: *cras,* "tomorrow"; *heri,* "yesterday"; *hodie,* "today." There is also a connection (in Wakese) between a life that is paradoxically both grim and evergreen and the final day on which one is fated to die. That mortal destiny and burial in a barrow are, of course, a fine how-do-you-do for anybody. I suggest that the interplay between the homophones *heri* and *hairy* in these passages contributes to Joyce's exploitation of pharaonic and Coptic Egyptian burial cults and their extension to HCE. A brief respite of military glory is present in a slightly more optimistic passage, in which the victorious HCE, just after "the brottels on the Nile" (*FW* 328.22), returns as "Heri the Concorant Erho" (*FW* 328.25). In short, the character of the hero of the *Wake* in particular and its author's view of the human condition in general are nicely summarized in one of Earwicker's "abusive names" in the "long list": "Hoary Hairy Hoax" (*FW* 71.5–15).

It should be obvious that—even for Joyce—the adventures of solitary ascetics in the sandy wilds of Egypt are not everyday reading. The rare manuscripts in which these tales have survived and the exotic languages in which they were composed are additional barriers. Corroborative evidence that Joyce was aware of this hagiographic tradition, however, can be found in the text of the *Wake* and in the notebooks in which he jotted scraps of information while the work was in progress.

First, a glance at some brief passages from the *Wake* itself. In the by-play between Issy, the Rainbow Girls, and Jaun, there is a report of an invocation to the slyly seductive preacher in which the reclusive women seek salvation. Someone is addressed in terms that resonate to the topic of the previous two paragraphs: "O salutary! Sustain our firm solitude . . . Hear, hairy ones!" (*FW* 454.18–19). During a later cross-examination of Yawn about a particular midsummer night in the park, there is a reference to "hermits of the desert" (*FW* 505.3). Finally, when St. Kevin retreats from the world, he has to make concessions to the topography and climate of Ireland. Thus, his "desert" is an island in a lake at "Glendalough-le-vert." But even there the "venerable Kevin, anchorite," excavates a cavity for his "altar *unacumque* bath" in "the arenary [sandy] floor" of his watery hermitage (*FW* 605.11–32). In all three of the passages, the character who is involved in these various manifestations is not HCE, but a manifestation of his ostensibly pious son Shaun. It would not, however, be an odd procedure in the *Wake* for Joyce to have transferred some of the qualities associated with isolated Coptic saints as well as some of the attributes of Osiris from the hairy father to the slickly smooth son.

Other examples of Joyce's familiarity with both the sources for and essential terminology of the edifying tales of desert recluses are found in the notebooks. The entry "curé d'Ars / father of the desert" (VI.B.28.216) refers to the nineteenth-century priest St. Jean-Baptiste Vianney. He was a pastor in a remote French village to whom thousands of troubled people flocked to confess their sins and to receive spiritual advice. Although the simple, uneducated priest three times fled to a life of solitude in a Carthusian monastery, he was induced to return to his post at Ars. The reputation of this modern holy man must have reminded Joyce of the early Christian monks in Egypt; or perhaps a source-document linked the French saint to the so-called fathers of the Egyptian desert. The second entry just cited does not seem to have left its mark on the *Wake*. But the curé himself is neatly commemorated as the putative author of "*Pease in Plenty* by the Curer of Wars, licensend and censered by our most picturesque prelates" (*FW* 440.l0–11).[18]

Another notebook entry joins the geographical designation for the Libyan Desert in Egypt and the area in which most of the early Coptic monks and hermits lived: "Desert Great / Thebaid" (VI.B.29.43). The latter term is derived from "Thebes," the ancient name of Luxor, the capital of Upper Egypt. Then and now, that city is one of the few major outposts of civilization on the Nile, between the great eastern and western deserts. Historians of Christianity argue that primitive monastic practices began in Egypt and spread to Syria, Italy, and Gaul and from there to Ireland. Irish monasticism was originally based on the severely Egyptian form practiced in what is now the coast of southern France. Joyce acknowledged this path of influence and recorded the note "Irish Thebiad" (VI.B.3.19). Although this entry is not crossed with crayon, I detect a compacted echo of the phrase in "a hiberniad of hoolies" (*FW* 138.11).[19]

A final archival index is the most emphatic evidence for Joyce's interest in the legends of the hairy anchorite:

Paul Hermit
ʳchained to bed of flowers
assaulted bites tongue (VI.B.1.120)

A well-known hagiographic "romance" variously titled *The Life of St. Paul of Thebes* or *The Life of St. Paul the First Hermit* was composed by St.

Jerome in the 370s A.D. This great translator of the Hebrew and Greek scriptures into Latin (the *Vulgate*) had himself lived for a while in solitude in the Syrian desert east of Antioch. According to Jerome, Paul fled from Thebes into the Egyptian wilderness to escape the persecutions of Christians ordered by Emperor Decius. He remained there as a total recluse (but was fed by a raven who brought bread) for nearly a century; his limbs were decayed with age, his hoary hair was totally unkempt. A divinely inspired visitor, St. Anthony (who is usually regarded as the first hermit), arrived at the remote cave just in time to bury Paul, whose grave was dug in the sand by two lions. In the thrust and details of this tale, it is easy to detect an affinity between the life (and death) of this St. Paul and that of St. Onuphrius. Both tales flow from the same pious sources in a way in which it is difficult to assign priority or to trace imitation.[20] What is important for my investigation of the link between the *Wake's* HCE and the Coptic solitary St. Onuphrius is establishing that Joyce knew something of the legendary tradition of the hairy Egyptian hermit. The notebook index just cited (and its source) provide oblique evidence for that claim.

In the introduction to his account of the hermit's life, St. Jerome supplies several paragraphs of historical setting. Paul fled into the desert during the persecutions of Decius (mid third century). The Roman methods of torture were cruel in the extreme; the body of one Christian youth was coated with honey, and the victim was then exposed, beneath the blazing sun, to the stings of flies. Another of the faithful was bound to a downy bed with ropes entwined with flowers. Next a pagan official ordered a beautiful harlot to pollute the body of the young Christian with a voluptuous embrace: "Unconquered by tortures he was being overcome with pleasure. At last with an inspiration from heaven he bit off the end of his tongue and spat it in her face as she kissed him. Thus the sensations of lust were subdued by the intense pain which followed."[21] While such enormities were being perpetrated by imperial officials in the lower Thebiad, Paul retreated in the deep desert.

There can be no doubt that Jerome's *Life of St. Paul the Hermit* is the ultimate source of the notebook index headed by "Paul Hermit." That ancient document, however, is not cited directly by Joyce; rather, he picked up the information from another trove of hagiographical trivia, a footnote in Edward Gibbon's unsympathetic treatment of Catholic reports of the tribulations of early martyrs.[22] The phrases "chained to bed of flowers" and "assaulted bites tongue" are the English historian's synopses of significant elements in adjacent episodes at the start of the *Life*. The specificity of the diction, not to mention the narrow focus on melodramatic sadism, is too striking to admit coincidence. In the *Wake* Joyce adapts the crossed entry to describe the situation of Yawn as the Four Old Men assemble to hold their star-chamber inquiry into his alleged crimes: the accused youth was "spancelled down upon a blossomy bed" (*FW* 475.8).

Although the second notebook entry cited above is not crossed, I suggest that it too was used in the text of the *Wake*. The setting for its appearance is the final perspective in which the Four Old Men view the act of intercourse by HCE and ALP. In this phantasmagoric section of the narrative, the hero seems to have become the freshly knighted Lord Mayor of Dublin, who is preparing to welcome the King to the city. Part of the ceremony involves a civic pageant with religious overtones. Meanwhile, the monarch (who may also be another manifestation of HCE) seems to be exposing his erection "and joking up with his tonguespitz to the crimosing balkonladies" (*FW* 569.1–2). This echoes Jerome's account of the Christian martyr who bit off the end of his tongue and spat it in the face of the harlot who kissed him. In the *Wake* passage, there is a "tip of the tongue" (*tungerspids* in Danish), the last part of which is shot out ("spits") into the prominent bust (*balcon* in French) of some crimson whores.[23] These ladies may be meant as minions of the "scarlet woman" in Revelation 17:4; in Protestant polemics that apocalyptic "mother of harlots" became a prime symbol of the Roman Catholic Church.

In the description of the setting of the scene for the King's arrival in the previous paragraph, I called attention to a "civic pageant, with religious overtones." That phrase needs some explanation. Here are Joyce's exact words: "(his scaffold is there set up, as to edify, by Rex Ingram, pageantmaster)" (*FW* 568.35–36). "Scaffolds" were the wooden platforms erected to serve as temporary stages for medieval mystery, miracle, and morality plays. These cyclic episodes from the Bible or the lives of saints were selected to edify the unsophisticated faithful. The plays were produced, usually by civic guilds, at pageants to celebrate religious feasts, the most important of which was Corpus Christi. Joyce recorded all of these details in one of his notebooks:

go to play (R C church)
Corp Xi cycles
public Urban IV
pageant (scaffolds) (VI.B.8.85)[24]

The royal and semi-liturgical thrust of Joyce's words is reinforced by the reference to "Rex Ingram" (*FW* 568.35). Mr. Ingram's Christian name,

"Rex," means "king" in Latin; he was the actor who starred as "de Lawd" in Marc Connelly's *The Green Pastures*. That 1930 play re-creates major moments in the Old Testament from the perspective of a rural, black community in Louisiana.[25] It is, quite literally, a modern mystery play.

Immediately before the passage from the *Wake* cited above, there are two additional, and previously undetected, references to a mystery play. The venue of this cryptic religious drama is ancient Egypt, the realm of "that illuminatured one, Papyroy of Pepinregn, my Sire, great, big King" (*FW* 568.34-35). The royal and divine lord who is the subject of the performance is Osiris (compare "my Sire" with "O Sire" [*FW* 566.29] in a nearby passage that is heavily indebted to the *Book of the Dead*). The primary clue for my Egyptian attribution here is "Pepi-," the name of a sixth-dynasty pharaoh (around 2300 B.C.) whose *Book of the Dead* was not written on a papyrus, but engraved on the walls of his royal pyramid. The hieroglyphic texts of Pepi were frequently cited and fully translated in books on ancient Egypt that Joyce certainly knew and from which he jotted entries in his *Wake* notebooks.[26] One such work has already been mentioned, E. A. W. Budge's *Osiris and the Egyptian Resurrection*. It has two long chapters on the "Mysteries" of Osiris, which (like later Christian mystery plays) were celebrated on the god's feasts at his special shrines, notably Abydos and Dendera in Upper Egypt.

All of this antiquarian detail from pharaonic, early Christian, and medieval sources *does* fit together—rather, it was made to fit together by Joyce in half a dozen lines in the *Wake* (568.34-569.2). The essential link in the chain of allusive evidence is the "mysteries" just mentioned. They are the thematic element that connects the royal pageants of Lord Mayor HCE, King Pepi and his temple texts, "my Sire" Osiris and his resurrection rituals, "de Lawd" in *The Green Pastures*, a king with an erect "canule," and the anonymous Christian martyr who bit off his tongue to avoid an erection.

The list of evidence-elements in the previous paragraph is, by design, more of a cascade than a catalogue. Conspicuously absent is a reference to the anchorite, St. Onuphrius, whose English name, "Humphrey," is after all the topic of this investigation. The Coptic recluse can, however, be reinserted into the process. His hagiographic vita is an archetypical instance of the legend of the "hairy anchorite." To establish that Joyce knew something of this tradition, it was necessary to identify and explain a number of references in the text of the *Wake* and several clusters of entries in various notebooks. A key element from the latter category was the three-element "Paul Hermit" index (VI.B.1.120). St. Jerome's Latin life of Paul is one of the most fully developed examples of the tale of the solitary penitent in the desert of Upper Egypt. Jerome's "historical" introduction includes the gory details of two martyrdoms during the reign of Emperor Decius. Joyce noted those instances of imperial cruelty, and (I argue) worked fragments of both into the text of the *Wake*.

The memorable "tonguespitz," in fact, is a Christian reversal of the re-membering of Osiris's severed limbs. According to Jerome, the pure youth's motive for self-mutilation was to avoid succumbing to sexual temptation. Since both of the notebook entries derived from the martyrs' tortures were applied to Shaun in the text, this motif may also have been meant to reverberate to the self-flagellation of Ireland's lacustrine anchorite, St. Kevin. Latin lives of that saint record that he lashed himself (and his tormentor) with nettles when a wanton woman assaulted his chastity: "smoothing out Nelly Nettle and her lad of mettle, full of stings" (*FW* 604.36).[27] Thus, like his use of Osiris, Joyce's adaptation of the Egyptian hairy hermit is sometimes applied to HCE and sometimes to his son Shaun.

This exercise in comparative onomastics traces archival and hagiographical detail from the Egyptian wilderness to Ireland and back. The essential point is the presentation of the evidence that HCE's byname "Honuphrius" is Latin for "Humphrey." That claim involves an examination of the life of the original H/Onuphrius, and its initial condensation in Gibbon's footnote. The Coptic saint—and his doppelgänger, Paul the Hermit—also make a distinct thematic contribution to the *Wake*. Their appearance and burial in the desert are among the more exotic elements in the work's frequent and typically twisted appropriation of material from the lives of the saints.

6

Irish and Other Celtic Saints

A major problem in dealing with Joyce's literary use of Celtic saints is the sheer number of hallowed candidates. A popular text from which Joyce took frequent notes reports that Cardinal Newman spoke of "the Irish multitude of Saints which the Book of Life alone is large enough to contain." An ancient manuscript cited in the same source divides the saints of Ireland "into three great orders," in the first of which were "350 in number, all bishops and all founders of churches."[1] In this categorization the other two orders are monastic pioneers and the isolated communities of semi-hermits. The document slights a most significant category of Irish saints: the numerous missionary-monks who introduced or reinforced the faith in Scotland and northern England and preserved Christian civilization throughout western Europe. These include St. Aidan at Lindisfarne, St. Columbanus in Gaul, St. Vergilius in Bavaria and Carinthia, St. Cathaldus in southern Italy, St. Donatus at Fiesole, and St. Gall in Switzerland.

As mentioned in my introduction, this chapter does not contain a review of the ongoing scholarship into St. Patrick's role in the fiction of Joyce. The Apostle of Ireland, himself a Brito-Roman missionary, appears all over *Finnegans Wake*, and the notebooks are packed with Patrician entries, many of which have been traced back to their documentary sources. Merely to survey this allusive and archival material—not to mention explicating phrases like "pawdry's purgatory" (*FW* 177.4) or "snakes in clover . . . for Patsy Presbys" (*FW* 210.26–27)—would be a monumental task. Thus, comment on St. Patrick is limited to a few references in chapter 9 to several pilgrimage-rituals associated with the veneration of Ireland's patron. On the other hand, the present chapter concludes with a fairly detailed review of the hagiographical source for and Joyce's literary use of St. Kevin's childhood miracles involving sheep and bones, and a more mature act of saintly chastity with nettles.

Joyce's earliest treatment of the holy heroes of his native land is in a 1907 lecture, delivered in Italian at the Università Popolare in Trieste. Three key pages of the English text of "Ireland, Island of Saints and Sages"[2] are little more than a chronological synopsis of almost a score of the country's missionaries, from Mansuetus to Sedulius the Younger (*CW* 157–59). Since it is sometimes difficult to determine precise dates in these hagiographical matters, I have opted to present my procession of premodern Irish saints in order of their appearance in Joyce's works, for which the chronology is more secure. In the case of the *Wake*, I begin with several clusters of thematic significance and move—with the exception of a terminal St. Kevin—to an alphabetic sweep of cleverly transformed figures from the history of the early Celtic church, including a few representatives from Wales and Brittany.

The opening story in *Dubliners* involves a young boy's reaction to the death of an old priest who "taught him a great deal" (*D* 10). Among the lessons are how to pronounce Latin properly, stories about the catacombs, and "the meaning of the different ceremonies of the Mass and of the different vestments worn by the priest." These data are what one might expect from a cleric who "had studied in the Irish college in Rome" (*D* 13). What is entirely missing in the priest's instruction is anything dealing with the earliest phases of the Celtic church; there is nothing about the Irish saints who were the glory of the island's nascent Christian heritage. I suggest that this omission of local hagiographical color is intended by Joyce to reflect Father Flynn's isolation from the life and heritage of the people whom he had once served as a parish priest. His ecclesiastical *Romanitas* embraces "the fathers of the church [who] had written books as thick as the *Post Office Directory*"; but it does not include the gripping tales of "that hermit of Aran who was called the dove of the church [St. Columkille]" (*CW* 236) or "Saint Brendan [who] weighed anchor for the unknown world . . . and, after crossing the ocean, landed on the coast of Florida" (*CW* 235).[3] Those expansively insular topics might have made even more of an impression on the bright young boy for whom people said Father Flynn "had a great wish" (*D* 10). There can be no doubt, however, that the folkloric thrust and tone of such narratives (even granting their saintly heroes) are remote from the seminary lessons likely to have been recalled by a learned alumnus of the Irish College in Rome.

At any rate, it is interesting to note a bit of allusive point, perhaps unintentionally injected into the first printed version of "The Sisters" by an overly scrupulous editor of the *Irish Homestead*. When an early version of Joyce's story (under the pseudonym "Stephen Daedalus") was accepted for publication in the August 13, 1904, issue, the text of the priest's death notice was altered to avoid any hint of topical realism: "St Catherine's Church, Meath Street" became a purely fictional parish, "St. Ita's Church." St. Ita is a widely venerated Irish holy woman who founded a religious community and a school for boys at Killeedy in Limerick. Among her pupils was the fabulous voyager St. Brendan. The substituted presence of St. Ita in a story involving the religious education of the young Dubliner is a tribute either to blind onomastic luck or to a finely tuned sense of hagiographical propriety on the part of the *Homestead's* editor.

Apart from the fleeting presence of a substituted Ita in "The Sisters," there are no early Celtic saints—and very few saints of any type—in *Dubliners*. Shortly before the last story in the collection was composed ("The Dead," during the summer of 1907), Joyce delivered the first of his three Trieste lectures. As previously mentioned, a section of this talk, "Ireland, Island of Saints and Sages," is specifically devoted to the "traces that the numerous Celtic apostles in almost every [western European] country have left behind them" (*CW* 157). Some of the exotic details—for example, that St. Fursey's "feast day is still celebrated at Peronne, the place where he died in Picardy" or that "the martyr Albinus directed [an institute of science] for many years in ancient Ticinum (now Pavia)" (*CW* 158–59)—are unmistakable evidence that Joyce had a documentary source close at hand.[4]

There is an obvious candidate for the source of Joyce's early information about the minutiae of Irish hagiography. E. A. Greene's book, *Saints and Their Symbols*, was in his Trieste library, and was definitely consulted for details in the Cyclopean catalogue. But the date of Joyce's copy ("twenty-seventh impression . . . 1913") makes it too late as a reference for the Trieste lecture. Another popular handbook, J. M. Flood's *Ireland: Its Saints and Scholars* (1917), is also disqualified for the same reason. Moreover, neither book supplies the necessary parallel details cited in the previous paragraph. An examination of the appropriate sections of the *Catholic Encyclopedia* and Butler's *Lives of the Saints*—both of which would probably have been difficult to consult in 1907 Trieste—reveals no relevant material. Thus, the search for Joyce's source of information for the lecture remains open.

The Stephen Dedalus of *A Portrait of the Artist as a Young Man* is not interested in Celtic saints. There is, of course, a transcendent Catholic ethos in the novel, but its locus is that of the Counter Reformation or the nineteenth-century Jesuit school and university—not the world of hermit-scholars, beehive cells, or wandering missionaries challenging Frankish warlords. At Clongowes Wood College young Stephen's religious icons were "the portraits of the saints and great men of the [Jesuit] order" (*P* 55); his teacher, in a discussion of aesthetics at University College, recalls "a sentence of Newman's in which he says of the Blessed Virgin that she was detained in the full company of the saints" (*P* 188). The matter and the vocabulary of both citations are far removed from those that characterize tales of St. Kevin's childhood miracles or St. Brendan's celebration of mass on the back of an Atlantic whale. Neo-Platonic aesthetics and Thomistic metaphysics are more important for *Portrait* than local hagiographical color.[5] Thus, most of the evidence in the rest of this chapter comes from *Ulysses* and especially the *Wake*.

In the absence of a section devoted to the life and works of St. Patrick himself, it is fitting to give pride of place in this chapter to two early saints who are almost as important as Ireland's patron. In fact, pious legend reports that Saints Patrick, Brigid, and Columba (Columkille) were all buried—or, more accurately, reburied—in the same tomb in Downpatrick. Archival entries for *Finnegans Wake* indicate that Joyce was aware of this tradition:

> Brigid, Columba, and SP / buried together (VI.B.1.106).
> . . . .
> Hi tres in uno tumulo tumulantur
> Brigida, Patricus atque Columba pius
> In Down 3 saints one grave do fill
> Patrick and Brigid and Columkille. (VI.B.1.164)

A slightly skewed transcription ("Columbella" for "Columkille") of the English version of the sepulchral couplet is crossed out in blue crayon in VI.C.3.169, but I have been unable to detect its collective presence in the text of the *Wake*. There are, however, two instances in the narrative in which Brigid and Patrick seem to be cited as saintly rivals. First, when Anna Livia Plurabelle lists the presents she has prepared for her offspring, she includes "snakes in clover, picked and scotched, and a vaticanned viper catcher's visa for Patsy Presbys" (*FW* 210.26–27). This gift packs together religious (and national) symbols, missionary miracles, a papal commission, an ethnic allusion to the inhabitants of the Northern section of Ireland's eastern neighbor, and an acknowledgment that St. Patrick is the grand old man (*presbyteros* in Greek) of the insular church. The nearby present for Ireland's premier female saint is quite a bit more utilitarian, "scruboak beads for beatified Biddy" (*FW* 210.29). St. Brigid founded her famous convent and school at Kildare, "church of the oak" in Irish. That institution is also commemorated in the second pair of comparative citations: "Girl Scouts from St. Bride's Finishing Establishment" (*FW* 220.3–4) are matched by "Components of the Afterhour Courses at St. Patricus' Academy for Grownup Gentlemen" (*FW* 221.1–2).

The association of an oak and St. Brigid in the previous paragraph leads to a brief excursus on early Irish social history—and on Joyce's uncanny ability to exploit opportunities for humor in the most unlikely places. There can be no doubt, etymologically and hagiographically, that the tree under which Brigid established her religious community at Kildare was an oak. That arboreal fact notwithstanding, Joyce twice transforms the tree into an elm in *Ulysses*. The first occasion is the Citizen's cry to save the trees of Ireland, a plea that serves to trigger the catalogue-report of the members of the wedding of Miss Fir Conifer of Pine Valley. The Citizen begs, "Save them ... the chieftain *elm* of Kildare with a fortyfoot bole and an acre of foliage" (*U* 12.1262–63; my emphasis). The second metamorphosis occurs in an Ithacan list of some of the most famous sites in Ireland, including "the pastures of royal Meath, Brigid's *elm* in Kildare, the Queen's Island shipyard in Belfast" (*U* 17.1976–77; my emphasis). I have no idea why Joyce repeated this bit of hagiographical misinformation. It would be difficult to argue ignorance, since his misapplication of the botanical epithet "chieftain" (elms are "Common," not "Chieftain" trees) in the first citation clearly points to an authoritative source.[6] Later in his career, Joyce engaged in significant (and reputably scientific) research about Irish trees for the *Wake*, especially the oldest, "the elm tree in the demesne of Howth Castle and Environs" (*Letters* III.309).[7] Whatever the source or the motive for the Ulyssean confusion about the genus of Brigid's tree, the text of the *Wake* emphatically restores the etymologically correct oak to its rightful place at the nunnery: "as tough as the oaktrees (peats be with them!) used to rustle that time down by the dykes of killing Kildare" (*FW* 202.30–31).

Brigid's saintly popularity in Ireland is second only to that of its patron, St. Patrick. A phrase from the *Wake* confirms that position of high honor. It appears immediately after the string of citations from an apocryphal gospel that links Issy and the Virgin Mary. Joyce then states that Issy "will blow ever so much more promisefuller, blee me, than all the other common *marygales* that romp round brigidschool" (*FW* 562.11–13; my emphasis). The italicized word is a Wakean compound of "Mary of the Gaels," a title given to St. Brigid as the special protectress of the Irish people. In less elevated terms, the saint lends her name to the flock of hens that surround Biddy Doran: "(and not one hen only nor two hens neyther but every blessed brigid came aclucking and aclacking)" (*FW* 256.5–6). Brigid's popularity is also reflected in the fact that she is the patron of many churches, as, for example, the initial element in a compound parish in a catalogue of Dublin churches: "Bride-and-Audeons-behind-Wardborg"

(*FW* 569.11; also note VI.B.44.103). An archival entry links St. Brigid with St. Foy (VI.B.10.51), whose gold-encased head is the principal relic in a famous pilgrimage church at Conques in the south of France on the route to Compostela.

A brief article by Edward Kopper suggests a folkloric reason for St. Brigid's special patronage of Issy and her February Rainbow Girls. According to a legend of uncertain date, the holy woman accosted St. Patrick and complained that the wards in her convent were not permitted any leverage in encouraging their shy lovers to propose marriage. Patrick reconsidered the ban on feminine initiative and allowed the girls this privilege once every seven years; Brigid threw her arms around his neck and begged Ireland's patron to extend the reversal of custom to leap years. He agreed—perhaps to escape Brigid's persuasive clutches.[8]

St. Columba (Latin for "dove") is better known by his Irish name, Columkille, "dove of the Church." According to tradition, Columkille was one of the illustrious students (later known as the Twelve Apostles of Erin) at St. Finnian's monastic school at Clonard. In the mid sixth century the saint founded many churches and Christian communities throughout Ireland. Columkille's most famous task, however, was establishing a monastery on the island of Iona, just off the west coast of Scotland, from which he and his companions preached the new faith to the Picts for over thirty years. His biography by a disciple, St. Adamnan, is one of the primary vernacular works of early Irish hagiography.[9]

According to legend—but not to the biography—Columkille's mission to Iona was penance for his copying a book of Psalms that was the property of St. Finnian. When Columkille refused to surrender the new manuscript to his mentor, King Diarmait was asked to mediate the dispute. His royal decision was in favor of St. Finnian, since "her calf belongs to every cow." Armed conflict followed, and a large number of warriors from the opposing clans were killed. For this reason, the copied book, which Columkille kept, was known as *Cathach* ("battle" in Irish). Several years later he went to Iona to make amends for his bloody stubbornness.

Joyce knew and used this anecdote. In an archival index on the Book of Kells,[10] several lines refer to this fraternal controversy: "pirates S. Finnian's / psalter (fingers light) / Cathach battle" (VI.B.6.56). The modern legal terminology of another entry is even more specific: "S. Finnian psalter / copyright noted / by Columba" (VI.B.22.131). Although neither item is crossed out, the incident clearly lies behind two neighboring phrases in the text: "Calomnequiller's Pravities" and "the mother of the book" (*FW* 50.9–12). The "marginal panels of Colum*killer*" (*FW* 122.25–26; my emphasis) also looks like an allusion to the illuminated text of the Psalms that the saint copied—and a hint of the deadly consequences of his refusal to accept King Diarmait's decision. Joyce also refers to the saint's penitential monastery on the island off Scotland: "He'd be as smug as Columbsisle Jonas wrocked in the belly of the whaves" (*FW* 463.31–32). Iona and the seafaring Hebrew prophet Jonah are linked in a note (VI.B.6.157),[11] and the Irish saint is cited as a model for Christopher Columbus in another entry (VI.B.28.169). Columkille is also conflated with the Roman agricultural writer Columela in "Columcellas" (*FW* 615.2–3).

In his list of notebook material that Joyce derived from Flood's book on Irish saints, Deane includes seven items, only one of which has relevant thematic significance. Flood reports that the Old Irish life of Columkille by Adamnan spread the saint's reputation so far that it "reached even to triangular Spain and Gaul and Italy." The note "ʳtriangular Spain" (VI.B.6.4) obviously comes from that source. Even though a connection with the Iberian peninsula has been elided, the phrase makes a minor contribution to the *Wake's* account of the arrival of snakes in Ireland: "They came to our island from triangular Toucheaterre beyond the wet prairie" (*FW* 19.13–14).[12]

A later tradition, which has no basis whatsoever in fact, attributes the gift of prophecy to St. Columkille. Joyce knew about this apocryphal tale and refers to it several times in the *Wake*: "As our revelant Colunnfiller predicted in last mount's chattiry sermon" (*FW* 324.26–27) and "till the timelag is in it that's told in the Bok of Alam to columnkill all the prefacies of Erin gone brugk" (*FW* 347.20–21). A final reference to the saint as a prophet is presented in the midst of an elaborate rhetorical introduction: "I have the highest gratification by anuncing how I have it from whowho but Hagios Colleenkiller's prophecies" (*FW* 409.26–28). Part of that citation is based on the notebook entry "ʳI have it from S Columkille's / prophecies." That item occurs as the apparent answer to another entry, "Who gave you the permit?" (VI.B.1.11).

In the notebook there follows an index, also crossed out in red, of ten lines, all of which are used in the adjacent text of the *Wake* as incidental components of the first four questions that correspond to the first four "stations of Shauns cross," or to the corresponding bumps of a barrel that rolls down the Liffey (*FW* 409.10; see *Letters* I.214). At least two of the archival entries show traces of a possible religious context: "It is written—there is a power / over and put upon from on / high by the Church" and a terminal "believe me, I say my prayers regularly" (VI.B.1.11). In the *Wake* these entries are murkily reflected in a scattered form (*FW*

409.36–410.2 and 411.12–18), but there is nothing that is aphoristic or cryptic in the expressions of their textual manifestation. They definitely do not sound like typical prophetic utterances. Thus, apart from pointing out the connection between the notebook index and text, there is nothing more to be said. What is necessary for further explication of the passage is an identification of its written source (presumably a book or article about St. Columkille's alleged prophecies) to determine the context of the excerpts. Without that sort of documentary base, additional comment about the exact meaning—not to mention the allusive force—of the index is pure speculation.

Columkille went to and was ordained at the famous school at Clonard founded by an earlier St. Finnian. He and eleven other companions from this monastic center—all destined to spread the faith by heroic means—became known as the Twelve Apostles of Clonard (or of Erin). Joyce includes scattered facts about these missionaries in an archival index during the same period as he was jotting down notes from Flood's book. The relevant entries include two cryptic phrases that are deployed in entirely distinct narrative contexts: "12 apostles of Clonard / ᵇfearless forehead / ᵇpainted eyelids / S. Senan" (VI.B.3.158; also see VI.B.6.183 and VI.B.41.101). The two crossed items are probably references to characteristics of the pagan tribes to whom the Irish apostles preached the new faith. In the *Wake*, a "fearless forehead" is applied to "Haromphreyld," one of HCE's aliases (*FW* 31.8–10); after one of her coy riddles Issy declares that Glugg/Shem's "eyelids are painted" (*FW* 248.16). For neither of these two phrases would even the most astute reader of the *Wake* have postulated an original religious source.[13]

St. Columkille is not the only Celtic holy man to whom the gift of divinely inspired prediction was attributed. The most famous collection of Irish "prophecy" is assigned, with no basis in historical fact, to St. Malachy (sometimes spelled "Malachi"). This twelfth-century bishop of Armagh worked ceaselessly to establish canonically correct procedures for assumption of episcopal offices throughout Ireland. The so-called *Prophecies of St. Malachy* (which allegedly named all future popes up to the end of the world) are a sixteenth-century forgery by an adherent of a candidate for the papal throne. Joyce's interest in this document is indicated by copies of different editions in both his Trieste and Paris libraries.[14] Several indubitable references to the predictions and their pseudonymous author are part of a long papacy index (VI.B.4.250–61) that was heavily mined by Joyce for the Mookse and the Gripes episode in the *Wake*. There the saint is specifically labeled "Malachy the Augurer" (*FW* 155.38), and his spurious list of the successors of St. Peter—it comprised 111 cryptic entries—is cited: "(secunding [close to "according to" in Latin] to the one one oneth of the prophecies)" (*FW* 153.1–2).

Interspersed through the notebook index cited in the previous paragraph are numerous Latin phrases that the author of the *Prophecies* used to identify future pontiffs. Danis Rose discusses the source of this index, its use in the *Wake*, and an identification of the popes that are so predicted.[15] Since readers can consult that piece for detailed information about Joyce's deployment of material attributed to this medieval Irish saint, I close my comments on Malachy by pointing out that one of the crossed archival entries, "^br^vatication" (VI.B.4.260), is based on the Latin noun *vaticanatio* which means "prediction," "augury." Joyce reused it in the nearby text in a batch of flashily Latinate words that terminate in "-ation," the suffix that creates abstract nouns from verbs, such as "retroraticination," "vatication," and "miserecordation" (*FW* 142.17–18, 19, 25). The Vatican Hill in Rome, destined to become the site of St. Peter's Church and the pope's residence, is so named because it was a spot favored by ancient Roman augurs to observe birds and offer predictions from their flight patterns.[16] One can be sure that Joyce, creator of Stephen Dedalus and his "curved stick of an augur" (*P* 225), appreciated the valid classical and papal application of this item in the notebook cluster.

The hagiographical scene now shifts from spurious pontifical prophecies to the fabulous narrative of the navigations of St. Brendan. He was a sixth-century monk, educated at St. Ita's school, who founded the famous monastery of Clonfort in Galway. Brendan's most notable achievements, however, took place on the high seas during the voyage he and his companions made to the Land of Promise. Also called "Hy Brasil," this land beyond the ocean is at least semitropical, with marvelous birds and fruit. In his 1912 article on the Aran Isles, Joyce claimed that St. Brendan "landed on the coast of Florida" (*CW* 235). Stops along the way included brief visits to the rock on which Judas Iscariot is marooned in enduring punishment and the island on which Paul the Hermit has lived for sixty years without a mouthful of food. On the way out and homeward the monk-navigators anchored their giant curragh and celebrated Mass on the moving "island" of Jasconius, actually the back of a whale. Translations of the *Navigatio Sancti Brandani*, the log of a saintly Sinbad the Sailor, were made into many European languages.[17]

Inge Landuyt and Wim Van Mierlo have discovered a documentary source for Joyce's notes on St. Brendan in a collection of lives of Irish holy men and women published to celebrate the fifteenth centenary of the introduction of Christianity into Erin.[18] This book, Frank Sheed's *The Irish Way*, was a gift to Joyce by his close friend Constantine Curran, who was the author of its essays on St. Laurence O'Toole and Blessed Mary Aikenhead.[19] Joyce took only a few notes from the book, but two of them concerning Brendan were crossed and placed in the *Wake*. The first entry joins the saint with the province of which he became the patron, "ᵇBrendan Kerry" (VI.B.34.146); the second names the goal of the long voyage, "ᵇHigh Brazil" (VI.B.34.146). Both items coalesce into the text's "Brendan's mantle whitening the Kerribrasilian sea" (*FW* 442.14–15). The fabulous trans-Atlantic land is also named "High Brazil Brandan's Deferred" (*FW* 488.24–25).

In addition to the pair of reused archival entries, there are several other thematically appropriate allusions in the *Wake* to St. Brendan. One links his voyage with the landfall of Viking explorers in the New World: "Vineland beyond Brendan's herring pool" (*FW* 213.35–36). The saint's parents, Fynlogue (or Findlug) and Cara, are named in "goodsend Brandonius, *filius* [Latin for "son"] of a Cara, spouse to Fynlogue" (*FW* 327.2–3).[20] There are also two archival notes that come from sources other than Sheed's collection of essays. One cluster itemizes what appear to be the provisions for a voyage: "Brendan's willow curragh / nuts and weeds for others / yoke of asses / BVM thistles / her milk" (VI.B.14.182). A final entry pushes the bold saint's explorations beyond the limits of the fabulous: "S. Brendan founded Chicago" (VI.B.6.75).

Another widely traveled Irish saint had little to do with the sea, nor could he be called a holy adventurer. Rather, St. Columbanus was a *peregrinus pro Christo*, a "wanderer, exile, pilgrim, missionary for Christ." In the late sixth century he and a dozen companions journeyed to the continent to spread the word of the Lord. They founded monasteries throughout Gaul, Germany, Switzerland, and northern Italy. His defense of his very strict rules and Irish ecclesiastical customs, as well as his excoriation of moral laxness in the Burgundian court, earned him the epithet *perfervidus*, "fiery" (*CW* 157–58). In fact, early in *Ulysses*, Stephen Dedalus recalls the saint as a witness to his own botched sojourn in Paris: "You were going to do wonders, what? Missionary to Europe after fiery Columbanus. Fiacre and Scotus on their creepystools in heaven spilt from their pintpots, loudlatinlaughing: *Euge! Euge!*" (*U* 3.192–94). An allusion to Columbanus may flash momentarily in an adjective at the start of a *Wake* passage that records one of Shaun's replies to a series of questions about his position as a postman: "—It is a confoundyous injective so to say, Shaun the *fiery* boy shouted, naturally incensed, as he shook the red pepper out of his auricles" (*FW* 412.13–15; my emphasis). After the attempted seduction of Chuff by the Rainbow Girls, his sinister brother Glugg/Shem rises to confess his sins and vows to reform, "praise Saint Calembaurnus" (*FW* 240.20–21). Contributing to the force of that invocation is wordplay involving the missionary's name and the French term, *calembour*, for a pun.

Several archival items mention significant events in St. Columbanus's career. The entry "S. Columbanus v S. Benedict" (VI.B.14.118) refers to the monastic regulations of the communities established on the continent by the Irish missionary; they naturally precipitated later conflict with the dominant European model, the Rule of St. Benedict. Columbanus died and was buried in a famous monastery that he founded in northwest Italy: "bishop of Bobbio abbot / of S. Columbanus" (VII.B.2.55). Another entry involves a self-inflating autobiographical comparison: "Columban to Boniface IV / JJ & G Rex)" (VI.B.17.24). During 1910 and 1911 Joyce had problems with the publisher George Roberts over certain passages in "Ivy Day in the Committee Room." At issue were some allegedly disrespectful references to King George V. After several delays in the appearance of *Dubliners*, Joyce decided to appeal directly to the king. He wrote a letter to Buckingham Palace and enclosed a proof-copy of the story with the "offensive" passage marked. On August 11, 1911, the secretary of George V replied that "it is inconsistent with rule for His Majesty to express his opinion in such cases" (*JJII* 314–15). In 612 St. Columbanus had written a long and passionate letter to Pope Boniface IV, demanding that the pontiff resolve some delicate issues of ecclesiastical policy. The letter is famous for its plain-spoken lack of diplomatic diction. At least in his notes for the *Wake*, Joyce saw a parallel between his appeal to the king and fiery Columbanus's letter to the pope. The entry was not transferred into the text.

St. Adamnan is best known for his life of St. Columkille, his predecessor as the (founding) abbot of Iona.[21] Joyce's only textual reference to the monk-hagiographer, however, focuses on a law that Adamnan forcefully supported at the Council of Birr (697). This provision, called the *cain Adomnain*, forbade attacks on women, children, and the clergy during times of war. Two archival notes refer specifically to this humane provision (VI.B.3.90 and VI.B.36.294), the second entry calling it the "law of Innocents." During the "Night Lessons" chapter of the *Wake*, an explanatory footnote is attached to "Adamman": "Only for he's fathering law I could skewer that old one and slosh her out" (*FW* 267.18 and F5). Here the adverb "only" is equivalent to "except"—and the saint's prohibition has (characteristically for the context) been skewed from combat to sex.

A recent article by Christine O'Neill examines the Joycean links between the ancient Irish pagan god Aegnus of the Birds and the eighth-century Christian saint Angus the Culdee.[22] The latter was an austere anchorite in the famous monastic community of Tallaght. His *Félire* (Calendar) is a metrical hymn of the annual festivals of the saints, a work of immense importance to the early history of Ireland. Both *Ulysses* and the *Wake* feature allusions to St. Angus, such as the triple invocation that immediately follows a reference to the controversy over the correct date for celebrating the Resurrection: "With easter greeding. Angus! Angus! Angus!" (*FW* 376.36–377.1).

Laurence O'Toole was a twelfth-century archbishop of Dublin. It was during his tenure that the major wave of Anglo-Norman adventurers attacked Ireland. After negotiating between King Rory O'Connor of Connacht and Henry II, he was forced into exile in Normandy, where he died and was buried at the monastery of Eu. St. Laurence's Irish name, Lorcan, is joined with that of St. Francis Xavier in an archival note (VI.B.43.72); the common element is their overseas death and burial. (Xavier was the Apostle of the Indies; his tomb is in Goa.)[23] Another note highlights St. Laurence's trip across the Irish Sea and the Channel to consult the English king: "ᵀlike Lowry O' / Twoheels between / the Dublin & / the Dieppe sea" (VI.B.34.124). His name is similarly distorted in an adjacent entry: "Larking o'Tooth" (VI.B.34.124). That type of onomastic wordplay underlies a number of the saint's appearances in the *Wake*: "larrons o'tootlers" (*FW* 5.3), "L.O. Tuohalls" (*FW* 77.2), "Scent Otooles" (*FW* 138.26), "send Larix U'Thule" (*FW* 235.19; also note VI.B.36.207), and "lairking o'toolers" (*FW* 510.18). In one of Joyce's several parodies of the Litany of the Saints, the blessed archbishop is commemorated in pseudo-Latin that approximates the standard formula of invocation: "Libera, nostalgia! Beate Laurentie O'Tuli, Euro pra nobis!" (*FW* 228.25–26). The beginning of that citation is appropriate for an exile, since nostalgia is literally "homesickness"; its end also doubly specifies his overseas burial at Eu, on the far western shore of Europe.

Early in 1938 Joyce started to work on what became the final section of the *Wake*. In a letter to Frank Budgen, he comments on "the hagiographic triptych in Part IV (S. L. O'Toole is only adumbrated)" (*Letters* I.406). In the first part St. Kevin is progressively isolated at Glendalough; then St. Patrick debates the Archdruid Berkeley. Explicit reference to St. Laurence O'Toole, in fact, is relegated to a single-sentence, line-and-a-half paragraph: "Lo, the land of laurens now orielising benedictively when saint and sage have had their say" (*FW* 613.15–16). In narrative terms, this is indeed a brief curtain call for the archbishop.[24] In lexical terms, on the other hand, the citation centers on what I am willing to wager is the English language's sole appearance of the present participle of a verb luminously created from the noun for a large bay window.

None of the standard handbooks of hagiography mention St. Mona, but she does play a minor role in Irish folklore—and in the *Wake*. As the tale goes, she rescued a hare that was being chased by the hounds of the foxhunting gentry. Thus, in some sections of Ireland, hares are known as "St. Mona's lambs," and children call on her to save rabbits that are being hunted down.[25] On three occasions in the *Wake* there are allusions to these country customs. After mentioning a "blue foux," Jaun addresses Issy as "Mona Vera Toutou Ipostila," and reveals that he dreams about hares, "a maurdering row, the fox!" and other animals hunted for sport (*FW* 449.11–22). Later in the same episode, Jaun inquires if "mona, my own love . . . making up to you . . . like the landskip from Lambay?" (*FW* 464.32–35). In another passage the saint merges with the moon: "Do you happen to recollect whether Muna, that highlucky nacht ["night" in German], was shining at all?" (*FW* 502.11–12). More questions follow, including "Of whitecaps any?" The answer is "Foamflakes flockfuyant from Foxrock to Finglas." That double-entendre triggers a relevant exclamation: "—A lambskip for the marines!" (*FW* 502.34–36). I have already discussed some saintly virgins whose coveted breasts became little Joycean "lambs"; here the chased rabbits and pursued fox, despite the protection of Mona their patron, are part of the same Wakean motif of sexually predatory behavior.

Saint Kevin

Excluding Patrick, the Irish saint given the most prominent role in *Finnegans Wake* is Kevin (Coemgen ["Well-born"] in Irish). A recent article by Christopher Bjork cogently lays out the genetic and textual evidence for several models used by Joyce in composing his portrait of St. Kevin.[26] One small area of the saint's life—and one that is quite significant in hagiographical terms—still needs to be explored. At a very late stage (1938) in the evolution of the *Wake*, Joyce added some typical "childhood miracles" to his account of the life of the patron of Glendalough. Before I investigate the source of that passage, it is necessary to give a bit of combined hagiographical and genetic background.

Probably the most familiar and certainly the most frequently cited segment of archival material from the *Wake* is a short but continuous unit from VI.B.3.42–45 (*JJA* 29.201–2 and 63.34–37). Jack Dalton's magisterial article presents the details of the additions to this early draft, as it was developed into the text of *FW* 605.4–606.12.[27] The initial sketch was transcribed, during the summer of 1923, by Nora Joyce at her husband's dictation; its three and a half pages constitute a single sentence that encapsulates the aquatic isolation of St. Kevin at Glendalough. Inserted above a number of lines in the primary text are some additions in Joyce's own hand. Most of these adjustments substitute a series of increasingly more honorific nouns-plus-epithets for the unspecific pronouns of the original: "holy Kevin," "very h[oly] K[evin]" "most holy K[evin]," "venerable K[evin]," "blessed K[evin]," "v[ery] blessed K[evin]," "St Kevin." To highlight the canonical crescendo in his choice and placement of terms, Joyce also excised the initial "St" that modified Kevin in the original opening of the passage, and placed it emphatically at the end. Shortly after this dictated-and-amended first draft, Joyce prepared three revisions, each with more elaborate adjectival and adverbial detail. These versions were followed by the famous fair copy, in ink, dispatched to Harriet Shaw Weaver on "16/vii/923," with a request that she prepare a typed copy (47488-24–27v [*JJA* 63.38a–38f]).

There is no evidence of any other authorial attention or adjustment to this core Kevin passage in book IV until early 1938. Then, after an almost fifteen-year hiatus in composition, Joyce added some interlinear words and phrases to a twelve-page, double-spaced, working typescript of the first two sections of the final book. On a separate sheet (47488-36v [*JJA* 63.60]) are four numbered additions in Joyce's hand. The last of these is the crucial minicatalogue of St. Kevin's childhood miracles. Prior to the special scrutiny of this passage, however, it is necessary to mention several other archival items dealing with the patron of Glendalough.

First, a series of notebook entries (VI.B.6.124) has been identified by Vincent Deane as coming from the *Catholic Encyclopedia* (4.9). Its nineteen lines, in Joyce's small, tight, source-recording hand, are an accurate digest of that article's synopsis of the data of St. Kevin's career, from his birth in 498 to the designation of the monastic and diocesan city at Glendalough and its seven churches as an important Irish pilgrimage center. The final bit of this meticulously recorded factual information seems to have made its way into the text of the *Wake:* Sevenchurches ... Glintalook" (*FW* 59.16–18) and "the Glendalough see" (*FW* 62.35–36).

Second, several entries label Kevin a consummate misogynist and illustrate his horror of sexual activity, as the following examples reveal:

- VI.B.3.132: "S Kevin had never / heard of a cunt / Kathleen is shocked."
- VI.B.6.40–41: "If Kevin had been / present / disgraceful scenes which

/ dishonored his [*in margin:* on / the bed / of] / conception he wd / have flatly declined / to be born at all."

- VI.B.10.73: "He simply had no / time for girls. He used / to say his sisters / were good enough for him."[28]

- VI.B.11.102: "called them by name / S Kevin did not know / 1 girl from another."

Third, a few scattered entries are related to the water motif pervading the Kevin passage in book IV:

- VI.B.2.9: "Kevin prays in water / 50 psalms."

- VI.B.2.15: "polynesian (Kevin)."

- VI.B.11.68: "polynesian / isolation / insular."

Next, I examine the key childhood passage itself, in which these diverse archival themes come together. Students of hagiography recognize that there is a common store of miracles that tend to get passed around and assigned to more than one saint's life. The attempted seduction of the desert hermit, the delivery of bread by birds to a fasting ascetic, or the reverent burial of a holy man's corpse by gentle animals are obvious instances of commonly used motifs.[29] In the discussion of St. Onuphrius/Humphrey, for example, I mentioned the ravens who supplied the saint with sustaining loaves and the marvelous events that led to his burial in the desert. Chapter 8 includes a brief reference to St. Benedict's method of avoiding sexual temptation: he stripped off his robes and rolled in a patch of briars that grew outside his hermit's cave. The persistent reappearance in various saints' lives of such motifs is a characteristic of hagiographical narrative. As one scholar puts it, "This sort of haphazard application of marvelous feats happened less through a desire of practicing deception, than from a motive of misconceived piety."[30]

The vacuum of information about the early years of the life of St. Kevin, for which there is nothing in terms of documented history, attracted masses of fabulous material. The richest surviving repository of this type of piously embellished information is a medieval Latin vita, most accessible in a 1910 edition prepared by Charles Plummer.[31] The straightforward vocabulary and syntax of this text would have presented absolutely no challenge to James Joyce. Nevertheless, since the additions to the *Wake* text show no major traces of a Latin-language origin (a display that would have been both congenial and customary for Joyce), I doubt very much that the original text of the vita is the direct source for Kevin's childhood miracles.[32] There is an alternative channel of influence—one that is supported by considerable internal, and some tantalizing archival, evidence.

In the late nineteenth century the Very Reverend John Canon O'Hanlon, M.R.I.A., published his nine-volume *Lives of the Irish Saints: With Special Festivals, and the Commemorations of Holy Persons, Compiled from Calendars, Martyrologies, and Various Sources, Relating to the Ancient Church History of Ireland*. Among the "Various Sources" are the several Latin vitae of Kevin. In fact, many pages of O'Hanlon's lengthy entry for the "Third Day of June: Article I.—St. Coemgin or Kevin, Abbot of Glendalough, County of Wicklow" are direct translations of various Latin episodes into English. O'Hanlon's work is specialized and packed with eccentric detail, but it is exactly the sort of text that would have tickled Joyce's bizarre hagiographical curiosity. I believe it is the immediate source of information for Joyce's Wakean re-creations of six extraordinary incidents in the early life of St. Kevin.

The first paragraph (one long and complex sentence) of the second section of book IV of the *Wake* is introduced by: "Of Kevin, of increate God the servant . . . the miracles, death and life are these" (FW 604.27–605.3). The paragraph that follows this formulaic introduction situates Kevin, with his portable altar, as he settles in his hip-bath on a "lacustrine yslet" in the midst of "Glendalough-le-vert." Near the end of the introductory paragraph is the cryptic, condensed report of five of the six miracles:

> shearing aside the four wethers and passing over the dainty daily dairy and dropping by the way the lapful of live coals and smoothing out Nelly Nettle and her lad of mettle, full of stings, fond of stones, friend of gnewgnawns bones and leaving all the messy messy to look after our douche douche, the miracles, death and life are these. (FW 604.34–605.3)

The clearest way of demonstrating the parallels between the passages in Canon O'Hanlon's study and the text of the *Wake* is to cite the actual textual evidence, after a brief indication of the context of the miracle.

1. O'Hanlon's life of Kevin reports that the youthful Kevin helped to tend his parents' sheep. One day some poor people, who had heard of his reputation for sanctity, came and begged him for food:

> . . . the holy youth delivered four sheep to those paupers. When evening came, and the flock had been counted over, still it was found, that the number of sheep remained complete. (O'Hanlon, 34)

shearing aside the four wethers (FW 604.34)

2. Another incident involves a typical hagiographical case of the supernatural feeding of a holy infant:

> ... a white cow was miraculously sent to his parents' house, each morning and evening. With the milk of this animal, the child was nourished ... two large vessels of milk were obtained from her each day.[33] (O'Hanlon, 33–34)

and passing over the dainty daily dairy (FW 604.34)

3. St. Kevin's first monastic retreat was at Lough Tay in Wicklow. There an older monk sent the young saint on an errand:

> "Brother, run quickly for the fire, and bring it with you." St. Kevin asked [how] ... his senior rather hastily answered: "In your bosom." ... Kevin placed ... some live coals in his bosom. And [then] the young novice threw this fire, on the ground, in the presence of his superior. Not alone his flesh, but even his garments, seemed to suffer no injury. (O'Hanlon, 37)

and dropping by the way the lapful of live coals (FW 604.35)

4. When the saint was in the full bloom of youth, he attracted the notice of an equally beautiful maiden.[34] She manifested great friendship toward him and began to visit the steadfast young monk's stone cell:

> This female ... endeavored to engage the love of this holy youth, by her looks, her words.... However, Kevin rejected these several advances ... [and] ... at once fled ... [and] sought concealment within a wood.... [He] buried himself among some nettles ... [and] repelled her further advances by striking her several times with ... a bundle of nettles. (O'Hanlon, 35)

and smoothing out Nelly Nettle and her lad of mettle, full of stings, fond of stones (FW 604.35–605.1)

5. Neither the detail nor the presentation of the fifth miracle in this series is very clear. At the end of the Nelly Nettle incident, Joyce's comment on Kevin's character is expressed in three similarly formed epithets: "full of stings" (his seduction-averting scourge), "fond of stones" (his beehive hut and traditional "bed" of stones), and "friend of gnewgnawns bones" (FW 604.36–605.1). The last of the three elements requires some textual comment. Joyce originally wrote "deadmen sbones" (47488-36v

[*JJA* 63.60]). The "deadmen" is crossed out and "gnewgnaw" is written in above it.³⁵

There are, especially in the Latin vita, several reports of Kevin's restoring dead humans to life.³⁶ The "sbones," then, might be an elided exclamation of awe at this impressive, but more or less conventional, miracle: "by God's bones!" From another perspective, however, in none of the hagiographical episodes have the "deadmen" been reduced (by corruption or predators) to mere "bones," newly gnawn or not. Thus, I suggest that for the final version of the fifth miracle included in Kevin's supernatural dossier, Joyce selected a far more exotic marvel, also reported in Canon O'Hanlon's text. One autumn the monks with whom the young saint was living hired many reapers to bring in the harvest. Generous portions of meat and beer were prepared to feed these laborers. Unexpectedly, a crowd of hungry pilgrims arrived, and Kevin gave them all of the reapers' food. The superior scolded Kevin, who then ordered the kitchen attendants "to collect all the bones" and to fill the empty tuns with water. After "he prayed with great fervor, . . . the water is stated to have become wine, while the bones were covered with an abundance of excellent flesh meat" (O'Hanlon, 40).

The primary beneficiaries of this culinary wonder are the reapers. The Latin noun in the original vita is *messores*. This standard term, which Joyce would have known without reference to the original text or a dictionary, seems to me a likely etymological trigger for the *Wake's* "messy messy" (*FW* 605.2). That is, I see and hear in these two words not only a redundant messy mess (English: a discombobulated heap) or mess (English, German: military dining hall), but also a harvest (Latin, Italian), fair (German), or mass (German, French)—and various permutations thereof. The presence of this sort of multilingual echo-pun is reinforced by the adjacent "douche douche" (*FW* 605.2). This phrase is more probably an evocation of a "sweet shower" (French) of water to be affused into Kevin's hip-bath or a fervent appeal from the catechumens for baptism (French)³⁷ than it is the reverberating chant (Italian) of a crowd of Mussolini's supporters. Moreover, since each of the five miracles mentioned in this passage is gracefully elided ("shearing aside," "passing over," "dropping by," "smoothing out," "leaving"), Joyce may be rushing through the messy improbability of these formulaic instances of "stupefacation" (*FW* 604.33), so that he can concentrate on Kevin's essential aquatic function—for Joyce's vita of Kevin now leaves the turbulent militancy of the saint-in-the-world for the crystalline serenity of a hermit's life at Glendalough. As a "recluse" there, the *"doctor insularis"* opts for a life of contemplating "continuously with seraphic ardor the primal sacrament of baptism or the regeneration of all men by affusion of water. Yee" (*FW* 606.7–12).

These are five of the six childhood miracles contained in Joyce's handwritten 1938 addition. The lines were inserted en bloc at the end of the first paragraph of the basic Kevin-sketch. Just before this supplement to the draft text, there is a shorter note, also in Joyce's hand: "whomamong the christener of his" (47488-36r [*JJA* 63.60]). This phrase also entered the *Wake*'s text at the same time as the longer addition, but it was placed slightly later in the episode, near the start of the second paragraph, where it introduces the final childhood miracle.

6. The trigger phrase "precreated holy angels" was present in the Kevin-node from its earliest stages of composition, the second expansion of the original sketch in July 1923 (47488-25 [*JJA* 63.380]). The inclusion of Kevin's "christener" among the primeval celestial creatures is the sixth wondrous event that Joyce lifted from O'Hanlon's life of the saint. An angel had appeared to Coenhella, Kevin's mother, and instructed her to have her infant baptized immediately after his birth. As the newborn child was being carried to a certain holy priest for him to administer the sacrament, an "Angel of God" accosted the group: "It is said, moreover, that Angel breathed on the child, and signed him. . . . Then praying, he bestowed a benediction on the future saint" (O'Hanlon, 32).

In a note to this incident, O'Hanlon comments on the strange omission of "an infusion or use of water," and remarks that "mere breathing alone"—albeit angelic—is not sufficient for the Christian initiation rite. If O'Hanlon could have foreseen Joyce's heavy emphasis in the *Wake* on Kevin's profound affection for water, he would have been even more perplexed by this unaccountable omission of this "necessary matter for baptismal ablution" (O'Hanlon, 32, n. 47).

The similarities in "plot" between O'Hanlon's narratives of these six miracles and Joyce's radically compacted versions cannot be mere coincidence. The details of source and adaptation just presented are the internal evidence. For archival evidence there is a 1935 notebook entry that, in my judgment, points indubitably to Joyce's direct use of *Lives of the Irish Saints*:

	Kevin		
	34	34	
p	36	36	
	37	37	(VI.B.47.57)

The three figures in the first column are crossed out, then rewritten in green crayon. I interpret these four lines as specifying a topic ("Kevin") and then recording three pages ("p / 34 / 36 / 37") on which basic information about that topic can be found.[38] In O'Hanlon's version of Kevin's life, the cow and the sheep appear on page 34; the nettles on page 35; the coals on page 37; the bones on page 40; and the angelic christening on page 32. Again, the close conjunction of the notebook page citations and the page numbers of O'Hanlon's narrative recounting Kevin's childhood miracles seems to me to preclude coincidence.

The entry on Kevin in volume VI of *Lives of the Irish Saints* runs from pages 28 to 90. In no other biography of which I am aware is so much attention given to the early—and more fabulous—career of the saint. Moreover, the Buffalo notebook (VI.B.47), in which this crucial entry is found, was compiled sometime in 1938, at more or less the same time as Joyce, after a considerable lapse, began once again to supplement his primary Kevin-node. These last two points do not prove the case for the identification of Joyce's source, but they do help to minimize reasonable doubt.[39]

Wales

A sixth-century abbot and bishop, St. David, is the patron of Wales. Heavily disguised allusions to his life, including reference to the saint's symbol (and the national emblem of Wales) in "the garlic leek" (*FW* 462.29–30), lurk in the passage roughly bounded by "Dave the Dancekerl" (*FW* 462.17) and "David R. Crozier" (*FW* 464.3).[40] There is also an uncrossed note citing two popular Welsh holy men: "S. David / S. Asaph" (VI.B.32.113). Another Welsh saint to merit Joycean recognition is Samson, the abbot-bishop of Dol. The account of his life and miracles is the earliest biography of a Celtic saint in Britain. An archival entry records what appears to be a modern edition of that life by the Society for the Promotion of Christian Knowledge: "S Samson of Dol / (SPCK)" (VI.B.8.87). A textual reference converts the saint into a trainer of racehorses and conflates him with his Old Testament namesake: "groomed by S. Samson and son, bred by dilalahs" (*FW* 523.17).

Brittany and Cornwall

Shortly before the Wakean entrance of St. Samson, another well-known figure in British-Celtic folklore reappears: "The man from St. Yves" (*FW* 523.8). In two other passages the saint has been blended into a traditional Christmas decoration: "And all the holly. And some of the mistle and it

Saint Yves" (*FW* 147.10–11) and "Saint Holy and Saint Ivory" (*FW* 556.3; also note the archival entry "S. Holy / & / S. Ives" [VI.B.15.cover verso]). St. Yves/Ives was a fourteenth-century priest and lawyer, famed for his clerical and legal integrity among the people of Brittany. In the English-speaking world he is best known as the presumed patron of the town in Cornwall from which came a "man with two wives."[41] In the *Wake* Joyce alludes to the town's location (and that of nearby Land's End) in "Saint Yves by Landsend cornwer, man" (*FW* 291.1–2).

In the index on the life of St. Kevin taken from the *Catholic Encyclopedia* (IV.92), one of the entries records that he was "ed.[ucated by] Petroc" (VI.B.6.124). Large numbers of ancient church dedications and place-names in Devon, Cornwall, and Brittany testify to the significance and popularity of the sixth-century abbot, St. Petroc. According to tradition, he was born in south Wales and founded a monastic community at Padstow (Petrocstow) in Cornwall. The Irish church commemorates him as the teacher of St. Kevin of Glendalough. His journeys took him on pilgrimages to Rome and Jerusalem, and he also served a stint as a hermit on an island in the Indian Ocean. In the expanded universe of the *Wake*, however, the wandering missionary-monk appears to have been circumscribed into a compound pun based on the biblical etymology of St. Peter's name: "petrock" (*FW* 203.31).

While on a recuperative trip to Brittany in the summer of 1924, Joyce became interested in the Breton language and folklore. Naturally, some of these observations were recorded in his notebooks.[42] A letter by Joyce sent to Valery Larbaud from Saint-Malo contains the following judgment on his foray into comparative linguistics: "And though Breton (when costumed and visited by tourists and blessed by Rome and câliné ["cajoled," "wheedled" in French] by S. Pseudonymous and Co) is probably more picturesque, of course Irish as a language is FAR SUPERIOR" (*Letters* I.218). An entry in a contemporary notebook also suggests that there was something slightly suspicious—at least in transmontane judgment—about the authenticity of the indigenous religious heroes of Brittany: "most Breton saints / not recognized by Rome" (VI.B.14.95).

The preceding chapter has involved a "[t]rip over the sacramental tea into the long lives of our [Celtic] saints and saucerdotes, with vignettes." Now it is time to "cut short into instructional primers by those in authority for the bittermint of your soughts" (*FW* 440.21–24). In so doing it is likely that I might have neglected an obscure Celtic holy man like "Saint Ultan of Arbraccan" (*U* 14.221).[43] The best solution to the danger of occasional omission is to redirect readers to Joyce's own summary of Ireland's saints and sages in his 1907 Trieste lecture (*CW* 153–74; also see *CW* 235–37). Those who prefer recapitulative challenges should try to figure out the Celtic patrons mentioned in the *Wake*'s two lists of Dublin churches (*FW* 569.5–11 and *FW* 601.21–28); each catalogue mentions a parish dedicated to a familiar but exiled archbishop, "S. Lorenz-by-the-Toolechest" (*FW* 569.6) and "S. Loellisotoelles" (*FW* 601.28).

Tradition hands down the names of four missionary bishops who came to Ireland shortly before St. Patrick: Saints Ailbey, Ciaran, Declan, and Ibar. The first three are commemorated in the *Wake:* "Ailbey and Ciardeclan, I learn, episcoping me altogether " (*FW* 484.23–24). In fact, Joyce began his list of insular heroes in his Trieste lecture by citing an earlier saint, from "the first century of the Christian era, under the apostleship of St. Peter. . . . The Irishman Mansuetus, who was later canonized, serving as a missionary in Lorraine" (*CW* 157). In the *Wake* he reappears in a passage packed with allusions to Celtic saints, on the same page as the quartet of pre-Patrician bishops: "owning my mansuetude before him" (*FW* 484.3; also note VI.B.22.14). His name means "gentle," "mild," or "quiet" in Latin; this etymology lies behind a second allusion, reinforced by paradox and alliteration: "mansuetudinous manipulator, victimisedly victorihoarse" (*FW* 472.19–20). Those characteristic instances of Joyce's triumphant manipulation of language and hagiography are a fit place to conclude a pageant that has progressed from fiery Columbanus to mild Mansuetus. The emphasis on early Celtic examples in this chapter is designed as partial justification of Joyce's claim that, during their late-night chat in the "Ithaca" chapter of *Ulysses,* Stephen Dedalus and Leopold Bloom thoroughly discussed "the progenitors of Ireland: their archaeological, genealogical, hagiographical, exegetical, homiletic, toponomastic, historical and religious literatures" (*U* 17.751–53).

7

Medieval to Modern Times

This chapter is a survey of Joyce's use of saints from the eighth through the twentieth centuries. To organize the presentation, I arrange the holy women and men to pass by in several loosely constituted affinity groups; others march to their own alphabetical drummer at the conclusion of the procession.

Scholastic Saints

As a system of philosophy, scholasticism grew out of attempts in medieval universities to examine and explain the tenets of faith by rational means. A sentence from the National Library episode in *Ulysses* neatly summarizes the classical (primarily Aristotelian) impetus to this movement: "—The schoolmen were schoolboys first, Stephen said superpolitely" (*U* 9.56). From St. Anselm (eleventh century) to Nicholas of Cusa (fifteenth century) the best minds of Europe were engaged in its methods and aims, as well as being energized by debate and controversy. Those matters—the topics, techniques, and testimonies of scholasticism—are fit subjects for historians of philosophy or curators of Western culture.[1] Here my focus is on those scholastics whose teachings and lives earned them the title of "saint." Many were also named "Doctors" of the Church, a title of intellectual as well as spiritual distinction.[2] Several of the major figures in this movement reappear as characters adapted to new situations, usually comic, in Joyce's work.

St. Albert the Great earned his epithet for the volume and scope of his studies in scripture, theology, logic, metaphysics, ethics, and especially the natural sciences. For this wide range of learning, he is known as "the Universal Teacher." His most famous student was, in fact, the greatest of all the scholastic philosophers, St. Thomas Aquinas. It is odd that St. Albert is never mentioned by Joyce; more explicable, however, is his quirky nomination of an Irishman as the primary mentor of Aquinas. It would certainly be rash to accuse Joyce of inventing chauvinistic data, but I have been able to discover nothing at all about "Petrus Hibernus, theologian who had the supreme task of educating the mind of the author of the scholastic apology *Summa contra Gentiles*, St. Thomas Aquinas" (*CW* 161).

In addition to being the most brilliant of medieval philosophers, Thomas Aquinas was also quite corpulent. There are a pair of references to the saint's girth in *Ulysses:* "Aquinas tunbelly" (*U* 6.385) and "Saint Thomas, Stephen smiling said, whose gorbellied works I enjoy reading in the original" (*U* 9.778–79). A frequently cited anecdote tells that, when he was still a Dominican novice, Thomas was unmercifully teased by his fellow friars. His size, reticence, and apparent intellectual slowness prompted them to call him "the dumb ox." That tempting epithet was noted only in an archival entry by Joyce (VI.B.31.236). The saint's belly and the suggestion that he is as dumb as a donkey or a horse do, however, come up in the *Wake:* "the latten stomach even of a tumass equinous" (*FW* 93.9). Here the English equivalent of the Latin *equinus* (belonging to a horse) triggers an expansive triple interpretation of "latten": in English, the word denotes a lathe, a thin strip; in Latin, paradoxically, it means something wide or broad (*latus,-a,-um*); finally, the term is a phonetic approximation of "Latin," the language in which Aquinas wrote his works. Several other equally demeaning nicknames are also applied to the philosopher: "bulldog of Aquin" (*U* 9.863), "san Tommas Mastino" ("the Mastif" in Italian) (*U* 16.887–88), and *"frate porcospino"* ("Friar Porcupine" in Italian) (*U* 9.863).

In one of their aesthetics discussions, Lynch reminds Stephen Dedalus, "After all Aquinas, in spite of his intellect, was a good round friar." Stephen replies that Thomas might be sympathetic to his comrade's Romantic views of art, because the philosopher was also a poet: "He wrote a hymn for Maundy Thursday. It begins with the words *Pange lingua gloriosi*" (*P* 210).[3] On the other hand, the views of Aquinas on hell that are cited by Father Arnall in the retreat sermon in *Portrait* are pointedly intellectual: "Saint Thomas, the greatest doctor of the church, the angelic doctor, as he is called, says that the worst damnation consists in this that the understanding of man is totally deprived of divine light" (*P* 127). One of Joyce's early essays mentions Aquinas's primary scholastic opponent: "John Duns Scotus (called the Subtle Doctor to distinguish from St. Thomas, the Angelic Doctor . . .) [who was] an unbeatable dialectician" (*CW* 154–55).

In the notebooks (but not in the text of the *Wake*) there are several references to Duns Scotus: "Aquinas v Scotus" and "Scotus v Aquinas" (VI.B.14.47 and 118); "dumbox / Duns Scotus & / S. Thomas" (VI.B.31.236). Since the core of the dispute between the two scholastics has absolutely nothing to do with saintliness, it is prudent to dismiss it with an apt quote from the *Britannica:* "The universal, as the form or essence of the individual, is called its *quidditas* (its 'what-ness' or nature); but, every man, for example, is this particular man, here and now. It is the question of the particularity, or 'this-ness' (*haecceitas*, as Duns Scotus afterwards named it) that embarrasses the Scholastics" (*EB* 24.354). This citation—especially in light of Stephen's fondness for "*quidditas*" (*P* 213)—is designed to generate some sympathy for Buck Mulligan's reaction to scholastic argument: "No, no.... I'm not equal to Thomas Aquinas and the fiftyfive reasons he has made out to prop it up. Wait till I have a few pints in me first" (*U* 1.546–48). Later, in the National Library, he is a bit more composed:

—Saint Thomas, Stephen began ...

—*Ora pro nobis,* Monk Mulligan groaned, sinking to a chair. (*U* 9.772–73; Joyce's ellipsis)

Enough, here and now, of fuzzy epistemological speculation. It is time to return to the sharp contours of medieval hagiography—in particular, to St. Bonaventure. Like Duns Scotus, he is also a Franciscan friar (in contrast to the two Dominicans, Albert and Aquinas). He is cited in the retreat scene as saying that "the bodies of the damned themselves exhale such a pestilential odour that ... one of them alone would suffice to infect the entire world" (*P* 120). The Belvedere College director of vocations also mentions St. Bonaventure's friendship with St. Thomas, even though he has some arch reservations about the propriety of Franciscan robes: "the capuchin dress ... was rather too ..." (*P* 154; final ellipsis is Joyce's). In the *Wake*, the Seraphic Doctor also makes a brief appearance as a fundamentally nominal tripartite question, "Bon a ventura?" (*FW* 207.26). Although he was never canonized, another Franciscan scholastic, William of Occam, appears momentarily in *Ulysses* as "invincible doctor" (*U* 3.123–24), the title awarded to him for his relentless reduction of logical obstacles.

Among the scholastic saints there lurks a sinner. Peter Abelard was a magnetic teacher of theology and philosophy at the cathedral school of Notre Dame in Paris during the early twelfth century. His most famous pupil was the brilliant young Heloise, who bore his child and became his secret wife. Her uncle and guardian, not trusting Abelard's promises to renounce his beloved, hired thugs to help him castrate the errant canon. With all advancement in the church now closed to him, Abelard retired to a series of monasteries. Meanwhile, Heloise had been established as the superior of the convent near Abelard's refuge, the oratory of the Paraclete. His *Historia Calamitatum* (A History of My Afflictions) inspired her to write several letters of devotion and resignation. The pair lie buried side by side in the cemetery of Père-la-Chaise in Paris.

Joyce's works contain several comments on the calamities of Abelard. The first is a smug rhetorical question in an essay written during his first year at University College: "And how can earthly intellects, if they blind their eyes to wisdom's epithets 'pudica, pacifica et desursum [chaste, peaceful and from above]' hope to escape that which was the stumbling-block with Abelard and the cause of his fall" (CW 24). In the *Wake* the philosopher and his lover appear together in a paragraph addressed to Shaun by Issy's maidens. They begin with "—Enchainted, dear sweet Stainusless, young confessor, dearer, dearest," and continue with "Sweet-staker, *Abel lord* of all our *haloease*, we (to be slightly more femmiliar perhips than is slickly more then nacessory), toutes *philomelas* as well as *magdelenes*" (FW 237.11 and 237.34–238.1; my emphases; also note VI.B.31.5). The presence of the virgin martyr Philomela and the repentant sinner Mary Magdalene underscores the fact that these Wakean maidens fully comprehend the nature of the temptations that they invite their confessor to share. There is also a muted allusion in "and what do ye want trippings for when you've Paris inspire your hat? *Sussumcordials* all round, let ye *alloyiss* and ominies" (FW 453.24–26; my emphases). The first italicized word is either disguised Latin for *sursum corda* (lift up your hearts) or Germano-Latin for "I am *(sum)* sweet *(süss)* for [your] heart *(cordi)*." The actual name of Abelard's sweetheart is phonetically revealed in the second italicized term.

St. Anselm is frequently called the "Father of Scholasticism" for his emphasis on the role of reason in support of faith. Although the motto *credo ut intelligam* (I believe so that I can understand) is his, Joyce selects a far more emotionally charged quotation from his works for inclusion in the retreat episode in *Portrait*. In hell, according to the Benedictine philosopher-saint, "the damned are so utterly bound and helpless that . . . they are not even able to remove from the eye a worm that gnaws it" (P 119). If the writings of St. Anselm (eleventh century) mark the beginning of scholasticism, the end of this mode of philosophical discourse is attributed to Nicholas of Cusa (fifteenth century). This Italian cardinal (like Giordano Bruno, who frequently cites him) is best known for his teaching about the coincidence of opposites, and that doctrine is the point of a Wakean reference: "Micholas de Cusack . . . by the coincidance of their contraries" (FW 49.34–36). His major work, *De Docta Ignorantia* (About Ignorance That Seems Learned), is also cited: "the learned ignorants of the Cusanus philosophism in which old Nicholas" (FW 163.16–17).

Supernaturally Powerful Women

In the history of the Western Church, there have been a number of highly influential female saints: mystics like Térèsa of Ávila, princesses like Elizabeth of Hungary, warriors like Joan of Arc. Although a few of these saints play minor roles in Joyce's fiction, his writings are not the place to discover frequent or emphatic allusions to supernaturally gifted women. There are, for example, only two references to Catherine of Siena. In addition to exerting great pressure on several popes to avoid the schism threatened by rival claimants to the papal throne in Rome and Avignon, Catherine experienced a series of rapturous visions, which attracted a large following. She also suffered periods of spiritual aridity and doubt (which is a likely reason for her choice as the patron of Father Flynn's parish in "The Sisters").[4] In 1970 the pope declared St. Catherine a Doctor of the Church, along with the great Spanish mystic, St. Térèsa of Ávila. In the retreat scene Joyce cites Catherine as an authority on the hideousness of devils; she wrote that, "rather than look again for one single instant on such a frightful monster, she would prefer to walk until the end of her life along a track of red coals" (P 123). This is the only appeal to a female expert in that episode, and there are no other references to this influential and popular saint in other works.

St. Elizabeth, daughter of the King of Hungary and wife of the Landgrave of Thuringia, was left a widow with three children when her husband died on the way to the Fifth Crusade. Turned out of the castle by her brother-in-law, Elizabeth continued to perform the works of charity for the poor that had won the love of all her subjects. As one of the few wives and mothers in the roster of female saints, she is pictured by Joyce as "Elizabeliza blessing the bedpain" (FW 328.36). Later in the *Wake* Elizabeth is also invoked to watch over the three children who are asleep in their beds: "Halosobuth, sov us!" (FW 561.8). A second Hungarian princess, Margaret, became a Dominican nun at an early age, refused marriage, and devoted the rest of her life to a series of increasingly horrifying penances of the flesh. This saint seems to be hardly the person for Issy to mention in her passionate farewell to Shaun, but it is difficult to argue with textual facts: "'twill carry on my hearz'waves my still waters reflections in words over Margrate von Hungaria" (FW 460.25–26).

A third saintly member of royalty is the Burgundian princess Clothilde, who married Clovis, the pagan king of the Franks. Her husband converted to Christianity after he defeated his Germanic rivals—a victory that he attributed to his prayers for help to his wife's God. There is a drawn-out allusion to the miraculous outcome of the battle in the *Wake*: "the rude hunnerable Humphrey, who was praying god of clothilides. . . . [vowed] no more of your maimed acts after this with your kowtoros and criados to every tome, thick and heavy, and our onliness of his revelance to your ultitude" (*FW* 325.27–35). Perhaps Joyce became aware of this story by inquiring about the life of the patron of St. Clotilde's church in Paris. He alludes to that local parish in a *Wake*-like piece that he published to promote the tenor John Sullivan in 1932: "From a Banned Writer to a Banned Singer" (*CW* 265).

The most militant female saint in the martyrology is certainly Joan of Arc. The first Joycean allusion to one of the patrons of France comes from *Stephen Hero*. Lynch is concerned—in fact, so concerned that his syntax is quite garbled—that the aesthetic Stephen might make "at least an assertion of that incorrigible virginity which the Irish race demands . . . from any Joan who would set it free as the first heavenly proof of fitness for such high office" (*SH* 151–52). In a 1924 note to Harriet Shaw Weaver, Joyce comments on George Bernard Shaw's refusal to subscribe to one of the deluxe editions of *Ulysses* because the price was too high. He concludes his comments: "A few days ago he [GBS] told a reporter he had made £10,000 out of Saint Joan or was it out of old Saint Mumpledum" (*Letters* I.221). The latter saint is not some legendary percussionist-martyr, but a reference to the song "Thump le Drum" from Shaw's play *Saint Joan*. The dramatic source of that allusion is confirmed by the appearance of "thunpledrum" (*FW* 162.3) in a passage that starts out with an appropriately Joannine sentiment: "(Tyrants, regicide is too good for you!)" (*FW* 162.1). The only other allusion to St. Joan associates the heroine with the postflood rainbow (*arc-en-ciel* in French): "when maids were in Arc" (*FW* 202.17–18).

Three far less imposing female saints conclude this section—but, however humble their backgrounds or accomplishments, each was honored while alive and canonized after meriting eternal life in heaven. I have already mentioned the textual and archival appearance of the first of these, St. Dympna, the patron of the insane and those with psychiatric disorders. The legends of her life are unclear and probably have evolved from a local folktale. At any rate, there is a hospital (founded in the fourteenth century) for the mentally ill at Gheel, near Antwerp, that still bears her saintly name.

Second, in the *Wake* there is an odd "roundtableturning, like knuts in a maze, the *zitas* runnind hare and dart" (*FW* 285.3–4; my emphasis). In fact there was a thirteenth-century Italian woman named "Zita" who was the faithful servant of a rich family. Her piety, patience, and the ability to perform modest miracles attracted wide attention. She is the patron saint of maidservants.

Last is St. Rose of Lima, Peru, the first person in the western hemisphere to be canonized. After working to support her parents, she became a Dominican nun and retired from the world. Her harsh, self-inflicted penances and her care for sick Indians and slaves won her recognition as a saint, and she became the patron of social workers and of South America. Rose marches, at the side of an Italian holy woman with the same name, in the "Cyclops" procession: "the saints Rose of Lima and of Viterbo" (*U* 12.1708). Joyce also commemorates her in the *Wake* with an appropriate linguistic flourish: "how buona the vista, by Santa Rosa" (*FW* 264.23–24).

British, Anglo-Saxon, and Anglo-Norman Saints

While there were undoubtedly scattered Christian communities in Roman Britain—St. Patrick was from one of them—the evangelization of the island really dates from the arrival of the Benedictine mission of St. Augustine and his fellow monks to the Angles in 597 (see chapter 4). Joyce would presumably have been less interested in pre-Conquest England than he was in the Celtic domains in Ireland and Scotland; nevertheless, there is a full-page Anglo-Saxon index in one of the *Wake* notebooks, a list, apparently in random order, of eight important early English saints (VI.B.10.99). None of these entries were crossed out, but some of the saints appear in the *Wake* from other sources and will be discussed later in this section of the chapter.

Another, longer, archival index is not limited, strictly speaking, to Anglo-Saxon material, but its content is relevant here. Earlier in the same notebook in which he entered much information about the cities of the world for "Haveth Childers Everywhere" (*FW* 532.6–554.10), Joyce jotted down a list of more than forty London churches (VI.B.24.144–49).[5] Two of the crossed items are used in the *Wake*: "ʳDunstan in the East / ʳEdmund K & Martyr" (VI.B.24.144; also note VI.B.11.126). The first entry refers to a church whose titular patron is St. Dunstan, the great tenth-century abbot of Glastonbury. After returning from an exile imposed by the king, Dunstan was appointed archbishop of Canterbury and is credited with restoring the Benedictine monastic rule in England. The second entry refers to another church dedicated to Edmund, a ninth-century king of the East Angles, who was killed defending his Christian realm from Danish invaders. His primary cult-center is at the abbey at Bury St. Edmunds. In the *Wake*, both of the churches and their saintly patrons are enshrined (the first with an appropriate cockney touch) as "Headmound, king and martyr, dunstung in Yeast" (*FW* 135.9–10).

There is a fourth saint lurking on the same page of the *Wake*, in the inconspicuously lowercase phrase "wilfrid's walk" (*FW* 449.8–9). St. Wilfrid (634–709) is one of the most important Anglo-Saxon saints. Guidebooks note "St. Wilfrid's Needle" in the crypt of the cathedral he founded at Ripon; the ability to crawl through this narrow hole was once taken as a proof of chastity. In the choir of Hexham Abbey, a monastery donated to the saint by Queen Ethelreda of Northumbria, there is a Saxon coronation stool known as "St. Wilfrid's Chair."[6] Although I find no references to "St. Wilfrid's Walk" in early English legend, as an abbot and a bishop Wilfrid conducted several famous visitations of his foundations throughout Northumbria and Mercia; these ecclesiastical tours of inspection are also called "walks." On that ground alone, however, it would be rash to claim a specific reference to the Anglo-Saxon saint in Joyce's "wilfrid's walk." But there is more—and absolutely definitive—evidence for significant hagiographical allusion here.

After basic education at the famous Celtic monastery at Lindisfarne, Wilfrid went to the continent for additional study. At Lyons he attracted the attention of Bishop Annemundus, who was so impressed that he offered his niece's hand to the young English pilgrim. Wilfrid demurred and traveled to Rome, where he became an ardent supporter of papal liturgical practice and Benedictine monasticism. After returning to England, he was the primary exponent of Roman (as opposed to Irish) practices and the Roman festal calendar at the Synod of Whitby (664).[7] Those personal and religious decisions by Wilfrid are translated by Joyce into Wakean terms, where they become part of Jaun's pitch to Issy: "I'd turn back as lief as not if I could only spoonfind the nippy girl of my heart's appointment, Mona Vera Toutou Ipostila, my lady of Lyons, to guide me by gastronomy under her safe conduct" (*FW* 449.9–12).

As I selectively interpret this passage, Jaun insists that he is committed to *one* ("Mona" in Greek), *true* ("Vera" in Latin), *universal* ("tout" in French; "tutte" in Italian), *apostolic* ("Ipostila" in pseudo-Romance) guide of his life and conduct. This ideal personification of Mother Church is, of course, closely modeled on the Roman Catholic formula recited in the Creed during a mass: "one, holy, catholic, and apostolic Church." The phrase "my lady of Lyons," then, in my interpretation, is not an appositive equivalent of "Mona . . . Ipostila," but a contrasting vocative to Issy as his Lyonese lady. She is the rival woman, the bishop's niece. Her hypothetical attractions are hypocritically rejected by Jaun in favor of a monastic life of strict Roman discipline, though "gastronomy" hints that he might be contemplating a less than total adherence to an abstemious refectory. In short, the sermonizer is pretending to imitate St. Wilfrid; thus he refuses an attachment with a lady of Lyons, despite the possibilities of nepotistic preferment and culinary delight.

Wilfrid may be the most prominent Anglo-Saxon saint in the *Wake*, but he is not the only one. The clue that leads to my next cluster of early English noble and holy people comes from a notebook: "ᵇS. Ermita / Mercia / wulf" (VI.B.41.193). During the seventh century the east central English kingdom of Mercia was ruled by King Wulfhere and his saintly wife, Queen Ermingild, who appears in the text as "(Ermina Regina!)" (*FW* 391.1). That parentheses is followed six lines later by "mercies" (*FW* 391.7), and the king and his realm appear nearby in adjacent lines, "Wulf! Wulf!" and "mercias!" (*FW* 385.17–18).

The phrase "peaces pea to Wedmore" (*FW* 391.27) on the same *Wake* page as the reference to the Mercian queen is additional support for an Anglo-Saxon presence. In 878 King Alfred agreed to the Peace of Wedmore, which defined the boundaries between his English realm and the territory conquered by invading Danes. Indeed, the entries "alfred / Peace of Wedmore" are also crossed out on the same page of the notebook as the genetic reference noted above.

Following the archival reference to the truce is another crossed entry, "ᵇBrownesberrow" (VI.B.41.193), transferred into the text as "brownesberrow" (*FW* 391.14). I suggest that this compound term is Joyce's translation into contemporary English of the archaic "Brunanburh," the site of a battle in which Ethelstan of Mercia ("yearl of mercies" [*FW* 391.7]) defeated Norse, Scottish, and British forces in 937. (The Norwegian contingent was led by Anlaf Guthfrithson of Dublin, who does not leave his mark on the notebook or the text.) In terms of the history of early English literature, the battle is commemorated by a celebrated mini-epic inserted into the *Anglo-Saxon Chronicle*.[8]

The only daughter of Ermingild and Wulfhere of Mercia was St. Werburga, who appears in a notebook entry alongside the most famous Irish female saint: "ᵇS. Brigid / S. Werburga" (VI.B.24.167). Werburga was guided in her religious life by her royal aunt, who was St. Ethelreda, the patroness of the aforementioned St. Wilfrid's monastery at Hexham. In the *Wake's* "ethelred" (*FW* 439.36) the Northumbrian queen shares the allusive spotlight with King Ethelred the Unready. Despite his epithet, that royal warrior was up for "the mossacre of St. Brices" (*FW* 390.1), a battle on November 13, 1002, in which English troops slaughtered Danish raiders. That date is the feast of Saint Brice, an early fourth-century bishop of Tours, sometimes commemorated in England as St. Britius, the Latinized form of his name.[9]

Joycean references to Queen Ethelreda's niece Werburga, also known as Werburgh, involve several strata of hermeneutical archeology. The feast days of Saints Brigid and Werburga are February 1 and 3, respectively; these dates bracket Joyce's own birthday, a fact he certainly would not have considered insignificant. The Church of Ireland parish named for St. Werburgh in south-central Dublin is famous for the noxious gas reputedly produced by coffins in its crypt (*U* 6.609–12). With Brigid, her notebook companion, St. Werburgh appears as a parish patron in a catalogue of Dublin churches in the *Wake*: "S. Mary Stillamaries with *Bride*-and-Audeons-behind-*Warborg*" (*FW* 569.10–11; my emphases). Lastly, I first see and hear a glimmer of her holy presence in "Werbungsap" (*FW* 269.20), a phrase that also advises in a learned language (*verbum sap. sat*) that this interpretative paragraph is sufficient for attuned fans of the *Wake*.

Another reference to an early English saint is deeply embedded in the sentence "It is scainted to Vitalba" (*FW* 600.22). McHugh glosses this item as a reference to *vita alba*, the botanical term for clematis, a perennial vine with bright-colored flowers (also note the earlier appearance of some "viridable ... branches of climatitis" [*FW* 59.11–13]). This interpretation seems entirely reasonable, but the next words in the text are "And her little white bloomkins, twittersky trimmed" (*FW* 600.22–23). Joyce's specification of white blossoms suggests that the word "scainted" in the original citation is not exclusively intended to designate the bright clematis, but also serves as an allusion to the proper name of a person who is "sainted"—and somehow connected with whiteness. St. Wit comes to mind. Her name means "white" in early English; one of several Latin adjectives for "white" is *alba*. The original portmanteau word "Vitalba" is thus another example of one of Joyce's favorite types of wordplay, *figura etymologica*, in which similar roots from different languages are juxtaposed.[10] St. Wit, patron of Whitchurch Canonicorum in Dorset, is also known as St. Candida, another Latin adjective meaning "white."

The following is a compact summary of the basis for this saint's cult:

Local tradition says she was a Saxon woman killed by the Danes on one of the occasions when they landed at Charmouth. (The Viking axe and longship carved on the late fourteenth-century church tower are evidence today of the legend.) Nothing more about her is known, though there is a holy well named after her at Morecombelake, a mile to the south, which yields clear cool waters said to heal eye-troubles. Dorset children still call the light blue starry flowers of the wild evergreen periwinkle "St Candida's Eyes."[11]

A "periwinkle" is not a clematis, and "light blue" is not white. On the other hand, the "bloomkins, twittersky trimmed" (in addition to their allusion to the young woman's bloomers) sparkle like "starry flowers." Moreover, St. Wit/Candida's connection with miraculous cures of eye-trouble would naturally appeal to the iritis-plagued Joyce. Granted that a specifically hagiographical cast in the Wakean citation is faint, it is surrounded by a distinctly Anglo-Saxon aura, "Saxenslyke . . . Anglesen . . . juties" (FW 600.24–25).[12] McHugh also plausibly suggests that the adjacent "slab . . . immermemorial . . . the white alfred" (FW 600.26–28) refers to the monumental White Horse carved into a hill near Wantage; it commemorates the victory by King Alfred the Great over the Danes, who, before their defeat on the Chalk Downs in 871, martyred St. Wit/Candida during one of their incursions into English realms.

Three other relevant saints (one Anglo-Roman, the other two Anglo-Saxon) appear in notebook entries, each involving a geographical factor interesting enough to warrant brief discussion. St. Alban was probably the first recorded Christian in Britain. A leading citizen of Verulanium (now St. Albans), a Roman town about twenty-five miles north of London, he sheltered a priest during the persecution by the emperor Diocletian. According to his hagiographical "life," Alban changed clothes with the priest, was arrested, tortured, and finally executed for refusing to worship the pagan gods. An uncrossed archival entry records the locus of the legend: "St. Albans (Verulanium) / London" (VI.B.19.147). St. Botolph was an early abbot of the monastery at Icanhoh, Lincolnshire. After his death, the site was renamed Boston (Botolph's Stone) in his honor. In another uncrossed note, Joyce appears—perhaps to create an instance of the stone-tree motif—to add another dimension to the saintly toponym: "S. Botolph / Boston (Lincs) / —Stump" (VI.B.38.88). St. Wolstan (or Wulfstan) was an eleventh-century abbot-bishop of Worcester. In the procession in *Ulysses*, "the monks of S. Wolstan" (U 12.1687) march beside contingents from far larger and more famous congregations and orders. After the Norman Conquest, Wolstan was the only English bishop to support King William; he also used his influence to fight the slave-trade from Bristol to Viking-controlled Ireland. Two notes cite the bishop: "S. Wolstan" (VI.B.9.147) and "ʳpriory S. Wolstan's / Rye Water / Celbridge" (VI.B.1.137). In the second note Joyce has transferred the original English site to its Irish namesake; there is a hamlet called St. Wolstan, with the remains of a small abbey, on the River Liffey near Celbridge, just west of Dublin. Although the Irish entry is crossed in red crayon, I have not been able to find it or its remains in the text.

St. Chad was a seventh-century bishop of the Mercians in the English Midlands. An archival note records that fact and his association with sacred wells: "Lichfield (S. Chad) / patron of wells" (VI.B.2.102). Like St. Kevin at Glendalough, he is said to have offered penitential prayers while standing in the icy waters of a spring near his episcopal oratory at Lichfield. The only shrine of this type that is mentioned in the *Wake* is Irish: "By the holy well of Mulhuddart" (*FW* 206.18; also note VI.B.6.109).

In the fantastic list of HCE's pseudonyms in Hosty's "Ballad," the pub keeper is appropriately called "Boniface" (*FW* 46.20; also note VI.C.5.222). In an earlier chapter I discussed the thematic reverberations of the names involved; here I wish to add that there is a genuine and important St. Boniface. He was English and christened Wynfrith; on becoming a monk, he took a Latin name, meaning "Doer of Good." As a missionary Boniface and his comrades brought the new faith to the Germanic tribes, to whom he proved the omnipotence of his God by cutting down the sacred oak of Thor. This Apostle of Germany baptized thousands and established monastic centers throughout the territory. As frequently happens, some of the natives did not appreciate the benefactions of the English interloper, and Boniface was martyred in the mid eighth century after many years away from home.

Before this review of Anglo-Saxon saints concludes, it is necessary to mention briefly a quintessential early English holy man. Not much is known about St. Swithin, bishop of Winchester and adviser to the kings of Wessex. What is important about St. Swithin is the state of the weather on his midsummer feast day. For that reason he is discussed in chapter 9 in the section on calendric hagiography.

Following the Norman Conquest of England in 1066, almost all of the positions of power in the church were occupied by the victors' candidates. Thomas à Becket, the son of well-to-do Norman parents, carried out several important missions for the archbishop of Canterbury. In time, Becket, who had attracted the patronage of King Henry II, was himself elevated to that position after resigning as Chancellor of England. During his tenure as archbishop, relations between the crown and the church deteriorated to such an extent that a rogue band of the king's knights rid their lord of the troublesome prelate—he was murdered in front of the altar in his cathedral in 1170. Thomas à Becket was immediately proclaimed a saint, and his tomb-shrine at Canterbury became England's premier pilgrimage center.[13]

On two occasions in the *Wake* Joyce links the Anglo-Norman bishop-martyr's name with that of St. Laurence O'Toole, the archbishop of Dublin, who also ran afoul of King Henry II and was exiled to Normandy. The first passage, "with larrons o'toolers clittering up and tombles a'buckets clottering down" (*FW* 5.3–4), may also contain a reference to the bloody and fatal sword-blow to the bishop's skull ("clottering down"). A second passage—ambiguously, in view of the former's martyrdom—states that "Messrs T. A. Birkett and L. O. Twohalls were made invulnerably venerable" (*FW* 77.1–3). The saint's family name also appears, irreverently toted, in "a bucket" (*FW* 211.8–9).[14]

That concludes the review of "Allenglisches Angleslachsen" (*FW* 532.10–11) saints from Roman times through the period after the advent of "William the Conk" (*FW* 31.14). Next comes a brief discussion of some holy men and women from the Christian East.[15]

Eastern Orthodox Saints

The allusive diversity of *Ulysses* is signaled early by a sentence of liturgical Latin as the novel's first line of dialogue (*U* 1.5). Not long afterwards comes a single Greek word, "Chrysostomos" (Goldenmouth) (*U* 1.26). Its contextual purpose is to highlight Buck Mulligan's expensive dental care: "his even white teeth glistening here and there with gold points" (*U* 1.25–26). Throughout the book Mulligan's nuggets of verbal wit also demonstrate that he is a master of repartee. The theme is picked up later in "Circe," in the multilingual names of Bloom's *"yellow and white children . . . : Nasodoro* [Goldennose], *Goldfinger, Chrysostomos, Maindorée* [Goldenhand]" (*U* 15.1821–27). The most famous Christian Greek orator was St. John Chrysostom of Antioch, the late-fourth-century theologian and patriarch of Constantinople. St. John is one of the four eastern Doctors of the Church; his sermons and explications of scripture are noted for their clarity, emotional power, and rhetorical point—hence the honorific epithet that is permanently associated with his name. An archival note, "Chrysostome / les fléaux" (VI.B.28.112–13), refers either to the verbal lashings (*fléaux* is "scourges" in French) he laid on the sinful behavior of various congregations or to the punishment inflicted on the saint himself during his imprisonment for criticizing the luxurious life of Empress Eudoxia.

In "Ithaca" when Bloom chants some Hebrew words, one of Stephen's reactions is to conjure up "the traditional figure of hypostasis, depicted by Johannes Damascenus . . . and Epiphanius Monachus" (*U* 17.783–84). The theological term "hypostasis" (substance, person) is the doctrinally correct way of explaining the complete union of divine and human natures in Christ. The theologian and hymnographer John of Damascus argued strongly against the destruction of sacred images during the iconoclastic controversy in the eighth century. Although he is a Doctor of the Eastern Church and a firm defender of the orthodox teaching about the hypostatic union of Christ's natures, what is essential to the passage in *Ulysses* is not doctrinal definition, but the physical appearance of the Lord: "leucodermic, sesquipedalian with winedark hair" (*U* 17.785). The first term is Greek for "white skinned"; the third term transfers a familiar Homeric epithet for the surface of the sea (*oinopa*) to the color of Jesus' hair. Joyce's ultra-Latinate middle term, "sesquipedalian," is, in my judgment, a conscious error (perhaps ascribable to the late hour and Stephen's considerable intake of drink) for the intended "six feet tall." As it stands, the word means "one-and-a-half-feet"—but Jesus was certainly more than eighteen inches tall.[16] (The other Eastern Christian cited as an authority for how Jesus looked is Epiphanius the Monk. He may be the famous fourth-century bishop of Cyprus, who was a defender of Christ's divine humanity against Arius and Origen.)

Although there is no hint of the fact in the text, St. John of Damascus is also the ultimate source for another Christological passage in *Ulysses*. In the midst of obstetrical bombast in "Oxen of the Sun," Stephen proposes a toast to virgin birth: "A pregnancy without joy, he said, a birth without pangs, a body without blemish, a belly without bigness" (*U* 14.309–11). An archival index reveals the unlikely Eastern origin for several of those phrases: "S. John Damascene / ʳBVM no pangs of childbirth / but passion / " [BVM] Wife (not consummated)" (*UNBM* 227:33–35). Three of John's most famous hymns, written in Greek, celebrate the Assumption of the Virgin Mary. I suggest that the notesheet phrases are lifted from an adjusted translation or a quoted paraphrase of one of those homilies or liturgical chants—even though the Eastern doctor would be tortured by the mocking twists applied by Stephen Dedalus to the citations. In that regard, it should be noted that Joyce uses the term "passion" with deliberate ambiguity; in the hymns of St. John, of course, it applies to the Virgin Mother's empathy with the suffering of her son—not to sexual ardor.

The monastic heritage of the Greek Orthodox Church is well known. Several of its most impressive monuments survive even now—for example, the remnants of the *lavras* (colonies of semi-hermits) and the communal foundations around Mount Athos, and the fortified monastery of St. Catherine, built by Emperor Justinian in the shadow of Mount Sinai. In Constantinople itself the most renowned monastery was founded by a rich Roman patrician named Studius (463). The ruins of the church, dedicated to St. John the Baptist, are the oldest surviving Christian sanctuary in the imperial city; the adjacent monastery was completely destroyed by an earthquake in the late nineteenth century. Its walls once sheltered Byzantium's greatest theologians and scholars; its Joycean memory is preserved only in an archival note: "S. John Studium" (VI.B.24.288).[17]

A compact cluster of Orthodox saints appears in the *Wake:* "after *liryc* and *themodius* soft *aglo* iris of the *vals*" (*FW* 528.23; my emphases). The italicized terms can be unscrambled (three are spelled backwards) to reveal "Cyril," "Methodius," "Olga," and "Slav." Saints Cyril and Methodius were brothers sent from Constantinople in the mid ninth century to convert the Slavs who had settled in the Balkans. Part of their heritage is the so-called Cyrillic alphabet, which is still the primary script for most Slavic languages, including Russian. St. Olga was the first Christian queen of the province of Kiev, the capital of the people who developed into what are today the Russians and Ukrainians. In an earlier paragraph that resounds with Slavic echoes, the saintly brothers are also present in the phrase "nawful curillass and I must slav to methodiousness" (*FW* 159.30–31).

A pair of uncrossed archival notes links "Cyril & Method" with "S. Josaphat" (VI.B.4.328). The latter is a seventeenth-century eastern Slav, whose mission was to unite the Orthodox Ukrainian church to Rome. As usual in that part of the world, long-standing ethnic pressures were probably more important than purely religious issues, but Bishop Josaphat was murdered by a mob that shouted, "Kill the papist!" He was canonized in 1867, the first saint of the Eastern rite to be formally recognized by the Roman Catholic Church. That distinction is not mentioned in the *Wake*.

In the "Night Lessons" chapter of the *Wake*, there is a truncated alphabetical list of some of the gods of the ancient Greeks: "Every letter is a godsend, ardent Ares, brusque Boreas and glib Ganymed like zealous Zeus" (*FW* 269.17–18).[18] Boreas is the Greco-Roman god of the biting north wind; here, however, the name does double duty as the first element (the nearby "glib" is the second) in an allusion to the Russian saints Boris and Gleb. They were the sons of St. Vladimir of Kiev, the first Christian king of that province,[19] and thus were the grandsons of St. Olga. When their father died, their older brother Svyatopolk murdered the two obstacles to his crown. The saints' heroic refusal to oppose their brother in battle won them saintly rank in the Eastern and Western church.

Modern Saints

Even after Emperor Constantine issued the Edict of Toleration (313), Christians were still occasionally killed by pagan zealots for their subversive beliefs. Sporadic outbreaks of persecution continue into the twentieth century, when a Polish Franciscan, for example, was murdered at Auschwitz and officially added to the martyrology in 1982.[20] So too, not all paragons of charity, piety, and theological learning are limited to the Middle Ages or the Counter Reformation. Several fairly modern saints participate in Joyce's fiction, and there is both textual and archival evidence that he kept informed about contemporary canonizations.

Some quite popular nineteenth-century saints lead the list. Bernadette (Maire Soubirous) saw apparitions of the Virgin Mary in a grotto near Lourdes, in the French Pyrenees. That site is now the most famous healing shrine in Europe, visited annually by thousands of pilgrims. Bernadette, who became a Sister of Notre Dame, died in 1879 and was canonized in 1933. She is commemorated in the *Wake* in a list of February saints (her first vision occurred on February 11, 1858). If my earlier suggestion of a sexual reference in the adjacent question about "Agatha's lamb" (*FW* 430.35) is correct, then Joyce intended an equally indiscreet inquiry in "and how are Bernadetta's *columbillas?*" (*FW* 430.35–36), since the word I have emphasized is Latin for "dovelets."

John Baptist Vianney was appointed a parish priest at Ars in 1818 and remained there until his death forty-one years later. During that period he worked ceaselessly to improve the lives of the people by establishing a school for girls and an orphanage. Despite the fact that his education was limited to the bare seminary requirements for ordination, the Curé of Ars attracted far-reaching attention as a sympathetic and insightful confessor. He was named a saint in 1925, and a few years later was declared the patron of parish priests. A short archival index indicates that Joyce was aware of the diabolical temptations suffered by Father Vianney, and of his unfulfilled desire to escape the world as a hermit: "curé d'Ars / father of the / desert / threw inkpot at S[atan??]" (VI.B.28.116). In the *Wake* the saint appears as an author: "*Pease in Plenty* by the Curer of Wars" (*FW* 440.10).

Sister Theresa of the Child Jesus, a Carmelite nun in Lisieux, France, died of tuberculosis at age twenty-four in 1897. Her spiritual autobiography, *The Story of a Soul,* was a sensational success; a basilica was built to accommodate pilgrims who visit her shrine to seek miracles through the intercession of this "ordinary" heroine of God's love. Joyce enshrined her in *Ulysses* before she was canonized (1925); hence she appears in the procession not as "Saint," but as "Blessed Sister Teresa of the Child Jesus" (*U* 12.1711).

Another French nun, Sister Margaret Mary Alacoque (1647–1690), also appears in two of Joyce's works as "Blessed." In "Eveline" a "coloured print of the promises made to her" hangs symbolically "on the wall above the broken harmonium" (D 37).[21] In the National Library episode of *Ulysses*, Buck Mulligan, "his pious eyes upturned," viciously takes the nun's name in vain: "Blessed Margaret Mary Anycock!" (U 9.646). Both titles are technically accurate, since Sister Margaret Mary was not canonized until 1920; the obscene pun in the distorted proper name is typical of its speaker and venue. It appears, however, that hagiographical verisimilitude has been sacrificed in the *Wake*, where the devout nun is still styled "Blessed Marguerite" (FW 146.12); a second reference omits any indication of her canonical status or rank, but merges her identity with the hospitable sisters of Lazarus: "marthared mary allacook" (FW 214.23; also note VI.B.31.5).

Even though she was practically an invalid for many years, Mother Mary Aikenhead of Cork founded a new community of sisters to work among the poor. Today the Irish Sisters of Charity also have convents in several other English-speaking countries. In the *Wake* their services to the most needy are acknowledged by their presence ("two sisters of charities on the front steps" [FW 362.25]) near the squalid precincts of HCE's pub. In 1884 Matt Talbot, a Dublin manual laborer and a chronic alcoholic, took the pledge never to drink again. He reinforced his determination with a severe regimen of prayer, daily mass, and fasting. Joyce summarizes this sort of penitential devotion: "three masses a morn and two chaplets [rosaries] at eve" (FW 410.34–35). Sometimes Talbot prostrated himself, face down on the floor of churches, to compensate for past sins and to ask for strength in his life of total abstinence. This routine continued until his death in 1925.

Cases for the eventual canonization of both Mother Mary Aikenhead and Matt Talbot are only in their preliminary stages, but their Irish supporters hope that both will someday be added to the official list of the saints. While that long ecclesiastical process is in progress, the upper-middle-class foundress and the reformed workingman can take pride in a small measure of literary fame. Both are enshrined in a Wakean footnote: "Says blistered Mary Achinhead to beautified Tummy Tullburt" (FW 262.F6; also note VI.B.16.80 and VI.C.1.38).

A wonderfully documented note by Anne Nolan in a leading Joycean journal identifies a nineteenth-century preacher-confessor whose work in Ireland merited notice not only by the Roman Catholic Church, but also in *Ulysses*. Father Charles of Mount Argus (1821–1893) was a Dutch-born Passionist priest; he arrived at the Order's church in Dublin in 1850 and spent most of the rest of his life ministering to the faithful there. Father Charles's reputation for sanctity was widespread and numerous miraculous cures have been attributed to him. Since his beatification by Pope John Paul II in 1988 the process of canonization continues.[22] Not far into the "Circe" chapter of Joyce's novel, Leopold Bloom is tested as a potential messiah by various characters—including Brini, a sham Papal Nuncio—in the fantasy at Bella's Nighttown whorehouse. One of the inquisitors demands that Bloom "perform a miracle like Father Charles" (U 15.1839).

In 1934 Joyce revised a draft of a section of chapter II.2 of the *Wake*, much of which was not included in the final text of the work. Near the end of the fourth paragraph of this abortive material, the following question occurs: "Why the fevilkins ask any Tossy Madden in Yesland or *Nervous Nelly of Holy God* whatever be her hoydennane" (my emphasis).[23] In *Ulysses* there is unmistakable indication that Joyce regarded the name "Nelly" as a suitable sobriquet for a cheap prostitute: "two gonorrheal ladies, Fresh Nelly and Rosalie, the coalquay whore" (U 9.1090–91). That occupation is confirmed by a ditty sung at the beginning of "Circe": "I gave it to Nelly / To stick in her belly, / The leg of the duck, / The leg of the duck" (U 15.55–59). In the *Wake*, Nelly's nickname is appropriately transformed into "flesh nelly" (FW 34.32), and she reappears as the prickly lass, "Nelly Nettle" (FW 604.36), who needs to be smoothed out for attempting to vamp pious Kevin.

The initial designation of "Nelly" as both "nervous" and "of Holy God" justifies a consideration of her unlikely inclusion in my list of latter-day Joycean saints. In 1903 a daughter was born to William and Mary Organ of Waterford, Ireland. After her mother's death, little Nellie was sent to an industrial school conducted by the Sisters of the Good Shepherd. It soon became obvious that she was seriously—indeed, incurably—ill, and she was confined to the infirmary. The moving story of her life (in which the priest-author frequently quotes Nellie's own words) was written not long after her death in 1908; it became immensely popular as the chronicle of a truly wondrous child. Throughout her suffering she remained cheerful. Although she was not yet old enough for her first Holy Communion, Nellie finally got her wish: "Mudder Prancis is goin' to bring me Holy God in de morning." As she grew weaker, she reported several familiar conversations with the divine presence in the eucharist that she was about to receive. These chats (duly reported in her baby-talk idiom) and her mode of addressing the Lord earned her the title "Little Nellie of Holy God." In 1910 the bishop of Cork and the children of St. Finbar's Industrial School petitioned the pope to make their young classmate a saint. Pius X sent the children his greetings and Apostolic Blessing, but an official process of canonization has apparently not been inaugurated.[24]

Somehow or other—perhaps on one of his trips back to Dublin in late 1909—it seems that Joyce heard about Little Nellie of Holy God, and that he was not impressed. It is, however, typical of his irreverent sense of humor that he converts the saintly child into a nervous hoyden in the *Wake*, then adds blasphemy to the injury by emphatically retaining her pitiful epithet, "of Holy God." The fact that this sentence was omitted from the final text of the *Wake* is more probably a matter of editorial oversight than of a sudden burst of hagiographical scrupulosity or parochial delicacy by Joyce.

In the introductory chapter I mentioned a spring 1924 notebook entry on St. Gabriel of Our Lady of Sorrows, a young Italian priest who was canonized in 1920. Although this item was not incorporated into the text of the *Wake*, it is additional evidence of Joyce's abiding interest in saints—especially those with slightly bizarre names. Another example of the same archival penchant involves a pair of twentieth-century martyrs, "Fr. Le Roux Rouvière / murdered by Eskimos / found wearing soutane & / vestments" (VI.B.6.138). Although this scenario sounds like an excerpt from the annals of the seventeenth-century French "Blackrobes" who met their doom at the hands of several North American Indian tribes, it is actually a far more contemporary martyrdom. Two Canadian priests, Guillaume Le Roux and Jean-Baptiste Rouviére, missionaries of the Oblate Order, were slain in the Northwest Territory by their hunter-guides. Both of the Inuit were caught and convicted; one of the murderers died in 1924—a fact that might have been reported in newspapers and there attracted Joyce's attention.[25]

Miscellaneous Saints

The following, in alphabetical order, are almost a score of saints who fit into none of the categories that I have adopted to organize my presentation. That is, they do not qualify as evangelists, apostles, virgin martyrs, Doctors of the Church, founders of religious orders, Celtic saints, or honorarily "canonized" archangels. At the same time, these holy men and women are by no means obscure or eccentric. St. Anthony of Padua, for example, is one of the most popular Catholic saints, and the area of his patronage is eminently practical. St. Olaf is a representative of Scandinavian Christianity; St. Wenceslaus is an archetypical central European.

- The early Franciscan friar St. Anthony of Padua was known as the greatest preacher of his age. He is the patron of the poor and is invoked to find lost objects and to ensure the safe delivery of messages. For his many miracles St. Anthony acquired the epithet "Thaumaturgus" (the Wonder Worker). In a 1925 letter to Ettore Schmitz, Joyce referred to the church of "il gran divo, Antonio Taumaturgo" in Trieste (*Letters* III.133; also see *Letters* III.166 and 473). Two pre-text notes for *Ulysses* also mention the saint: "s. Anthony of Padua" (V.A.2.12) and "ᵗthaumaturgic" (V.A.2.28).[26] In *Ulysses,* the only "Wonderworker" is "the world's greatest remedy for rectal complaints," obtainable by mail from London; indeed, the prospectus for that anti-flatulence device makes the explicit claim that it is "thaumaturgic" (*U* 17.1819–25). St. Anthony's dossier records no miraculous cures in this regard.

Joyce knew the Italian expression of thanks to the saint for his unexpected gifts: "*Troppa grazia, San Antonio*" (Too much grace). A version of this phrase appears in a March 24, 1940, letter to Ettore Settanni: "Un po' di poesia, Sant'Antonio ma non troppa!" (A bit of poetry, but not too much). Another variation appears in a November 8, 1927, letter to Ezra Pound: "Troppa Grossa, San Giacomone!" (Too fat, Saint Jimmy) (*Letters* III.473 and 166).

On the other hand, in the *Wake,* there are several allusions to the saint's well-attested guidance of letters sent in the mail. That protection was devoutly elicited by the initials "S.A.G." (Saint Anthony Guide) on the back of an envelope. The most expansive Joycean reference to this mission includes notice of the novelist Anthony Trollope, who established the royal postal system in Ireland: "Not the phost of a nation! Nor by a long trollop! I just didn't have the time to. Saint Anthony Guide!" (*FW* 409.6–7; also note VI.B.40.40). Early in the work there is a huge envelope, "superscribed and subpencilled by yours A Laughable Party, with afterwrite, S.A.G., to Hyde and Cheek, Edenberry" (*FW* 66.16–18). Near the end of the book the petition is reduced to its basics: "Send Arctur guiddus!" (*FW* 621.7–8). A cryptic hagiographical notebook entry is also obliquely pertinent to St. Anthony's function as protector of the post: "S. Delay / S. Miscarriage (SAG)" (VI.B.8.120). Since there are no official saints to whom one can appeal to *delay* a menstrual period or to cause a *miscarriage,* Joyce has reversed the customary ejaculation to St. Anthony in these two entries, while connecting the gynecological functions with the General Post Office. Sometimes a delay in the regular cycle is a bad omen; and for some people a safe delivery is not desirable—hence the temporary archival canonization of spontaneous abortion.

• Near the head of the procession of saints in "Cyclops" is an unfamiliar Spanish holy man, "S. Isadore Arator" (*U* 12.1689–90). His Latin epithet means "plowman" or "farmer." Nothing reliable is known of his life, but many miracles are ascribed to him. The saint's symbol is a sickle, as is recorded in a note: "S. Isadore reaper" (VI.B.5.91). His partner in the procession is "S. Cyr" (*U* 12.1689); the French national military academy is located in the town of St.-Cyr. If, by the juxtaposition of these two obscure saints, Joyce intended to imply that swords will be beaten into plowshares, his attempt at hagiographical allegory has remained understandably unappreciated.

- According to tradition, when the young Hubert was pursuing prey in the forest one Good Friday, a stag with a crucifix between its antlers appeared before him. The hunter realized that he was being called to a more noble career. Shortly thereafter Hubert became a missionary priest, and eventually a "hunter" of souls and a bishop of the diocese of Liege, which included the densely wooded area of the Ardennes. In one of the accusations of HCE, incriminating evidence is produced, some of it distinctly Belgian: "This is a bulgen horesies; this is wollan indulgencies, this is flemsh . . . Hubert was a Hunter, *chemins de la croixes* ["ways of the crosses" in French]" (*FW* 376.4–7).[27] A second phrase is most probably meant to refer to the holy bishop's relics, although it might also pack an allusion to the animal remains that the young Hubert left strewn in the forest: "Holybones of Saint Hubert" (*FW* 31.25).

- *The Golden Legend* reports that a stag appeared in the forest and warned another holy hunter, St. Julian, that he would kill his mother and father. To avoid that fate, he fled from his home. Meanwhile, his parents came to console his wife, and she told them to sleep in her own bedroom. When Julian finally decided to return home, he discovered a couple beneath the covers in his wife's bed and imagined that she had taken a lover. He slew the sleeping pair. After discovering his tragic error, Julian and his wife moved into the forest, where they aided poor travelers and ferried them freely across a river. Once Julian rescued a leprous old man and placed him in his own bed. At that act of charity, the stranger rose and revealed that he was a messenger from God—Julian's penance had been accepted.[28] The saint is the patron of innkeepers, ferrymen, and hospitals. "S. Julian" (*U* 12.1690–91) is in the first group of saints in the *Ulysses* catalogue. The *Wake*'s "St Jilian's of Berry, hurrah there for tobbies!" (*FW* 406.24–25) adds a bit of hagiographical local color: "Berry" is the name of a former province in France where the legendary events took place; "toby" is an archaic term for a mug of ale—an appropriate refreshment to be offered to a weary traveler by a saintly innkeeper in the forest.

- St. John of the Cross was a sixteenth-century reformer of the Carmelite order; he is best known, however, as a mystical theologian and poet. His penetrating lyric, *The Dark Night of the Soul*, has long been recognized as a spiritual masterpiece. A brief reference to this work appears in Joyce's

1912 lecture on William Blake (*CW* 221). Although there is only a single explicit allusion to the Spanish saint in the *Wake* ("jam of the cross" [*FW* 448.8]), a 1921 letter to Miss Weaver indicates that Joyce had the poem on his mind as a thematic parallel (*Letters* I.281). As a confessor-adviser, John was much in demand by nuns in the convents of the strict Carmelites; in fact, completely unsubstantiated charges of sexual impropriety were hurled at him by his enemies from the relaxed faction of the order. That accusation and St. John's "incamination" of the night suggest some obvious affinities with the *Wake*. A brief monograph by Marion Cumpiano thoroughly—and with verve—explores those parallels.[29] Since it would be rash to attempt a summary of her detailed comparative analysis, I recommend that all readers locate a copy of that original study and see how a competent comparatist deals with intertextual evidence.

- In the mid sixteenth century, another John, a middle-aged Iberian reprobate, decided to amend his life. The conversion had such extreme emotional consequences that he was confined as a lunatic. After being released, John received the assistance of the archbishop of Granada to set up a shelter and hospice for those in desperate need, the homeless, prostitutes, and the dying. After John's death the epithet "of God" was added to his name, and those who followed his example of charity are known as the Brothers Hospitaller of St. John of God, an order that is in no way connected with the crusader Knights Hospitaller.

Several archival notes record the name of this hospitaller saint; one has a curious introduction: "Hebr. Lat & Gr. & John of G" (V.A.2.12).[30] Before he saw the light, John was an uneducated soldier; after his conversion, he dedicated himself to the sick and poor, not to linguistics and grammar books. An off-the-wall explanation for the odd connection between biblical and classical languages and the saint is the fact that a leading hospital for the insane in Dublin was named after him: "Sure, he's out in John of God's off his head, poor man" (*U* 12.55). From the context it is difficult to determine whether the gentleman in question is suffering from *delirium tremens* or is just plain mad. At any rate, although there is certainly no necessary cause-and-effect relationship between the study of an ancient language and lunacy, in forty years of hanging around departments of classics in several universities, I have noticed an inordinate number of people who drink too much and have decidedly crazy ideas. Joyce may have made the same observation.

- The patron saint of Leopold Bloom is fittingly inserted into the procession in "Cyclops" in the midst of eight holy men whose names are borne by other male characters in *Ulysses*:

S. Martin of Tours [Martin Cunningham] and S. Alfred [Alfred Bergan] and S. Joseph [Joseph J. O'Molloy] and S. Denis [Denis Breen] and Cornelius [Corny Kelleher] and S. Leopold and S. Bernard [Barney Kiernan] and S. Terence [Terry Ryan] and S. Edward [Ned Lambert]. (*U* 12.1694–96)

Joyce makes no attempt at matching the actions or personalities of these Dublin stalwarts with their patron saints, but he does opt for direct nominal correspondence for the next member of the procession, "S. Owen Canicula" (*U* 12.1696). The ferocious watchdog at Barney Kiernan's pub is called Garryowen; in this section of the text, his canonized namesake is given an impressive-sounding epithet. The force of Joyce's pseudo-hagiographic moniker is, however, significantly reduced when it is traced to its Latin source: *caniculus* is Latin for "puppy."

Bloom's patron is St. Leopold, although none of the several saints who carry that name behave anything like the hero of *Ulysses*, nor does he himself ever allude to a patron. One of several possible namesakes, St. Leopold of Austria was a medieval prince who was the benefactor of three great abbeys but refused the imperial crown. He also had eighteen children. In "Ithaca," a hypothetical new home for the current inhabitants of 7 Eccles Street is given the imposing title "Bloom Cottage. Saint Leopold's. Flowerville" (*U* 17.1580).

The closest involvement Bloom himself has with the cult of the saints is the honorary presence of "*saint Stephen's iron crown*" (*U* 15.1439), the national relic of his ancestral Hungary, at his mock coronation in "Circe." Among those in attendance at this momentous event is "*the chapter of the saints of finance in their plutocratic precedence of order*" (*U* 15.1418–20), but Joyce does not include any details about these holy capitalists. When Bloom is actually crowned, his expanded royal names are announced: "Leopold, Patrick, Andrew, David, George, be thou anointed!" (*U* 15.1489–90). The names of the final four saints in this list constitute a hagiographical Union Jack, incorporating the patrons of Ireland, Scotland, Wales, and England.

- In his *Annotations*, one of several glosses that McHugh offers for "O Mr Mathurin" (*FW* 335.35) is "St Mathurin: patron of fools." I have not been able to track down any information about this French saint and his reputed foolishness. Joyce was at least aware that there was "a commemorative plaque [to St. Fiacre] in the church of St. Mathurin in Paris" (*CW* 158).

- St. Olaf was an eleventh-century king of the Norwegians. Along with leading Viking raids for the Normans and against the Danes, he converted to Christianity and brought many of his people with him. An archival cluster includes St. Olaf along with other Scandinavian patrons, St. Halvard of Oslo, Brigetta and Eric of Sweden, Knute and Ansgar of Denmark (VI.B.18.63). Two later entries in the same notebook name "S. Clement Dane / Olaf the Saint" in what looks like a list of London churches with Scandinavian connections. Since another Norse warlord, Olaf the White ("Olaf the Hide" [FW 100.26]), raided Dublin and set up a Viking kingdom there in 852, it is difficult to distinguish specific references to St. Olaf in the *Wake*. A brief article attempting to do that stretches the thin textual evidence beyond the point of credibility.[31] In my judgment, the only secure allusion is "Olaph the Oxman" (*FW* 132.17–18); the epithet can be modulated into "Ostman," a term for a Viking, or it may refer to his royal (and hagiographical) emblem, an ax held in the paws of a lion.

- The next item is included primarily to illustrate one of the difficulties of hagiographical research in general, and its application to the work of James Joyce in particular. An uncrossed pair of notebook entries reads: "popular confessor / San Raymondus—by Moors" (VI.B.2.39). Standard manuals of the lives of the saints offer three likely candidates, all Iberians from the thirteenth century. Raymond Lull, a Franciscan who was imprisoned and deported from Tunis by the Moors, wrote more than three hundred treatises (many in Arabic) on all aspects of philosophy, science, and theology.[32] He was beatified in 1853, but has not been named an official saint.

Raymond Nonnatus (the "Not Born," because he was delivered by a caesarian section) was a Mercedarian priest, a Spanish order that specialized in ransoming Christians who had been enslaved by Muslims. He narrowly escaped death in Algeria for conversion of Islamic citizens, and was later created a cardinal. The circumstances of his birth make him the patron saint of midwives.

St. Raymond of Peñafort was a Dominican who preached throughout Spain to Moors and Christians who were former slaves in Islamic territory. According to some sources, St. Raymond worked closely with St. Peter Nolasco in founding the Mercedarians in his native land. He was famed for his charismatic oratory, and became a confessor to the pope and a codifier of canon law. After contracting a serious illness in Rome, he returned to die in Barcelona—but managed (perhaps miraculously) to live, administer, and write for another thirty-five years.

If pressed for a choice of which of the three Raymonds (all of whom were involved with the Moors) is embedded in the archival note cited above, I would select the last, the long-lived Catalonian friar. My reason is a crossed note that appears tangentially, three lines below the original citation: "ʳangel of death kicked / lost the bucket" (VI.B.2.39). A variation of that statement is used in the *Wake* as one of the answers to the riddle "when is a man not a man? . . . when the angel of death kicks the bucket of life" (*FW* 170.5 and 12–13).

- St. Roche (Roch, Rock, Rocco, Roque) was very popular in premodern times, since he was invoked to ward off epidemics and especially the plague. Born in France, he cared for—and miraculously cured—victims of the plague that was decimating Italy, until he himself was infected. Abandoned by everyone except his dog, Roche decided to return to his home, but he was so disfigured by the disease that he was not recognized. Jailed as an impostor or spy, Roche died in prison, where his corpse was finally identified by a cross-like red birthmark on his chest.

Kopper suggests an echo of that recognition device in "Peter Roche, that frind of my boozum" (*FW* 449.16).[33] In her monologue Molly recalls seeing "the Spanish cavalry at La Roque" (*U* 18.398). The reference is to the actual town of San Roque, six miles north of the British Lines, to which the whole of the Spanish population fled after the colonial occupation of Gibraltar. That identification is confirmed by an archival note: "caval. San Roque" (*UNBM* 511:45). I suggest a bit of intentional irony in Joyce's allusion to the refugees' choice of a patron saint for their town-in-exile. Gibraltar is "the Rock" in any language; the municipality of San Roque, then, magnanimously honors both a genuine saint and the hallowed home from which the Spaniards have been driven by British invaders.

- St. Vincent Ferrer of Valencia was instrumental in bringing an end to the great Western Schism by advising that the antipope, Benedict XIII, his former patron at Avignon, be deposed. His primary apostolate was preaching and converting thousands in Spain. In an index of transcribed notes that concern the career of St. Vincent, several entries are crossed out. The first, "ʳhairshirt" (VI.C.12.154) undoubtedly refers to a penance that the Dominican friar imposed upon himself; it reappears in the *Wake* as one of the Four Old Men describes someone who wears a "cheapshein hairshirt" (*FW* 387.5). The second item seems to deal with Vincent's homeland, "ᵍVF creates Catalan / question" (VI.C.12.154). Despite the specific nature of that entry, I have not been able to detect its placement in the *Wake*; in fact, there is nothing about Catalonia, its language, or separatist politics in the entire work. This is another instance in which knowing the documentary source of a notebook index might help in determining the contextual meaning of an individual entry. But, again, source identification does not necessarily help to determine text usage, since Joyce is usually far more interested in sound or sense wordplay than he is in thematic propriety or historical verisimilitude.

- St. Wenceslaus is one of the patrons of the Czech people. He became ruler of Bohemia in the early tenth century and initiated friendly overtures with the German emperor. King Wenceslaus was killed by his semi-pagan brother and is usually counted as a martyr, even though political motives outweighed the religious reasons for his murder. In the *Wake* he is called "Whencehislaws" (*FW* 539.29–30); since he is responsible for constructing the first walls of Prague, he appears alongside other historic erectors at the start of the Masterbuilder section. There appear to be no Joycean echoes of the Christmas carol "Good King Wenceslaus"—who is carefully to be distinguished from his namesake, the "bad" King Wenceslaus IV, who ordered the execution of St. John of Nepomuk (see chapter 9 for an allusion to the latter's putative relics).

8

Founders and Religious Orders

Previous chapters contain numerous references to the procession of saints in the "Cyclops" chapter of *Ulysses*. That section of the novel is noteworthy for several extended catalogues: "the tribal images of many Irish heroes and heroines of antiquity" (*U* 12.175–99), "the picturesque foreign delegation known as the Friends of the Emerald Isle" (*U* 12.554–69), "the clergy present" at a discussion of "the revival of ancient Gaelic Sports" (*U* 12.889 and 927–38), "the fashionable international world" who attend the wedding of the "grand high chief ranger of the Irish National Foresters, with Miss Fir Conifer of Pine Valley" (*U* 12.1266–79), and the abbreviated titles, honors, and societies of "the right honourable sir Hercules Habeas Corpus Anderson" (*U* 12.1892–96). By far the longest and most impressive list of dignitaries in the chapter, however, is that comprised of eighty-one saints, genuine and bogus, plus the "eleven thousand virgins" who accompany St. Ursula (*U* 12.1689–1712). (After this procession Joyce includes a list of appropriate symbols and emblems.) Leading the catalogue of holy women and men are representatives of almost thirty of the most important orders and societies in the Roman Catholic Church, some marching with their founders (*U* 12.1679–88). In what follows I concentrate on the larger Joycean field for the presentation of those formal religious groups of Catholic men and women, from the Benedictines to the Poor Clares and the Irish Christian Brothers.[1]

In several cases (the "Premonstratensians" and "Vincentians," for example), the catalogue is the only occasion in Joyce's works in which the order appears. (In these instances I recommend that readers consult the brief and accurate entries for each of these groups—and for some of the solo saints in the procession—in Gifford and Seidman's *"Ulysses" Annotated*, 368–74). What all the standard handbooks omit in their analyses of this passage is an identification of Joyce's source of information about the more esoteric items in his list. Where did he find out about the "sons of poor Francis, capuchins, cordeliers, minimes and observants and the daughters of Clara" (*U* 12.1684–85)? Those terms for the various branches of Franciscan friars and nuns appear, in exactly the same order, in E.A. Greene's compact guide *Saints and Their Symbols*. Joyce had a copy of this book in his Trieste library,[2] and obviously went to it for information and terminology while composing this section of *Ulysses*.

Not merely the names of several Franciscan congregations, but also the various Benedictines, Augustinians, Carmelites, and Dominicans (*U* 12.1679–86) come directly from the appendix, "Notes on the Monastic Orders, and the Habits by Which They Are Distinguished," in Greene's book.[3] Even though some of the various orders mentioned have representatives in or around Dublin, and even though Joyce's personal knowledge of the minutiae of his Catholic heritage was encyclopedic, every now and then he needed a bit of documentary assistance, especially (I suspect) in the case of "the children of Peter Nolasco" (*U* 12.1682). This group was founded in Spain in the early thirteenth century to ransom Christians taken captive by the Moors. Greene calls them the "Order of Mercy"; their religious function is more clearly illustrated by the title "Mercedarians," a term that comes from the Latin noun *merces, mercedis* (pay, cost, fine). In later times the members of this order dedicated themselves to more general works of charity. The Dublin that Joyce presents in *Ulysses* and the *Wake* has fallen victim to many invaders, but the city scarcely needed a resident Catholic order to buy its citizens back from Muslim pirates.

The Benedictines

Apart from the Mercedarians, a number of the other groups that appear in the Ulyssean catalogue also pop up in different Joycean venues. The temporal primacy and historical influence of the Benedictine order is acknowledged by their position at the head of the procession in "Cyclops." St. Benedict, the patriarch of Western monasticism, established his first community at Subiaco, near Rome, in the early sixth century. His "rule," according to which the monks divide their time between prayer, work, and study, is still followed by Benedictines ("black monks," from the color of their habit) all over the world. His sister, St. Scholastica, founded a parallel order of nuns. She and her brother were buried in the same grave.

Joyce naturally perverts this relationship by casting Jaun, at the start of his homily to Issy, in the role of the saintly founder: "nor could he forget her so tarnelly easy as all that since he was brotherbesides her benedict godfather" (*FW* 431.17–18; also note VI.B.3.49). The fraternal link is confirmed by the almost immediate mention of "his scholastica" (*FW* 431.23), who (Jaun recalls) used to write him letters "and would be telling us a*nun* . . . thy oldworld tales" (*FW* 431.30–31; my emphasis). In fact, the prolonged duration of Jaun's not very spiritual advice to Issy may owe its genesis to a well-known anecdote told about St. Benedict and his sister. Sometimes he would walk from his monastery at Monte Cassino to visit Scholastica at her nunnery. On what was to be the last of these meetings, she begged her brother to stay the night. When Benedict refused, Scholastica wept and prayed. Her tears were miraculously transformed into a wild storm, which convinced her brother to stay so that they could pass "the whole night in holy conversation and mutual edification." Three days later St. Scholastica died.[4]

The presence of the ostensibly colloquial adverb "tarnelly" (for "eternally") in Jaun's introduction to his sermon to his sister also stimulates Joycean hagiographical reverberations. According to *The Golden Legend*, the devil sent an image of a woman to torment Benedict when he was a young hermit. The saint stripped off his robe and rolled in thorns to drive away the vision, "and from that time on he no longer felt the temptations of the flesh."[5] Joyce does not associate a thornbush with St. Benedict; rather, that natural deterrent to lust is obliquely applied to the Wakean "Nelly" who attempts to vamp St. Kevin at Glendalough.

In a *Wake* notebook there is an uncrossed entry on one of the most famous Benedictine monasteries in Europe: "Mont S. Michel en Normandie / Benedictine S. Aubert / 708" (VI.B.14.15). In the early eighth century St. Aubert, the bishop of Auranches in Normandy, was instructed in a series of dreams to build a shrine to St. Michael the Archangel on a rocky island in the tidal bay. This pilgrimage site was later crowned by the magnificent Gothic monastery dedicated to its patron. Joyce's story "The Dead" contains an allusion to another monastic foundation, Mount Melleray. Mrs. Malins informs the dinner guests that her son, Freddy, "will visit Mount Melleray, in a week or so"—for the unstated purpose of drying him out under the watchful eyes of the monks. A Protestant guest, Mr. Browne, is astonished to hear that the members of that community "never spoke, got up at two in the morning and slept in their coffins" (*D* 200–201). The monks in question are Trappists, officially Cistercians, a reformed, ultra-strict branch of the Benedictine family, known as "white monks" from the color of their habits. They do not, in fact, sleep in their coffins.

St. Bernard of Clairvaux (the mountainous site of one of the order's first monasteries) is the most famous of the founders of the Cistercians. He argued strenuously for both monastic and papal reform and preached in favor of the Second Crusade. St. Bernard is cited several times in *Ulysses*, once mistakenly as the author of a famous homily in honor of the Virgin Mary (*U* 14.290–97). As a Doctor of the Church Bernard's title is "Doctor Melifluous," since the words that flowed from his mouth were as sweet as honey (*mel* in Latin). An archival note combines this title and the highly distorted name of Ireland's first Cistercian foundation, Mellifont Abbey: "abbayse / ᵇmellifond" (VI.B.23.49).⁶ The crossed element shows up in the text in a phrase that acknowledges its etymology: "moonmist would be melding mellifond indo his mouth" (*FW* 477.30). Another Cistercian monastery—the only one still functioning in England, Mount St. Bernard's Abbey in Leicestershire—is twisted into an archival "Mt. St. Barnyard" (VI.B.29.21; also note VI.B.1.106).

There are several other branches of Benedictine monasticism that march in the Cyclopean procession: "Carthusians and Camaldolesi . . . Olivetans, Oratorians and Vallombrosans." Only a few scattered references to one of these spin-off orders appear in Joyce's work.

In 1084 St. Bruno and six companions withdrew to the Grande Chartreuse, a deserted spot in the mountains near Grenoble. Their monastery consisted of a chapel and a separate hut for each member, since the group wished to combine the way of eremitic and communal life. This first Charterhouse (as Carthusian foundations are called in English) set the pattern for future establishments: individual two-story cells, each with a small garden, situated along three sides of a rectangular cloister; the church and a meeting room for no more than twenty-four monks was located on the fourth side. The monks devoted their entire day to prayer, meditation, and study; all service and labor in the community were done by the order's brothers, who lived in a dormitory outside the cloister.⁷ The Carthusian motto reflects the order's pride in its rigorous adherence to the rule: *numquam reformanda quod numquam deformata* (what has never been deformed never needs to be reformed). In "Grace" Mr. Cunningham predictably misapplies this attribute: "the Jesuit Order was never reformed. It never fell away" (*D* 163–64).

In the *Wake* there is an isolated incident in which "The Nolan of the Calabashes . . . was as much incensed by Saint Bruno" (*FW* 336.33–35). Other Wakean references make it highly likely that Joyce intends an evocation of the fiery reformer Giordano Bruno the Nolan (from the city of Nola in Italy), rather than a snapshot of the founder of the Carthusians swinging a smoking censer. At the same time, that passage incorporates an allusion to St. Bruno's pipe tobacco, as is confirmed by the address of a "Mr G.B.W. Ashburner, S. Bruno's Toboggan Drive" (*FW* 369.7–8). Also mentioned in the *Wake* are the "Elder Charterhouse's duckwhite pants" (*FW* 137.21); their color is correct because St. Bruno's monks wore white habits.

In *Ulysses* Leopold Bloom passes a Catholic church, but is disappointed at hearing no music: "They had a gay old time while it lasted. Healthy too, chanting, regular hours, then brew liqueurs. Benedictine. Green Chartreuse. Still, having eunuchs in their choir that was coming it a bit thick" (*U* 5.406–8). Although his idea about the composition of monastic choirs is totally confused, Bloom is correct about their production of expensive cordials. Each community had to support itself: some baked bread; others raised sheep for wool; some distilled liqueurs from secret formulas—and named them after their orders.

A tangential figure in the Benedictine tradition deserves mention: Cassiodorus, the sixth-century Roman politician and scholar. When he left the service of a conquering Ostrogothic king, he retired to one of the monasteries that he had founded, adopting the rule of St. Benedict, on his ancestral estates in Vivarium, in southern Italy. There Cassiodorus compiled a history of the Church and designed a program of study for monks that included secular and sacred literature. He can thus be considered the father of monastic humanism, one who began the process of preserving the classics during the long medieval twilight of learning and science. In the *Wake* Joyce placed "Cassiodorus" at the end of a minor catalogue—beginning with Pliny the Younger and his uncle, Pliny the Elder—of ancient Roman encyclopedists and technical writers (*FW* 255.18–21). The learned statesman-monk is not an official saint, but Cassiodorus's role in the miraculous conservation of the West's cultural heritage merits respectful scrutiny by a canonization committee.

Throughout medieval Europe Benedictine monasticism, with isolated cloisters to which the monks were bound for life and in which all activity was subject to their founder's rule, was a bastion of security and civilization. In the early thirteenth century, however, the rise of cities brought new challenges to the mission of the Church. There was a call for priests, teachers, and preachers to confront the world, not to retreat from it—followers of the Lord who would move among the people, to minister to the physical as well as spiritual needs of the poor and the sick. Two new orders developed in response to that change in socioeconomic conditions, the Dominicans and the Franciscans. Members of both groups are called "friars," a term derived from the Latin noun *frater* (brother).

The Franciscans

St. Francis was born in Assisi, in central Italy, into a wealthy merchant family. After a carefree early life, he answered a call from Christ by dedicating himself to poverty and the service of the urban poor. Others soon joined the founder to form an "order of Lesser Brothers" (*Ordo Fratrum Minorum*).⁸ St. Clara, also of Assisi, joined him to found a kindred community of nuns, known in English as the "Poor Clares." After a failed attempt to convert Muslims in Egypt during the Fifth Crusade, Francis returned to Italy to reiterate, in the face of some internal opposition by backsliding friars, the order's renunciation of property and to inspire its rapid spread across Europe. He received the stigmata, lesions corresponding to the five wounds of the crucified Christ. His *Canticle of the Sun* and a collection of the legends associated with the saint and his early followers, *The Little Flowers of St. Francis,* are well known.⁹ He was canonized shortly after his death, and in 1979 Pope John Paul II proclaimed the preternaturally "green" Francis a patron of ecologists.

By far the most detailed of any of Joyce's references to St. Francis appears in a section of *Stephen Hero* that was not incorporated into *Portrait,* but reappears momentarily in *Ulysses* (*U* 3.107–8). In Marsh's Library in Dublin, Stephen read old books in Italian: "He had begun to be interested in Franciscan literature. He appreciated not without pitiful feelings the legend of the mild heresiarch of Assisi. He knew, by instinct, that S. Francis' love-chains would not hold him very long but the Italian was very quaint. Elias and Joachim also relieved the naïf history" (*SH* 176). Francis is called a "mild heresiarch" because his enthusiastic preaching and insistence on necessary poverty for his order—and by extension, for the whole church—were quite disturbing to the ecclesiastical establishment who controlled enormous wealth and property.

The two other Franciscans mentioned in the previous paragraph are important figures in the early history of the order. Elias of Cortona was Francis's vicar and helped to formulate a revised version of the rule. When he eventually became the leader of the order, his personal life was not guided by the principle of poverty, but the picture of Friar Elias as the betrayer of the Franciscan ideal is an exaggeration. Joachim of Flora was a late-twelfth-century Cistercian abbot and mystic. His apocalyptic prophecy that the reign of the Holy Ghost (to commence in 1260) would bring a new era of spiritual liberty and political anarchy inspired the zealot branch of the Franciscans, the Spirituals, to denounce all authority. This created a schism in the order, and a number of ultra-radicals (scornfully called "Fratricelli" [Teeny-weeny Brothers]) were condemned as heretics, and some were burned at the stake.¹⁰

In *Portrait* Stephen self-consciously casts himself as one of these errant friars. He recalls an exchange with Emma Clery:

—You are a great stranger now.

—Yes. I was born to be a monk.

—I am afraid you are a heretic. (*P* 219)

That recollection triggers a reverie: "A monk! His own image started forth a profaner of the cloister, a heretic franciscan, willing and willing not to serve, spinning like Gherhardino da Borgo San Donnino, a little web of sophistry and whispering in her ear" (*P* 219–20). That sinister-sounding scholar was a radical Franciscan Spiritual who composed a companion to the works of Joachim of Flora, entitled *The Introduction to the Eternal Gospel*. Many of the Fratricelli practiced severe corporal abuse, and some roamed from city to city flagellating themselves. That form of penitential exhibitionism explains the title of a book that Jaun recommends as spiritual reading to Issy, "With Flageolettes in Send Franciesland" (*FW* 440.20–21; also note VI.B.34.72).

In *Portrait* Stephen's climactic confession of his sins takes place in an unnamed "chapel" (*P* 141); in the earlier version, after receiving absolution, the hero "went every Sunday evening to the church of the Capuchins whither he had once carried the disgraceful burden of his sins to be eased of it" (*SH* 177). In *Portrait* the Jesuit director of vocations speaks to Stephen about "the dominican and franciscan orders and of the friendship between saint Thomas [a Dominican] and saint Bonaventure [a Franciscan]. The capuchin dress, he thought, was rather too . . ." (*P* 154; Joyce's ellipsis). His apt pupil picks up the allusion to the long, dangling cowls worn by that branch of the Franciscan family. He also grasps the comment on that habitual breach of decorum by the friars:

—Les jupes.

—O. (*P* 115)

Capuchins are so called because their cowl is topped by a pointed hood, *caputium* in monastic Latin (from *caput*, "head").[11]

In the early days of the order, the typical Franciscan habit was gray, made of undyed homespun material. Later, most branches of the order adopted a brown habit, usually worn with a rope or cord around the waist. That cincture supplies the name by which a branch of Franciscan friars is called, "cordeliers" (*U* 12.1685; also note "corded friar" [VI.B.14.38]).[12] The two colors of the habits are also confirmed in *Ulysses*: "friars, brown and grey, sons of poor Francis" (*U* 12.1684). In the *Wake*, one of the Four Old Men is addressed as "Jimmy, my old brown freer" (*FW* 588.13); a bit later a pidgin-English sentence indicates that a guest of St. Patrick is a "cassock groaner fellas of greysfriaryfamily" (*FW* 611.9). That identification is reinforced by an archival note: "grey friars OSF" (VI.B.15.188). In the second catalogue of Dublin churches, it might seem that "Bruno Friars" (*FW* 569.9) was dedicated to St. Bruno, the founder of the Carthusians. Not so; the phrase that designates the Church Street parish of the Franciscans uses the Italian adjective *bruno* for the first element in "Brown" Friars.[13] Probably the most familiar local church in the *Wake* is the initial Adam and Eve's (*FW* 3.1), so called after a tavern that once stood on the site. The official name of that Liffey-side parish is St. Francis of Assisi.

In the Glugg-Chuff episode of the *Wake*, Issy needs some sympathy, since her beau seems to have cooled. She is willing to follow him just about anywhere. "But if he'll go to be a son of France's she'll stay daughter of Clare" (*FW* 226.9–10; also note VI.B.29.127). That citation joins St. Francis with St. Clare, who founded the order of Franciscan nuns. As a notebook entry indicates, the nuns are sometimes called by their Latin title, "°Sorores Minores [Sisters Minor]" (VI.B.29.127), but they are more often known as "Poor Clares" in recognition of their strict adherence to the founder's rule of self-denial.[14] Joyce does not allude to the Franciscan nuns' poverty, but he acknowledges the serenity and purity of their life by investing Issy "with a cheek white peaceful as, wen shall say, a single professed claire's" (*FW* 290.20–21). Later, in a typical twist of this image of innocence and purity, unmistakably Franciscan terms appear in a couplet inserted in the midst of the tale of Tristan's and Isolde's loveplay: "sister soul in brother hand, the subjects being their passion grand" (*FW* 394.24–25).

A final allusion to the life of St. Francis links the Umbrian founder-friar with an Athenian philosopher-martyr. In the marginal list of suggested essay topics in "Night Lessons," the name "*Socrates*" is keyed to "Devotion to the Feast of the Indulgence of Portiuncula" (*FW* 306.L3 and 23–24). "Portiuncula" is the name of a small chapel and some scattered huts in the plain near Assisi. Throughout his life St. Francis used that humble retreat as the site of important meetings to determine the direction of the growing order of his fellow friars. At that location in 1216, Francis received from Pope Innocent III the so-called Indulgence of Portiuncula, permission to continue and expand his mission of service to the poor.

There may be other solutions to this odd phrase linking Socrates and Portiuncula,[15] but it is distinctly possible that Joyce intended to underscore the aggressive poverty of both the saint and the philosopher. That factor is significant in Socrates' *Apology*, his defense against the charges brought by fellow citizens who had been stung by the gadfly's logic and integrity. As part of his case, the philosopher denies accepting fees for his teaching of the youth of the city. Then, after being found guilty, Socrates has the opportunity to avoid the death penalty by proposing a suitable fine. In court he contends that, if he had any money, losing it would not bring him any harm; but, as it is, he has no money to hand over—except for a *mina* of silver. That sum (less than $100) infuriates the jurors, and they sentence the philosopher to drink hemlock. In short, just as Socrates honestly pled poverty to the Athenian court in the face of death, so too does Francis demand poverty from Christian Europe as the price of eternal life. Naturally, then, the ancient wise man would join the medieval friar in celebrating the latter's permission to preach his message of salvation, the Indulgence of Portiuncula.[16]

The Dominicans

The same notebook page that identified "greyfriars" as Franciscans also records another color-coded piece of information about religious orders:

> black friars & white
> domin   carmel (VI.B.15.187)

The first group of friars cited in that entry takes their everyday title from the name of their founder, St. Dominic. He was a Spanish priest whose special mission was to convince the Albigensian heretics in the southern part of France of the theological error—and civic disruption—stemming from their extreme view that all matter was evil. Dominic's primary method was persuasion; thus the order he founded in the early twelfth century to further his task was officially called *Ordo Praedicatorum* (the Order of Preachers). Like the contemporary Franciscans, Dominicans worked primarily among the people, in cities. Their order, however, was far more intellectually oriented (Thomas Aquinas and Giordano Bruno were both Dominicans), and many members taught at the growing urban universities or served on ecclesiastical courts. The Dominicans wear long black cowls over their white habits—hence the designation "black friars." In "Nausicaa" Gerty MacDowell wonders whether handsome, young Father Conroy would visit her convent, "if ever she became a Dominican nun in their white habit" (*U* 13.451–52).

The *Wake* contains a pair of references to Dominicans and their founder that seem to have no contextual relevance (*FW* 187.11 and 580.5). Two other instances emphasize the order's titular mission as preachers: "*Domin-*

ical Brayers" (*FW* 342.11) and "orational dominican" (*FW* 432.7), the latter in the exordium of Jaun's eloquent speech to Issy. (Joycean wordplay underlies the apparent repetition of epithets here; the Latin adjective meaning "associated with Sunday" is *dominicanus,-a,-um*, referring literally to the Lord's Day—and its customary sermons.) The legend that the Virgin Mary instructed St. Dominic to use the rosary in his campaign against the Albigensians is apocryphal; nevertheless, the order did much to spread the use of that Marian devotion. Joyce alludes to that dedication in a passage in which the lisp concurrently undercuts the order's reputation for oratorical polish: "the dominican mission for the sowsealist potty was on at the time and he thought the rowmish devowtion known as the howly rowsary might reeform ihm" (*FW* 72.23–25). Another legend holds that Dominic introduced the cultivation of bees into Ireland. That gift is commemorated obliquely in the *Wake* by the nearby appearance of "honeycomb," "Melosedible" (*mel, melis* is "honey"; *edibilis* is "able to be eaten" in Latin), and "the Baden bees of Saint Dominoc's" (*FW* 422.25–29). The section on Dominic in *The Golden Legend* is packed with tales of every type of miracle, but there is no mention of bees or Ireland.[17]

Finally, a Latin pun explains another allusion in the *Wake:* "demonican skyterrier" (*FW* 424.3). A literal translation of the Latin phrase *domini canes* is "dogs, hounds of the Lord"; that pun is appropriate, since the *Dominicani* (followers of Dominic) were relentless in tracking their spiritual quarry, to free them from the devil and bring them to heaven. A similar play on words occurs in the saint's "life" in *The Golden Legend* (which was composed by a Dominican friar). Just before her son was born, Dominic's mother dreamed that she carried in her womb "a little dog which held a lighted torch in his mouth, and when the dog came forth from her womb, he set fire to the whole fabric of the world."[18] Jacques Mercanton, one of Joyce's friends during the Paris days, recalls that, while admiring the Jesuits, he considered the Dominicans "narrow, obtuse, tangled up in their own, truly the barking dogs of the Lord."[19] In his 1932 Wakesque promotion of the career of the tenor John Sullivan, Joyce alludes to several anti-Catholic arias in Meyerbeer's *Huguenots:* "And woops with him through the window tallyhoed by those *friers pecheurs* who are selfbarked. *Dominie's canes.* Can you beat that, you papish yelpers? To howl with the pups!" (*CW* 266; my emphases). The two italicized phrases mock the Dominicans, multilingually: their title in French is "Frères Prêcheurs" (Friars Preachers); the pseudo-Latin slightly twists the standard canine insult cited above.

The Carmelites

As the introduction to the Ulyssean procession indicates, the completely legendary "founder" of the Carmelite Order was an Old Testament prophet who defeated King Ahab's Baal priests on Mount Carmel: "the children of Elijah" (*U* 12.1682). Whatever its original form, the European order was reorganized after the Crusades by an English friar, St. Simon Stock. Carmelites are sometimes called White Friars because they wear a white mantle over their dark brown habit.

According to a much-disputed legend, the Virgin Mary appeared to St. Simon and promised salvation to all who wore her scapular. That object is two small squares of brown-trimmed cloth with an image of the Virgin, connected by two pieces of string; it is worn over the neck, lying on the chest in front and between the shoulder blades (*scapulae* in Latin) in back, under a shirt or dress. The connection between the Carmelite friar and this once-popular item of devotional wear is established in an archival note: "S. Simon Stock / Scapola [Italian for shoulder blade]" (VI.B.26.98).

There are a number of references to scapulars in Joyce's fiction. The customer just ahead of Leopold Bloom in the porkbutchershop is his neighbor's young maid. Bloom observes her "Sodachapped hands" and speculates: "Crusted toenails too. Brown scapulars in tatters, defending her both ways" (*U* 4.175–77).[20] Near the end of "Nausicaa," Bloom muses about the dangers that sailors face at sea: "The anchor is weighed. Off he sails with a scapular or a medal on him for luck" (*U* 12.1156–57). Since the nominally Jewish Bloom is confused about a "tephilim" (he means "mezuzah") in the next line of text, it is strange that he twice demonstrates a fairly accurate grasp of the function of a scapular. In "Circe" one of the composite whores remembers her pure youth: "I was confirmed by the bishop and enrolled in the brown scapular" (*U* 15.2227–28). Perhaps the "enrollment" is specifically recalled because Elijah, the prophet of Mount Carmel (now a fictional spokesman for Reuben J Antichrist), has just sought to save the "sisters dear" (*U* 15.2216–24) at that point in the festivities.[21] In the *Wake* the Carmelite talisman is also mentioned twice: once along with "falsehair shirts, God-forsaken scapulars" (*FW* 183.18) and a second time amid other more familiar religious paraphernalia, "Scapulars, beads and a stump of a candle" (*FW* 376.5–6).

A well-known center of Carmelite nuns, the Tranquilla Convent, was in Rathmines (*U* 8.143–44) and another was in New Ross, County Wexford (*U* 12.1247). The former shows up again in "Circe," where "THE NYMPH" is dressed in the *"nun's white habit, coif and hugewinged wimple"* of a professed sister of that house (*U* 15.3433–35). In *Stephen Hero* Cranly arranges that he and Stephen attend Good Friday services "in the Carmelite Church, Whitefriars St where, he said, the office was much more homely" (*SH* 118). In the list of Dublin churches near the end of the *Wake*, two are staffed by Carmelite priests: "S. Clarinda's" (*FW* 601.22) is the church of the Discalced branch of the order on Clarendon Street; "S. Waidafrira's" (*FW* 601.27) is White Friars, the Carmelite Priory on Angier Street. In a previous list of churches and religious edifices, the Tranquilla Convent appears beside "Agilhetta" (St. Agatha's Church, North William Street) without titular distortion (*FW* 569.14).

The Discalced (shoeless) Carmelites mentioned above are the rigorous, reformed branch of the order founded by St. Teresa of Ávila. Joyce pays a backhanded tribute to the austerity in dress and diet of these friars and nuns in Jaun's promise "to get me an increase of automoboil and footwear for these poor discalced" (*FW* 448.29–30). In *Portrait* Stephen Dedalus tries an ad hominem attack against Lynch during one of their arguments about aesthetics: "—I speak of normal natures. . . . You also told me that when you were a boy in that charming carmelite school you ate pieces of dried cowdung" (*P* 205). When TAFF and BUTT are introduced in the *Wake*, the descriptions hint that each might have tangential connection with the Carmelites. TAFF is a representative of the reformed branch, since he looks "*through the roof towards a relevution of the karmalife order*" (*FW* 338.6). BUTT, with his "*clergical appealance*," looks like a "*pied friar*" (*FW* 338.11–12). That latter term is properly applied to a branch of the Franciscans, but it can also refer to the Carmelites since they wore a brown habit with a white mantle. Neither of the pair of disputants acts very austere or contemplative, even though TAFF may have won some pontifical approval when he "*was popsoused into the monkst of the vatercan*" (*FW* 339.34–35).

The Jesuits

Jesuits are neither monks nor friars. Although they take vows of personal poverty, chastity, and obedience to their superiors, members of this order do not live in cloistered monasteries with regular hours of communal prayer and chant; they are not bound to a single place (Benedictine "stability"). Like the friars, however, the Society of Jesus is primarily an urban order—Jesuits then and now teach in universities, run elite high schools, are physicians, editors, labor experts. The early Society was also very much a product of its times: the Council of Trent (1545–63) was convened to prepare the Roman Catholic Church to confront the rapid spread of Protestantism. The Jesuits, founded in 1534, were imbued with the zeal and the perspectives of the Counter Reformation. Many Jesuits also traveled far as missionary pioneers. Matteo Ricci and his companions won the respect of Mandarin scholars at the imperial court in Beijing by explaining the function of Western scientific instruments and theories. The ill-fated communes established for the Guarani in Paraguay were a Jesuit project. The most conspicuous ways, however, by which the Society of Jesus fulfills the demands of its motto, *ad maiorem Dei gloriam* (to the greater glory of God), are intellectual enterprise and excellence.

From 1888, when he was enrolled as a boarding student at Clongowes Wood College, to his graduation from University College in 1902, Joyce's formal education was under the Society's auspices. Those years—and their lifelong reverberations—have been fully documented in several books.[22] Joyce's remarks about the Society range from his description of the Jesuits as "black lice" (*Letters* II.160) to his answer to a friend who asked what he retained from his education: "to arrange things so that they can be grasped and judged."[23] My purpose in this section of the chapter is to examine the impact of Jesuit saints on Joyce's life and works. There is considerable material to sift: since their foundation by St. Ignatius in 1534, the Society of Jesus has produced "38 saints, 134 Blessed, 36 Venerables and 115 Servants of God."[24]

Ignatius Loyola was a soldier in his native Basque province of the Iberian peninsula. While recuperating from a serious leg wound, he was so moved by reading the lives of Christ and the saints that he resolved to dedicate himself to the Lord's work. Ignatius spent time at universities in Spain and earned a degree at Paris; there he collected his first followers from fellow students. The *Spiritual Exercises* are a series of meditations and guides to a life of Christian denial and perfection; this text forms the basis for the content and conduct of Jesuit retreats. The *Ratio Studiorum* (Method of Studies) was developed by the first-generation Society as the pedagogical rationale and program for its mission in secondary education. Ignatius was canonized within three-quarters of a century after his death on July 31, 1556, a date Joyce remembered throughout his life.

During his interrogation, Shaun reveals that his brother Shem temporarily "went into the society of jewses" (*FW* 423.36), then tried the Dominicans (*FW* 424.3–4). Balancing that highly irreverent distortion of the official title of the Jesuit order is the falsely modest—but absolutely true to life—identification of one of his sources by the retreat master in *Portrait*. Although he specifically cites "Saint Catherine of Siena" (*P* 123), "Pope Innocent the third" (*P* 128), and "saint Augustine" (*P* 129), Father Arnall opts for collegial anonymity for the most lurid description of the punishment that awaits unrepentant sinners: "—A holy saint (one of our own fathers I believe it was) was once vouchsafed a vision of hell" (*P* 132).²⁵ (Always lift an eyebrow whenever anyone is "vouchsafed" something!) In the *Wake* Joyce reverts to his habitual practice of perverting the proper names of the high and mighty. Shaun says that a mob tried to attack Shem on "the deathfête of St. Ignaceous Poisonivy, of the Fickle Crowd (hopon the sexth day of Hogsober, killim our king, layum low!)" (*FW* 186.12–14). Here St. Ignatius Loyola is conflated with Charles Stewart Parnell, who died on October 6, 1891, annually commemorated as Ivy Day.

It was the custom in Jesuit schools to write the abbreviation of the order's motto, A.M.D.G., at the top of exam papers and essays; L.S.D. (*Laus Semper Deo* [Praise to God Always]) was added at the end of academic exercises. This practice is followed by Stephen Dedalus on the sheet on which he tries to compose a love poem to Emma Clery (*P* 70–77; also see *P* 108). In the *Wake* Joyce combines the two pious phrases with the common Sterling-block monetary abbreviation "l.s.d." (*libra* [pound], shilling, *denarius* [pence]): "*Ad majorem l.s.d! Divi gloriam*" (*FW* 418.4).²⁶ Other nice examples are "At maturing daily gloryaims!" and "Lawdy Dawdy Simpers" (*FW* 282.6 and F2), as well as "Ellers for the greeter glossary of code" (*FW* 324.21).

The seals of most Jesuit schools and universities include the central figure from the coat of arms of St. Ignatius's noble family, the Loyolas. The figure is a wolf on its hind legs leaning against a large pot, with its forepaws on the vessel's top rim. As in many heraldic devices that emblem is a rebus, a series of figures in which words (or syllables) are "spelled" out by things (*rebus* in Latin).²⁷ The Spanish word for a wolf is "lobo"; for a large pot, "olla"; combined and slurred, the two "things" form the family's name, *lobo y olla*, Loyola. The nearest I can come to a Joycean re-creation of that heraldic name-device in the *Wake* begins with a twist of the saint's given name into "eggnaggy" (*FW* 26.3), followed by a confused report of the zodiacal signs of Finn/HCE: "Your heart is in the system of the She*wolf*. ... Your *olala* is in the region of sahuls" (*FW* 26.12–14; my emphases).

St. Francis Xavier was one of Ignatius's earliest recruits into the infant group of Jesuits; in the mid sixteenth century he sailed to Asia as the Society's first—and greatest—missionary. After making many converts to Christianity in southwest India, Xavier traveled to Malaya, Japan, and China. Those voyages are summarized by the Rector of Belvedere College in *Portrait* as he announces that the annual retreat will be dedicated to Francis Xavier, the school's patron saint and the Apostle of the Indies (*P* 107–9). The Jesuit church on Gardiner Street in Dublin was also dedicated to Xavier (*U* 16.1747–48; *FW* 569.7 and 601.21), and a pun on the saint's surname is probably intended in "egg saviour" (*FW* 483.23). There is an archival reference to "S / Francis gift of tongues / (cause of canonization)" (VI.B.12.35), one of the miraculous gifts that were cited to authenticate Xavier's sainthood.[28]

After he has been unfairly pandied early in *Portrait*, Stephen Dedalus decides to appeal that prefectorial injustice to the Rector of Clongowes. To get to the office of that august father, Stephen must pass along a "narrow dark corridor," on the walls of which hung portraits of "saint Ignatius Loyola holding an open book and pointing to the words *Ad Majorem Dei Gloriam* in it, saint Francis Xavier pointing to his chest . . . [and] the three patrons of holy youth" (*P* 55–56).[29] Each of these young Jesuit saints merits a brief biographical paragraph, followed by collective comments.

St. Stanislaus Kostka died in 1568, when he was only eighteen years old. According to tradition, the sickly Polish youth walked from Vienna to Augsburg and from there to Rome so he could begin his studies in the Jesuit novitiate, a vocation that his noble parents disapproved. He died the next year on the feast of the Assumption and was beatified shortly thereafter.

St. John Berchmans came from a poor Flemish family. In 1618 he was sent to Rome for his studies in the Jesuit college, where his intellectual brilliance and application marked him as the star pupil. His health was shattered by the strain of preparing for a public disputation covering the entire field of philosophy and another display at the Greek College. He died at twenty-two, but was not canonized until 1888. This is the reason John Berchmans is styled "blessed" when Stephen passes his portrait at Clongowes (*P* 56), but has correctly been elevated to "S[aint]" in the Cyclopean procession (*U* 12.1704–5).

Although St. Aloysius Gonzaga was the heir to the family title of Marquis of Castiglione, he decided that the life of a courtier in Medici Florence did not suit him. He too was a brilliant student at the Roman College, but he volunteered to work in a hospital during an attack of the plague and became infected. He was twenty-three when he died in 1591; he was canonized in the early eighteenth century. Joyce's continuing interest in the young Jesuit's saintly career is certified by the term "singularly illud" (*FW* 153.24) inserted into the text of the Mookse-Gripes episode. The phrase is a lightly disguised version of "*Singulare Illud* (That Extraordinary Thing)," the opening words of a document issued by Pope Pius XI in 1926 proclaiming St. Aloysius Gonzaga a patron of youth.[30]

Extrapolations from those data could suggest that the trio of Jesuit saints hold up to Christian youth the following models of behavior: running away from home, courting breakdowns of health by cramming for exams, and exposing oneself to level-four viruses. That cynical twist to the abbreviated lives of the three heroic patrons of holy youth is wildly prejudicial, but there can be no doubt that Joyce permits several of his fictional characters to express severe reservations about the saints' exemplary value. Late in *Portrait*, for example, Cranly protests to Stephen that a mother's love is enduring. When Stephen replies that "Pascal . . . would not suffer his mother to kiss him as he feared the contact of her sex," Cranly calls Pascal a pig. Stephen retorts, "—Aloysius Gonzaga, I think, was of the same mind." Cranly calls him a pig, too, even though Stephen objects that the "Church calls him a saint" (*P* 242). The saint's vaunted avoidance of any possible temptation from women lies behind Joyce's decidedly ironic evocation of his patron on several occasions. In 1906 the young artist wrote to his brother that "if I put down a bucket into my own soul's well, sexual department, I draw up Griffith's and Ibsen's . . . and St. Aloysius' . . . water along with my own" (*Letters* II.191). Years later, Joyce wrote to Miss Weaver that he hoped to "pass through the fires of purgatory as quickly as my patron S. Aloysius" (*Letters* I.137).

When Issy's entourage of maidens addresses Shaun, one of their cloying vocatives is "dear sweet Stainusless, young confessor" (*FW* 237.10; also note VI.B.31.5). Although he did not live long enough to be ordained and thus be permitted to hear confessions, it is difficult to miss an allusion to Stanislaus Kostka here. Within the same paragraph his hallowed youth is praised again: "You are in your puerity. . . . Return, sainted youngling, and walk once more among us!" (*FW* 237.25–30). In another episode, Shem is accused of fratricide by Shaun. The twin immodestly refers to himself as a pure victim, "Immaculatus . . . our handsome young spiritual physician that was to be, seducing every sense to selfwilling celebesty" (*FW* 191.13–17; also note VI.B.31.11). The term "spiritual physician" is a cliché in hagiographical texts; nevertheless, its application to the Shaun-Stanislaus figure might be seen as appropriate in the context of the saint's fatal service to the sick in a Roman hospital. Later, the specter of a plague is more explicitly raised by TAFF: "amalthouse for leporty hole! . . . Sling Stranaslang" (*FW* 338.20–22).

Jesuit novices were once instructed to preserve "modesty of the eyes," that is, to avoid looking directly at another's—especially a woman's—face. After his retreat and spiritual rehabilitation in *Portrait*, Stephen Dedalus (who a few pages later will consider a call to enter the Society of Jesus) anticipates Jesuit deadening of the senses: "In order to mortify the sense of sight he made it his rule to walk in the street with down cast eyes. . . .

His eyes shunned every encounter with the eyes of women" (*P* 150). The documentary source for this sort of pietistic bilge could be any one of the numerous edifying "Lives" that rolled off parochial presses in the late nineteenth and early twentieth centuries. For example, the official biography of the third of the patrons of holy youth, St. John Berchmans, appeared shortly after his canonization in 1888. One of the saint's most marked attributes is the "caution with which he guarded his eyes ... they were constantly cast downward.... His sight was so completely under his control, that it was never directed but as he pleased, and so little liberty did he allow it, that several persons who had lived years with him scarcely knew the color of his eyes."[31]

Stanislaus Joyce (whose patron saint was ineluctably Stanislaus Kostka) is blunt in his criticism of similar types of self-willed mortification: "Jesus was no eunuch priest. We find something fanatical or foolish always in those who are eternally virginal, something invigourous, unvirile, sentimental. Compare, for instance, a St. Augustine with a St. Aloysius."[32] Embedded in Stanislaus's final comment are the names of two of James Joyce's patron saints: Augustine of Carthage, a confessed sinner and a renowned philosopher-theologian, and Aloysius of Castiglione, a stainless youth and abstemious Jesuit. The former name was selected for Joyce by his parents at his baptism; the latter was his own choice at his confirmation. There is no section on onomastic prophecy in the *Ratio Studiorum*, and that arcane subject is not addressed in the standard Jesuit curriculum; nonetheless most people figure out that—in real life, as opposed to fiction—names rarely forecast achievement.

Miscellaneous Founders and Orders

In the mid eighteenth century Alphonsus Liguori founded a congregation of priests known as the Redemptorists; a cognate group for women is the Redemptoristines. After his "conversion" in *Portrait*, Stephen Dedalus often visited the Blessed Sacrament; his guide for these spiritual communions "was an old neglected book written by saint Alphonsus Liguori, with fading characters and sere foxpapered leaves" (*P* 152). In "Circe" Bloom encounters a Nymph-nun and accuses her of some sexual perversion involving "good mother Alphonsus" (*U* 15.3467). Gifford and Seidman suggest some connection with "AE" (see *U* 8.529) and cite a church and convent of the Redemptoristines in St. Alphonsus Road.[33]

St. Francis de Sales became bishop of Geneva at the beginning of the seventeenth century, a difficult period for the Church in that Calvinist area. His devotional writings are still widely read,[34] and he is the patron saint of authors and journalists. In the middle of the nineteenth century, Dom John Bosco founded an order of priests and brothers whose mission is the education of poor young men. This Society of St. Francis de Sales, popularly known as the Salesians, has schools (many with a vocational curriculum) all over Europe and the Americas. In the *Wake* notebooks there are several references to these dedicated men: "Salesian / rigorist" (VI.B.14.188); "his pen tends / S. Francis de sales / ... nolo episcopari [I do not wish to be made a bishop]" (VI.B.25.69–70); and "St. Frances de Sales / Abelard" (VI.B.31.13). Although none of these entries became part of the *Wake's* final text, a few comments are in order. Joyce acknowledged the saint's power in a humorous aside in a 1934 letter to Lucia: "(Saint Francis de Sales, protector of writers, pour a little ink into this inkstand!)" (*Letters* I.342).[35] Although he was most successful as bishop of Geneva, Francis genuinely wished to avoid that important post and remain a humble priest. The last entry links the saint with Abelard—both are remembered as intellectuals and as confessors of women.

Near the end of the "Aeolus" chapter in *Ulysses,* Stephen Dedalus tells the "Parable of the Plums." One of the Dublin biddies involved in this high adventure has "the lumbago for which she rubs on Lourdes water, given her by a lady who got a bottleful from a passionist father" (*U* 7.949–50). In the *Wake* a second reference to that order of priests is slightly altered: Jaun reveals that, if he ever abandoned his dedication to Issy and the Rainbow Girls, he would "be tempted rigidly to become a passionate father" (*FW* 457.6–7). That confession involves more than his fervent desire to beget children. Rather, carnal procreation can also be interpreted as a metaphor for a religious vocation. In the early eighteenth century St. Paul of the Cross founded an order formally known as the Congregation of Discalced Clerks of the Most Holy Cross and Passion of our Lord Jesus Christ—Passionists, or the Passion Fathers, for short. These men (and an allied congregation of Passionist nuns) lead lives of great austerity and harsh penance as they seek to convert the most hardened sinners and criminals.

The final founder in this list is lifted directly from the Cyclopean procession: "the confraternity of the christian brothers led by the reverend brother Edmund Ignatius Rice" (*U* 12.1687–88). This group of men who teach in Catholic boys' schools was organized in 1802, at first in Waterford, then throughout Ireland, and now in North America, Australia, and many missionary countries. In *Portrait,* after young Stephen leaves the Jesuit boarding school, Mr. Dedalus arranges with the Rector to enroll his bright son in the Society's school in Dublin, Belvedere College. Simon Dedalus comments on the less expensive alternative: "Christian brothers be damned! . . . Is it with Paddy Stink and Mickey Mud? No, let him stick to the Jesuits in God's name since he began with them. They'll be of service to him in after years. Those are the fellows that can get you a position" (*P* 71).[36]

As a matter of fact, after all his achievement in their schools, the Jesuits did not "get [Stephen Dedalus] a position." At the end of *Portrait* he leaves, jobless, for Paris; in *Ulysses* he has a temporary appointment as a history teacher in Mr. Deasy's private school in Dalkey. Nevertheless, no reader of Joyce's fiction would be tempted to label his heroes (or their creator) Dominican "skyterriers" or Franciscan "flageolettes"; on the other hand, the following string of drunken epithets seems to suit at least Stephen Dedalus quite well: "Jesified, orchidised, polycimical jesuit!" (*U* 14.1486–87). As for the primary males in the *Wake*, they show no signs of having been "jesuistically formed at first"; but, in their darker moments, HCE and the twins may have occasionally "genuflected aggrily toewards the occident" (*FW* 120.21–22) and the saintly founders whose orders helped to shape the Western heritage.

9

Relics, Symbols, Pilgrimages, and Feasts

This chapter deals with the realia of Joyce's literary use of hagiography: relics, artistic symbols, rituals, pilgrimages, and feasts. It begins with an examination of tangible mementos of a saint's earthly life (bones, clothes, books, material that has touched the tomb or body) and ends with a Joycean martyrology (a list of the days on which his saints began their heavenly life). In hagiographic terms, a *dies natalis* (day of birth) celebrates the Christian hero's martyrdom or death; in most cases it is the saint's official feast day.

Relics

The ultimate relic is that which Catholic tradition assigns to the sixth Station of the Cross. There, as Jesus was being led through Jerusalem to be crucified on Mount Calvary, a pious woman, Veronica, wiped his sweaty, bloody face with her linen veil. A life-portrait of the Savior was miraculously impressed on the cloth. Even Veronica's name is part of the process, since it is sometimes thought to be a slightly skewed anagram of the Latin words *vera* (true, genuine) and *icon* (image, picture).[1] In the *Wake* there are two obvious references to this primary relic: "Veronica's wipers" (*FW* 204.30) and "veronique" (*FW* 458.14). A third allusion can be related to Veronica only through an archival note that includes her name: "° Spitz on the iern / Veronica" (VI.B.8.23). In the *Wake* this becomes: "Spitz on the iern while it's hot" (*FW* 207.21–22). I understand the connection between the entry and the image to involve a test of the temperature of a flat iron. On the *via crucis* Veronica presumably did not take that housewifely precaution, since there can be no doubt that alleged reproductions of the image of Christ's face on her veil resemble the scorch on a piece of cloth.

In another archival note Joyce is even more scornful in his choice of a metaphor to apply to the divine relic captured by Veronica: "obscenity of religious arts veronica's towel butchers apron" (VI.B.5.31). The bloody stains impressed on each piece of cloth are the basis of the comparison. The *Wake* contains a pair of slightly more muted adaptations of this notebook entry. The first repeats the "spit" of a previous citation and transfers the possession of the relic to the pontifical Mookse: "he was the holy sacred solem and poshup spit of her boshop's apron" (*FW* 158.29–30). (There is also an allusion here to an ecclesiastical "apron," a shortened form of a cassock that is worn by Anglican bishops, deans, and archdeacons.) The second textual application occurs as the washerwomen spread their clothes out to dry near the end of the Anna Livia chapter: "Else I'd have sprinkled and folded them only. And I'll lie my butcher's apron here" (*FW* 213.25–26). Here any trace of the original archival context, which is artistic and religious and which establishes a blasphemous comparison to Veronica's veil, has totally disappeared.[2]

Even more bizarre than Joyce's treatment of the legendary portrait of Christ on Veronica's veil is the passage in *Ulysses* that discusses the proper respect to be shown to an actual relic from the body of the infant Jesus. The gospel of Luke reports that Jesus, like all Jewish males, was circumcised shortly after his birth (Luke 2:21). In "Ithaca" Stephen Dedalus ponders: "the problem of the sacerdotal integrity of Jesus circumcised (1 January . . .) and the problem as to whether the divine prepuce, the carnal bridal ring of the holy Roman catholic apostolic church, conserved in Calcata, were [sic] deserving of simple hyperduly or of the fourth degree of latria accorded to the abscission of such divine excrescences as hair and toenails" (*U* 17.1203–9; my ellipsis; also note *UNBM* 191–92:57–65).

The diction of this passage accurately mimics the convoluted terminology of treatises that once explored pressing matters of this sort. In plainer English, Stephen initially wonders if the loss of his foreskin disqualifies Jesus from becoming a priest who can validly officiate at the eucharistic liturgy. The answer to this improbable perplexity (priestly "integrity" prohibits the ordination of men who have lost a major limb) is certainly "no." The second perplexity involves the proper level of veneration to be accorded to the "divine prepuce." Is it *dulia* (the respectful "servitude" shown to saints' relics), *hyperdulia* (the "extreme servitude" shown to relics of the Virgin Mary), or *latria* (the "worship" shown only to relics of Christ).[3] Here—based on the analogy of hair and toenails—the answer seems reasonable and clear: "the fourth degree of latria." In his preparatory note on the material incorporated into the text of this passage, Joyce concluded with two additional queries: What would be the disposition of these sacred relics (the foreskin, hair, and toenails) "after end of world?" This is a problem that could keep professors of relicology busy for centuries. Joyce, relying on his study of astral metamorphoses in classical mythology, comes up with a brilliant suggestion: "Constellation?" (*UNBM* 192:64–65).

St. Helena, the mother of the first Christian emperor, went to the Holy Land in 326 to locate and honor the places that had been hallowed by the earthly presence of the Lord. Her paramount achievement in Jerusalem was the recovery of the cross on which Jesus had been executed three centuries before. The *Wake* commemorates Helena's discovery with precise festal terminology: "the one true cross, *invented* and *exalted*" (FW 605.9–10). The words printed in italics are based, respectively, on the Latin verbs "to find" (*invenire*) and "to raise up" (*exaltare*). The feast of the Invention of the Cross—and the miracle by which it was distinguished from the crosses of the two thieves crucified with Jesus—was once celebrated on May 3; the feast of the Exaltation of the Cross—and its glorious return from Persian captivity in the seventh century—is celebrated on September 14. Reputed pieces of this relic are treasured throughout the Christian world, as Joyce acknowledges in the phrase "a fragment of their true crust" (FW 165.36–166.1). Finally, pseudo-Greek is brought into phonetic and graphic play in the exclamation, *By the hross of Xristos*" (FW 342.18).[4]

An archival note refers to another treasured relic of Jesus' divine mission: the Holy Grail. According to tradition, the chalice used to hold the master's wine at the Last Supper was entrusted to Joseph of Arimathea.[5] Medieval legends bring this disciple, who also assisted in the burial of Christ (Matthew 27:57–60), to England, where he built a chapel to enshrine the precious vessel. The site of Joseph's chapel later became Glastonbury Abbey, and various versions of the legend of the grail become entwined with tales about King Arthur. Joyce briefly notes the basic facts of this romance in an early notebook: "Joseph of Arimathea / brought holy graal [*sic*] to / Glastonbury . . . but staff flowered" (VI.B.6.167). The final element in the index refers not to Joseph of Arimathea, but to St. Joseph, the foster father of Jesus. His "flowering staff" miraculously identified him as a suitably chaste protector of the Virgin Mary, as was discussed in chapter 2.

A covert allusion to a famous relic of the Society of Jesus may be intended in one of the details included in the Rector's announcement of the retreat in *Portrait*. The priest reminds the students at Belvedere of "the story of the life of saint Frances Xavier," the patron of the college, who is "said to have baptized as many as ten thousand idolaters in one month. It is said that his right arm had grown powerless from having been raised so often over the heads of those whom he baptized" (P 107–8). After Xavier died of fever on the island of Sancian, off the coast of China, his body was returned to Goa, in southeast India, and buried there—except for his right arm. That limb, now honored as a powerful relic of the Apostle of India, was taken to Rome, encased in a gold and silver reliquary, and placed in a shrine in the Gesu, the primary Jesuit church in the Eternal City.

In the Roman Catholic Church it is customary to place a relic of a saint in the stone that forms the central part of the altar at which Mass is celebrated. An archival note acknowledges this tradition: "Martyrs beneath altar / as in heaven, so on earth / I/xi / (ignoti)" (VI.B.2.24). The final Latin word means "the unknown" and undoubtedly refers to the unknown martyrs who, like unknown soldiers, are commemorated on a communal feast day, November 1, All Saints Day. The phrase "as in heaven, so on earth" probably refers to the martyrs' celestial place of honor near the throne of God—as well as to their terrestrial monuments in eucharistic altars.[6] The fact that the venerable Kevin in the *Wake* had been "graunted the praviloge of a priest's postcreated portable *altare cum baleno*" (FW 605.7–8) means that he could carry into the watery wilds of Glendalough his own personal altar (with its saint's relic) and built-in bathtub to ensure his penitential purification.[7]

In *Ulysses* the term "relic" is twisted out of a religious context, and applied to a counterfeit specimen. When the whore Zoe lifts Bloom's shriveled potato-prophylactic from his pocket in "Circe," he demands its return: "(*with feeling*) It is nothing, but still, a relic of poor mamma" (*U* 15.3513). In the *Wake* there are a number of references to the relics of saints, none of them uttered with any reverence. My introductory chapter cites that most conspicuous cluster of relics in Joyce's last work, a series of symbolic mementos ranging from "*the girtel of Izzodella the Calottica*" to "*the great belt, band and bucklings of the Martyrology of Gorman*" (FW 349.20–24). Articles of clothing worn by saints are frequently the objects of veneration—or the agents of miraculous intervention. Among such relics I can cite the archival veil of St. Agatha of Sicily (VI.B.17.93); it is carried forth to stem the flow of lava from Mount Aetna.

The phrase "Sainte Andrée's Undershift" (FW 147.26–27) is the focus of several pulses of allusive energy. The fundamental reference is architectural: there is a London church, St. Andrew Undershaft, as confirmed by the adjacent "Fibsburrow churchdome" (FW 147.26).[8] Contemporary literature is also involved: Andrew Undershaft is the arms-manufacturing father of the heroine of Shaw's *Major Barbara*. Joyce's change of the saint's gender to feminine fits the narrative context in the *Wake*: Issy is addressing her mirror-image and swearing "by all [she holds] sacred from my world and in my underworld of nighties and naughties and all the other wonderwearlds!" (FW 147.27–28). Thus, whatever else may be implied in the "Undershift," it is also a piece of the saint's treasured underwear, a worthy object of Joycean veneration. There is an archival parallel to St. Andrée's relic: "chemise de / S. Jeanne des Anges" (VI.B.28.119). After a careful search through hagiographical sources, I have not been able to identify either St. Jeanne or her sanctified undergarment.

According to Neapolitan tradition, a phial of the blood of the martyr St. Januarius liquefies three times a year as it is solemnly displayed in front of the altar in the city's cathedral. Joyce mixes a mention of this religious phenomenon with an obscene twist of the saying "See Naples and die." In the *Scribbledehobble* notebook he jotted down the following list of desiderata: "⁸I just wanted to see, W's cunt and S. Gennaro's blood 1000 candles & invocation before they liquefy" (*Scribbledehobble* 165 [901]). In an August 5, 1928, letter to Valery Larbaud, Joyce alludes to Neapolitan excess in their patron's celebration. The occasion was a trip to Chartres with Adrienne Monnier: "She drove us there lately and lit a candle for me. But I would need as many as Gennaro himself."[9] Joyce does not directly allude to this wonder in the *Wake*, but he seems to have confused the saint's miraculous blood with another common topic of hagiographic lore, the weeping or sweating statue: "though still the graven image of his squarer self . . . , perspiring but happy . . . , by the holy januarious" (*FW* 429.13–16).

Not only is a relic placed in every Catholic altar stone, but also many monasteries and local churches can boast a collection of bones, garments, and other mementos of the saints. A fictional example of such a collection is the description of the treasury of reliquaries in Umberto Eco's *The Name of the Rose*:

> There was, in a case of aquamarine, a nail of the cross. In an ampoule, lying on a cushion of little withered roses, there was a portion of the crown of thorns; and in another box, again on a blanket of dried flowers, a yellowed shroud of the tablecloth from the last supper. . . . two links of the chains that bound the ankles of the apostle Peter in Rome, the skull of Saint Adalbert, the sword of Saint Stephen, the tibia of Saint Margaret, a finger of Saint Vitalis, a rib of Saint Sophia . . . the engagement ring of Saint Joseph, a tooth of the Baptist, Moses' rod, a tattered scrap of very fine lace from the Virgin Mary's wedding dress.[10]

This excerpt is not a wild exaggeration. Similar catalogues could be drawn up for the treasures in many actual abbeys and cathedrals. In fact, during the later Middle Ages, especially in the aftermath of the Crusades, there was a brisk east-to-west and south-to-north trade in relics. Visitors to Jerusalem and Rome brought back pious souvenirs of their tours. Enterprising abbots, bishops, pastors, and mayors saw an opportunity to attract pilgrims—and consumers—to venerate newly acquired relics. This demand generated a supply of authentic and fake pieces.[11]

In the "Circe" chapter of *Ulysses,* Joyce records the inception of a new relic cult, involving a martyr of Ireland's persecution by her English overlords. When the Demon Barber, Rumbold, hangs the Croppy Boy, the heroic youth's body reacts with a *"violent erection"* from which spews *"gouts of sperm . . . on to the cobblestones."* Three matronly spectators (each, curiously enough, with an aristocratic Anglo-Irish name) *"rush forward with their handkerchiefs to sop it up"* (*U* 15.4548–52). The blasphemous twist is typical, but there is hallowed precedent for this scene. At the execution of an early Christian, the faithful frequently rushed past pagan sentries to dip pieces of cloth into the martyr's blood. Such relics were kept as precious and tangible reminders of the price paid by the Lord's ultimate witnesses; their veneration was a source of spiritual grace.

James Joyce and Umberto Eco were, of course, not the first authors to detect and exploit an occasionally humorous aspect in relics. As august and orthodox a Catholic prelate as John Henry Cardinal Newman indulged in an occasional burst of comic hagiography. He is reported to have suggested to fellow members of the Oratory that they begin to assemble relics of the early members of their group: "a gin bottle or cayenne phial of the Venerable Serve di Dio [Servant of God], il Padre Wilfredo Faber, an old red biretta of Eminence C. Robert Coffin, and a double tooth and the knuckle bone of St. Aloysius of Birmingham."[12]

A fitting coda, with an absolutely authentic patina of local color, is Joyce's own eyewitness testimony. In a November 20, 1906, letter written to Stanislaus from Rome, he describes his attendance at a ceremony in St. Peter's Square:

> At the close of the service a priest came out on a high balcony under the dome and exhibited the sacred relics, the lance [that pierced Christ's side on the cross], the piece of the cross, and the towel of Veronica. This he did by marching from one end to the other of the balcony with each relic in turn and holding it over the parapet at each end while a bell rang and the procession knelt in the center of the nave. The upper part of the dome was rather dark and the towel looked rather like a thing out of Tussaud's. (*Letters* II.195)

Symbols

Closely related to relics are the symbols traditionally associated with the saints, especially in their artistic representations. The primary emblem of St. Patrick, to cite an obvious example, is the three-leafed shamrock that he used in his preaching to the pagan Irish to illustrate the central Christian mystery of the Trinity, one God in three distinct Persons. This omnipresent modern symbol of Ireland and its tourist industry, not surprisingly, hardly appears in Joyce's work. A rare example—framed by references to "Sants and sogs" (*FW* 613.6) and "saint and sage" (*FW* 613.16)—occurs as an invocation during ALP's flow to the sea: "Shamwork, be in our scheining!" (*FW* 613.10); another instance briefly flashes in the midst of other Patrician references: "snakes in clover . . . and a vaticanned viper catcher's visa" (*FW* 210.26–27). Stanislaus Joyce's Triestine wife compensated for this lack of indigenous patriotic fervor in the male members of the family. In an October 7, 1924, letter to Miss Weaver, Joyce wrote: "My sister is a devotee of S. Patrick and keeps his statue on her mantlepiece. She gave me a breast-plate in the new Irish colours with part of his famous prayer on it cut in the form of a shield" (*Letters* III.108).

Symbols of divine love are frequent in Christian poetry and art. The Sacred Heart (a bleeding human heart pierced by a crown of thorns and transfixed with a sword) is an object of devotion by several medieval mystics and by Mrs. Kernan of "Grace" (*D* 158). Its significance is clear, even blatant, but Leopold Bloom is critical of the artistic execution of this emblem on a statue in Glasnevin cemetery: "The Sacred Heart that is: showing it. Heart on his sleeve. Ought to be sideways and red it should be painted like a real heart. Ireland was dedicated to it or whatever that" (*U* 6.953–56).[13] On the other hand, in "Oxen of the Sun" a remarkable command of subtle Christian symbolism is shown in a comment made about the hypocrisy of Bloom's sympathy for the difficult delivery of Mrs. Purefoy's baby. Although he himself has attempted "illicit intercourse with a female domestic," Bloom is said to be acting like "a censor of morals, a very pelican in his piety" (*U* 14.921–23; also note *UNBM* 179:55). The pelican is frequently depicted as a symbol of the eucharist because (according to tradition) it rips open its own breast so that its young can feed on the flesh and blood.

The most elaborate string of hagiographic symbols in *Ulysses* occurs in "Cyclops" immediately following the last of the saints ("S. Ursula with eleven thousand virgins") in the grand procession. Joyce then supplies additional information about this spectacle:

> And all came with nimbi and aureoles and gloriae, bearing palms and harps and swords and olive crowns, in robes whereon were woven the blessed symbols of their efficacies, inkhorns, arrows, loaves, cruses, fetters, axes, trees, bridges, babes in a bathtub, shells, wallets, shears, keys, dragons, lilies, buckshot, beards, hogs, . . . boxes of vaseline, bells, crutches, forceps, stags' horns, watertight boots, . . . eyes on a dish, wax candles, aspergills, unicorns. (*U* 12.1712–19; my ellipses)

In this cascade, only the buckshot and the boots seem to be original interpolations by Joyce. The rest of the implements (including those elided) are lifted directly from a thirty-page alphabetical list of "Symbols Distinguishing the Saints in Art" from a popular book by E. A. Greene; Joyce owned a copy while he was at work on *Ulysses*. Although Gifford and Seidman do not mention this handbook as Joyce's source of information here, they do an excellent job in linking these symbols with the appropriate saints.[14] Particularly ingenious is their suggestion that the "watertight boots" are the symbols of blessed Gabriel Conroy and his revered "goloshes" (*D* 180–81). Emboldened by that identification, I thought of associating the "buckshot" with Haines, the trigger-happy Saxon interloper in the Martello tower, but his wildly brandished gun (*U* 1.57–62) is most probably meant to be a revolver, not a shotgun.[15]

The emblems of the four evangelists are frequently seen in church art: Matthew, winged man or angel; Mark, lion; Luke, bull or ox; John, eagle. The Four Old Men in the *Wake* often assume the characteristics of the gospel writers, as in "Father Mathew and Le Père Noble and Pastor Lucus and Padre Aquilar" (*FW* 184.34–35). Here each of the evangelists is given the customary title of a parish priest in, respectively, English, French, German, and Spanish. That title alone is sufficient for Matthew's traditional symbol (a man or an angel); Mark's lion is represented by "Noble," an allusion to the status of the king of the beasts; the pasture in which Luke's bull grazes is suggested by "Pastor"; the Spanish word for "eagle" is *aquilar*. The list of the four Fathers is followed by a coda that may have some significance in terms of symbolism in religious art: "—not forgetting Layteacher Baudwin!" (*FW* 184.35). In nativity scenes and crèches, an ass and an ox usually overlook the infant Jesus lying in the manger. The source of this traditional symbolism is a "prophetic" verse from the Old Testament: "The ox knoweth his owner, and the ass his master's crib" (Isaiah 1:3). McHugh points out that "Baldwin" is the name of the ass in the Reynard cycle and that *Baudet* is French for "ass." I suggest that the presence of Luke's ox in the list of the evangelists triggered the addition of Baudwin's etymological ass.

A full-page index in a fairly late (mid-1933) notebook lists each of the twelve apostles and a symbol:

Peter	a key	Thomas	spear
Andrew	cross	James L	*bat*
James G	staff	Matthew	*wallet*
John	cup	Jude	*club*
Philip	cross	Simon	saw
Bartholomew	knife	Matthias	*halberd*

(VI.B.43.63; my emphases)

The italicized items are different symbols from those traditionally assigned to these apostles.[16] Of these, the *wallet* assigned to Matthew the Evangelist is the easiest to explain. As just mentioned, this apostle is customarily represented by an angel (or winged man), sometimes by a spear with which the pagan officials executed him. Justification for a symbolic wallet, however, can be found in his own gospel: before being called by the Lord, Matthew was a publican, a collector of taxes (Matthew 9:9–13, 10:3). Thus, a large pouch to safeguard his receipts would be an appropriate reminder of his pre-apostolic occupation. The anomalous *bat* associated with St. James the Less is undoubtedly Joyce's shorthand for the traditional fuller's pole (perhaps shaped like a cricket bat) with which he was martyred. The medieval spear-with-battle-ax (halberd) attributed to Matthias is anachronistic, but textually moot: the only "halberdiers" in all of Joyce's works are the decidedly secular honor guards for Major Tweedy in "Circe" (*U* 15.4611).

Since none of the notebook entries was actually transferred into Joyce's text, concern about the eccentricity of several of the symbols is not a pressing critical task. Nevertheless, two conclusions can be drawn from the index: first, hagiographic symbology, especially in the *Wake* archives, is not an exact science; second, as is almost always the case, a documentary origin for Joyce's odd data does exist. *Brewer's Dictionary of Phrase and Fable* is a reference work that Joyce is known to have consulted for other bits of esoteric information.[17] The list of apostolic symbols (featuring the problematic *fuller's pole/bat*, *club*, and *halberd*) in this popular compendium of literary trivia corresponds precisely to the roster in the notebook—except for Joyce's unique wallet for Matthew.

Pilgrimages

During the biographical prelude to the recitation of his ballad, Hosty calls for some supernatural deliverance from the ills that plague him, "through

Sant Iago by his cocklehat" (*FW* 41.2; also note VI.B.36.319). The appeal is directed to the apostle St. James the Greater (Sant Iago), the patron of Spain, whose tomb at Compostela, in the far northwest of that country, is his primary cult center. According to tradition, the martyred saint's body sailed in its stone sarcophagus from Jerusalem to the Iberian peninsula, and there, in revivified form, it led the long reconquest of that land from the Moors. His shrine at Compostela became the goal of medieval pilgrimages. The saint's best-known symbols are the scallop shell and the broad-brimmed hat worn by travelers. Joyce compresses both emblems into the aforementioned "cocklehat" as well as into an oath later uttered by Kate to affirm her confidence in HCE's amorous nature: "And if he's not a Romeo you may scallop your hat." That exclamation is immediately followed by a reference to a French pilgrimage site, "the fane of Saint Fiacre!" (*FW* 81.10–11).[18]

Near the conclusion of "Night Lessons" as the three youngsters prepare for bed, Shaun plans ahead: "Foremaster's meed will mark tomorrow when we are making pilscrummage to whaboggeryin with staff, scarf and blessed wallet" (*FW* 305.31–306.1). In other words, the trio intends to go on a pilgrimage to visit "Heavysciusgardaddy" (*FW* 306.3), their overweight sugar daddy whose "gift" (*FW* 306.4) may contain a toxic surprise—*Gift* is the German noun for "poison." This passage commands attention for more than its implication of a threat lurking in pilgrimage and its bilingual wordplay; there is also a genetic dimension that illustrates an unusual aspect of Joyce's use of notebook material.

Some background information is necessary. Medieval pilgrims—to Compostela, Canterbury, Rome, Jerusalem—would equip themselves with a staff to help them traverse the rough roads and a "wallet" pack to carry food, a few clothes, and their "scrip" (a certificate that they were genuine pilgrims deserving the aid of the authorities and religious hospices on their journey). Joyce noted this equipment in an early notebook: "pilgrim gets blessed / wallet & staff" (VI.B.2.46). Although these two entries were not crossed out in the notebook, they probably contributed to the initial version (late 1924) of book III.3, as Yawn lies low, "brief wallet to his side, and arm loose, by his staff of citron" (*FW* 474.3–4).

From the perspective of Joyce's quirky modes of consumption, what is significant about these archival notes took place a decade later. Sometime between 1933 and 1937, the unused entries in most of the VI.B. series of notebooks were transcribed into a second set (VI.C.1–18). Joyce's amanuensis for this task, Madame France Raphael, understandably made many errors in dealing with the author's often crabbed handwriting, not to mention the esoteric nature of many of the entries. These transcription mistakes are called "Raphaelisms."[19] Just such an error was made in the case of the pilgrimage entries just cited. Madame Raphael's version reads: "ᵍpilgrim gets blessed / wallet and *scarf*" (VI.C.2.43; my emphasis). When Joyce went through the secondary notebook, he picked out these entries, drew a green line through the Raphael transcription, and added the material to the evolving text of the *Wake*. In this case, Joyce seems to have recalled the exact wording ("staff," not the transcribed "scarf") of the original note written in the autumn of 1923. For some reason, however, he did not discard the archival mistake, but incorporated it into the narrative, alongside the staff.[20] Thus, when the Earwicker children plan their own weird pilgrimage, the definitive text of the *Wake* has them outfitted with a scarf as well as the traditional—and original—gear (*FW* 306.1).

To prove that they had actually completed their journeys to hallowed sites, medieval pilgrims wore emblems that symbolized the shrines: a scallop shell for Compostela (see *U* 2.215), a palm branch for Jerusalem. The emblem for the latter destination became the basis of a term for pilgrims in general ("palmers") and is included in the midst of the alliterative circumstances that are posed to Yawn during his interrogation: "a shuler's shakeup or a *plighter's palming* or a winker's wake" (*FW* 514.19–20; my emphasis). The italicized words are the key to the wordplay: *Pilger* is the German noun meaning "pilgrim," as is corroborated by the phrase "your pilger's fahrt" (*FW* 248.13–14), the last two words of which are literal German for "pilgrimage."

Two sets of archival notes indicate that Joyce was aware that pilgrimages had created a bull market in—and the bucket shops for—sham relics. The first entry is brief and to the point: "ᵇʳpilgrim false / relics" (VI.B.3.144). The second directly transfers the practice of honoring the remains of the saints to the two major characters in the *Wake*: "ᵍrelics of ⊓ / & △ / the Livites" (VI.B.27.44). In the text the latter entries are reduced to an exclamation, "Relics of pharrer and livite" (*FW* 578.5–6). There is a suggestion here that HCE and ALP have turned to a life of religious service: in the Old Testament the Levites were ministers in the temple at Jerusalem. One of the certain signs that an interred body was actually that of a genuine saint, not a marketable fake, was the fact that a fragrant odor issued from the tomb. Hence the formulaic description in hagiographic literature: "So-and-so died in the odor of sanctity." In the *Wake* Joyce has Jaun use the phrase in a mild threat to Issy near the end of his sermon: "So don't keep me now for a good boy for the love of my fragrant saint, you villain . . . or I'll first murder you but, hvisper, meet me after" (*FW* 460.4–8; also note VI.C.1.71).

Not all pilgrims sailed to the Holy Land, crossed the Alps, or completed the long trek to Compostela. Since at least the twelfth century St. Patrick's Purgatory at Lough Derg (Red Lake), in County Donegal in Ulster, has been the primary locus of Irish pilgrimage; the site is included in a Cyclopean list of the beauties of Ireland (*U* 12.1458–59). According to legend, at this site St. Patrick slew a monstrous serpent, whose blood dyed the waters as it sank beneath the waves. Tradition also holds that Patrick entered a subterranean cave on an island in the lake and was granted a vision of the souls of the dead expiating their sins in Purgatory. The modern pilgrimage (more than 20,000 faithful visit Lough Derg during July and August each year) involves three days of prayer, fasting, and barefoot visits to the "beds" (shallow pits in the rocky surface) dedicated to Saints Brigid, Brendan, Catherine, Columba, Patrick, Davog, and Molaise.[21] Special Wakean attention is paid to one of these pilgrimage shrines: "Saint Kevin's Bed" (*FW* 40.36) appears in a cluster of Dublin hospitals.

A long index in a *Wake* notebook (VI.B.6.153) indicates that Joyce investigated the details of this penitential ritual. In the text there are several references to the site. The first occurs in a description of HCE during his nighttime lovemaking with ALP: "Derg rudd face should take patrick's purge" (*FW* 582.28–29). Shortly after this dubious combination of spiritual and medical advice comes an odd parentheses: "(private judgers, change here for Lootherstown! Onlyromans, keep your seats)" (*FW* 582.33–34). A gloss by McHugh clears up the mystery here. He notes an anecdote from P. W. Joyce's book *English as We Speak It in Ireland* that served as the model for these two sectarian exclamations. On the railway to Hell [so the story goes], the conductor comes through the passenger cars shouting, "Catholics, change here for Purgatory; Protestants, keep your places." In the *Wake*, the destinations are reversed: the Protestants avoid damnation by interpreting the bible privately, as recommended by Luther; Catholics have a direct route to Hell, perhaps because they demand exclusive privileges as members of the "Holy Roman" Empire.

A second allusion involves a home remedy recommended by ALP as she begins her trip to the sea: "a good allround sympowdhericks purge, full view" (*FW* 618.15). A direct reference is included in Shaun's condemnation of his brother, Shem: "his pawdry's purgatory was more than a nigger bloke could bear" (*FW* 177.4; also see VI.B.1.71). Shaun himself is later called "a litterydistributer in Saint Patrick's Lavatory" (*FW* 530.10–11; also note VI.B.26.113). Etymologically speaking, the substitution of terms is not as shockingly blasphemous as it first appears: in Latin the verbs *lavo, lavare* and *purgo, purgare* both mean "to cleanse," "to wash away"; in religious texts both terms are applied to the removal of moral stains.

During the "Stations of the Cross" section of the *Wake,* Shaun is asked about his mission of delivering the infamous letter. One of his replies during this interrogation involves parodic allusions to some of the rituals of the Lough Derg pilgrimage. He claims that he must avoid "unnecessary servile work of reckless walking of all sorts for the relics of [his] time" (*FW* 411.3–4). Indeed, a voice has commanded, "Go thou this island, one housesleep there, then go thou other island, two housesleep there, then catch one nightmaze, then home to drearies" (*FW* 411.6–8). In Lough Derg there are two significant islands, Saints Island (the site of Patrick's original vision of Purgatory) and Station Island (the site of the modern basilica and the seven saints' beds). During the first night of their stay on the island, pilgrims do not sleep; the second night is spent in communal dormitories; on the third morning, pilgrims are ferried off the island to return home. "His hungry will be done! On the continent as in Eironesia" (*FW* 411.11–12). Hunger is an essential part of the penance; the initial fast (thirty-six hours) is broken by hot water (sometimes flavored with pepper) and dry bread. During medieval times, pilgrims came from all over Europe—including two Hungarian noblemen who left detailed accounts of their visions of the punishments of the souls in Purgatory.[22] Joyce's coinage "Eironesia" for "Ireland" is appropriately built of a Gaelic root, *Eir-* (the name of the country), and a Greek root, *-nesia* (island). Perhaps the sound of the first element is almost meant to offer a less mythological, more scientific explanation of why the namesake waters of Lough Derg appear red—traces of *iron* ore in the lake bed.

The paragraph in which these excerpts just cited appear concludes: "regular, genuflections enclosed.... Happy Maria and Glorious Patrick, etc., etc. In fact, always, have I believe. Greedo! Her's me hongue!" (*FW* 411.17–21). The rituals at Lough Derg prescribe the recitation of three "Our Fathers," three "Hail Marys," and one "Creed" at each of the saints' beds, all repeated three times, twice while kneeling. In short, Joyce's genuflections, invocations, "etc., etc.," and a perverted *Credo* are meant to be Shaun the Post's mocking boast that, if he were able to fulfill the obligations of pilgrimage to Lough Derg, he has the stamina to carry the letter.

Another native Irish pilgrimage site is Croag Patrick (Patrick's Mountain) in County Mayo. On the first Sunday in August, 60,000 pilgrims (many without shoes) climb the 2,200-foot summit to commemorate St. Patrick's original defeat of the pagan harvest god and the ancient fertility goddess who dwelt there.[23] Among the catalogue of Ireland's scenic wonders in *Ulysses* is "Croagh Patrick" (*U* 12.1452), and an echo of the site is heard in "Cliopatrick" (*FW* 91.6); both names also suggest another seductive woman of the pre-Christian era, Cleopatra.

A primary Irish Marian shrine makes a brief appearance in *Ulysses:* one of the women in the "Parable of Plums" is reported to rub on "Lourdes water" (*U* 7.979) to soothe her lumbago. An interesting article links the apparition of the Virgin Mary at the Catholic church in the village of Knock (August 21, 1879) with several important trends in modern Irish history.[24] A large basilica (as well as an international airport) has been constructed to facilitate contemporary pilgrimages to this site in County Mayo, but—despite the Wakean outline of a "Knock Knock" joke (*FW* 330.20–32)—there is only a muted allusion to this popular pilgrimage center in Joyce's last book. After several references to Marian feasts and titles, one of the Four Old Men advises HCE, "Knock and it shall appall unto you!" (*FW* 528.21). On the other hand, an archival note cited in the calendar list below (for February 11) compactly unites the Irish and the French locations of an appearance by the Virgin Mary.

Feasts

One of the most mind-bogglingly complex articles in the eleventh edition of the *Encyclopaedia Britannica* is that devoted to the calendar. In its sixteen double-column pages (*EB* 4.987–1004) there are subheadings for topics such as "Luni-solar Periods" and "Cycle of Indiction," twelve elaborate tables, and countless calculations that enable those so inclined to determine the date of Easter for all eternity. Joyce, of course, was so inclined. Several of his archival notes deal with the method of computing the annual occurrence of the feast of the Resurrection. The first entry gives both a Hebrew date (on which Passover was celebrated at the time of Christ) and its astronomical determinant: "Parasceve 14 Nisan / ^{b}1 full moon after spring / equinox" (VI.C.12.118). In Christian terms, "Parasceve" (literally, the Greek word for "preparation," that is, the day before the Sabbath) is Good Friday; Easter is the following Sunday. In terms of the modern calendar, this feast can thus occur at the earliest on March 22 and at the latest on April 25. There is a crossed note with these dates (VI.B.35.20), which reappears in the section of the text that describes the fortunes of HCE: "he can get on as early as the twentysecond of Mars but occasionally he doesn't come off before Virgintiquinque Germinal" (*FW* 134.12–13)—the final phrase combines Latin (for "twenty-five") and the name of a springtime month in the French Revolutionary calendar.

The basic astronomical factor in the Easter equation appears as "the first equinarx in the cholonder" (*FW* 347.2–3); that allusion is expanded, in cross-cultural terms of calculation, as "the calends of Mars, under an incompatibly framed indictment of both the counts (from each equinoxious points of view)" (*FW* 85.27–28). Another archival note records the fact that the extraordinarily rare occasion of the Western Christian and the Eastern Orthodox celebration of Easter on the same Sunday "will not recur / again till 2199" (VI.B.35.21). I have not been able to find a source that verifies Joyce's contention—nor have I been able to determine when the last such concurrence of the holy day was.

My introductory excerpts clearly show that Joyce's interest in calendars primarily involves the recurrent feasts of the church; saints' days are significant components of this annual cycle.[25] Generally speaking, the appropriate date on which Western Christian martyrologies (official lists of saints) honor heroes of the faith is their *dies natalis* (day of birth). Again, for hagiographical purposes, the "birth" is not the date on which the saints entered the world, but the day when martyrdom or natural death began their eternal lives. Saints' days, as well as the major feasts of Christmas (December 25) or the Annunciation (March 25), are *fixed* feasts; they occur on the same calendar date each year. *Movable* feasts, like Easter and the holy days dependent on the commemoration of the Resurrection, fall on different dates in different years. For example, the Third Sunday of Lent occurs five weeks before the variable date of Easter, and the Ascension is celebrated on a Thursday, forty days after Easter.[26]

In his lengthy description of HCE in the *Wake*, Joyce includes the following obituary notice that combines elements from fixed and movable feasts: "on Christienmas at Advent Lodge, New Yearland, after a lenty illness the roeverand Mr Easterling of pentecostitis, no followers by bequest, fanfare all private" (*FW* 130.7–10). In short, Joyce took pains to authenticate his fictional dates. The designation of the first Bloomsday in 1904 as occurring on "the sixteenth day of the month of the oxeyed goddess [Juno] and in the third week after the feastday of the Holy and Undivided Trinity" (*U* 12.1111–12) is right on the mark, in both mythological and ecclesiastical terms.

According to Stephen Dedalus (at least during his postretreat surge of piety in *Portrait*), even the days of the week have specific religious significance: Sunday was dedicated to the mystery of the Holy Trinity, Monday to the Holy Ghost, Tuesday to the Guardian Angels, Wednesday to Saint Joseph, Thursday to the Most Blessed Sacrament of the Altar, Friday to the Suffering Jesus, Saturday to the Blessed Virgin Mary (*P* 147).[27] A quick way of honoring the appropriate divine or saintly dedicatee is to utter a fast prayer: "Suffering Jesus save me," "Saint Joseph, grant me a happy death." The official name of such miniprayers is "ejaculation," literally something that is "shot out." On the same page of the text as the previous passage, Stephen reveals that "[h]is daily life was laid out in devotional areas. By means of ejaculations and prayers he stored up ungrudgingly for souls in purgatory centuries of days and quarantines and years" (*P* 147). In the *Wake*, the more common sexual connotation of this term is intended: a long list of the debris that litters the floor of Shem's den includes "seedy ejaculations" (*FW* 183.23)—but even this phrase occurs just five lines after some marginally pious "falsehair shirts" and "Godforsaken scapulars" (*FW* 183.18).

In her reminiscence of meetings with Joyce, Carola Giedion-Welcker recalls that he frequently "wore a lilac necktie—a color that he loved and whose Passional significance this former Jesuit student believed in." (On most Sundays in Lent and Advent the priest wears purple or violet vestments for Mass.) In a footnote to that bit of information about Joyce's liturgical elegance, his friend also remarks: "Here, as with many other instances in his life, a symbolic reference was made that hovered between the personal and the ritualistic. Thus Joyce observed and celebrated certain days according to his own calendar, on which ecclesiastical and historic dates as personal memories were marked."[28]

The process of marking important Joycean dates as distinctly as possible involves a number of factors. Too frequently the controlling principle for their inclusion into the fictional text appears to be completely haphazard: "the feast is a flyday" (*FW* 5.24). The clearest and most economical way of presenting the details of Joyce's use of the church calendar, especially the saints' days, is to put them in a month-by-month list, with appropriate references and comments. Before presenting that calendar, however, I give two final examples to demonstrate the complexity of the hallowed enterprise.

In a previous chapter I discussed Joyce's long archival index of material from the life of St. Martin of Tours. In addition to that compilation of hagiographical detail (and strange expressions), there are two unrelated references to the saint's feast day, November 11, in the *Wake*; the first, a very late (1938–39) addition to the text, confirms the date (and its coincidence with Armistice Day): "The uneven day of the unleventh month of the unevented year. At mart in mass" (*FW* 517.33–34); the second specifies the season, "martian's frost" (*FW* 581.14).[29] In England and Scotland, Martinmas in November was also a day for settling outstanding accounts, hiring servants, and holding special markets. In the old Roman martyrology that is still maintained in the Anglican Book of Common Prayer, St. Martin had a second feast day in the summer, July 4. That duplication may explain Joyce's use of "frost" to specify the date in the second phrase cited.

There is also another genetic aspect that deserves mention here to illustrate Joyce's skill in his manipulation of saints' days. In one of the preliminary accounts of HCE's alleged crime in the park, the unseasonable weather is mentioned as "attenuating circumstances . . . as an abnormal *Saint Swithin's* summer . . . a ripe occasion to provoke it!" (*FW* 34.27–29; my emphasis and ellipses). St. Swithin's day (July 15) is an appropriate summer date; moreover, Swithin is one of several traditional "weather-saints" (see his entry in July in the list below). In his first-draft version of this passage, however, Joyce specified the date as "S Martin's summer," and only later changed it to "Saint Swithin"³⁰—presumably selecting a more conspicuously summertime saint to make the unusual heat (and the ripening occasion) more emphatic factors in the evidence for (or against) the accused. A second reference is clear ("Swithun's Day" [*FW* 178.8]), but the third is lightly camouflaged ("saints withins" [*FW* 520.16]).

What follows is a month-by-month list of textual and archival feasts that are explicitly marked as significant by Joyce; the roster includes a number of feasts that were used to date Joyce's letters.

January

1: "Jesus circumcised (1 January) holiday of obligation" (*U* 17.1203–4).

February

1: "1/2 Brigid's deer" (VI.B.14.210); "Bridgetmas" (VI.B.29.45).

2: "Presentation 2/ii" (VI.B.11.84 and *FW* 528.19); "ᵇpurification" (VI.B.17.93);*³¹ see Luke 2:22–25; in German the feast is called "Maria Lichtmesse" (*Letters* II.436).

3: "3/2 S. Blaize / ᵒwool throat" (VI.C.568) [*FW* 381.26].

5: "ᵇAgatha . . . / a /mazon/illa / 5/2 her veil saved Catania / from Etna" (VI.B.17.93)*; "pankin 5/ii shewbread" (VI.B.32.37).

10: "ᵇScholastica . . . / Sister of Benedict 10/2" (VI.B.17.93).*

11: "apparition Knock 11/2" (VI.B.17.93):* In 1879–80 a series of visions of the Virgin Mary and miraculous cures were reported at the village of Knock in County Mayo, Ireland; a likely Wakean allusion to this shrine is cited earlier in the pilgrimage section of this chapter (*FW* 528.21). The date in the archival note is connected to the most famous European site of apparitions by the Virgin, Lourdes in southeastern France; the feast of Our Lady of Lourdes is celebrated on February 11, since the first vision appeared on that day in 1858.

12: "Servite 12/2" (VI.B.17.93):* The Servites are a religious order founded in 1240 by seven wealthy men of Florence; February 12 is the feast day of the Seven Founders.

13: "Ides of Valentino's" (*FW* 289.28): The phrase conflates the patron of lovers, St. Valentine (whose feast is celebrated on February 14), the movie idol Rudolph Valentino, and the ancient Roman Ides of February (February 13).

29: "――29/2" (VI.B.13.12): No major saints have a February 29 feast day; in leap year St. Leander or St. Oswald may be honored on this day, but neither seems to participate in any sort of Wakean festivals.

March

1: Joyce frequently remembers Frank Budgen's birthday, which fell on St. David's Day (*Letters* III.394 and 468); "David 1/III" (VI.B.1.27).

1–15: "Mary's lent (1–15 March)" (*Scribbledehobble* 51 [45]): I find no reference to this pre-Easter period in any of Joyce's works; the Eastern Orthodox Church observes a period of fasting (fifteen days) before the feast of the Assumption (Dormition) of the Virgin (August 15).[32]

17: In *Ulysses* the members of the Fraternal Order of the Emerald Isle have an "animated altercation" about whether "the eighth or the ninth of March was the correct date of the birth of Ireland's patron saint" (*U* 12.572–74); St. Patrick's actual feast day is firmly fixed to March 17. In a postscript to a March 16, 1935, letter to his sister Eileen (whose third child was named "Patrick"), Joyce wrote: "I did not know that Irish Paddies celebrate their *onomastico* [saint's nameday]. However, if it gives you and him pleasure, I will send him a line for tomorrow. I mean Patrick" (*Letters* III.350). Also see a "thank-you" to Miss Weaver in a March 25, 1925, letter (*Letters* III.117).

"17 March / = Deluge / Entry into the Ark" (VI.B.4.186): No date is given for this event in the story of Noah in the Old Testament.

"°17th of Joseph" (VI.C.10.144 and *FW* 274.L3): The feast of St. Joseph is March 19; the Eastern Orthodox Church commemorates the chaste Old-Testament patriarch Joseph (who rebuffed Potiphar's wife) on the Monday in Passion Week, six days before Easter.

19: At the end of a March 19, 1935, letter to his son, George, Joyce wrote, "I think that's all the news I have this day of Our Lord (it is really S. Joseph's)" (*Letters* III.351).

25: "Annunciation 25/iii" (VI.B.11.84 [*FW* 528.19–20]); "ʳ 25/3 Lady

Day" (*UNBM* 227:41 [*U* 14.516]); "till ladiest day" (*FW* 365.5). "Lady Day" is the Anglican term for the commemoration of the archangel Gabriel's message announcing her maternity to the Virgin Mary.

27: "—baptist / 27/3" (VI.B.12.72): This entry occurs in a list of saintly Johns, but there is no feast honoring the Baptist on March 27; that date is the feast day of St. John the Egyptian, a fourth-century deserthermit.

April

29: The only saint's day noted for the month of April is tenuous in the extreme. Ellmann reports that Joyce acknowledged Beckett's 1939 presentation copy of *Murphy* with a bad limerick; it is dated "Paris / S. Catherine [19]39" (*JJII* 701). If the feast is that of Catherine of Siena, then April 29 is the correct date for the gift book; if Catherine of Alexandria is intended, the occasion must be deferred until November 25, 1939.

May

1–7: "°1st week in Mary" (VI.C.10.144): Although May 1 (and, by extension, perhaps the entire first week of the month) is traditionally dedicated to the Virgin Mary, the meaning of this entry is not clear; it does not appear to be a mistaken transcription by Madame Raphael for "1st week in May." In the text only "in the week" remains (*FW* 70.1–2); that phrase is balanced by "the first deal of Yuly" (*FW* 70.3), which probably owes its genetic origins to the previous entry: "2d Prentis [*sic*] Blood / (July)" (VI.C.10.144).

3: "the one true cross, invented" (*FW* 605.8–9): The feast (May 3) commemorating St. Helena's discovery (*inventio* in Latin) of the cross was discontinued by the Roman Catholic Church in the calendar reforms of 1960.

6: "John 6/v" (VI.B.4.298): May 6 commemorates the occasion when the evangelist St. John was tortured by Emperor Domitian, but miraculously escaped alive; the basilica of St. John Lateran in Rome marks this hallowed spot.

12: "on the last feast of the Ascension, to wit, the twelfth day of May of the bissextile year one thousand nine hundred and four" (*U* 17.94–95): The Ascension is a movable feast that did indeed occur on May 12 in 1904. (The term "bissextile" [twice six] means that 1904 was a leap year, since in Roman times February 24, the sixth day before the calends of March, was counted twice to accommodate the intercalary day.)

"feast of Saint Pancreas" (*FW* 550.12–13): The youthful martyr, St. Pancras (after whom a famous London railway station is named), is honored on May 12.

21: "21 May (Whitsun Eve)" (*U* 17.1376–77): The date on which this book in Bloom's bookcase was borrowed from the lending library is correct for the day before the movable feast of Pentecost (Whitsun) in 1904.

23: "Sam Dizzier's Feedst" (*FW* 408.22–23; also see *FW* 471.7): St. Desiderius (known in France as Didier or Dizier) was an early-seventh-century bishop of Vienne, martyred in retaliation for his reproaches to members of the royal family for their scandalous conduct; his feast is celebrated on May 23.

June

5: "5 June S. Kevin abbot" (VI.B.5.49).

8: "S Medard 8/6" (VI.B.9.61; also note VI.C.19.232): Medard and Godard are legendary twin brothers who were born, consecrated bishops, died, and ascended into heaven on the same date (June 8); they are commemorated at *FW* 185.20–31 and *FW* 433.34–35. St. Medard, like the English St. Swithin (VI.B.4.326–31), is a "weather-saint" in the French tradition (see *EB* 26.238); Joyce alludes to this custom in a 1937 letter to Constantine Curran: "S. Médard (who has just sent us a shower which means 40 days rain)" (*Letters* I.391–92).

9: "Kenlia 9/6" (VI.B.6.9): This minor saint shares the feast day with St. Columba.

21: "21 June (S. Aloysius Gonzaga)" (*U* 17.655–56).

24: "John 24/6" (VI.B.4.98); "24/vi __ " (VI.B.14.217); "S. John's Well 24/6" (VI.B.41.207): This is the date on which the Church celebrates the birth of John the Baptist, as noted in the *Wake*, "Juhn that dandyforth" (*FW* 473.10); another archival entry is one day late, "[25/]6 S. John" (*UNBM* 227:42).

July

1: "first deal of Yuly" (*FW* 70.3): In addition to its connection (fixed and movable) with the feast of the Most Precious Blood, July 1 is also the day on which a fairly recent Irish martyr is commemorated. Oliver Plunket was named archbishop of Armagh and Primate of All Ireland in 1669. During the renewed persecution of Catholics by King Charles II, he was arrested and accused of participating in a treasonous "Popish Plot" to murder the sovereign. He was found guilty and hanged, drawn, and quartered at Tyburn in 1681. Since Plunket was not canonized until 1975, during Joyce's lifetime he was styled "Blessed" Oliver Plunket. The saint's feast day is July 1, the date of his execution. A prime factor in my suggestion that Joyce's "first deal in Yuly" refers to Plunket's martyrdom is the emphatic appearance of his perjurious accuser in the nearby text: "Titus . . . Oates!" (*FW* 70.14, 18); for additional Joycean comment on this "most lying knave," see *CW* 119–120.

2: "Visitation 2/vii" (VI.B.2.19): This feast commemorates the meeting between Elizabeth, the mother-to-be of John the Baptist, and the Virgin Mary (Luke 1:39–45).

1–3: "2nd Precious Blood / July" (VI.B.26.98): This entry is the primary form of the transcribed version already cited for May 1–7; another entry reads "1/7 feast of Precious Blood" (VI.B.10.63); both refer to a once *movable* feast (first Sunday in July) that became *fixed* (July 1) only after the reform of the liturgical calendar in 1917. Thus, in terms of the composition of this notebook (1928), Joyce's anachronistic date of "2nd . . . July" is probably meant to reflect the fictional date of the death of Father Flynn in the *original* text of "The Sisters" published in the *Irish Homestead* in 1904.[33]

4: St. Martin: His feast (and its secular significance) was discussed just before the start of this catalogue.

15: "Swithun Winchester 15/7 / christening apples" (VI.B.9.61) [*FW* 433.35]: This entry refers to the English folk tradition that is encapsulated in the lines:

> St. Swithin's day if thou dost rain
> For forty days it will remain;
> St. Swithin's day if thou be fair
> For forty days 'twill rain no mair.[34]

A 1931 letter to Adrienne Monnier from Joyce is dated "St Swithin le Bandit" (*Letters* I.305), but I have found no hagiographical or folkloric reasons to account for the epithet that labels the saint a thief.

22: "22 July" (VI.B.31.12): This unspecified archival date is the feast of St. Mary Magdalene.

25: "James 25/vii" (VI.B.4.298): On this date the church commemorates the apostle St. James the Great.

29: "Felix Day" (*FW* 27.13–14): July 29 is the feast day of St. Felix, who (with St. Regula) is a patron of the city of Zürich—this holy pair literally keeps matters, especially those involving bank accounts, in "felicitous order." Joyce provides his own translation of these Latin saint-names in a July 17, 1933, letter to Frank Budgen, in which he announces "Am back here in the city of S.S. Felix and Regula (= Prosperity and Order)" (*Letters* I.336).

31: "last of the scorchers" (*FW* 433.2): July 31 is the feast day of the founder of the Society of Jesus (Jesuits), St. Ignatius Loyola, whose name is slightly distorted in the heading of a July 31, 1925, letter to Miss Beach: "S. Ignaceous' Day" (*Letters* III.122).

August

1: "August one" (VI.B.33.12): In the text of the *Wake* (*FW* 521.33), this notebook entry is not capitalized, thus appearing to have been transformed into an honorific title. On August 1 the Christian church commemorates some Old Testament saints, the seven Maccabee brothers who fought for the liberation of Israel from foreign domination and were martyred in the second century B.C. The possibility of a muted hagiographical allusion is supported by the exclamation that immediately follows: "Fairplay for Finnians!" (*FW* 521.33).

10: "feast of St. Lawrence (Martyr), 10 August" (*U* 17.1116 and *UNBM* 455:17): The summer feast of St. Lawrence occurs during the season of frequent showers of meteors, as the text of *Ulysses* notes.

12: "ᵍS. Grouse 12/8" (*Scribbledehobble* 158 [805]) [*FW* 449.27]: The saint (a.k.a. St. Partridge) is fictional, but his "feast" occurs on the opening of the bird-shooting season in England and Scotland.

"ᵇᵏ Tithing of our Lord / Lammas Day" (VI.B.29.126); "God's tithe" (VI.B.44.66) [*FW* 541.9]: Lammas Day is another of the old quarter-days once observed in England and Scotland; the name is derived from the Anglo-Saxon for "loaf-mass," since worshipers presented a loaf of bread at mass as a symbolic offering of their first-fruit tithes.[35]

16: "Apparition [of Virgin Mary on Mount Carmel] 16/viii" (VI.B.2.19): This minor Marian feast shares the date with St. Joachim, the Virgin's father, and St. Roche, the patron of those afflicted with the plague.

19: "S.S. Johannes": This signature (Saint John) appears at the end of an August 19, 1904, letter, written in dog Latin from John F. Byrne, apologizing for his inability to loan Joyce a pound. It is probably pure coincidence, but August 19 is the feast of St. John Eudes, a seventeenth-century French priest who founded an order to teach in seminaries.

September

1: "1 September" (VI.B.31.128): On this day the Church celebrates the feast of St. Fiàcre and St. Giles.

8: "the feast day of Madonna Bloom, September 8. . . . Didn't you know that she was born on the same day as the Virgin Mary?": Joyce's friend Jacques Mercanton reports this conversation with the author, who confirms the date by citing the eight roses [correctly, poppies] that Blazes Boylan sent Molly Bloom (*U* 18.329).[36]

14: "the one true cross, . . . exalted" (*FW* 605.8–9): This date is dedicated to both the recovery and the praise (*exaltatio* in Latin) of Christ's cross.

19: "S. Eve 19/ix" (VI.B.2.14): This archival entry, occurring in the middle of a cluster of notes about the garden of Eden, refers to an obscure female saint, as well as to Adam's wife; September 19 is more familiarly the feast of St. Januarius (of the liquefying blood).

25: "[25/]9 conc. John" (*UNBM* 227:4): This date (or, more accurately, June 24) occurs nine months before the birth of John the Baptist; hence it is the feast of his conception by Elizabeth (Luke 1:24–25).

27: "27.9 S. Cosme = / Priapus": I can think of no conceivable reason for the equation of St. Cosmas, a legendary physician-martyr who treats the sick for no fee, with the ancient Roman god whose mighty phallus protected gardens from fruit thieves. Yet, Joyce somehow noticed that the British ambassador to Naples wrote a paper in 1781 comparing the pagan cult to contemporary local practice.

29: "⁰michelmassed" (VI.B.15.178, VI.B.27.133, and *FW* 23.16); "All Angels' Day" (*FW* 26.6): the named archangels (Michael, Gabriel, Raphael) and the anonymous heavenly host are honored on September 29; Michaelmas was the autumn quarter-day for settling accounts in England and Scotland. Joyce dates letters on "Michaelmass" in 1904 and 1920 (*Letters* II.57 and III.23).

October

6: "S. Michael & All Angels 6/x / ʳdate easily capable of rememberence by all" (VI.B.11.48) [*FW* 39.3]: In the light of the previous item in this calendric list, which gives the *correct* date for Michaelmas (September 29) another reason must be found to explain Joyce's archival claim that this date should stick in everyone's memory. The alternative is easy: October 6 is the date on which Charles Stewart Parnell died, as is confirmed by a Wakean citation: "sexth day of Hogsober" (*FW* 186.12 and VI.B.8.110). Perhaps Joyce's note confuses October ("x") with September ("ix"), since September 6 is the feast of the Miracle of the Archangel Michael in Colossae in the Eastern Orthodox Church. On October 6 the Western Church celebrates the feast of St. Bruno, founder of the Carthusians, or St. Foi (Faith), the gold reliquary of whose head is the glory of the pilgrimage church at Conques, in the south of France. For Ireland, however, October 6 is forever Ivy Day.

24: "S. Raphael / Oct 24" (VI.B.36.296): The archangel once had an individual feast on this day, but now Raphael is honored with St. Michael on September 29.

31: "allhorrors eve" (*FW* 19.25): This date is Halloween, the night before All Saints (All Hallows) Day; an archival note refers to special evening prayers for the dead: "black vespers / 31/10" (VI.B.32.37).

November

1: "any saints day" (VI.B.22.1/2); "Pantheon (1/xi)" (VI.B.19.96): The second archival entry is Greek for "all of the god-like saints." The major feast of All Saints' Day is twice commemorated in the *Wake*: once in an Oxfordian milieu, "All Saints beat Belial!" (*FW* 175.5), and a second time in a French version: "Toussaint's" (*FW* 455.5). A letter to Count Carlow is dated "1 November 1937 All Saints" (*Letters* III.408).

2: "the night of Allclose" (*FW* 207.32);[37] "Allso's night" (*FW* 488.24); this is Joyce's version of All Souls' Day, celebrated on November 2.

4: "4/ix S. Emeric" (VI.B.8.82): This saint is the son of St. Stephen, the first Christian king of Hungary, who is also cited in this same archival cluster.[38]

12: "S Columbanus 12 Nov" (*Scribbledehobble* 88 [401]).

13: "S. Brice's Day" (VI.B.7.142): Brice succeeded St. Martin as bishop of Tours; he is remembered in England because King Ethelred II the Unready ordered a general massacre of all Danes in the country on the saint's day in 1001; I cannot explain why the *Britannica* gives "December 2" (*EB* 1.290) as the date of the slaughter since November 13 is the feast day in both Roman Catholic and Anglican martyrologies.

14: "—A triduum before Our Larry's own day" (*FW* 517.35): The feast of St. Laurence O'Toole is celebrated three days (*triduum* in Latin) after that of St. Martin (November 11), the occasion that is the festal point of reference for this phrase.

15: "S. Finian of Moville (15/xi)" (*Scribbledehobble* 88 [401]): This note misapplies the feast day of St. Fintan of Rheinau, an Irish youth kidnapped by raiders, who became a wandering pilgrim on the continent.

25: See April 29 above.

December

3: "saint Francis Xavier whose feast day is Saturday" (*P* 107, 109); "feast of Saint Francis Xavier" (*U* 17.144); "third of snows" (*FW* 433.2): The famous Jesuit missionary to the Far East is honored on December 3.

6: Joyce began a 1934 letter to his son George with a reference to his grandson and one of the European dates for seasonal gifts: "This being San Nicolo I hope you have given Stevie something in our name" (*Letters* III.332).

8: "Take your first thoughts away from her, Immacolacion" (*FW* 528.20–21): Even though this statement is spoken by Issy to her mirror-image, it may refer (since it is uttered in a Marian context) to the Virgin's immaculate conception; this feast (December 8) celebrates the fact that Mary was born free of the original sin that all humans inherit from our first parents, Adam and Eve.

13: Joyce concluded a December 1933 letter to Stanislaus with this postscript: "Santa Lucia '33[.] Her candle is burning quietly in the drawing room. She has had rather a job looking after my occhi ['eyes' in Italian]" (*Letters* III.294).

25: "[25/]12 Xmas Birth" (*UNBM* 227:44); "Deiparation BVM 25/12" (VI.B.2.19); "Nativity 25/xii" (VI.B.11.84): All of the terms in these archival notes are ways of indicating Christmas.

26: A 1909 postcard from Joyce (in Dublin) to Nora (in Trieste) is dated "S. Stephen's Day" (*Letters* II 282).[39]

27: "John 27/12" (VI.B.4.298); "John beauty 27/12" (VI.B.12.72): December 27 is the feast of the apostle St. John the Evangelist; the theological brilliance of his works (traditionally, the fourth gospel, Revelation, and three epistles) earned him the epithet "the Divine," but I know of no source that mentions his "beauty."

31: "Sylvester" (*FW* 473.3): The last day of the year is dedicated to St. Sylvester, whose name is embedded in a passage including references to December, January, February, and perhaps March ("Walker").[40]

Movable Feasts

Septuagesima Sunday (ninth Sunday ["seventy" days in Latin] before Easter):

"steptojazyma's culunder buzztle" (*FW* 578.22); nearly the same components appear earlier in the text, but separated by several lines: "culunder buzzle . . . Steploajazzyma Sunday" (*FW* 102.10, 15).

Laetare Sunday (fourth Sunday of Lent):

"°Laetare / Sunday rose" (VI.B.17.91): On this day the regulations of the fast are suspended, and joyful music and flowers are included in the ceremonies; the clergy also wear rose-colored vestments at Mass, at which each member of the congregation was exhorted to "rejoice" (*laetare* in Latin) at the approach of Easter.

Pentecost or Whit Sunday (the descent of the Holy Spirit on the apostles to strengthen their faith [Acts 2:1–4], "fifty" [in Greek] days after Easter):

"ᵀpenticoatrically" (VI.B.34.37): This crossed entry may refer to the feast—or to a characteristic item in Issy's wardrobe, "her petticoats" (*FW* 466.33) and "Petticoat's ableep" (*FW* 561.31); in *Portrait* Stephen attends the "Whitsuntide play" (*P* 73), a Jesuit tradition, at Clongowes Wood College. In a September 3, 1933, letter to Frank Budgen, Joyce mentions his use of the "Old Catholic" schismatics in the developing fable of the Mookse and the Gripes: "they have the eucharist under two species but the faithful received the cup only at Whitsun" (*Letters* III.284). The catalogue of Leopold Bloom's books in "Ithaca" includes "*The Stark-Munro Letters* by A. Conan Doyle . . . lent 21 May (Whitsun Eve) 1904" (*U* 17.1375–77). A characteristically Joycean touch is likely intended in the emphatic citation of the exact date here, since the novel is about the loss of a young man's faith, an ironic counterpoint to its having been borrowed on the eve of Pentecost. In her monologue Molly Bloom says, "Whit Monday is a cursed day" (*U* 18.953), perhaps because her husband was stung by a bee on that day (see *U* 17.1449 for confirmation of the sting and the actual date, "23 May 1904"). At the start of his sermon to Issy and her Rainbow Girls, Jaun alludes to his love of the "lithurgy";

then calls attention to the fact that it is "[s]everal sindays after whatsintime" (*FW* 432.32–33).

Gaudete Sunday (third Sunday of Advent):

"Gaudete . . . / Sunday rose" (VI.B.17.91); as on Laetare Sunday in mid-Lent, the faithful are told to "rejoice" (*gaudete* in Latin), since the end of the pre-Christmas fast is near.

The preceding list documents Joyce's attention to the hagiographic aspects of the "redletter calendar" (*FW* 456.34), on which important feast days are noted in emphatic color. It concludes a chapter that presents textual and archival references to outlandish relics, authentic and bogus symbols, aberrant pilgrimages, and intricate festal calculations. Those data—from Joyce's letters, notebooks, and fiction—supply proof for the flashy claim that introduces the marvelous life of St. Kevin in the *Wake:* "*Hagiographice canat Ecclesia*" (*FW* 604.19). A creative translation of that Latin HCE-acrostic passage might run: "The Church sings its cycle of feasts by celebrating the saints."

Fictitious Saints

An archival index links the following entries: "Panis angelicus / Military soup / Sartorial cabbage / ʳlives of the Saints" (VI.B.3.131). The clue to the conjunction of these items is paradox: incorporeal angels do not eat bread (*panis* in Latin); an army is not noted for its cuisine; fancy clothes are not made from scraps of cloth ("cabbage" in the obsolete terminology of tailors); nor does the typical biography of a saint resolutely document the verifiable events of a real life. Rather, many hallowed tales have been spun out "in the long lives of our saints and saucerdotes, with vignettes, cut short into instructual primers by those in authority for the bitterment of your soughts" (*FW* 440.21–23; also note VI.B.4.169). Joyce occasionally goes one step beyond even the flexible frontiers of official hagiography. Just as he temporarily appropriates several traditional but undocumented saints, so too does he invent his own bogus holy men and holy women. This chapter brings examples from both categories into the critical spotlight, and concludes with a detailed analysis of Joyce's thematic use of several items from the life of St. Jingo as retold in *The Ingoldsby Legends*.

The most memorable (and euphonious) cluster of fictitious Joycean saints are "S. Anonymous and S. Eponymous and S. Pseudonymous and S. Homonymous and S. Paronymous and S. Synonymous" (*U* 12.1696–98).[1] This sextet appears early in the procession of Christian heroes in "Cyclops." They follow the tracks of "S. Owen Caniculus" (*U* 12.1696), who is a canonized and Latinized—*caniculus* means "puppy"—stand-in for the Citizen's "bloody mangy mongrel, Garryowen" (*U* 12.119–20).

Another saint with a fortuitous name is invoked by Buck Mulligan in "Oxen of the Sun," when he calls to witness "all and several by saint Foutinus his engines that he was able to do any manner of thing that lay in man to do" (*U* 14.236–37). St. Pothinus (also Photinus, Fotinus) was indeed the first Christian bishop of Lyons in the late second century. Hagiographical sources indicate that he was aged and infirm, but stalwart in proclaiming his faith. Gifford and Seidman note that in later times the people of Lyons honored a statue of St. Foutin (*sic*) as a thinly Christianized reincarnation of a priapic fertility-fetish: they poured wine over the image's genitalia and used the resulting vinegar as a cure for barrenness.[2] I do not know the origin of this folkloric extension of the bishop's powers, but Joyce's specific citation of "his engines" and the interjection of the verb "lay" facilitate a possible sexual interpretation of the passage. In the light of Joyce's pervasive attention to etymology, the spelling of the saint's name in the text ("Foutin") may well be intended as wordplay—and thus an additional marker of the priapic purpose of the invocation. The Latin verb *futuo,-ere* and its French derivative *foutir* are the crude terms for "to have sexual intercourse, to fuck." Joyce deployed this term on several occasions: "footootoo is the supine / of the verb to top to come" (VI.B.17.58) and its bilingual application in the *Wake*, "(fouyoufoukou!)" (*FW* 320.5). There is only a short leap from this type of lexico-grammatical acrobatics to the creation of a saint whose "engines" were the hallowed prototypes of those used by Buck Mulligan, Ireland's self-styled "*Fertiliser and Incubator*" (*U* 14.660).

Naturally, there are considerably more opportunities for Joyce to insert bogus saints into the *Wake*. A pair of these are borrowed from the tradition of identifying a significant date by the name of the saint assigned to it in the church calendar. In addition to the feast of "Saint Grouseus" (*FW* 449.27) cited in my introduction to mark the opening of the British bird-shooting season on August 12, there is the custom of noting St. Tibb's Eve. Since St. Tibb is entirely fictitious, she or he has no official feast; its eve is therefore the equivalent of the "Twelfth of Never." Joyce nevertheless twice commemorated the occasion: ALP is reported to be capable of chattering "tell Tibbs has eve" (*FW* 117.19); HCE is not to go to Cork "till Cantalamesse [Candlemas, February 2, Joyce's birthday] . . . or Saint Tibble's Day" (*FW* 236.7–8). Another instance of willful perversion of an established feast is "S. Pivorandbowl" (*FW* 351.14). Underlying that phrase is a reference to Saints Peter and Paul, whose joint feast is celebrated on June 29. The apostolic pair are not only compressed into a single unit, their commemoration is also converted into an occasion for inconsequential fun-and-games, as has been explained in chapter 3.

Joyce demonstrates his feeling for hagiographic authenticity and for geographic accuracy with a reference to Molly Bloom in "Cyclops." She appears in the midst of a cluster of female saints at the end of the procession as "S. Marion Calpensis" (*U* 12.1710). The epithet is the Latin adjective for one of the ancient Pillars of Hercules, now known as Gibraltar.

The *Wake* also contains a number of examples of Joyce's invention of saints entirely new to any official list. The most conspicuous is "Sant Pursy Orelli" (*FW* 243.34), the eponymous patron of one of the manifestations of the work's hero, Humphrey Chimpden Earwicker, HCE. His last name is associated with the common European insect the earwig, *persse-oreille* in French. As mentioned in the introduction, "Saint Mowy of the Pleasant Grin" (*FW* 252.7) is another holy man whose name has been twisted topsy-turvy in Joyce's saintly epithet. Several other Wakean canonizations of this general type include "Saint Annona's Street and Church," which is located "by the old tollgate" (*FW* 44.6). In Latin *annona* is the price of grain—and by extension the surcharge imposed on the import of food, just the sort of additional fee to be paid at an ancient tollgate. Another alimentary reference can be heard "in the pit of his St Tomach's" (*FW* 53.31), which also contains a jab at St. Thomas Aquinas's girth.

Two additional fictitious saints are also tangentially connected with eating. Near the end of his Lenten sermon to Issy, Jaun recalls pleasant times at the dining table: "The crisp of the crackling is in the chawing. Give us another cup of your scald. Santos Mozos!" (*FW* 455.35–36). In Spanish *mozos* are the waiters who serve food and drink in the cantinas. There may also be a deeply buried allusion to the real St. Moses the Black, a fourth-century Ethiopian who was a servant in an Egyptian household. After being dismissed by his master for thievery, he became the leader of a gang of robbers. Finally Moses repented, joined a monastery, and was martyred by a band of raiding Berbers. At the end of the same paragraph in which Jaun refers to the holy "Mozos," he announces that he must leave and that he will not let anyone stand in his way: "By the horn of twenty of both of the two Saint Collopys. . . . I'll nurse him till he pays me fine fee. Ameal" (*FW* 457.1–4; my ellipsis; also note VI.B.5.18). Edward Kopper makes the ingenious suggestion that the saintly "Collopys" are an allusion to "Collop Monday," the day preceding Shrove Tuesday, the last day before Lent. On that day Catholics would eat their final steaks and chops ("collops," colloquially) before the rigorous fast and abstinence in preparation for Easter.[3]

Archival Imposters

A number of phony saints lurk in the leaves of the *Wake* notebooks. I have already mentioned Joyce's invention of two ersatz patrons of maternity: the anticipatory "S. Delay" and the absolving "S. Miscarriage" (VI.B.8.120). Another pair of entries identifies some unfamiliar agents of supernatural (or even divine) promotion of female charm: "ᵇSaviour of the Hair / ᵇRedeemer of the Complexion" (VI.C.1.163–64). A newly minted Marian title also deserves citation: "ʳN. D. du Bon Marché" (VI.C.7.31). The French phrase (Our Lady of the Good Buy) sanctifies the actual name of a famous

Parisian department store and is transferred to the text as the "jotty young watermark" of ALP's letter paper (*FW* 112.32). In a January 20, 1926, letter to Miss Weaver, Joyce includes some local humor from the French capital: "I will just add an epigram I made. To a person asking if I go to church: O, yes, I go to mass every morning at Notre Dame de Siam and to vespers every evening at Saint Louis le Debonair" (*Letters* I.239). The long roster of official saints named "John" is inflated by an archival canonization of the author of spicy and often ribaldly anticlerical tales, "S. Giovanni Boccaccio" (VI.B.10.16). "S. Sophistory" (VI.B.27.90) could serve as the patron of the clever use of specious precedent or as an embodiment of the symbolic role of Constantinople's premier church in Eastern Christian history.

Although it is difficult to read the entry, I think that a notebook entry invents and invokes a new Spanish saint, "Por San Robo" (VI.B.15.2), as the patron of "Holy Robbery." That suspicion is supported by an adjacent appeal, "By S. Jakob," the son of the patriarch Isaac; according to the Old Testament, Jacob deftly expropriated the birthright of his elder twin, Esau, in exchange for a bowl of pottage (Genesis 25:29–34).

Joyce's appropriation of the names of trees for the participants in the wedding of "Miss Fir Conifer of Pine Valley" is one of the well-known set pieces in "Cyclops" (*U* 12.1266–95). Another archival entry illustrates his continued interest in this theme, with a hagiographical twist: "Ste. Baume / Magnolier" (VI.B.22.22). Between Marseille and Toulon in southeast France there is a limestone ridge known as the Massif de la Ste. Baume. The French noun *baume* means "balm," "unguent," and by extension "consolation"; in Provence the term also denotes a "grotto" or "cavern." Thus, the area cited in the archival note is not under the special patronage of some holy woman; rather, it is so named either for resinous products used to make chrism used in church rituals or for a sacred cave in one of its ridges. Moreover, the entry indicates that magnolia trees are found in this region, allowing Joyce to engage in concurrent cross-cultural wordplay in which the French toponym is converted into a German noun (*Baüme* means "trees"), followed by a specific example (*Magnolier*, also in German) that is noted for its fragrant flowers.

The final pair of invented saints from the *Wake* notebooks exemplifies a common category of hagiographical onomastics: abstract terms or characteristics that are used as proper—and properly descriptive—names. Perfect illustrations of this principle in action are two absolutely historical, third-century Carthaginian martyrs, St. Perpetua and St. Felicitas. The former was a young married woman who, after refusing to renounce her faith, heroically faced the attacks of wild beasts and the executioner's sword.

The latter was a youthful slave who calmly awaited death with her noble companion in the arena. Their Latin names, Felicitas (Prosperity, Happiness) and Perpetua (Everlasting), appear side by side in the prayer to martyrs during the eucharistic portion of the Mass. The liturgy thus reminds Catholics that the two brave women dwell among the saints in heaven, united in perpetual felicity. An equivalent example in the Joycean archives falls short of that standard of perfection, despite the bureaucratic determination implied in the name: "S. Thruanthru / papers not in order" (VI.B.14.119). Another personified saint, however, refuses to tolerate any detour in her march toward the pearly gates: "S. Notwithstanding" (VI.B.12.133).

St. Jingo

Gengulphus (also called Gandolfus, Gongolfus, Gingulfus, Jingo) straddles the categories of real and imaginary saints. Several martyrologies include an entry for Gengulphus, called a martyr, who lived during the reign of King Pepin the Short, Charlemagne's father. What is important for this saintly Frankish noble, however, are not the verifiable facts of his life, but its later re-creation in two disparate, yet strangely kindred works of imaginative literature. The first is a 582-line hagiographic epiclet, *Passio Sancti Gongolfi Martiris* (The Suffering of Saint Gongolfus the Martyr), in Latin elegiac couplets, by a tenth-century Benedictine nun, Hrotsvitha of Gandersheim. For my purposes, only the conclusion of Hrotsvitha's pious plot is important. After Gengulphus has been cuckolded by his wife and murdered by her lover, the relics of his corpse bring about many miraculous cures for those who visit his tomb: blind eyes are opened, deaf ears hear, crippled legs walk. The widow scorns these manifestations of the deceased Gengulphus's supernatural power by declaring that "the outermost segment of her own spine"—that is, her backside—could perform equal signs. From that moment on, whenever the unrepentant adulteress tried to speak, her words "sounded like a foul peal of farts," and she became a laughing-stock for the rest of her life.[4]

Although it is certain that Joyce would have appreciated the odd mixture of moral edification and earthy divine retribution in this tale, there is absolutely no evidence that he knew Hrotsvitha's verses. On the other hand, definite archival and textual clues indicate that Joyce was familiar with—and made use of—another equally earthy verse narrative of the life, death, and miraculous afterlife of the Burgundian saint. That evidence is found in the following notebook index:

S. Niklaus
Rich Barham

Fictitious Saints 185

    naked / students arising / from a tub of / pickled pork /
        blessed by S. N.
    S. Gengulphus
    S. Jingo
    Jingo (Basque)
    Queen Jingo
    Basques in Wales (VI.B.4.15–16)

    My search for the documentary source of the notebook entries in this curious assembly of names and a central incident began with a survey of the standard compendia. Butler does not include this saint in his roster of their lives, and Baring-Gould's terse account supplies no relevant material; even the usually undiscriminating pages of *The Golden Legend* pass over the adventures of Gengulphus. The next volume I pulled from the shelf was Joyce's favorite source of omnibus information, the eleventh edition of the *Encyclopaedia Britannica*. In that work's index the only reference to "Gengulphus" directed me to an article on "Jingo" (*EB* 6.417–18). After a brief paragraph on a legendary third-century empress of Japan by that name (Joyce's "Queen Jingo"), the article turned to various derivations suggested for the English oath "By Jingo" or "By the living Jingo." The first explanation offered is attributed to a literary joke by Richard Harris Barham in *The Ingoldsby Legends*. The *Britannica* article adds a comment that some etymologists suggest the word is a corruption of "Jainko," the Basque name for God. These items establish, beyond doubt, that the encyclopedia was Joyce's source for the notebook items cited above.

    The literary reputation of Barham (1788–1845), a country gentleman and priest in the Church of England, rests on his stories of "mirth and marvels." Many of these pieces, marked by ingenuity of rhyme and wordplay, are tales of grisly violence, rank superstition, and incredible twists of plot. A number of the most popular *Ingoldsby Legends* are, not by accident, very much like "genuine" saints' lives. Joyce knew these stories, as is indicated by several archival references to "The Jackdaw of Rheims" (*Scribbledehobble* 17 [13], VI.B.3.63–64, VI.B.31.262, VI.C.9.228).[5] Barham's "A Lay of St. Gengulphus" (published in 1840) is separated from Hrotsvitha's work by nearly a millennium, and there is nothing to suggest that he consulted her verses. Rather, it is most likely that both authors took the details of their plots from an original Latin vita. It is, nonetheless, a remarkable coincidence that a Saxon nun and an English parson-squire should create verse versions of an otherwise insignificant saint's life, and that both tales should display a moralizing comic—indeed scatological—bite.

The larger thematic relevance of "A Lay of St. Gengulphus" to the *Wake* is obvious. In a section of chapter 4, I discussed the life of Nicholas of Myra with an emphasis on the saint's resurrection of the murdered bodies of three young men from a barrel of brine. That wonderful deed is a crucial link between all the narratives involved. Joyce's notebook entries and Barham's tale both mention this miracle by the Near Eastern bishop as a parallel to St. Gengulphus/Jingo's fantastic reintegration of his own mutilated corpse. What is important for my fictitious hagiographical purposes here are the details of that feat and the moral lessons derived from it.

While the pious Gengulphus is on a pilgrimage to the Holy Land, his Lady Wife takes up with a Learned Clerk. The pair murder the unsuspecting husband on his first (and unexpected) night home. They dispose of the evidence by dismembering the corpse and hiding the pieces all over the estate. When the Prince Bishop arrives with his retinue and demands to be entertained, they are treated to an elaborate feast. Gengulphus's head, which had been thrown down the well, reappears and, on the victim's command, his entire body is reassembled, naturally to the consternation of the guilty pair and supranaturally to the amazement of the guests. Although a reward is offered for the apprehension of the persons responsible for the crime, the energy of local authorities is directed more to bluster than to detection. Meanwhile, the reconstituted limbs of Gengulphus begin to perform anatomically fitting cures. A "single touch of his precious Great Toes" healed chilblains and gout; a prayerful salute to the still-scarred nape of Gengulphus's neck rendered zealous petitioners safe from sore throat. The murdered pilgrim is declared a saint, and his hallowed limbs are encased in a shrine.

Finally, Gengulphus's bristly beard (the only portion of his body that had not been restored) grips his wife with quill-sharp tentacles when she sits in a certain chair. (The murderers had stuffed the saint's beard into its cushions.) For the rest of her life, then, she must bear this mordant "Bustle." Barham concludes his spoof of hagiographic grotesqueries with three stanzas of "Morals." The first advises returning pilgrims to send advance notice of their returns. The second admonishes learned clerks to stick to the "study of the *Vitae Sanctorum*." The third warns "gay ladies" to remember Gengulphus's wife and to reflect on the "moral enforced by her terrible tale."[6]

In *Ulysses* there are two instances of the oath invoking the saint's nickname (U 6.866 and U 15.2959); it is repeated parenthetically in the *Wake*, "(and by jingo ...)" (FW 67.2). The notebook entry "Rich Barham" and the immediately subsequent item about the three butchered youths are not crossed out in the primary index, but I suggest that their conjunction precipitates the text's "barbarihams" (*FW* 518.28). This odd compound joins the author's name with some "bare hams"—as in the naked shanks of the clerks in the brine barrel—and labels the crime that placed them there as "barbaric."

In a 1928 letter to Joyce, Ezra Pound complained about his frustration with Italian bureaucracy: "to swear . . . even by the tits of St. [*sic*] Marie des Paluds in the Genoa consulate requires a minimum of four hours."[7] The fictional guarantor of the truth of Pound's deposition is St. Mary of the Marshes; in a Joycean context she would probably have been invoked as "Our Lady of the Bogs." Generally speaking, however, that irreverent relic and title—like the tales of Sister Hrotsvitha and Parson Barham—nicely epitomize the spirit and gusto of Joyce's imaginary saints.

Sources and Parallels

After a thorough tour of the festal mansions inhabited by Joycean saints, I turn to more mundane aspects of conventional criticism. My special interest in the archival notes for *Ulysses* and *Finnegans Wake* has triggered frequent reference to their documentary sources; a summary roster of this background material helps to bring Joyce's compositional strategies into sharper focus. I also present a brief survey of several modern works in which hagiography and its scholarly trappings are part of the fictional action, usually with a humorous twist. The final paragraphs in this chapter draw some general conclusions about Joyce's vigorously comic scouring of "all the sinkts in the colander" (*FW* 432.36).

Sources

In the preface to his twelve-volume lives of the saints, the Reverend Sabine Baring-Gould writes of treading wearily "in the romance world of Irish hagiology, where the footing is as insecure as on the dark bogs of the Emerald Isle."[1] He goes on to acknowledge the inestimable help given by the "great storehouse" of information stocked by generations of Bollandists, the Jesuits whose *Acta Sanctorum* (Records of the Saints) were begun in 1643 and have yet to be completed. Baring-Gould also tips a nod to Father Alban Bulter's *Lives of the Saints*, an eighteenth-century monument to Roman Catholic research and piety. In his Trieste lecture on Ireland, Joyce acknowledges "the learning and patience of . . . leisurely Bollandist[s]" (*CW* 154), and many years later has the ostentatiously pious Shaun cite the "pleasures of a butler's life" (*FW* 189.8–9). There is, however, no biographical or archival evidence that Joyce himself actually consulted either of these massive works of scholarly reference; the "Father Butler" in "An Encounter" is a grammar-school teacher of Roman history (*D* 20).

In this regard, a quirky antiquarian essay by a member of Dublin's literati deserves brief mention; its author inhabits both the real and the fictionalized worlds in which Joyce's early works were composed. In 1905 John Eglinton, an assistant at the National Library, who appears in *Ulysses* as an affected interlocutor in the "Scylla and Charybdis" chapter, published an article entitled "The Island of Saints." Two points stand out in his torturous—and conspicuously undocumented—paragraphs. First, the ancient Celtic bards, converted by the magnetic power of Patrick's personality, were Ireland's initial saints, just as the sacred places of Druidism became the shrines of the monks. Second, Christianity never learned to express itself in Irish; the Celtic language still babbles of the fancies of its youth before Patrick, and only after the introduction of English did Ireland become a pious nationality. Although Joyce owned copies of Eglinton's essays,[2] there is no indication that the librarian's eccentric ideas contributed anything either to "Ireland, Island of Saints and Sages" or to the comedic aspects of the hagiography in Joyce's later fiction.

The documentary source of the information about the heroes of the early Irish church for Joyce's 1907 lecture in Trieste remains a mystery. The initial misinformation about the Phoenician antecedents of the Irish language and the Egyptian origins of Druidism points to some popular nineteenth- or early-twentieth-century work with introductory comments on the murky prehistory of the Emerald Isle. Two popular and specifically hagiographical works certainly supplied data for the procession of saints in *Ulysses* and for numerous archival and textual references in the *Wake*: E. A. Greene's *Saints and Their Symbols* and J. M Flood's *Ireland: Its Saints and Scholars*.[3] For the career of St. Patrick, Joyce used several studies, none of them remarkable for original research; when he did dip into academic treatises, his purpose was usually to glean odd phrases or anomalous facts. An exception to the rule of avoiding scholarly tomes is a late (1938) and highly selective foray into Canon O'Hanlon's comprehensive life of St. Kevin for several examples of the holy man's childhood miracles.[4] For incidental information on all aspects of hagiography—as on every topic under the sun—Joyce could also turn to the volumes of the *Encylopaedia Britannica* (eleventh edition, 1910–11); the original edition of the *Catholic Encyclopedia* (1907–12) supplied arcane minutiae of church history and practice. A handful of footnotes in Edward Gibbon's monumental *Decline and Fall of the Roman Empire* also made minor (but characteristically titillating) contributions to the project.

Jacques Mercanton reports a reaffirmation (see *P* 80) of Joyce's "admiration for Newman, the greatest of English prose writers"—especially for his sermons.[5] Perhaps the most famous of all the future cardinal's sermons is "The Second Spring," delivered on July 13, 1852, to mark the restoration of the Roman Catholic hierarchy in England and Wales. In the middle of that work (which was once assigned for memorization in Jesuit classes in oratory and declamation) is a ringing catalogue of English saints and martyrs, from St. Augustine of Canterbury, through St. Wilfrid of York, St. Cuthbert of Durham, St. Swithun of Winton, St. Chad of Lichfield, and ending with St. Richard of Chichester.[6] Newman's list comprises only twenty-two members, but the renown of its author and the significance of its occasion may well have contributed to the shape of Joyce's more expansive Dublin procession of saints in *Ulysses*.

In short, for his references to the deeds and memory of the saints, Irish and otherwise, Joyce certainly used all the help he could get. This material did not reappear in his fiction to argue fine points of antique ecclesiology or to chasten the hearts of his readers. Thus, popular, even propagandistic sources of ready data were usually preferred to cumbersome compendia of scrupulously documented hagiographical research. Joyce was neither a preacher nor a devil's advocate in an official process of canonization, but a writer of fiction looking for relics of local color or devoutly perverse turns of phrase in the lives of the saints. In countless instances his leisurely patience with this material was crowned with just the right burst of hallowed extravagance.

Parallels

It would be possible to draw up a considerable list of historical novels—none of them a masterpiece, but all with some cachet as popular fiction—modeled on the lives of the saints: Henryk Sienkiewicz's *Quo Vadis* is a narrative of Peter and the apostolic church; the hero of Frederick Buechner's *Godric* is the far-traveled hermit of Finchdale, near Durham, while another of his popular novels recreates the adventures of St. Brendan; Graham Greene's *The Power and the Glory* follows a flawed martyr through revolutionary Mexico; Robert Hugh Benson's apocalyptic *The Lord of the World* involves the last pope and the advent of the antichrist; Sheri Holman's *A Stolen Tongue* is a recent best-seller about medieval pilgrims and the quest for a purloined relic of St. Catherine of Alexandria and Sinai.[7]

Far fewer titles would appear on a list of novels that feature a central character dedicated to the advancement of hagiographic scholarship. There are, however, some shining examples. The fictional hero of Robertson Davies's *The Deptford Trilogy* (1970–75), Dunstan Ramsay, has published a popular volume, *A Hundred Saints for Travellers*, and is working on a more substantial monograph, *The Saints: A Study in History and Popular Mythology*. During the first novel of the trilogy, Ramsay's article on St. Wilgefortis-Kümmernis (the bearded princess and virgin martyr) is accepted by the Jesuit editor for publication in *Analecta Bollandiana*.[8]

A considerably more fervent hagiographer appears in the highly autobiographical fiction of Joris Karl Huysmans. In a 1903 review of a totally undistinguished French religious novel, Joyce makes a brief comparison: "Huysmans is daily growing more formless and more obviously comedian in his books [so] that Paris has begun to be wearied by the literary oblate" (*CW* 123). The final term in that excerpt is an allusion to Huysmans's latest book, *L'Oblat*, the fourth novel in the sequence *Là-Bas* (1891), *En Route* (1895), and *La Cathédrale* (1898). The tetralogy traces the spiritual career of M. Durtal from Satanism through a Trappist retreat, an aesthetic interlude at Chartres, and a period as a lay attendant at a Benedictine monastery. A common stylistic device in all these works is the catalogue of useless information, usually about ecclesiastical trivia, that Huysmans injects on every other page of each of these self-reflecting novels, presumably to prove that he has done his contextual homework. For readers who need a compact review of the names and missions of various Catholic religious orders, for example, the following paragraph is sufficient:

> The Jesuits, Franciscans, Redemptorists, Dominicans, and others preach, give missions and retreats; others keep schools; others, like the Sulpiciens and the Lazarites manage seminaries. Others, again, take care of the sick, or, like the Carthusians and the Cistercians, make reparation for the evil and the sin that is in the world; finally, others, like the Benedictines of the Congregation of France devote themselves especially to the service of the Liturgy and to praising God.[9]

Nowhere in the novels of Huysmans are such excrescences more frequent or more pronounced than in the avalanche of religious data that overpowers the text of *The Cathedral*. For the elevation of a new bishop, the streets of Chartres are enlivened by a procession of nuns in habits of every hue, choirs in surplices, seminarians in cassocks, priests in vestments, and the consecrand himself, with mitre and crozier.[10] Durtal is treated to several pages of initiation into the varieties of "the odour of sanctity": "Saint Treverius exhaled a fragrance compounded of roses, lilies, balm, and incense; Saint Rose of Viterbo smelt of roses; Saint Cajetan of orange blossom; Saint Catherine Ricci of violets; Saint Teresa by turns of lily, jasmine and violet; Saint Thomas Aquinas of incense; Saint Francis of Paul of musk." The other side of these fragrances was the stench of the demons: "the essential odour of the devil is amply recorded in the life of Christina of Stumbela . . . [as] has been preserved by the Bollandists." This introduction to the tortures of that holy woman is followed by several paragraphs of explicit description of every type of "infernal filth."[11]

Other items of hagiographical trivia recorded in Huysmans's novel include an item about "Saint Lawrence [O'Toole] of Dublin, who, by way of food, was content to dip his bread in the water clothes had been washed in." There are interesting catalogues of the diseases assigned to various saints for healing and the members of the human body as allegorical emblems, including the fact that "the nose meant discretion. . . . The knees the sacrament of penance. . . . The bowels the mysterious precepts of the Lord . . . [and] the bones hardness of heart."[12]

Just before summarizing the infinite details of the life and tribulations of Mother Mary Margaret [Van Valckenissen] of the Angels—including the fact that her corpse did not decompose, "but assumed the golden brown colour of a date"—Durtal reveals his own desire to write the life of Lydwine of Schiedam.[13] In a factual pursuit of fiction, Huysmans translated his character's wish into print and, just before the publication of *The Oblate*, produced a full-scale life of Blessed Lydwine of Schiedam.[14] Since that fervent Dutch nun was never canonized, the work is not, strictly speaking, a formal hagiographic vita; nevertheless, it is, in deed and intent, a work of serious scholarship, even though the emphasis on its subject's physical and psychological traumata reads like a recherché parody of the genre, composed by a God-struck author with a barely latent sadomasochistic streak.[15] Although Joyce does not mention the life of Blessed Lydwine, he is certainly correct in labeling the later works of Huysmans as the books of an unwitting "comedian." It is one thing to list the allegories and types of Virgin Mary in the Old Testament; it is another thing to end a novel with a prayer to the "Holy Temptress of men, Our Lady of the Pillar, Virgin of the Crypt." The former endeavor is an exercise in traditional Catholic exegesis; the latter choice of diction (at least in its English translation) is a Freudian lapse of laughable proportions.

For all of the reasons presented in the last few paragraphs—including his citation in one of Joyce's early reviews—I am convinced that Huysmans's pervasive and frequently eccentric hagiography was a model for some of the saintly shenanigans in *Ulysses* and *Finnegans Wake*. Indeed, Atherton suggests direct Wakean allusion both to a dinner party at which all the food ("caviare, truffle jellies"), servers ("naked negresses"), and table settings were black and to the title of *La Cathédrale:* "a blackfrinch pliestrycook . . . a cathedral of lovejelly" (*FW* 486.17–18).[16]

During the same year (1929) that versions of the "work in progress" (III.3–4) were appearing in *transition*, that Parisian journal also published Gertrude Stein's *Four Saints in Three Acts*. The plot, diction, and hagiographical point of this libretto, subtitled "An Opera to Be Sung," go nowhere, laboriously. Given the mutual indifference between Joyce and Stein (with the notable exception of "gert stoan" [*FW* 287.19]), the probability of literary allusion to her work in the *Wake* is very low. Although *Four Saints* features a minor catalogue of genuine and imaginary holy men and women in its prelude and intermittently thereafter, Stein's primary hagiographical achievement is tedious invocation of Saint Ignatius and Saint Therese. Joyce's "Alis, alas, she broke the glass!" (*FW* 270.20–21) and Stein's "Pigeons on the grass alas" share a common exclamation and catchy iambic conclusion, but there is no textual or archival evidence to suggest saintly parody.[17]

Frank McCourt's recent best-selling memoir of his childhood in Limerick also involves some surrealistic hagiography. To avoid the rain one day, the young McCourt dips into the local library. There he discovers the shelf loaded with the volumes of Butler's *Lives of the Saints* and begins to peruse the "stories about virgins, martyrs, virgin martyrs." Those topics prompt several trips to the dictionary to check out the meaning of "inviolate chastity," "intercourse," and "intromission." The lexical wild-goose chase propels him back to the narrative of "St. Christina the Astonishing who takes ages to die." She flings her amputated breasts at the Roman judge, who "goes deaf and blind"; finally the magistrates "have her head cut off and that does the job." St. Christina's feast is July 24. In honor of the lurid details of the saint's last hours, McCourt adds that day to the anniversary of his own patron, St. Francis of Assisi (October 4). When the rain stops, the librarian gives the boy a note to take home to his mother: "I think, Mrs. McCourt, you might have a future priest on your hands and I will light a candle in hopes it comes true."[18]

Conclusion

If writers as different as those just discussed—not to mention Cardinal Newman, in an unguarded comment on modern relics—could pluck potentially comic material from the dusty bins of hagiography, so could James Joyce. McCourt's encounter with Butler's *Lives* involved vocabulary-building, reproductive biology ("the copulative organ of any male animal"), and sadistic contempt of imperial Roman courts. Davies's research into the cult of a supranaturally hirsute virgin martyr triggered the introduction into his plot of the bearded lady of *Le grand Cirque forain de St. Vite*. Huysmans's fascination with parochial Flemish holy women and obscure apparitions may have been intended to steer his neurasthenic hero away from black masses and into an aesthetically pleasing cloister, but they are, in contextual terms, faintly ridiculous.

In his early works, Joyce's deployment of hagiography is never blatantly heterodox, usually more ironic than overtly comic. The alteration of dates (July 1 to 2) in versions of "The Sisters" ensures that the fallible Father Flynn dies on the movable Feast of the Most Precious Blood; the shadow of the stalwart St. Tarcisius falls across the beginning of "Araby." Both of these inconspicuous allusions to the heroic traditions of Western Christianity are designed as muted contrasts to the humdrum rhythms of daily life in Dublin. The apparently casual mention of Francis Xavier's "powerless" right arm in *Portrait* is a covert reference to the saint's potent relic, exhausted by record-setting baptisms.

It is appropriate (and providential) that no important saints are commemorated on June 16, thereby permitting a new feast to take its title from its Ulyssean patron—a name forever fragrant in fictional sanctity. The procession of prelates, priests, and saints in "Cyclops" is a primary contribution to the roster of Joycean hagiography. The holy men and women on parade in *Ulysses* are accompanied by suitable emblems, symbols, and relics. Their function in that section of the novel is mock-heroic counterpoint—grand, but enough off-kilter to generate a laugh from the connoisseur of religious trivia.

By far the most concerted statement about saints by Joyce in his pre-*Wake* years is a 1907 lecture in Trieste on Ireland's cultural and political history. The audience and the medium (the talk was delivered in Italian) precluded subtle humor, although Joyce does seem to twit the Gaelic League for the fact that, until recently, the "only Irish grammars and dictionaries that existed in Europe . . . were the works of Germans" (*CW* 155). The primary thrust of the first section of Joyce's presentation is his accolade of the Celtic missionaries who introduced Christianity and the remnants of classical learning into northern Europe. Brave Irish monks (and an occasional British colleague, like St. Boniface) denounced the tribal religions, chopped down holy oaks, baptized pagan Gauls, Franks, and Germans by the droves, and set up monasteries. Joyce demonstrates that his remote ancestors, as it were, participated, spiritually and intellectually, in the growth of European culture. In his catalogue of the achievements of these "wanderers for Christ" there is no hint that a putatively anti-colonial Joyce was embarrassed by either the motives or the hegemonic results of their divinely inspired mission.

Saints and their paraphernalia are scattered throughout *Finnegans Wake,* with only the usual attempts to disguise their hallowed presence in that traveling circus of cross-cultural wonders. Founders and confessors jostle Celtic navigators and a Persian recusant; the genders of holy men and women are miraculously transformed, while hermits are exhibited in urban carnivals. All feasts are movable and, by the "Holybones of Saint Hubert" (*FW* 31.25), no relic is authentic. In a sustained and profane comedy of the universal condition, the realm of the sacred is turned topsy-turvy—like St. Peter on his cross in Neronian Rome.

The evidence presented in the foregoing chapters illustrates the many aspects of Joyce's manipulation of hagiography. His success in that curious enterprise is accurately mirrored in a tribute written in honor of St. Jerome. In the turbulent fourth century, to prepare for his translation of the Bible into Latin, the language of Western Christianity, Jerome retired into the desert to learn Hebrew, Greek, and Aramaic. Joyce's friend (and one of the translators of *Ulysses* into French), Valery Larbaud, composed a homage to the venerable patron of that project. At the end of his essay, Larbaud visualizes Jerome, scholar and saint, listening to the compliments:

> From heaven on high, surrounded by his court of glossaphile, grammarian and lexicographic angels . . . who work under his guidance on the never ending Dictionary of *all* languages ever spoken or to be spoken by Adam's children, he is listening kindly.[19]

Not to cut the point too finely, that scenario can be applied, equally and equitably, to James Joyce and his mastery of "haggiography" (*FW* 234.12).

Notes

1. Introduction

1. *JJII* 581, n., and 798, n. 17.
2. *Letters* III.180.
3. For Beach's invitation (6/23/28), a facsimile of Fitzgerald's reply, and the drawing, see Fitzgerald, *Correspondence*, 218; a facsimile of Joyce's note (7/11/28) is reproduced on 219. Also see *Letters* III.180 for Joyce's note and a photograph of Fitzgerald's sketch (illustration 27, after page 192).
4. Joyce himself also contributed to the process of exaltation; in a letter to Edmond Jaloux (7/23/39) that includes a comic verse, he refers to himself as "Mr. James Saint-James," "Joyce Saint James," and "James Saint Joyce"; see Joyce, "Trois lettres a Edmond Jaloux," *L'Herne: Joyce*, 137.
5. See Knowles, *Enterprises*, and the memoir by Herbert Thurston, in appendix I to Attwater's edition of Butler's *Lives of the Saints*, IV.651–66.
6. See Giraldus, *Ireland*, nos. 107 and 105.
7. The calendar that is cited as marking the Irish St. Fursa "as the precursor of Dante Alighieri" (*CW* 236) could not be a reference to Gorman's martyrology, which was composed a century before Dante's birth.
8. Giedion-Welcker, "Meetings," 268–69. By pure coincidence, Alban Butler, the author of the famous eighteenth-century *Lives of the Saints*, notes the following fact in his preface: "The duke of Joyeuse, marshal of France, owed his perfect conversion to the reading of the life of St. Francis Borgia" (*Lives* I.xxxii).
9. See the detailed entry on "Patron Saints" in the *Catholic Encyclopedia* XI.562–67; its section on Ireland notes a local exception in the "titles" of churches in Dublin: although they all had appropriate patrons, a parish was customarily "known simply by the name of the street in which it is situated, as 'the Jesuit church in Gardiner Street'" (564).
10. For a discussion of these details and other elements in this story and its revisions, see Schork, "Liturgical Irony," 193–97.
11. See Tylenda, *Jesuit Saints*, 190–93.
12. Byrne, *Silent Years*, 86–87; and *Letters* I.137; also note, *P* 242, and *U* 17.1707.
13. Stanislaus Joyce, *Complete Dublin Diary*, 89.
14. In a November 11, 1921, letter to Miss Weaver, Joyce notes birthday coinci-

dences for the first serial publication of *Portrait* and for the start and finish of *Ulysses* (*Letters* III.52).

15. Joyce's probable source for this calculation was the "Calendar" article in the *Britannica* (*EB* 4.1001). This section of the *Wake* was indeed composed in the summer of 1927 (47473-128v [*JJA* 47.112] and 47473-70 [*JJA* 47.118]).

16. The phrase is used in the title of an article that attempts (without much success) to determine the "dramatic" date (April 1, 1904) that Joyce intended for the action of the *Wake;* see Bates, "Feast," 174–87. Another, equally unconvincing, stab at the *Wake's* date is found in Gordon, *Plot Summary,* 37–43.

17. See Rose's brief discussion of this index and some of its odd attribution of symbols in *JJA* 39.xv.

18. When Joyce found a notebook entry that could be used in the evolving text, he usually crossed out that item with a colored pencil; uncrossed entries (few of which appear in the text) are valuable as traces of Joyce's archival imagination at work and at play.

19. See Schork, "Priestly Penrose," 564–66, for comment on the saint's conspicuous "modesty of the eyes."

20. See Rose, *Textual Diaries,* 71–72.

21. See Schork, "Eastern Orthodox Church," 116–19.

22. Butler's *Lives of the Saints,* which occasionally revels in the gory details of a martyrdom, does not disappoint in this instance. In two pages the reader is taken through the excision of each finger and toe, hand and arm, foot and leg; when Jacob's Christian comrades came to collect the relics of his body, they were directed to precisely twenty-eight different spots where these pieces had been scattered (*Lives* IV.415–16). In the interests of mathematical accuracy and anatomical verisimilitude, I must point out that the executioners finally beheaded Jacob—and likely would not have omitted specific attention to the "bough" at the base of his saintly "trunk." Thus the total of all pieces to be located and placed in a hallowed tomb should be thirty.

23. See P. Brown, *Cult,* for a brilliant discussion of the origins of this process in Latin Christianity; a lively account of the illegal trade in relics is found in Geary, *Furta Sacra.*

24. See Schork, "Victorian Hagiography," 296.

25. The French word is cognate with the Middle English "mow" (grimace); "jeremiad" is derived from the name of the vituperative Old Testament prophet Jeremiah.

26. Two examples of recent source-based genetic studies of Patrician material in the *Wake* are Skrabanek, "Nightmare Confession," and McHugh, "Dean Kinane."

27. See Deane, "Wellspring," 1–27.

28. For textual and bibliographic details, see Schork, "Sheep, Bones," 151–62; also note a cameo appearance of Canon O'Hanlon in *Ulysses,* as he celebrates Benediction at Mary, Star of the Sea, Church in "Nausicaa" (*U* 13.448, 492, and following).

29. Curtius, *European Literature,* 425–28.

30. Although my perspective and approach are different, my views in this matter seem quite similar to those of Father Robert Boyle, who quotes Joyce's comrade,

Frank Budgen, to more or less the same effect (see *Pauline Vision*, 78–79). On the other hand, Beryl Schlossman's quirky presentation of the evidence for Joyce's Catholic *jouissance* does not, in my judgment, cohere (see *Catholic Comedy*, ix–xxvi and throughout).

2. Archangels; Saints in the Gospels

1. For brief comment on this topic, see Schork, "Citron," 414–18; neither the background nor the interpretations of Moseley, *Joyce and the Bible*, can be regarded as authoritative.

2. In Joyce's Trieste library there were four Bibles: the Authorized Version (King James), an Italian translation, a Vulgate (Latin) edition, and a volume of Old Testament apocrypha (see Gillespie, *Trieste Library*, 48–49 [52–55]); the only even marginally scriptural text recorded as present in his Paris library was a collection of New Testament apocrypha (see Connolly, *Personal Library*, 29 [211]).

3. For a discussion of some of the details of the Miltonic version of the defeat of the bad angels, see Hogan, *Milton*, and Schork, "Nodebinding," 69–83.

4. Attwater and John, *Penguin Dictionary of Saints*, 255.

5. See Troy, *Mummeries*; Rose, *Chapters*; and Bishop, *Book of the Dark*, 86–125 and his exhaustive notes.

6. See text and illustrations in Silverman, *Ancient Egypt*, 133–37.

7. After a painful eye operation in June, Joyce spent July and August of 1924 (when notebook VI.B.14 was composed) in Brittany, but there is no evidence that he visited Amiens, a distance of well over 200 miles.

8. The *Penguin Dictionary of Saints* also suggests that a reminiscence of the archangel Michael's role as "the receiver of the souls of the dead" may lie behind a "contemporary popular song, of American Negro folk origin, 'Michael, row the boat ashore! Alleluia!'" Since there is no evidence that Joyce knew this song, contemplation of the problem is prudently left to comparative musicologists. If he had heard about Michael rowing the boat, Joyce would have been able to make the connection with Charon, the Greco-Roman ferryman who transported the souls of the dead across the River Styx into the underworld.

9. See Walzl, "Gabriel and Michael," 17–31, for the first of several attempts to construct an onomastic allegory from Joyce's choice of these significant names in the final story of *Dubliners*.

10. In a comment on Joyce's use of flower symbolism, Stuart Gilbert quotes Madame Blavatsky to the dubious iconographic effect that the "sprig of lilies placed in the hand of the archangel who offers them to the Virgin Mary . . . have precisely the same meaning" as the lotus (*Study*, 44).

11. The preface to Mary's biblical reply to the angel, "Behold the handmaid of the Lord" (Luke 1:38), is echoed several times in the *Wake*: "Behose our handmades for the lured!" (*FW* 239.10); "behoves you handmake of the load" (*FW* 278.11–12); "behold, she had instantt with her handmade as to graps the myth inmid the air" (*FW* 561.26–27; also note VI.C.3.56).

12. See McHugh, "Protevangelium," 20; Joyce's source of information is Orr's translation of New Testament apocrypha (Connolly, *Personal Library*, 29 [211]); there are two archival loci for entries from this source: VI.B.11.25 and VI.C.1.97–98.

13. The gospels also mention that Jesus was a carpenter: "Is this not the carpenter, the son of Mary?" (Mark 6:3). That tradition is reflected in a *Ulysses* note ("ᵇHe told her J. C. was a Socialist carpenter" [*UNBM* 502:6]) and in the text ("he [Bloom] said about Our Lord being a carpenter . . . and the first socialist" [*U* 18.175–78]).

14. For the possibility of a blasphemous imputation of sexual perversion on St. Joseph's part, see Gifford and Seidman, *"Ulysses" Annotated*, 556.

15. See Ryan, *Golden Legend*, II.153.

16. There is an amusing anecdote about Joyce's recitation of the dance of Salome passage from Flaubert's "Herodian"—and his pedantic quibble about an inappropriate adverb—in Parandowski's memoir (see "Meeting," 159–60).

17. In the *Wake* an isolated "Zachary" appears beside an equally biblical—and elderly—"Toobiassed" (*FW* 580.8), but I see no necessary connection with the Baptist's aged father.

18. As a matter of eponymous hagiographical fact, the historical church of San Giovanni fuore Porta Latina is dedicated to Saint John the Apostle and Evangelist, not the Baptist. The *Portrait* passage appears in the "diary" section, but the assigned date (March 21) for the comment on Cranly has no connection with feasts for any of the scores of St. Johns honored by the Church.

19. See Ryan, *Golden Legend*, II.137–39, for legends on the discovery of John's head.

20. In several European languages variations of the word "lazar" denote a leper; the etymology depends on another New Testament Lazarus, the miserable beggar in Luke 16:19–31. St. James the Less was the patron of those inflicted with the disease; hence "through Sant Iago by his cocklehat, good Lazar, deliver us" (*FW* 41.2).

21. See Gifford and Seidman, *"Ulysses" Annotated*, 90, for additional comment on this passage, including a reference to the dubious "old master." It is also interesting to note that Edouard Dujardin, the author of *Les Lauriers sont coupés*, visited Zürich in 1917 to produce his play *Marthe et Marie*. He and Joyce, however, did not meet at that time (*JJII* note 411).

22. Since she has loaned her name to colleges at Oxford and Cambridge, as well as to a period in the Old Stone Age, there are undoubtedly other oblique allusions to Magdalene's tenure as a university patron in the *Wake*. My review covers those with obvious New Testament origins.

3. The Apostolic Age

1. For a Homeric-Hesiodic prefiguration of the *Wake's* contrastive use of a rock and a tree, see Schork, *Greek*, 66–67.

2. A footnote in McHugh's *Annotations* mentions C. K. Ogden, *Notes in Basic English on the Anna Livia Phirabelle Records*, and comments, "(J appears to have collaborated in the production of these notes [for Joyce's recording of an early version of this episode])"; also see *JJII* 637.

3. In ecclesiastical history, Peter and Paul do not espouse rival positions, nor do they play a prominent typological role in Joyce's chronicle of the acts of the frequently combative Shaun and Shem (see Devlin, "Self and Other," 31–50). An archival note links their apostolic relics: "Palladius, relics of Peter Paul" (VI.B.14.37); the source of Joyce's information here is a nineteenth-century life of St. Patrick (see McHugh, "Dean Kinane," 26).

4. Earlier in the same chapter of *Ulysses*, there is a reference to the authority of the man "that holdeth the fisherman's seal, even that blessed Peter" (*U* 14.250–51). Although the canonical and apocryphal scriptures contain no hint that St. Peter was ever involved in the chemical-condiment trade, Joyce suggests just that. Along with some fellows named "Acetius [Vinegary] and Oleosus [Olive-Oily] and Sellius Volatilis [Salty Swifty]," the Fisher of Men appears as "Petrus Papricus [Rocky Peppers]" (*FW* 161.25–26). For interesting insight into the socioeconomic status of those involved in the Galilean fish industry, see Murphy-O'Connor, "Fishers."

5. It is interesting to note that the "prophecies" of pseudo-Malachy (a number of which appear in *FW* 155–57) forecast that the name of the *last* pope before the destruction of the world will be *Petrus Romanus* (see Rose, "Prophetia," 27–28).

6. During his seven-month stay in Rome from the end of July 1906 to early March 1907, Joyce paid several tourist's visits to St. Peter's (*Letters* II.145 and 152). In the first *Wake* catalogue of Dublin parishes, there is also a church dedicated to Peter's colleague, "Paull-the-Aposteln" (*FW* 569.8). In *Ulysses* the phrase "Paul's men" (*U* 14.537) appears in a cluster of archaic terms referring to low-life characters. Gifford and Seidman gloss the phrase as "loungers" who once gathered in "the nave of St. Paul's [Church] in London" (*"Ulysses" Annotated*, 423). An archival note records a minutia of apostolic topography: "S. Paul without the Walls / to our doors" (VI.B.19.82). The Church of St. Paul outside the Walls is one of the four patriarchal basilicas in Rome. When Catholic bishops make their required quinquennial visits *ad limina apostolorum* (to the doorsteps of the apostles) to the Holy City, they traditionally visit this basilica, containing the tomb of St. Paul.

7. Joyce is correct in noting that the same pun is present in the Aramaic word for "stone," *cephas*, as is recorded in John's version of Peter's call (John 1:42) (see *Oxford Companion to the Bible*, 695).

8. It may be just coincidence, but on the same page of the *Wake* it is revealed that "to all his foretellers he [HCE] reared a *stone* and for all his comethers he planted a *tree*" (*FW* 135.4–5; my emphases). The inclusion of "Peter Roche" (*FW* 449.16) in another cluster of saints' names may appear to be nothing more than a bit of Greco-Anglo-Gallic wordplay (*roche* is French for "rock"), but there is a genuine St. Roche who is discussed in a later chapter.

9. Ryan, *Golden Legend*, I.315.

10. McHugh records that the term "romescot" (*FW* 159.19), which appears in the heavily papal "Mookse and Gripes" episode, is Old English for "Peter's pence."

11. See Schork, *Latin*, 95–96.

12. See Hart, *Structure and Motif*, 245.

13. For a somewhat different view, from a far more informed theological perspec-

tive, see the comments of the distinguished Jesuit critic Robert Boyle. His book, *James Joyce's Pauline Vision: A Catholic Exposition*, is filled with suggestions of every sort; most of his insights, however, are more germane to a study of the biblical contributions to Joyce's fiction.

14. I owe this citation to Gifford and Seidman, *"Ulysses" Annotated*, 571. St. Paul's persistent travels to spread the word are held up to a bit of humor in *Stephen Hero*. Stephen said to Maurice: "Protestant Orthodoxy is like Lauty McHale's dogs; it goes a bit of the road with everyone. —It seems to me that S. Paul trained that dog, said Maurice" (*SH* 112).

15. See Gillespie, *Trieste Library*, 94–95 (161); Joyce's first note from these volumes is from I.55, the second from I.413.

16. See Schork, "Graphic Exercise," 3513–54.

17. See Schork, *Latin*, 249–51.

18. Kopper, "Joyce's *FW*," item 34; for a comment on the gruesome details of Bartholomew's execution, see Ryan, *Golden Legend*, II.112–13.

19. Joyce's comment is to the point here: "Whether he [Wilde] was innocent or guilty of the charges brought against him, he undoubtedly was a scapegoat" (*CW* 203–4); see Schork, "Sheep, Goats," 200–211.

20. Slote, "Wilde Thing," 107. Two earlier studies are Walton, "Wilde at the *Wake*," 300–312, and Pesch, *Wilde about Joyce*.

21. Hanks and Hodges, *A Dictionary of Surnames*, 185; the Irish name is derived from a root *flaith(eamh)* meaning "prince," "ruler." Thus, there is an additional contrast between a royal name (Irish) and a typical servile name (Greek).

22. See Walton, "Wilde at the *Wake*," 306–10.

23. The evidence for a covert canonization of HCE as a "Hairy Hermit" of Egypt is presented in the final section of chapter 5.

24. The title *De Profundis* (Out of the Depths) is traditionally assigned to Psalm 130 (Vulgate 129) from its opening words in Latin. Joyce plays with this phrase: "in this profundust" (*FW* 535.29), "deprofound" (*FW* 58.9), "upers the deprofundity" (*FW* 394.31), and, in a passage filled with references to Wilde and his works, "Hence his deepraised words" (*FW* 536.25).

25. The complete text of the document is in Wilde, *Letters*, 423–511; for a discussion of its purposes and impact, see Ellmann, *Oscar Wilde*, 510–15.

26. Wilde, *Letters*, 513. There is also a marvelous anecdote about Wilde's performance in a perfunctory Oxford examination in Divinity: he was asked to translate Acts 27 from Greek into English; when told to stop, Wilde said to the examiner (Professor W. H. Spooner) that the story "was all about a man named Paul, who . . . was caught in a terrible storm . . . but do you know, Mr Spooner, he was saved . . . and I thought of coming to tell you" (cited from Ellmann, *Oscar Wilde*, 64–65).

27. Suetonius, *Life of Augustus*, 68: *solitusque sit crura suberere nuce ardenti, quo mollior pilus surgeret.*

28. For other examples of use of Suetonius' *Lives*, see Schork, *Latin*, 69–72, 210–11. For an oblique treatment of the general topic of Joyce's deployment of homosexual themes, see Rabaté, "Sodomy," 159–66.

29. It is also possible to see another pervasive Wakean theme at work in the passage being discussed. "Toumaria" sounds like "tomorrow"; the first five letters of "*Antea*ch" spell the Latin adverb meaning "beforehand," "prior." The pair of words suggests a time-warp in which tomorrow is placed before ("prepositus") the past. The Russian root *slom* means "to tear," "to destroy"; the *Wake*'s "slomtime" may signal a destruction of conventional distinctions in time. If one wishes to avoid multilingual philological motifs here, there is also the possibility that "Toumaria" is meant to suggest "Samaria"; after Saul's conversion the "churches throughout Judea, Galilee, and *Samaria* were now left in peace" (*Acts* 9:31; my emphasis).

30. For a compact discussion of the form and variations of this document, see McCarthy, "Last Epistle," 725–33.

31. The "holey corner" is close to the phrase "hole and corner," which means "secretly"; "holi-poli" might be Greek for the "entire city" (*holē polis*) or the "mob" (*hoi polloi)*; "whollyisland" refers to all of Ireland or to the famous monastic holy island of Lindisfarne.

32. In the nearby mention of "Paoli's where the poules go" (*FW* 117.24–25), McHugh detects a reference to Hamburg's Sankt Pauli red-light district.

33. There is nothing similar to this type of allusion in *Ulysses*; the occasional references to the Pauline epistles are fairly straightforward (e.g., *U* 12.1489, *U* 14.226). In his 1912 broadside "Gas from a Burner," Joyce alludes to a play by George Moore, *The Apostle*, in which St. Paul and Christ meet: "And a play on the Word and Holy Paul / And some woman's legs that I can't recall" (*CW* 243). The reference is to Eunice, the mother of Timothy, one of Paul's early disciples (cf. 2 Timothy 2:25). In the preface to his drama, Moore hypothesizes on the possibility of a romance between Eunice and Paul.

34. The names are a very late (1938) addition to the text; see *JJA* 55:448, 471, 534.

35. See footnotes 4 and 5 in Slote, "Wilde Thing," 103.

36. The term "christlikeness" is applied to HCE in this passage, and it is true that Wilde evokes the example of Christ and the man "who would lead a Christ-like life" (Wilde, *Letters*, 476–89); on the other hand, there is an early archival item that needs to be mentioned here: the entry "Christlikeness" (VI.B.2.24) appears in the midst of a list that has to do with religion, not Oscar Wilde. Also note the report that Wilde regarded Major J. O. Nelson, the warden near the end of his term in Reading jail, as "the most Christlike man I ever met" (Ellmann, *Oscar Wilde*, 507). This mixture of archival and allusive urges caution in the area of general conclusions from selective evidence.

37. See Mink, *Gazetteer*, 373, for geographical data; for "kish-lak," see Partridge, *Dictionary of the Underworld*, 387.

4. The Early Church

1. *Apologeticus* 50.13; also see VI.B.1.102 for a compact Joycean list of pagan luxuries that Tertullian forbids (its immediate source is a passage from Gibbon, *Decline and Fall*, chapter 15, footnote 90).

2. This entry, from a January–February 1924 *Wake* notebook, is a very early use of the ⌐⌐ siglum.

3. There is no evidence that Joyce knew the fifteenth-century *Legends of Holy Women* by Osbern Bokenham, but no fan of hagiography should miss the modern translation by Sheila Delany, *A Legend*.

4. Saints Agatha, Juliana, and Eulalia are officially commemorated during February.

5. In Christian art the severed breasts often look like small loaves of bread or pastries. A Joycean note confirms this perspective: "pankin 5/ii shewbread" (VI.B.32.37); a "pankin" is a small earthenware pan or bowl; February 5 is St. Agatha's feast day; "shewbread" are the loaves placed on the sacred table as an offering to Yahweh (Exodus 25:30).

6. Ryan, *Golden Legend*, I.157; St. Agatha's cult also spread to Dublin, where a church was dedicated to her, on William Street, North (*U* 10.111, *FW* 569.14, *FW* 601.20). Although there is no archival evidence that Joyce used the information, *The Golden Legend* derives the name of a kindred virgin martyr, St. Agnes, from *agna*, the Latin noun for "lamb," and has her appear after her death with "a lamb whiter than snow standing at her right hand" (I.101–3).

7. Ryan, *Golden Legend*, I.193.

8. McHugh glosses "tubberbunnies" with "Tobberbunny: village, Co. Dublin ('milk well')"; what is intended by "tuggerfunnies" is unclear.

9. As Gifford and Seidman indicate, St. Barbara is also associated with towers (*"Ulysses" Annotated*, 527); hence the nearby presence of *"the high barbacans of the tower"* (*U* 15.4690).

10. For another possible model for Joyce's Francophone bearded lady, see Schork, "Apollinaire," 166–72.

11. An inconspicuous endnote is the proper venue for comment on the former saint Philomena. Her cult began when the bones of a young woman, a veil with traces of what was assumed to be blood, and an inscription ("Peace be with you, Philomena") were discovered in a Roman catacomb. Devotion to her memory is a product of the nineteenth and early twentieth century, but nothing at all is known of her life and the word "Philomena" itself may not be a proper name, but a Greek participle for "beloved [woman]." In a revision of the Roman Catholic martyrology in 1961, Philomena was removed from the list of saints. That latter-day ecclesiastical decision could not have disbarred her Wakean selection as the baptismal patroness of "Philomena O'Farrell" (*FW* 212.12–13).

12. This material (which is the topic of a long notebook index [VI.B.4.256–60]) has also tickled the fancy of several contributors to *AWN*; see Atherton, "Sus in Cribro," 111–13, and Rose, "Prophetia," 27–28; the latter piece identifies Joyce's likely source for the prophetic mottoes. Inge Landuyt (Antwerp) has also identified two popular French guidebooks on the Vatican and Pope Pius XI as the sources (in several long indices in notebook VI.B.3) of Joyce's information on pontifical details.

13. I cite this version of the well-known anecdote from the *Britannica* article on Gregory (*EB* 12.566).

14. There is a purely classical parallel to this motif, the Spartan boy who hid a vicious fox cub in his tunic to avoid detection; see Hopkins, "Spartan Boys," 222–24.

15. Hahn, "Tarsicius," 381–85. In *Stephen Hero* (195) there is a reference to *Callista*, Cardinal Newman's 1856 novel about the church of the martyrs.

16. Ryan, *Golden Legend*, II.67; see Curtius, *European Literature*, 125–26.

17. See Ryan, *Golden Legend*, II.240. One of his closest Parisian friends reports that Joyce "was astonished that Saint Denis meant nothing to the French" (Mercanton, "Hours," 219). From both national and devotional points of view, I cannot explain Gerty MacDowell's exclamation in "Nausicaa": "holy saint Denis" (*U* 13.395). In his Trieste lecture on Ireland's saints and sages, Joyce himself confused the Parisian Dionysius with his namesake, "Dionysius, the pseudo-Areopagite" (*CW* 160).

18. Two other notebook entries involve St. Denis, at least tangentially: "^{g}beheaded squelette / ^{g}no ghost (S. Denis)" (VI.C.13.51). The word "squelette" refers to the custom of beheading the corpses of suspected vampires to prevent them from continuing to wander the earth. In Sheridan Le Fanu's ghost story "Carmilla" (which Joyce certainly read) the remains of several vampires are decapitated. In the reuse in the *Wake* of two notes just cited, no specifically vampiric circumstance is indicated: "and prompt poor Marcus Lyons to be not beheeding the skillet on for the live of ghosses" (*FW* 397.21–22).

19. Gibbon, *Decline and Fall*, chapter 39, footnote 100; I have translated the French: "La distance n'y fait rein; il n'y a que le premier pas qui coute."

20. See Ryan, *Golden Legend*, I.238–42.

21. In addition to the impressive Ionic columns of the church's facade, Stuart Gilbert reports that it is the only church in the Irish capital with an inscription in Greek (*Study*, 371). In the first catalogue of Dublin churches in the *Wake*, Joyce specifically acknowledges this distinction: "S. George-le-Greek" (*FW* 569.7).

22. See Aravantinou, *Ta Hellenika*, 121–39, and Schork, *Greek*, 240–44.

23. See Schork, *Sacred Song*, 196–206.

24. For Gibbon's view of the incident, see *Decline and Fall*, chapter 16; the skeptical historian's caustic footnotes to this chapter are the sources for several other Joycean allusions; more—and more sympathetic—detail about the alleged miracle is found in Ryan, *Golden Legend*, II.188–92.

25. The best-known version of this incident is found in *The Golden Legend* (II.188–92), which includes the exact number of soldiers slain; briefer notice also occurs in another familiar source, Gibbon, *Decline and Fall*, chapter 16, footnote 144.

26. See Etter, *Zürcher Stadtheiligen;* Joyce offers these literal translations of the patrons' names in a 1933 letter from Zürich to Frank Budgen (*Letters* III.336).

27. For the immediate documentary source of this item, see Rose, "Kells," 6–7 and 12.

28. Even Leopold Bloom was able to cite the authority of these great teachers of Christian doctrine. In "Nausicaa" when the ceremony at Our Lady, Star of the Sea, Church causes him to wonder about several "mysteries," Bloom concludes his reverie with: "Liberty and exaltation of our holy mother the Church. The doctors of the Church: they mapped out the whole theology of it" (*U* 5.439–41).

29. Another possibility—but one lacking thematic resonance—is an allusion to Ambrosius Aurelianius, a fifth-century leader of the Britons against the Saxons.

30. Stanislaus Joyce, *Brother's Keeper*, 162; also see 224, and several citations in *Dublin Diary*, 93, 100, 116.

31. The fact that Joyce's middle name, given at baptism by his parents, is "Augustine" is of minor consequence; whereas his personal choice of "Aloysius" as a confirmation name is significant, as has been mentioned.

32. Parandowski, "Meeting," 159.

33. See Morse, *Alien*, 21–37, 127–39; Schlossman, *Catholic Comedy*; and Kimbell, "St. Augustine," 375–78; the best short introduction to this topic remains Atherton, *Books*, 140–43.

34. An odd archival note reads: "TSE bishop of Hippo" (VI.B.31.25). The initials must refer to T. S. Eliot, one of whose early poems (with distinct allegorical overtones that make it a commentary on the "True Church") is entitled "The Hippopotamus" (*Complete Poems*, 30–31).

35. Atherton, *Books*, 143–44.

36. As McHugh indicates, "huffsnuff" denotes someone quick to take offence; the application to Constantinople is particularly appropriate in a religious context, since the patriarch in the imperial capital was frequently at odds with the doctrinal positions of other Christians in the Middle East and Egypt. Joyce picked up this odd term from Sainéan, *La langue de Rabelais*, II.402 (see Jacquet, *Joyce et Rabelais*, 32). In fact, two of the three *OED* references to "huffsnuff" come from Urquhart's seventeenth-century translation of the French work.

37. During that period Jerome lived mainly in a monastery in Bethlehem, and his relationships with the bishops of Jerusalem were not always cordial.

38. Ryan, *Golden Legend*, II.213.

39. Atherton's case that the translation of Jerome's letter 127 comes from Wright, *Select Letters* (*Books*, 144) is strong here.

40. In a May 1905 letter to Stanislaus from Trieste, Joyce describes some boats anchored in the canal: "[T]he prow of every sailing ship has an image of some saviour, Saint Nicholas or the Madonna or Jesus walking on the waters" (*Letters* I.90).

41. Schork, "By Jingo," 104–27.

42. I cite these verses from Jones, *Saint Nicholas*, 251; Jones reports every detail of this component of the saint's legend, 123–40, 247–52.

43. Verrimst, *Rondes*, 305–7; see Connolly, *Personal Library*, 41 (302). There is an archival index (VI.B.33.48–49, 63–65, 70, 87–88, 176–77, 190–93 and VI.C.6.172, 189) from this source, but none of the entries come from the St. Nicholas song; see Deane, "Song Hoard," 12–24.

44. In a late notebook the entry "ᵇkilderkin" (VI.B.41.117) appears in the midst of long lists of Swedish words and references to Finn MacCool, but there is no connection between the archaic English term and either of these indices.

45. See Deane, "St. Patrick," forthcoming.

46. Van Mierlo, "St. Martin," 29–44.

47. Connolly, *Personal Library,* 25 (186).

48. See Fleming, "Saltmartin," 14; the phrase "Blessed shield Martin" (*FW* 624.21) may be connected with the saint's protection.

49. In my judgment, each of the "three logically separate propositions" that constitute Rose's "theoretical matrix" for the *Wake* notebooks is too extreme. In particular, the adverb "implicitly," which modifies "was intermediated" in the third proposition, is just too vague (see Rose, *Diaries,* 16–19). On the other hand, Rose's ideas about the creative use of notebook entries are far more valid than the expansively subjective norms applied by David Hayman and some of his disciples.

5. The Hairy Hermit

1. McGinley, *Love Letters,* 55–56. For a scholarly and fascinating study of the role of the stylite in late antiquity, see P. Brown, "Holy Man," 80–101.

2. One of his notes for *Ulysses* is evidence that Joyce was aware of the origin and extent of these practices: "1/4 of Egypt. adults monks / 365 monasteries" (*UNBM* 358:63–64).

3. Gibbon, *Decline and Fall,* chapter 29, note 32; this information comes from one of the lives of the Desert Fathers who reveled in records of this type.

4. The version in the text of the *Wake* appears to be an example of a "Raphaelism": an alteration of information from an original VI.B note caused by a mistaken transcription in a VI.C entry (see Rose, *Diaries,* 169–81). In his initial note Joyce wrote "S. Sylvania washed only / tips of fingers at 60" (VI.B.16.116). Madame Raphael's version mistakenly transcribes the numeral "60" as "fd" (VI.C.1.53). When Joyce converted the VI.C. entry (it is crossed out with red crayon) into text, he expanded the abbreviation into "ford" and ignored the sixty years.

5. See Ward, *Harlots,* for the texts and a thorough discussion of notable examples of this type of sin and repentance.

6. Ryan, *Golden Legend,* I.227–29.

7. On this topic see Culleton, *Names and Naming.*

8. O Hehir and Dillon, *Classical Lexicon,* 390.

9. Connolly, *Personal Library,* 25–27 (191); four pages of Father Matharan's text are reproduced between pages 30–31.

10. For example, H. L Kavanagh's 1906 translation, *The Life of St Humphrey (Saint Onnofrius) Hermit: By the Abbot Paphnutius;* also see Paphnutius, *Histories.*

11. Williams, *Oriental Affinities,* 84.

12. For a fascinating modern discussion of themes and variants in these "hagiographic romances," see Elliott, *Roads to Paradise,* 51–76, especially figure 1 (56).

13. Note the "Theban recension . . . and the Bug of the Deaf" (*FW* 134.35–36). For a discussion of Joyce's use of these documents, see Rose, *Chapters;* Troy, *Mummeries;* and the chapter "Inside the Coffin" in Bishop, *Book of the Dark,* 86–125, 405–15.

14. The original spelling of "hon*u*phreum" was changed to "honophreum" at a late stage (47475-210 [*JJA* 46:194]).

15. See Budge, *Book of the Dead,* I.53–54. Troy includes an illustration of the

funeral "wake" (*veillée funèbre*) of Osiris-Unnefer at Abydos (*Mummeries*, figure II [33]).

16. Kavanagh, *Life of Humphrey*, 14–15.

17. Elliott, *Roads to Paradise*, 99.

18. This latter-day pseudo-hermit was well known enough to have been mentioned in *Ulysses*. When Stephen Dedalus passes in front of Clohissey's, we are informed that one of the tattered volumes in a second-hand pushcart is *Life and Miracles of the Curé of Ars* (*U* 10.838–39).

19. These words occur in the catalogue of the attributes of HCE. Here Joyce more likely intends a "narrative" suffix in "hiber*niad*" (as in *Iliad*) than a "geographical" designation. Thus, the phrase is probably to be interpreted as "an Irish epic tale of wild parties [McHugh's gloss on 'hoolies']," not "an area in Ireland serving as a refuge of 'holy' monks and hermits."

20. See Williams, *Oriental Affinities*, 119–22, and Elliott, *Roads to Paradise*, 71–74.

21. Jerome, "Life of St. Paul," VII.299; another popular work in which Jerome's "Life of Paul" has been followed closely is the section on the hermit in *The Golden Legend* (Ryan, I.84–85).

22. See Gibbon, *Decline and Fall*, chapter 16, footnote 65; other nearby items in notebook VI.B.1 also come from Gibbon's chapters 15 ("The Progress of the Christian Religion") and 16 ("The Conduct of the Roman Government towards the Christians"). Near the beginning of my discussion of the Hairy Hermit, I also cite another of Gibbon's footnotes as the Joycean source for an intriguing detail about St. Sylvanus/ia. Also see Schork, "Footnotes," forthcoming.

23. The translinguistic details here come from McHugh, *Annotations*.

24. I have not been able to discover the specific source of Joyce's information here; it could have come from any general discussion of the origin and development of European drama from its liturgical roots.

25. For archival evidence of Joyce's familiarity with this play, see Deane, "Green Pastures," 56–60.

26. See Rose, *Chapters*, 17 (VI.B.40.142); Troy also calls attention to "Beppy's realm" (*FW* 415.36) (*Mummeries*, 73–74).

27. See my comments on St. Kevin in chapter 6.

6. Irish and Other Celtic Saints

1. The source of Joyce's information (and my citations) is Flood, *Ireland: Its Saints and Scholars*; for a discussion of the archival use of this short book, see Deane, "Wellspring," 1–27, especially entries VI.B.3.19–20 for the "three orders."

2. The formulaic title is parodied a number of times in the *Wake*: "saint to sage" (*FW* 53.8–9), "Saint Scholarland" (*FW* 135.19), "saints and sages" (*FW* 388.36–389.1) "long lives of saints and saucerdotes" (*FW* 440.21–22; also note VI.B.3.131 and VI.B.35.42), "sager . . . saint" (*FW* 612.23–24), "Sants and sogs" (*FW* 613.6), and "saint and sage" (*FW* 613.16). Just before the procession of religious orders and saints in "Cyclops," the owner of Barney Kiernan's comments on Leopold Bloom's

Jewish heritage: "—That's the new Messiah for Ireland! Says the citizen. Island of saints and sages!" (*U* 12.1642–43).

3. Both citations come from the English translation of Joyce's 1912 article "The Mirage of the Fisherman of Aran," for *Il Piccolo della Sera*, Trieste (*CW* 234–37). In this piece Joyce also lists several other saints (Enda, Finnian, and Fursa) who were once hermits in the Aran Islands.

4. For a modern scholarly discussion of the monastic settlement and the development of the Christian community in Ireland, see Bitel, *Isle of the Saints*.

5. On the other hand, professionals and serious amateurs were certainly involved in archeological and folkloric investigation (Madame Wilde) and scholarly research (Canon O'Hanlon) at this time.

6. See the comments and references in Gifford and Seidman, *"Ulysses" Annotated*, 352.

7. For a report of some brilliant archival detective work regarding this reference, see Rose, *Textual Diaries*, 150–68.

8. See Kopper, "More Legends," 120.

9. For a history of Iona and its daughter foundation, with a text and translation of the life of Columkille, see Herbert, *Iona, Kells, and Derry*.

10. For a discussion of archival references to the Book of Kells and their documentary sources, see Rose, "Kells," 1–13.

11. An erroneous entry connects Iona with Columbanus (VI.B.6.157). Earlier in the same notebook there may be a reference to a source for Joyce's information, "Victor Bramford / S. Columba" (VI.B.6.131), although I have been unable to locate an author with this name.

12. See Deane, "Wellspring," 8–9.

13. Rose and O'Hanlon suggest a source for this index: Benedict Fitzpatrick, *Ireland and the Making of Britain* (see *Understanding FW*, 335).

14. Gillespie, *Trieste Library*, 175 (345) and Connolly, *Personal Library*, 31 (234); also see the comment by Atherton, *Books*, 265.

15. Rose, "Prophetia," 27–28.

16. See Schork, *Latin*, 99–102, 120.

17. See Webb, *Lives of the Saints*, 33–68; Severin's *The Brendan Voyage* investigates a possible stratum of fact in this tale of a fantastic ocean trip. An entry in one of Joyce's notebooks illustrates the popularity of this saint: "P. C. [Police Constable] in X reads / life of Brendan" (VI.B.26.11); in *Scribbledehobble* (79 [301]) a parenthetical entry links the Irish sailor-saint with another famous explorer of the New World: "(cf Columbus & Brendan)."

18. See Landuyt and Van Mierlo, "Catholicism, Nationalism," forthcoming.

19. See Connolly, *Personal Library*, 34 (268).

20. An archival note may also refer to St. Brendan's mother: "Cara / as good as a / Agatha" (VI.B.24.64). In Latin *cara* means "dear," "beloved"; in Greek *agatha* means "good," "noble."

21. For the most recent scholarship on this document, see Herbert, *Iona*.

22. O'Neill, "Aegnus," 279–93; in the midst of a long notebook index on St. Patrick,

there are several entries on St. Angus, including a list of his books (VI.B.14.47).

23. See Landuyt and Van Mierlo, "Catholicism, Nationalism." In the final text of the *Wake*, "Lorcan" has been supplanted by Xavier's fellow Jesuit "ignitious Purpalume [St. Ignatius Loyola]" (*FW* 433.1).

24. See the comment in Rose, *Textual Diaries*, 133.

25. See Kopper, "More Legends," 119–20.

26. Bjork, "'Sinted Sageness,'" 86–100; for general comment on the Kevin section of the *Wake*, see Swartzlander, "'On the Verge,'" 475–85.

27. Dalton, "Advertisement," 119–37; for an excellent summary of Dalton's conclusions, see Rose and O'Hanlon, *Understanding*, 322–25, note 6.

28. An expanded version of this entry appears at the end of some extra-draft material on the back of the first (1923) expansion of the core-node (47488-24r [*JJA* 62.38b]); for its source (interviews in the London *Daily Sketch* for December 22, 1915, about the Bywaters-Thompson murder case), see Deane, "Bywaters," 185.

29. An old, but still reliable, general introduction to hagiographical tropes and techniques is Delehaye, *Legends*. For an up-to-date narratological reading of the highly thematic lives of early saints—including a Wakesque St. Onuphrius—see Elliott, *Roads to Paradise*.

30. The writer of this sentence is an Irish priest, Reverend John A. O'Hanlon, whose detailed life of St. Kevin is discussed and cited throughout the rest of this article; the quote is from his *Lives of the Irish Saints*, VI.30. This scholarly priest appears in *Ulysses*. In a typical touch of historical verisimilitude, he celebrates the Benediction service at his parish, the church of Mary, Star of the Sea: "Father Conroy handed the thurible to Canon O'Hanlon and he put in the incense and censed the Blessed Sacrament" (*U* 13.490–92). That ceremony provides the liturgical background for "Nausicaa."

31. Plummer, *Vitae Sanctorum Hiberniae*, I.234–57.

32. On the other hand, two of Joyce's entries in a Buffalo notebook are in Latin (probably *not* from a source, but his own "shorthand" summation of a significant theme): "Kevin lavat" (Kevin washes/bathes himself) (VI.B.2.80) and "Kevin quid monstrum" (Kevin what monstrous thing) (VI.B.2.80). While I detect no evidence in these notes for a direct reference to a Latin vita, Kevin does bathe in the lake at Glendalough (*vita* xxx [Plummer I.249–50]), and an angel does appear there to repel a bestial monster—and to warm the water for the praying saint (*vita* xviii [Plummer I.243]).

33. A second "dairy" miracle is also recorded: a cow used to visit the hollow tree in which the hermit Kevin lived for a while in his youth. She licked the saint's garments, "daily," and "gave an almost incredible quantity of milk" (O'Hanlon, 39).

34. This episode, transferred to the saint's stony "bed" at Glendalough, is probably the inspiration of another legendary attempt at seduction: the tragic punishment of Kathleen, as immortalized in Thomas Moore's *Irish Melodies*.

35. In all of the surviving textual witnesses to this passage, including the November 29, 1939, galley proofs (47488-208 [*JJA* 63.301]), the final words are

"gnewgnawn sbones." If the final edition's variant, "gnewgnawns bones," is *not* a very late typographical error, it was introduced into the text on the missing duplicate set of galley proofs (late 1938, early 1939). If, on the other hand, the switch of "s" from the start of "sbones" to the end of "gnewgnawn" is purely a printer's error, it was not detected or marked in either the typed list of corrections (47488-238 [*JJA* 63.338]) or the "Buffalo Errata" (VI.H.4.b.30 [*JJA* 63.380]).

36. These include two beheaded females, who become nuns in their new life (Plummer xi; O'Hanlon, 41–42), and a single suffocated male, who becomes a monk (Plummer xv; O'Hanlon, 43–44). In the *Wake* there is a related allusion to the folktale of St. Kevin's gift of miraculous longevity to an animal, the goose of King O'Toole: "old Kong Gander O'Toole of the Mountains" (*FW* 557.6–7).

37. It is also very likely that the Irish language makes a contribution to the thematic wordplay here. On the *Wake*'s first page there is a Shem-Shaun "bellowed mishe mishe to tauftauf" (*FW* 3.9–10); McHugh's annotation suggests: "mise" = me (Irish) and "tafuen" = to baptize (German), a motival cry that neatly links the end with the beginning.

38. In 1938 Joyce was working furiously to complete the *Wake*; moreover, his eyesight was severely impaired. Thus, it is unlikely that he himself read through O'Hanlon's work to glean additional data on St. Kevin; rather, one of his Parisian friends, his informed "research assistants" (see *JJII* 698–99), probably summarized the pertinent data and reported their source.

39. The best single article on the transcendent function of the Kevin section in the *Wake* is Norris, "Last Chapter," 11–30; reprinted in McCarthy, *Critical Essays*, 212–30.

40. See Kopper, "More Legends," 42.

41. There may be some doubt about the patronage of the Breton saint since the *Britannica* cites a fifth-century Irish virgin, St. Hya or Ia (*EB* 24.10). At the end of "Eumaeus" in *Ulysses* Joyce also mocks the tony sound of a pair of other Cornish saint-towns: "catchy tenor solos foisted on a confiding public by Ivan St Austell and Hilton St Just and their *genus omne*" (*U* 16.1850–52); in the *Wake* the stage names are deflated: "Hilton St. Just (Mr. Frank Jones), Ivanne Ste Austelle (Mr. J. F. Jones)" (*FW* 48.11–12).

42. See Aubert, "Breton Proverbs," 106–8, and Rose, "Breton in Λa/b," 90–92.

43. According to Gifford and Seidman, Ultan (perhaps an uncle of St. Brigid) was a seventh-century missionary to the Netherlands and a patron of orphans; see *"Ulysses" Annotated*, 412.

7. Medieval to Modern Times

1. For the influence of scholastic philosophy on Joyce's works, see Noon, *Aquinas*, and Staley, "Religious," 154–68.

2. In one of his Trieste lectures, Joyce refers to "John Duns Scotus (called the Subtle Doctor to distinguish him from St. Thomas, the Angelic Doctor, and from St. Bonaventura, the Seraphic Doctor)" (*CW* 154).

3. There are two famous hymns entitled *Pange, lingua:* one by Venatius Fortunatus (sixth century); the other attributed to Aquinas; see Schork, *Latin,* 199 and 271, n. 25.

4. See Schork, "Liturgical Irony," 193–94.

5. For information on the documentary sources of this important episode in the *Wake,* see Rose and O'Hanlon, "The H.C.E. Project," in *Understanding FW,* 331–40. While similar in intent and use, the church index is *not* part of that project, nor is its source the *Britannica* article on London (*EB* 16.941–42).

6. Spence, *Cathedrals and Abbeys,* 254 ("Needle") and 230 ("Chair").

7. The following passage exemplifies Wakean concern with the peculiar Irish form of tonsure (front area of head shaved) and Celtic differences with Rome over the date of Easter: "a particularist prepenary pondering on the roman easter, the tonsure question" (*FW* 43.11–13; also note VI.C.5.183). The single reference to the site of this synod, "Whitby hat" (*FW* 587.11), appears to have no connection with the ecclesiastical controversy.

8. See *Anglo-Saxon Chronicle* translated by Garmonsway, 106–10.

9. There is an archival reference: "S. Brice's Day / Ethelred" (VI.B.7.142). In his *Annotations* McHugh indicates that the saint's feast is celebrated on "2/12"; the correct date is November 13. This minor bit of misinformation comes from the *Britannica* article on "Aethelred II" (*EB* 1.290).

10. The *Wake* abounds in examples: the Greco-French "Peter Roche" (*FW* 449.16) has already been discussed; "domestic economy" (*FW* 545.5) combines the Latin and Greek roots for "house" (see Schork, *Greek,* 268–71). There is no apparent thematic connection between "Vitalba" and "white life" (*FW* 148.28).

11. Adair, *Pilgrim's Way,* 50.

12. Also note several obvious Anglo-Saxon names in the HCE-acrostic catalogue at *FW* 88.21–23; the leaders of the Germanic incursion into Britain are commemorated as "hanguest or hoshoe" (*FW* 63.22), "Hengegst and Horsesauce" (*FW* 272.17), and others. It may be pure coincidence, but one of Joyce's favorite prose stylists, Cardinal Newman, prepared a detailed prospectus for a "Catalogue of English [mostly Anglo-Saxon] Saints" (1843–44); another rhetorical catalogue of pre-Conquest saints is a feature of Newman's famous sermon "The Second Spring" (1850), which Joyce certainly knew, even if he did not directly imitate it.

13. An archival note records an Oxford tradition involving St. Thomas à Becket: "101 knells even / S.T. Of Canterbury / Tom Quad" (VI.B.22.187). Each evening at 9:05, the great bell in Tom Tower at Christ Church, the largest college at Oxford, is rung 101 times in memory of the original number of its students; that bell is named after the sainted archbishop.

14. In 1534 another former Chancellor of England, Thomas More, was executed for his opposition of King Henry VIII. He was proclaimed a martyr-saint, and can briefly be glimpsed in a *Wake* passage bristling with Catholic-Protestant antagonism: "by gramercy of justness, I mean veryman and *more*mon, stiff and staunch for ever" (*FW* 534.13–14; my emphasis). A recent article amasses the evidence for a deeply subsurface parallel to the character Richard Rowan of *Exiles:* St. Richard of

Wick, a thirteenth-century bishop of Chichester, who earned the enmity of King Henry III (see Bauerle, "Historical Counterparts," 104–11).

15. For an extended discussion of Joyce's knowledge and use of Eastern Christianity, see Schork, "Eastern Orthodox Church."

16. I have not been able to locate Joyce's documentary source for this information on the physical appearance of Christ; for icon painters in the Orthodox tradition, *the* authority is a seventeenth-century manual attributed to an artist-monk from Mount Athos, Dionysius of Fourna.

17. The *Britannica* is Joyce's source of information for the Constantinopolitan index in which the entry appears (*EB* 7.6).

18. For a discussion of this passage, see Schork, *Latin,* 76.

19. An archival note commemorates the initial conversion of large numbers of Russian pagans: "mass baptism / in Dnieper" (VI.B.28.34).

20. Father Maximilian Kolbe volunteered to take the place of another prisoner in a starvation cell; see Woodward, *Making Saints,* 144–47.

21. See Torchina, "Joyce's 'Eveline,'" 22–28. In a series of visions St. Margaret Mary was instructed how to promote proper veneration of the Sacred Heart of Jesus (*D* 158 and *U* 6.594) and the practice of receiving communion on nine consecutive first Fridays of the month (*D* 37 and 137); for a summary of the "promises" see Kennedy, "Another Root," 271–72, and Keen, "June Sixteenth," 94–96.

22. Nolan, "Father Charles," 841–45; the note reproduces four pages from a pamphlet produced for pilgrims visiting Blessed Charles's shrine at Mount Argus in Dublin.

23. Hayman, *First-Draft Version,* 153: MS 47478-281.

24. My information comes from the booklet published in 1911, "Little Nellie of Holy God: The Story of the Life of a Saintly Irish Child," written by a "Priest of the Diocese of Cork." My thanks to Vincent Deane for sending me a copy of this rare document.

25. See *Canadian Encyclopedia* XX.1701; I owe this reference to Geert Lernout (Antwerp).

26. See Herring, *Notes and Drafts,* 87:37 and 103:44.

27. One of Joyce's friends in Paris, Arthur Power, reports the following anecdote: "Our family arms are of French origin—a stag bearing a cross between its antlers, taken from the legend of St Hubert, with a device underneath: *Per Crucem ad Coronam* [Through the Cross toward the Crown]" (Power, *Conversations,* 13).

28. My synopsis is based on the version in Ryan, *Golden Legend,* I.127–28; Joyce also knew Flaubert's *Le Légende de Saint-Julien-l'Hospitalier* (see Brunazzi, "La Narration," 123–31.

29. Cumpiano, *Saint John;* Jaurretche's recent "Waking to Obscurity,"154–82, does not seem to me to shed much light on the topic.

30. Herring, *Notes and Drafts,* 86:20, 100:6; note a Latin version at VI.B.18.143.

31. Kopper, "Saint Olaf," 35–39.

32. In a 1903 review of a book on Giordano Bruno, Joyce mentions Bruno's "commentaries on the art of Raymond Lully" (*CW* 133).

33. Kopper, "More Legends," 42.

8. Founders and Religious Orders

1. Since catalogues are a staple of epic poetry and its imitations, there is no need to cite a literary model for Joyce's heroic list of monks and friars. At the same time, one of Rabelais's chapters in *Gargantua and Pantagruel* begins: "nine transports . . . laden with monks, Jacobins, Jesuits, Capuchins, Hermits, Augustines, Bernardins, Celestins, Theatins, Egnatians, Amadeans, Franciscans, Carmelites, Minims, and other holy brethren" (*Gargantua*, 490).

2. See Gillespie, *Trieste Library*, 109 (199).

3. Greene, *Saints*, 189–90.

4. Ryan, *Golden Legend*, I.192–93.

5. Ryan, *Golden Legend*, I.187. In an archival note Joyce records a cryptic secular parallel to this practice: "Shane O'Neill buries se ["himself" in Latin] in nett[les]" (VI.B.2.80). Since this O'Neill was a profligate Irish rebel (see U 12.178), the incident—if my decipherment of the final word is correct—is puzzling.

6. The uncrossed first entry triggered analogous, alphabetic wordplay in the nearby "ᵍabbe's seize" (VI.B.23.50); other archival references include "Malady Cistercian / & Clair Vaux / S. Bernard" (VI.B.1.106).

7. A short notebook index deals with these matters: "Carthusian S Bruno / Synod Charters. 1 a year / brothers work all day" (VI.B.1.49). The second item refers to the annual meeting of all the order's abbots.

8. An archival note takes the comparative humility of the Friars Minor to its superlative degree: "a monk of / S. Francis / Fyrer [sic] *minimus*" (VI.B.15.60; my emphasis).

9. *The Golden Legend* contains a charming version of the saint's life and miracles, especially his conversations with "sister birds" and "brother birds." When tempted, Francis scourged himself and rebuked his body, "See here, brother ass! Either behave yourself or take a beating!" When his final hour came, he said, "Welcome, my sister Death!" (Ryan, *Golden Legend*, II.220–30).

10. Umberto Eco's 1980 novel, *The Name of the Rose*, is set in this period of fragmentation in the Franciscan community.

11. The capuchin monkey is named after its hoodlike crown of hair; the coffee-with-milk drink is called "cappuccino" because its color is about the same as a brown Franciscan habit.

12. It is worth noting here that Molly Bloom's recollection of a passage in *Ruby of the Ring* that has someone being hung up on "a hook with a cord flagellate" (U 18.494–95) has nothing whatsoever to do with Franciscan penitential practice.

13. Joyce, habitually, covered every patch of fraternal color: "*pied friar*" (FW 338.11–12) refers to a small order of mendicants that was disbanded in 1243; they were presumably so called because their robes were black (or brown) and white. The geographical spread of the Franciscans is also acknowledged in "Fran Czeschs" (FW 423.36).

14. Despite the thrust of their title, the Ulyssean "Little Sisters of the Poor" (U 12.549–50) are not Franciscan Poor Clares; they are a group of Sisters of Charity

who run orphanages, old-age homes, and hospices and perform other types of public good works. Most convents of Poor Clares are strictly cloistered and contemplative.

15. See Schork, *Greek*, 143.

16. Stanislaus Joyce would not have appreciated his brother's joint allusion to St. Francis and Socrates. In a section of his diary, he contrasts Jesus and the saint: Jesus is far more intellectual than "simple . . . poor . . . St. Francis" (*Dublin Diary*, 88–90).

17. Ryan, *Golden Legend*, II.44–58.

18. Ryan, *Golden Legend*, II.44–45. For archival entries on the births of St. Dominic and St. Francis, see McHugh, "Dean Kinane," 25; Joyce's source of information was an incidental comment in a nineteenth-century life of St. Patrick.

19. Mercanton, "Hours," 299.

20. A German classicist-Joycean has recently suggested an ingenious parallel between this Dublin woman's "brown scapulars" and the "saffron peplos" characteristically worn by Eos, the Homeric goddess of the dawn (see Lohmann, *Kalypso*, 131–32).

21. In a 1906 letter written to Stanislaus from Rome, Joyce makes some comments on recent developments in church-state politics on a grand scale: "The next thing we hear will be the emperor William's [Wilhelm II of Germany] enrollment in the brown scapular" (*Letters* II.160).

22. For the earlier period, see Bradley, *Schooldays*; Sullivan's *Joyce among the Jesuits* also covers his university studies.

23. Suter, "Reminiscences," 64.

24. Tylenda, *Jesuit Saints*, xxiv; for a synopsis of the terminology, see my preface.

25. James Thrane has thoroughly analyzed Joyce's primary source for the "Hell" sermon in the retreat (*P* 117–35). That anonymous Jesuit saint and his clock that ticked "ever, never; ever, never" (*P* 132) are not included in *Hell Opened to Christians*, by the Italian Jesuit, Petro Pinamonti. Thus, I suspect that that paragraph and its putative author are a figment of Joyce's accurately imitative Jesuitical imagination (see Thrane, "Sermon," 172–98).

26. See Schork, *Latin*, 242.

27. For extensive comment on and examples of Joyce's use of the rebus in the *Wake*, see O'Shea, *Heraldry*.

28. For the source of this information, see McHugh, "Dean Kinane," 25. In another part of the world, early Jesuit missionaries to Paraguay encouraged the Indians on their *reductiones* to cultivate and market the *maté* plant, the leaves of which are used to brew a drink sometimes called "Jesuits' tea," as is reported by Joyce in the *Wake* (*FW* 382.7; also note VI.B.41.261).

29. In the second list of Dublin churches in the *Wake*, "S. Ruadagara's" (*FW* 601.23–24) hides the name of the Church of the Three Patrons, Rathagar.

30. The source of the notebook entry, "⁸Singulare illud" (VI.B.4.331), that lies behind this entry has been discovered by Inge Landuyt (Antwerp) in a popular French book on Pius XI.

31. See Father Boero's biography, *St. John Berchmans*, 77–81, and Schork, "Penrose," 563–66.

32. Stanislaus Joyce, *Dublin Diary,* 89.

33. Gifford and Seidman, *"Ulysses" Annotated,* 509.

34. Francis de Sales is the source of Cardinal Newman's motto, *cor ad cor loguitur* (heart speaks to heart). That saying lies behind the comment in "Wandering Rocks" about the religious throwaway placed in Bloom's hand: "Heart to heart talks" (*U* 8.7); see Schork, "Newman," 112–13. Boyle, *Pauline Vision,* 87–88 and O'Shea, *Heraldry,* 151, suggest other echoes.

35. In a 1915 letter to Michael Healy, Joyce wrote that he was trying to discover "the patron of men of letters . . . to remind him that I exist; but I understand that the last saint who held that position resigned in despair and no other will take the portfolio" (*Letters* I.86).

36. See Bradley, *Schooldays,* 81–82; Stanislaus Joyce states that he and his brother actually spent several months in a Christian Brothers' school during 1892 (*Brother's Keeper,* 70; see also 82–83 for a later attempt by the Dominicans to poach James Joyce from the Jesuits).

9. Relics, Symbols, Pilgrimages, and Feasts

1. For a version of the legend in which the impression takes place before the Passion, see Ryan, *Golden Legend,* I.212.

2. Joyce when younger was not so jaded in his judgments about religious art; see his 1899 essay "Royal Hibernian Academy 'Ecce Homo' [of Michael Minkacsy]" (*CW* 31–37).

3. A later archival note repeats this term: "latreia" (VI.B.27.13); the source is the section of the *Britannica* article on the Eastern Orthodox Church that deals with the proper veneration of icons (*EB* 20.335). (Dirk Van Hulle [Antwerp] recalled my attention to this notebook cluster.)

4. The key to Joyce's translingual ploy here is the modern Greek pronunciation of the letter *chi* (X); see Schork, *Greek,* 255.

5. Some legends about the Holy Grail say that this cup was further sanctified by being used by Joseph to catch the blood flowing from Jesus' wounds on the cross. An archival note also shows that Joyce knew of the tradition that wood from the Tree of Life from the Garden of Eden played a significant role in Jewish history, including the crucifixion: "Tree=Ark=Temple=Cross" (VI.B.2.14).

6. In the *Wake,* heaven and earth appear side by side with a relic in Jaun's sermon to Issy and her schoolmates. He advises them, "Rely on the relic. What bondman ever you bind on earth I'll be bound 'twas combined in hemel [*Himmel* is "heaven" in German]" (*FW* 435.22–23). Here Joyce is playing with Christ's apostolic commission to the Apostle Peter (Matthew 16:19) and linking it to an unspecific relic in his narrative—the allusive and contextual force of which eludes me.

7. For discussion of Joyce's source and model for "the privilege of [a] portable altar" (VI.B.10.13), see Bjork, "Sinted Sageness," 87–90.

8. In the "National Library" chapter of *Ulysses,* Stephen Dedalus briefly recalls meeting John Millington Synge "in rue Saint André des Arts" (*U* 9.577). None of

the various saints named Andrew is associated with the arts; rather, as an aside in a recent article points out, the original name of this Paris street was rue Saint André des Arcs (see Maguire, "Irish Historical Memory," 309–10). Another hagiographical mystery is generated by this correction, since the saint is not known as a patron of bows or arches.

9. J. Brown, "French," 43.

10. Eco, *Name of the Rose*, 423.

11. See Geary, *Furta Sacra*; note "pilgrim false relics" (VI.B.3.144).

12. Ker, *Newman*, 347; also see the reference to a parody of one of Newman's writing projects, "Saints of the Desert," in *Punch* (March 1866), 574.

13. For discussion of the classical dimensions of Bloom's critique of the sculptor's technique, see Schork, *Latin*, 89–90.

14. See Gillespie, *Trieste Library*, 109 (199); Gifford and Seidman, *"Ulysses" Annotated*, 374–77.

15. See Ellmann's comments on Samuel Chevinix Trench, the model for Haines (*JJII* 172–75).

16. The editor of the notebook discusses these anomalies in his introduction to the facsimile volume (*JJA* 39.xv).

17. Atherton, *Books*, 33, 87, 209. Joyce's source-collection, first compiled by Ebenezer Cobham Brewer in 1870, has been marginally updated and frequently reprinted; in my edition the apostolic symbols are described on page 42. I found an explicit contemporary reference to this source, plus a two-page citation of the symbols themselves, in an otherwise undistinguished 1999 crime novel, Boris Starling's *Messiah* (216–17). In this British thriller an obsessed serial killer dispatches his victims on their patron saints' days, with the appropriate instruments of the apostles' martyrdom. The lead detective discovers the hagiographic key to the murderer's bizarre modus operandi in "a very old edition" of *Brewer's Dictionary of Phrase and Fable*.

18. St. Fiacre was a wandering Irish monk who built a garden hermitage at Meaux, in France, from which women were strictly forbidden.

19. For a complete discussion of these archival phenomena (and many entertaining examples), see Rose, *Textual Diaries*, 168–81.

20. All the accoutrements (including the scarf) were inserted into the text at the same time in late 1934 (47478-203 [*JJA* 52.284]).

21. For a general description of the site and the pilgrimage, see Dames, *Mythic Ireland*, 22–42; detailed historical background is given in Haven and de Pontfarcy, *Medieval Pilgrimages*.

22. See Haven and de Pontfarcy, *Medieval Pilgrimages*, 120–68.

23. See Dames, *Mythic Ireland*, 167–69.

24. T. Brown, "Magic Lantern," 791–98.

25. An uncrossed notebook entry records several basic types of "calendar / legal / ecc[lesiastical] / civil" (VI.B.5.136); in the *Wake* Joyce shows his mastery of the "comple anniums of calendrias, gregoromaios and gypsyjuliennes" (*FW* 553.16–17).

26. On at least one occasion, Joyce's precise date for a movable feast serves to confirm the year in which a notebook was composed: "23 June / S. Heart Feast of Universal Church" (VI.B.10.63). In the calendar of the Catholic Church, the Sacred Heart is specifically honored on the Friday after the second Sunday after Pentecost (Pentecost, or Whit Sunday, occurs seven weeks after Easter). Thus the year in which this very early notebook was written is 1922, in which June 23 was the designated date for the movable feast of the Sacred Heart. For another example of the significance of the date of a movable feast (in Joyce's first published story), see Schork, "Liturgical Irony," 193–97. It is also necessary to be cautious in applying internal indicators of the date of composition; the entry "ᵇholy year (1925)" (VI.B.26.81; see FW 569.13) appears in a notebook that was certainly written in the summer of 1928. Inge Landuyt discovered the source (a popular book on Pope Pius XI published in 1928) for the archival entries (VI.B.4.326–31) on this Jubilee celebration at Rome (also see Schork, "Genetic Criticism," forthcoming).

27. In a liturgical passage in the *Wake*, there is a truncated list of the days of the week: "from Manducare Monday up till ferrier's siesta" (FW 433.6–7); *feria sexta* is the ecclesiastical Latin term for Friday, and *feria quinta in cena Domini* (the fifth day at the Lord's Supper) is the term for Maundy (Holy) Thursday.

28. Giedion-Welcker, "Meetings," 260.

29. For the alien spelling of the saint's name as "Martian" also note the entry "Martin (Marsicolae [Latin for 'inhabitants of Mars'])" (VI.B.3.105).

30. See Hayman, *First-Draft*, 63; the date of this version (47472-97b [*JJA* 45.99]) is August–September 1923; the change to "Saint Swithin" takes place in early 1927.

31. Those entries marked with an asterisk are part of the heavily crossed out index headed by "February" in VI.B.17.93, discussed in the section on virgin martyrs in chapter 4.

32. See the *Britannica* article on "Fasting" (*EB* 10.97).

33. In the revised version of the story that appears in the text of *Dubliners*, the date is altered to "1st July" (*D* 12); for a discussion of the implications of and reasons for this change, see Schork, "Liturgical Irony," 193–97.

34. See the informative article in *EB* 26.238.

35. For more information on Lammas Day, see *EB* 16.130.

36. Mercanton, "Hours," 237.

37. For the connection between this date and Joyce's reading from "Anna Livia Plurabelle" on November 2, 1927, see Nash, "Date," 557.

38. In England November 5 is Guy Fawkes Day, to commemorate the discovery and quashing of the Catholic Gunpowder Plot on that date in 1605. Joyce alludes to the date in "remember the filth of November" (*FW* 87.4); for comment on the text, see Higginson, "Notes on the Text," 452.

39. In England the first weekday after Christmas is a holiday, Boxing Day, on which gifts are left for the postman and milkman; in a multicultural list of the months in the *Wake*, December appears as "the christymansboxer" (*FW* 142.11).

40. See Schork, *Latin*, 249–51, for a discussion of Joyce's etymological allusions to the names of ancient Roman months.

10. Fictitious Saints

1. In this passage the Greek root -*onymous* (involving a name) combines to form several standard English adjectives as well as the less familiar "Eponymous" (giving a name) and "Paronymous" (differing in spelling and meaning, but sounding the same—as "where," "wear," "ware").

2. Gifford and Seidman, *"Ulysses" Annotated*, 413.

3. Kopper, "More Legends," 42; another possible source for the allusion is the two Collopy brothers who played rugby on the Irish national team (see Atherton, "Sport," 61).

4. The key Latin phrases that I have translated are *mira mei miracula dorsi / Proferat extrema denique particula* (571–72) and *Ergo dedit sonitum turpi modulamine factum* (575) (Hrotsvitha, *Opera*, 53). An English hagiographer appends a footnote to his treatment of the career of St. Gengulphus: "It is impossible, even in Latin, to give the account of the miraculous punishments inflicted on the murderer and the wife" (Baring-Gould, *Lives*, 5.153). For a recent study of every facet of Joyce's literary deployment of farts, see O'Shea, "By Dad," 398–403.

5. See Schork, "By Jingo," 123–24.

6. Barham, *Ingoldsby Legends*, 156.

7. Spoo, "Unpublished Letters," 595.

11. Sources 'and Parallels

1. Baring-Gould, *Lives*, l.vi.

2. See Gillespie, *Trieste Library*, 88 (146–47), for entries on *Bards and Saints* (1907) and *Anglo-Irish Essays* (1917).

3. For the evidence for the former, see chapters 8 and 9; for the latter, see Deane, "Wellspring," 1–28. Landuyt and Van Mierlo deal with another similar work in "Catholicism, Nationalism."

4. See chapter 6 and Schork, "Sheep, Bones," 151–62.

5. Mercanton, "Hours," 217.

6. Newman, *Sermons*, 169–70; Newman had this material at his fingertips, since in 1843–1844 he had prepared an extensive calendar of English saints from the second to the fifteenth century for a projected series on their lives.

7. I mention Michèle Roberts, *Impossible Saints* (1997), only to dismiss it; its central "story of Josephine," loosely modeled on the life of St. Teresa of Ávila, is interspersed with surrealistically kinky revisions of the lives of eleven female saints (several of whom are mentioned in my discussion of virgin martyrs). If there were a secular version of the *Index of Prohibited Books*, this effort would top the list for pathological poor judgment.

8. Davies, *Deptford*, 146–50, 168–70, 185; for possible reference to St. Wilgefortis in the *Wake*, see the section on virgin martyrs in chapter 4.

9. Huysmans, *Oblate*, 237.

10. Huysmans, *Cathedral*, 147.

11. Ibid., 298–302.

12. Ibid., 51 and 331.

13. Ibid., 94–101.

14. Huysmans, *Saint Lydwine*.

15. The title of the chapter that discusses this period in the authoritative biography of the author is "The Hagiographer" (see Baldrick, *Life*, 290–310).

16. Atherton, *Books*, 257; the citation is from Huysmans, *Against Nature*, 27.

17. The citation from Stein's work comes from *Last Operas*, 467; *Four Saints*, with music by Virgil Thomson, was first produced in 1934 in New York. For brief comment on Joyce and Stein, see *JJII* 528–29.

18. McCourt, *Angela's Ashes*, 285–86. McCourt's library source has conflated several tales. The historical St. Christina lived, long after the Roman persecution, in thirteenth-century Belgium; she earned her epithet by such "astonishing" feats as a return to life after a tour of hell, purgatory, and heaven. Moreover, she so despised the odor of fellow creatures that she climbed trees to avoid any human contact. Some of the tortures in McCourt's account of Butler's life seem to have worked their way into his text from the tale of another St. Christina (herself the product of hagiographical compression) as narrated in *The Golden Legend* (I.384–87).

19. Larbaud, *Homage*, 44.

Bibliography

Adair, John. *The Pilgrim's Way: Shrines and Saints in Britain and Ireland*. London: Thames and Hudson, 1978.
The Anglo-Saxon Chronicle, translated by G. N. Garmonsway. London: J. M. Dent and Son, 1962.
Aravantinou, Manto. *Τά 'Ελληνικά τοῦ Τζαίημς Τζόυς* (*Ta Hellenika tou Tzaimes Tzoys* [*The Greek of James Joyce*]). Athens: Hermes, 1977.
Atherton, James S. *The Books at the Wake: A Study of Literary Allusions in James Joyce's "Finnegans Wake."* Carbondale and Edwardsville: Southern Illinois University Press, 1974.
———. "Sport and Games in *Finnegans Wake*." In *Twelve and a Tilly: Essays on the Occasion of the 25th Anniversary of "Finnegans Wake,"* edited by Jack P. Dalton and Clive Hart, 52–64. Evanston: Northwestern University Press, 1965.
———. "Sus in Cribro." *AWN* 9.6 (1972): 111–13.
Attwater, Donald. *A Dictionary of Saints*. Harmondsworth: Penguin, 1965.
Attwater, Donald, and Catherine R. John. *The Penguin Dictionary of Saints*. 3d ed. Harmondsworth: Penguin, 1995.
Aubert, Jacques. "Breton Proverbs in Notebook VI.B.14." *AWN* 15 (1978): 86–89.
Baldrick, Robert. *The Life of J.-K. Huysmans*. Oxford: Clarendon Press, 1955.
Barham, Richard Harris. *The Ingoldsby Legends*. London: Macmillan, 1911.
Baring-Gould, Sabine. *The Lives of the Saints*. Rev. ed. Edinburgh: John Grant, 1914.
Bates, Roland. "The Feast is a Flyday." *JJQ* 2 (Spring 1965): 174–87.
Bauerle, Ruth. "The Historical Counterparts for Rowan and Hand: Why 'Doggy' Justice Lives in Surrey." In *A Collideorscape of Joyce: Festschrift for Fritz Senn*, edited by Ruth Frehner and Ursula Zeller, 104–14. Dublin: Lilliput Press, 1998.
———. *The James Joyce Songbook*. New York and London: Garland, 1982.
Bishop, John. *Joyce's Book of the Dark: "Finnegans Wake."* Madison: University of Wisconsin Press, 1986.
Bitel, Lisa M. *Isle of the Saints: Monastic Settlement and Christian Community in Early Ireland*. Ithaca: Cornell University Press, 1990.
Bjork, Christopher. "'Sinted Sageness': Some Sources for Kevin in *Finnegans Wake*." In *Probes: Genetic Studies in Joyce*, edited by David Hayman and Sam Slote, 85–100. European Studies in Joyce 5. Amsterdam: Rodopi, 1995.
Boero, Father. *The Life of St. John Berchmans*. New York: P. J. Kenedy and Sons, n.d.

Bokenham, Osbern. *A Legend of Holy Women*. Translated by Sheila Delany. Notre Dame: University of Notre Dame Press, 1992.

Boyle, Robert. *James Joyce's Pauline Vision: A Catholic Exposition*. Carbondale: Southern Illinois University Press, 1978.

Bradley, Bruce. *James Joyce's Schooldays*. New York: St. Martin's, 1982.

Brown, John. "*Ulysses* into French." In *Joyce at Texas,* edited by Dave Oliphant and Thomas Zigal, 29–59. Austin: Humanities Research Center, University of Texas Press, 1983.

Brown, Peter. *The Cult of the Saints: Its Rise and Function in Latin Christianity.* Chicago: University of Chicago Press, 1981.

———. "The Rise and Function of the Holy Man in Late Antiquity." *Journal of Roman Studies* 61 (1971): 80–101; reprinted in Peter Brown, *Society and the Holy in Late Antiquity,* 103–52. Berkeley and Los Angeles: University of California Press, 1982.

Brown, Terence. "Joyce's Magic Lantern." *JJQ* 28 (Summer 1991): 791–98.

Brucolli, M. J. *Some Sort of Epic Grandeur.* New York: Harcourt Brace Jovanovich, 1986.

Brunazzi, Elizabeth. "La Narration de l'autogenèse dans 'La Tentation de saint Antoine' et dans 'Ulysses'." In *James Joyce 2: "Scribble" 2: Joyce et Flaubert,* edited by Claude Jacquet and Andre Topia, 123–31. Paris: Lettres Modernes, 1990. (*La Revue des lettres modernes* 953–58).

Budge, E. A. Wallis. *The Egyptian Book of the Dead.* New York: Dover, 1967.

———. *Osiris and the Egyptian Resurrection.* New York: Dover, 1973.

Budgen, Frank. *James Joyce and the Making of "Ulysses" and Other Writings.* Oxford and New York: Oxford University Press, 1972.

Butler, Alban. *The Lives of the Fathers, Martyrs, and Other Principal Saints.* Boston: D. and J. Sadlier, 1855.

———. *Lives of the Saints.* Edited and revised by Donald Attwater and Herbert Thurston. New York: P. J. Kenedy and Sons, 1962.

Byrne, John Francis. *Silent Years: An Autobiography with Memoirs of James Joyce and Our Ireland.* New York: Farrar, Straus and Young, 1953.

The Catholic Encyclopedia. New York: The Encyclopedia Press, 1907–12.

Connolly, Thomas E. *The Personal Library of James Joyce: A Descriptive Bibliography.* Buffalo: University of Buffalo Press, 1957.

Culleton, Claire A. *Names and Naming in Joyce.* Madison: University of Wisconsin Press, 1994.

Cumpiano, Marion. *Saint John of the Cross and the Dark Night of "Finnegans Wake."* A Wake Newslitter Monograph 8. Colchester: A Wake Newslitter Press, 1983.

Curtius, Ernest Robert. *European Literature and the Latin Middle Ages.* Translated by Willard R. Trask. New York: Harper, 1963.

Dalton, Jack P. "Advertisement for the Restoration." In *Twelve and a Tilly: Essays on the Occasion of the 25th Anniversary of "Finnegans Wake,"* edited by Jack P. Dalton and Clive Hart, 119–37. Evanston: Northwestern University Press, 1965.

Dalton, Jack P., and Clive Hart, eds. *Twelve and a Tilly: Essays on the Occasion of the*

25th Anniversary of "Finnegans Wake." Evanston: Northwestern University Press, 1965.
Dames, Michael. *Mythic Ireland.* London: Thames and Hudson, 1992.
Davies, Robertson. *The Deptford Trilogy: Fifth Business, The Manticore, World of Wonders.* Harmondsworth: Penguin, 1983.
Deane, Vincent. "Bywaters and the Original Crime." In *"Finnegans Wake": Teems of Time,* edited by Andrew Treip, 165–204. European Joyce Studies 4. Amsterdam: Rodopi, 1994.
———. "Greek Gifts: *Ulysses* into Fox in VI.B.10." *JSA* 5 (1994): 162–75.
———. "*The Green Pastures* in VI.B.33." *AFWC* 4 (Spring 1989): 56–60.
———. "Song Hoard: Four Indexes: Indexes One and Two: *Rondes et chansons populaires* in VI.B.33 and VI.C.6." *AFWC* 6 (1990–91): 12–24.
———. "St. Patrick." *AFWC* 8: forthcoming.
———. "The Wellspring of the Saints: J. M. Flood in B.3." *AFWC* 7 (1991–92): 1–27.
Delahaye, Hippolyte. *The Legends of the Saints: An Introduction to Hagiography.* Translated by V. M. Crawford. New York: Fordham University Press, 1962.
Devlin, Kimberly. "Self and Other in *Finnegans Wake:* A Framework for Analyzing Versions of Shem and Shaun." *JJQ* 21 (Fall 1983): 31–50.
Dunleavy, Janet E., ed. *Re-Viewing Classics of Joyce Criticism.* Urbana and Chicago: University of Illinois Press, 1991.
Eco, Umberto. *The Name of the Rose.* Translated by William Weaver. San Diego and New York: Harcourt Brace Jovanovich, 1983.
Eliot, T. S. *The Complete Poems and Plays, 1909–1950.* New York: Harcourt, Brace, 1952.
Elliott, Alison Goddard. *Roads to Paradise: Reading the Lives of Early Saints.* Hanover: University Press of New England, 1987.
Ellmann, Richard. *The Consciousness of Joyce.* London: Faber and Faber, 1977.
———. *Oscar Wilde.* New York: Knopf, 1987.
———. *Ulysses on the Liffey.* New York: Oxford University Press, 1973.
Etter, Hansueli F., et al., eds. *Die Zürcher Stadtheiligen Felix und Regula.* Zürich: Büro für Archäologie, 1988.
Ferrer, Daniel. "The Freudful Couchmare of Ld: Joyce's Notes and the Composition of Chapter XVI of *Finnegans Wake.*" *JJQ* 22 (Summer 1985): 367–82.
Ferrer, Daniel, and Claude Jacquet, eds. *Writing Its Own Wrunes for Ever: Essais de Génétique Joycienne.* Tusson: Du Lérot, 1998.
Fitzgerald, F. Scott. *Correspondence of F. Scott Fitzgerald.* Edited by M. J. Bruccoli and M. M. Duggan. New York: Random House, 1972.
Fitzpatrick, Benedict. *Ireland and the Making of Britain.* New York and London: Funk and Wagnalls, 1922.
Fleming, Bill. "Holy Saltmartin (419.08)." *AFWC* 2 (Autumn 1986): 14.
Flood, J. M. *Ireland: Its Saints and Scholars.* Dublin: Talbot Press, 1917. Reprinted: Port Washington: Kennikat Press, 1970.
Frehner, Ruth, and Ursula Zeller, eds. *A Collideorscape of Joyce: Festschrift for Fritz Senn.* Dublin: Lilliput, 1998.

Geary, Patrick J. *Furta Sacra: The Theft of Relics in the Middle Ages.* Princeton: Princeton University Press, 1978.

Gibbon, Edward. *The Decline and Fall of the Roman Empire.* London, 1776–88.

Giedion-Welcker, Carola. "Meetings with Joyce." In *Portraits of the Artist in Exile: Recollections of James Joyce by Europeans,* edited by Willard Potts, 253–80. San Diego and New York: Harcourt, Brace, Jovanovich, 1986.

Gifford, Don, with Robert J. Seidman. *"Ulysses" Annotated: Notes for James Joyce's "Ulysses."* Rev. ed. Berkeley and Los Angeles: University of California Press, 1989.

Gilbert, Stuart. *James Joyce's "Ulysses": A Study.* New York: Vintage, 1958.

———. *Reflections on James Joyce: Stuart Gilbert's Paris Journal.* Edited by Thomas F. Staley and Randolph Lewis. Austin: University of Texas Press, 1993.

Gillespie, Michael Patrick, with Erik Bradford Stocker. *James Joyce's Trieste Library: A Catalogue of Materials at the Harry Ransom Humanities Research Center, The University of Texas at Austin.* Austin: University of Texas Press, 1986.

Giraldus, Cambrensis. *History and Topography of Ireland.* Rev. ed. Harmondsworth: Penguin, 1982.

Glasheen, Adaline. *Third Census of "Finnegans Wake": An Index of the Characters and Their Roles.* Berkeley and Los Angeles: University of California Press, 1977.

Gordon, John. *"Finnegans Wake": A Plot Summary.* Syracuse: Syracuse University Press, 1986.

Greene, E. A. *Saints and Their Symbols.* Rev. ed. London: Whittaker and Co., 1909.

Hahn, H. George. "Tarsicius: A Hagiographical Allusion in Joyce's 'Araby'." *Papers on Language and Literature* 27 (Summer 1991): 381–85.

Hanks, Patrick, and Flavia Hodges, eds. *A Dictionary of Surnames.* Oxford: Oxford University Press, 1988.

Hart, Clive. *Structure and Motif in "Finnegans Wake."* Evanston: Northwestern University Press, 1962.

Hartshorn, Peter. *James Joyce and Trieste.* Westport: Greenwood Press, 1997.

Haven, Michael, and Yolande de Pontfarcy. *The Medieval Pilgrimages to St. Patrick's Purgatory: Lough Derg and the European Tradition.* Enniskillen: Clogher Historical Society, 1988.

Hayman, David, ed. *A First-Draft Version of "Finnegans Wake."* Austin: University of Texas Press, 1963.

———. "'Scribbledehobbles' and How They Grew: A Turning Point in the Development of a Chapter." In *Twelve and a Tilly: Essays on the Occasion of the 25th Anniversary of "Finnegans Wake,"* edited by Jack P. Dalton and Clive Hart, 107–18. Evanston: Northwestern University Press, 1965.

Herbert, Máire. *Iona, Kells, and Derry: The History and Hagiography of the Monastic "Familia" of Columba.* Oxford: Clarendon Press, 1988.

Herring, Phillip F. *Joyce's Notes and Early Drafts for "Ulysses": Selections from the Buffalo Collection.* Charlottesville: University Press of Virginia, 1977.

Higginson, Fred H. "Notes on the Text of *Finnegans Wake.*" *Journal of English and Germanic Philology* 55 (1956): 451–56.

---. "The Text of *Finnegans Wake.*" In *New Light on Joyce from the Dublin Symposium,* edited by Fritz Senn, 120–35. Bloomington and London: Indiana University Press, 1972.
Hogan, Patrick Colm. *Joyce, Milton, and the Theory of Influence.* Gainesville: University Press of Florida, 1995.
Hopkins, Lisa. "Spartan Boys: John Ford and Philip Sidney." *Classical and Modern Literature* 17 (Spring 1997): 217–29.
Hrotsvitha. *Opera.* Edited by Karl Strecher. Leipzig: B. G. Teubner, 1906.
Huysmans, Joris K. *The Cathedral.* Translated by Clara Bell. London: Dedalus; New York: Hippocrene, 1989.
---. *The Oblate of St. Benedict.* Translated by Edward Perceval. London: Dedalus, 1996.
Ignatius Jubiläum. Feldkirch: Stella Matutina, 1990.
Jacquet, Claude. *Joyce et Rabelais: Aspects de le création verbale dans "Finnegans Wake."* Paris: Didier, 1973.
James Joyce 2: "Scribble" 2: Joyce et Flaubert. Edited by Claude Jacquet and André Topia. Paris: Lettres Modernes, 1990. (*La Revue des Lettres Modernes* 953–58).
Jaurretche, Colleen. "Waking to Obscurity: *Finnegans Wake* and John of the Cross's Dark Night." *JSA* 8 (1997): 154–82.
Jerome, St. "Life of St. Paul the Hermit." In *The Principal Works of St. Jerome.* Translated by W. H. Fremantle. In *A Select Library of Nicene and Post-Nicene Fathers of the Christian Church,* edited by Philip Schaff and Henry Wace, VII.299–303. Grand Rapids: Eerdmans, 1954.
Jolas, Eugène. "My Friend James Joyce." In *James Joyce: Two Decades of Criticism,* edited by Sean Given, 3–18. New York: Vanguard, 1948.
---. *Sur Joyce.* Translated by Marc Dachy. Paris: Plon, 1990.
Jones, Charles W. *St. Nicholas of Myra, Bari, and Manhattan: Biography of a Legend.* Chicago: University of Chicago Press, 1978.
Joyce, James. "Trois Lettres a Edmond Jaloux." In *L'Herne: James Joyce,* edited by Jacques Aubert and Fritz Senn, 137–39. Paris: L'Herne, 1985.
Joyce, Stanislaus. *The Complete Dublin Diary.* Edited by George H. Healey. Ithaca and London: Cornell University Press, 1971.
---. *My Brother's Keeper.* Edited by Richard Ellmann. London: Faber and Faber, 1982.
Kavanagh, H. L., trans. *The Life of St. Humphrey (Saint Onnafrius). By the Abbot Paphnutius.* London: Burns and Oates, 1906.
Keen, William P. "June Sixteenth Once Again." *JJQ* 14 (Fall 1976): 94–96.
Kennedy, Sister Eileen. "Another Root for Bloomsday." *JJQ* 6 (Spring 1969): 271–72.
Kenner, Hugh. *Ulysses.* Rev. ed. Baltimore: Johns Hopkins University Press, 1987.
Ker, Ian. *John Henry Newman.* Oxford: Clarendon Press, 1988.
Kimbell, Jean. "St. Augustine and Love in Bloom." *JJQ* 25 (Spring 1988): 275–78.
Knowles, David. *Great Scholarly Enterprises: Problems in Monastic History.* London and New York: Nelson, 1963.
Kopper, Edward A. "Joyce's *Finnegans Wake.*" *Explicator* 22 (January 1964): no. 34.

———. "More Legends in *Finnegans Wake*." *AWN* 6.3 (June 1969): 39–43.

———. "Saint Olaf in *Finnegans Wake*." *AWN* 6.3 (June 1969): 35–39.

———. "Three More Legends in *Finnegans Wake*." *AWN* 4.6 (December 1967): 119–20.

Landuyt, Inge, and Wim Van Mierlo. "Catholicism, Nationalism, and Exile: *The Irish Way* in VI.B.34." Forthcoming.

Larbaud, Valery. *An Homage to Jerome, Patron Saint of Translators*. Translated by Jean-Paul de Chezet. Marlboro, Vermont: Marlboro Press, 1984.

Lernout, Geert. "Czarnowski's *St Patrick* in VI.B.14." Forthcoming.

Litz, A. Walton. *The Art of James Joyce: Method and Design in "Ulysses" and "Finnegans Wake."* Oxford and New York: Oxford University Press, 1968.

Lohmann, Dieter. *Kalypso bei Homer und James Joyce*. Tübingen: Stauffenberg, 1998.

Maguire, Peter A. "*Finnegans Wake* and Irish Historical Memory." *Journal of Modern Literature* 22 (Winter 1998–99): 293–327.

McCarthy, Patrick A. "The Last Epistle of *Finnegans Wake*." *JJQ* 27 (Summer 1990): 725–33.

———. "Stuart Gilbert's Guide to the Perplexed." In *Re-Viewing Classics in Joyce Criticism*, edited by Janet Dunleavy, 23–35. Urbana and Chicago: University of Illinois Press, 1991.

McCourt, Frank. *Angela's Ashes*. New York: Scribner's, 1996.

McGinley, Phyllis. *The Love Letters of Phyllis McGinley*. New York: Viking, 1954.

McHugh, Roland. "Angelic Wisdom." *AFWC* 1 (Autumn 1985): 2–4.

———. *Annotations to "Finnegans Wake."* Rev. ed. Baltimore and London: Johns Hopkins University Press, 1991.

———. "Dean Kinane in VI.B.14." *AFWC* 1 (Winter 1985): 21–32.

———. "Protevangelium." *AFWC* 1 (Autum 1985): 20.

———. *The Sigla of "Finnegans Wake."* London: Edward Arnold, 1976.

Mercanton, Jacques. "The Hours of James Joyce." In *Portraits of the Artist in Exile: Recollections of James Joyce by Europeans*, edited by Willard Potts, 206–52. San Diego and New York: Harcourt, Brace, Jovanovich, 1986.

Mink, Louis O. *A "Finnegans Wake" Gazetteer*. Bloomington: Indiana University Press, 1978.

Moore, George. *The Apostle*. London: Maunsel, 1911.

Morse, J. Mitchell. *The Sympathetic Alien*. New York: New York University Press, 1959.

Moseley, Virginia. *Joyce and the Bible*. De Kalb: Northern Illinois University Press, 1967.

Murphy-O'Connor, Jerome. "Fishers of Fish, Fishers of Men." *Bible Review* 15 (June 1999): 22–27, 48–50.

Nash, John. "The Date of Joyce's ALP Reading." *JJQ* 34 (Summer 1997): 557.

Newman, John Henry. *Sermons Preached on Various Occasions*. London: Burns, Oates, 1870.

Nolan, Anne. "Father Charles of Mount Argus, 1821–1893." *JJQ* 29 (Summer 1992): 841–45.

Noon, William T. *Joyce and Aquinas*. New Haven: Yale University Press, 1957.
Norris, Margot. "The Last Chapter of *Finnegans Wake:* Stephen Finds His Mother." *JJQ* 25 (Fall 1987): 11–30. Reprinted in *Critical Essays on James Joyce's "Finnegans Wake,"* edited by Patrick A. McCarthy, 212–30. New York: G. K. Hall, 1992.
O Hehir, Brendan. *A Gaelic Lexicon for "Finnegans Wake."* Berkeley and Los Angeles: University of California Press, 1967.
O Hehir, Brendan, and John M. Dillon. *A Classical Lexicon for "Finnegans Wake": A Glossary of the Greek and Latin in the Major Works of Joyce*. Berkeley and Los Angeles: University of California Press, 1977.
O'Hanlon, John. *Lives of the Irish Saints: With Special Festivals, and the Commemorations of Holy Persons, Compiled from Calendars, Martyrologies, and Various Sources, Relating to the Ancient Church History of Ireland*. Dublin: James Duffy; London: Burns, Oates; New York: Catholic Publishing Society, 1890–97.
O'Neill, Christine. "Aengus of Birds and Angus the Culdee: The Pagan and His Christian Namesake." In *A Collideorscape of Joyce: Festschrift for Fritz Senn*, edited by Ruth Frehner and Ursula Zeller, 279–93. Dublin: Lilliput Press, 1998.
O'Shea, Michael. "'By Dad, youd not heed that fert?': Joyce's Anterior Monologue, or a Paean in the Erse." In *A Collideorscape of Joyce: Festschrift for Fritz Senn*, edited by Ruth Frehner and Ursula Zeller, 398–403. Dublin: Lilliput Press, 1998.
———. *Joyce and Heraldry*. Albany: State University of New York Press, 1986.
The Oxford Companion to the Bible. Edited by Bruce M. Metzger and Michael D. Coogan. New York and Oxford: Oxford University Press, 1993.
Paphnutius. *Histories of the Monks of Upper Egypt and the Life of Onnofrius*. Edited and translated by Tim Vivian. Cistercian Studies 140. Kalamazoo: Cistercian Publications, 1993.
Parandowski, Jan. "Meeting with Joyce." In *Portraits of the Artist in Exile: Recollections of James Joyce by Europeans*, edited by Willard Potts, 153–62. San Diego and New York: Harcourt, Brace, Jovanovich, 1986.
Partridge, Eric. *A Dictionary of the Underworld*. 3d ed. London: Routledge and Kegan Paul, 1968.
Pesch, Josef. *Wilde about Joyce*. Munsteraner Monographien zur englischen Literatur. Frankfurt am Main: Peter Lang, 1992.
Plummer, Charles. *Vitae Sanctorum Hiberniae*. Oxford: Clarendon Press, 1910.
Potts, Willard, ed. *Portraits of the Artist in Exile: Recollections of James Joyce by Europeans*. San Diego and New York: Harcourt, Brace, Jovanovich, 1986.
Power, Arthur. *Conversations with James Joyce*. Edited by Clive Hart. Chicago: University of Chicago Press, 1982.
A Priest of the Diocese of Cork. *Little Nellie of Holy God: The Story of the Life of a Saintly Irish Child*. Cork: City Printing Works, 1911.
Rabaté, Jean-Michel. *James Joyce, Authorized Reader*. Baltimore and London: Johns Hopkins University Press, 1991.
———. "On Joycean and Wildean Sodomy." *JJQ* 31 (Spring 1994): 159–66.
Rabelais, Francois. *Gargantua and Pantagruel*. Translated by J. M. Cohen. Harmondsworth: Penguin, 1985.

Roberts, Michèle. *Impossible Saints*. Hopewell, N.J.: Ecco Press, 1997.
The Roman Missal in English. 3d ed. New York, Cincinnati, and Chicago: Benziger Brothers, 1925.
Rose, Danis. "Breton in /\a/b." *AWN* 15.6 (1978): 90–92.
———. *Chapters in Coming Forth by Day*. A Wake Newslitter Monograph 6. Colchester: A Wake Newslitter Press, 1982.
———. "Kells-Dublin-Rome-Trieste-Zurich-Paris." *AFWC* 2 (Autumn 1986): 1–13.
———. "Prophetia." *AWN* 10.2 (1973): 27-28.
———. *The Textual Diaries of James Joyce*. Dublin: Lilliput, 1995.
———, ed. *James Joyce's The Index Manuscript: "Finnegans Wake" Holograph Workbook VI.B.46*. Colchester: A Wake Newslitter Press, 1978.
Rose, Danis, and John O'Hanlon. *Understanding "Finnegans Wake": A Guide to the Narrative of James Joyce's Masterpiece*. New York and London: Garland, 1982.
———, eds. *James Joyce. The Lost Notebook*. Edinburgh: Split Pea Press, 1989.
Ryan, William G., trans. *The Golden Legend: Readings on the Saints*, by Jacobus de Voragine. Princeton: Princeton University Press, 1993.
Sainéan, Lazare. *La Langue de Rabelais*. Paris: De Coccard, 1922–33.
Schlossman, Beryl. *Joyce's Catholic Comedy of Language*. Madison: University of Wisconsin Press, 1985.
Scholes, Robert E., compl. *The Cornell Joyce Collection: A Catalogue*. Ithaca: Cornell University Press, 1961.
Scholes, Robert, and Richard M. Kain, eds. *The Workshop of Daedalus*. Evanston: Northwestern University Press, 1964.
Schork, R. J. "'All the sinkts in the colander': *Finnegans Wake*, 1939." *Éire-Ireland* 24 (Winter 1989): 121–28.
———. "Apollinaire with Tirésias in the *Wake*." *Journal of Modern Literature* 17 (Summer 1990): 166–72.
———. "By Jingo: Genetic Criticism of *Finnegans Wake*." *JSA* 5 (1994): 104–27.
———. "Feldkirch in *Finnegans Wake*." *Montfort* (Dornbirn-Bregenz) 41.3/4 (1984): 308–11.
———. "Genetic Criticism: A Primer." Forthcoming.
———. "Gibbon in the *Wake*: A Note on Footnotes." Forthcoming in *JJQ*.
———. "A Graphic Exercise in Mnemotechic." *JJQ* 16 (Spring 1979): 351–54.
———. *Greek and Hellenic Culture in Joyce*. Gainesville: University Press of Florida, 1998.
———. "James Joyce and the Eastern Orthodox Church." *Journal of Modern Greek Studies* 17 (May 1999): 107–24.
———. "Joyce and Newman: *Ulysses* 151." *American Notes and Queries* 23 (1985): 112–13.
———. "Kennst Du das Haus Citrons, Bloom?" *JJQ* 17 (Summer 1980): 407–18.
———. *Latin and Roman Culture in Joyce*. Gainesville: University Press of Florida, 1997.
———. "Liturgical Irony in James Joyce's 'The Sisters'." *Studies in Short Fiction* 26 (Spring 1989): 193–97.

———. "'Nodebinding Ayes': Milton, Blindness, and Egypt in *Finnegans Wake*." *JJQ* 30 (Fall 1992): 69–83.

———. "Romanos' Elijah: An Apocalyptic Prophet." *Patristic and Byzantine Review* 9 (1990): 41–48.

———. *Sacred Song from the Byzantine Pulpit: Romanos the Melodist*. Gainesville: University Press of Florida, 1995.

———. "Sheep, Bones, and Nettles: St. Kevin's Childhood Miracles." In *Writing Its Own Wrunes for Ever: Essais de Génétique Joycienne*, edited by Daniel Ferrer and Claude Jacquet, 151–62. Tusson: Du Lérot, 1998.

———. "Sheep, Goats, and the *Figura Etymologica* in *Finnegans Wake*." *Journal of English and German Philology* 92 (April 1993): 200–211.

———. "Significant Names in the *Wake* 46.20 and 371.22." *JJQ* 34 (Summer 1997): 505–16.

———. "*Ulysses*' Priestly Penrose." *JJQ* 31 (Summer 1994): 563–66.

———. "Victorian Hagiography: A Pattern of Allusions in *Robert Elsmere* and *Helbeck of Bannisdale*." *Studies in the Novel* 21 (Fall 1989): 292–304.

———. "The *Wake*'s Hairy Anchorite: St Humprey/Onuphris." In *A Collideorscape of Joyce: Festschrift for Fritz Senn*, ed. Ruth Frehner and Ursula Zeller, 270–77. Dublin: Lilliput, 1998.

Senn, Fritz. *Inductive Scrutinies*. Edited by Christine O'Neill. Dublin: Lilliput, 1995.

———. *Joyce's Dislocutions: Essays of Reading as Translation*. Edited by John Paul Riquelme. Baltimore: Johns Hopkins University Press, 1984.

———. "Nausicaa." In *James Joyce's "Ulysses": Critical Essays*, edited by Clive Hart and David Hayman, 277–311. Berkeley and Los Angeles: University of California Press, 1974.

———. "Trivia Ulysseana IV: 'Taxilonomy'." *JJQ* 19 (Winter 1982): 154–58.

Severin, Timothy. *The Brendan Voyage*. London: Hutchinson, 1978.

Silverman, David P., ed. *Ancient Egypt*. New York: Oxford University Press, 1997.

Skrabanek, Petr. "St. Patrick's Nightmare Confession." *AFWC* 1 (Autumn 1985): 5–20.

Slote, Sam. "Wilde Thing: Concerning the Eccentricities of a Figure of Decadence in *Finnegans Wake*." In *Probes: Genetic Studies in Joyce*, edited by David Hayman and Sam Slote, 101–22. European Studies in Joyce 5. Amsterdam: Rodopi, 1995.

Spence, Keith. *Blue Guide: Cathedrals and Abbeys of England and Wales*. London: Benn; New York: Norton, 1984.

Spoo, Robert. "Unpublished Letters of Ezra Pound to James, Nora, and Stanislaus Joyce." *JJQ* 29 (Summer 1992): 841–45.

Staley, Thomas F. "Religious Elements and Thomistic Encounters: Noon on Joyce and Aquinas." In *Re-Viewing Classics of Joyce Criticism*, edited by Janet E. Dunleavy, 155–68. Urbana and Chicago: University of Illinois Press, 1991.

Starling, Boris. *Messiah*. New York: Onyx, 1999.

Stein, Gertrude. *Last Operas and Plays*. Edited by Carl van Vechten. New York: Reinhard, 1949.

Suetonius. *The Twelve Caesars*. Translated by Robert Graves. Baltimore: Penguin, 1957.
Sullivan, Kevin. *Joyce among the Jesuits*. New York: Columbia University Press, 1958.
Suter, August. "Some Reminiscences of James Joyce." In *Portraits of the Artist in Exile: Recollections of James Joyce by Europeans*, edited by Willard Potts, 61–66. San Diego and New York: Harcourt, Brace, Jovanovich, 1986.
Swartzlander, Susan. "'On the verge of selfabyss': The St. Kevin Section of *Finnegans Wake*." *JJQ* 25 (Summer 1988): 475–85.
Thrane, James R. "Joyce's Sermon on Hell: Its Sources and Its Background." *Modern Philology* 57 (February 1960): 172–78.
Torchina, Donald T. "Joyce's 'Eveline' and the Blessed Margaret Mary Alacoque." *JJQ* 6 (Fall 1968): 22–28.
Troy, Mark L. *Mummeries of Resurrection: The Cycle of Osiris in "Finnegans Wake."* Studia Anglistica Upsaliensia 26. Uppsala: Acta Universitatis Upsaliensis, 1976.
Tylenda, Joseph N. *Jesuit Saints and Martyrs: Short Biographies of the Saints, Blesseds, Venerables, and Servants of God of the Society of Jesus*. Chicago: Loyola University Press, 1984.
Van Mierlo, Wim. "St. Martin of Tours." *AFWC* 7 (1991–92): 29–44.
Verrimst, V.-F. *Rondes et chansons populaires illustrées avec musique et accompagnement*. Paris: A. Lahure, n.d.
Walton, Franklin. "Wilde at the Wake." *JJQ* 14 (Spring 1977): 300–312.
Walzl, Florence L. "Gabriel and Michael: The Conclusion of the 'The Dead'." *JJQ* 4 (Fall 1966): 17–31.
Ward, Benedicta. *Harlots of the Desert: A Study of Repentance in Early Monastic Sources*. Cistercian Studies Series 106. Kalamazoo: Cistercian Publications, 1987.
Warner, Marina. *Alone of All Her Sex: The Myth and Cult of the Virgin Mary*. New York: Alfred A. Knopf, 1976.
Webb, J. F., trans. *Lives of the Saints: The Voyages of St. Brendan; Bede: Life of Cuthbert; Eddius Stephanus: Life of Wilfrid*. Baltimore: Penguin, 1965.
Wilde, Oscar. *The Letters of Oscar Wilde*. Edited by Rupert Hart-Davis. New York: Harcourt, Brace, and World, 1962.
Williams, Charles A. *Oriental Affinities of the Legend of the Hairy Anchorite: Part II: Christian*. Urbana: University of Illinois Press, 1927.
Woodward, Kenneth L. *Making Saints: How the Catholic Church Determines Who Becomes a Saint, Who Doesn't, and Why*. New York: Simon and Schuster, 1990.

Index

Abbreviations used: f, feast; m, monastery; o, order; p, pilgrimage.

Abelard, Peter (philosopher) 110–11, 151
Adam 19, 79, 177, 195
Adamman (St.) 91–92, 96
Aegnus of the Birds 97
Agatha (St.) 51–53, 123, 156, 169 (f), 204nn.5, 6
Agnes (St.) 204n.6
Aidan (St.) 86
Aikenhead, Mary (Blessed) 95, 124
Ailbey (St.) 107
Alban (St.) 118
Albert the Great (St.) 108
Albigensians (heretics) 145
Albinus (St.) 88
Alexandria 66
Alfred the Great (king) 118
All Saints' Day (All Hallows) 176 (f)
All Souls' Day 176 (f)
Aloysius Gonzaga (St.) 6, 148–49, 172 (f)
Alphosus Liguori (St.) 150
Ambrose (St.) 57, 64
Ambrosius Aurelianius (British warlord) 206n.29
Amiens 20, 199n.7
Ananias 39
Anastasia (St.) 54
Andrew the Apostle (St.) 9, 36, 156, 161
Anglo-Saxons 114–20
Angus the Culdee (St.) 97
Annunciation (Lady Day) 21, 167, 170–71 (f)
Anselm (St.) 108, 111
Ansgar (St.) 131

Anthony of Egypt (St.) 75–76
Anthony of Padua (St.) 125–27
Antioch 44, 66, 120
Anubis 20
Apollonia (St.) 5
Aran Islands 2, 87, 94, 209n.3
Archangels 18–19
Arian (heretic) 10
Asaph (St.) 105
Ascension (feast) 171–72 (f)
Assumption (feast) 170 (f)
Atherton, James 66, 192
Attila the Hun 55
Attwater, Donald xii
Aubert (St.) 136
Augustine of Canterbury (St.) 56–57, 61, 190
Augustine of Hippo (St.) 6, 10–11, 64–66, 116, 150
Augustinians (o) 134
Augustus (Roman emperor) 43

Barat, Madeleine Sophie (St.) 62
Barbara (St.) 54, 204n.9
Barham, Richard H. 67, 72, 184–87
Baring-Gould, Sabine 184, 188
Barnabas the Disciple (St.) 44
Bartholomew the Apostle (St.) 36–37, 161
Basil of Caesarea (St.) 10
Beach, Sylvia 1
Beckett, Samuel 171
Becket, Thomas à (St.) 119, 212n.13
Bede (Venerable) xii

Index

Belshazzar (king) 21
Belvedere College 4, 6, 11, 17, 147, 151, 155
Benedict (St.) 51–52, 57, 96, 100, 135–39, 169
Benedict XV 10
Benedictines (o) 57, 134–38, 145, 191
Benson, Robert H. 190
Bernadette of Lourdes (St.) 123
Bernard of Clairvaux (St.) 136, 214n.6
Black Friars (Dominicans) (o) 142
Blaise (St.) 60, 169
Blake, William 65, 129
Boanerges. *See* Sons of Thunder
Boethius (St.) 60
Bollandists 2, 188, 191
Bonaventure (St.) 110, 140, 211n.2
Boniface (St.) 119, 194
Boniface IV (pope) 96
Book of Kells 91
Book of the Dead 78–79, 84, 207n.13
Boris (St.) 122
Bosch, Hieronymus 75
Botolph (St.) 118
Boxing Day (holiday) 218n.39
Boyle, Robert 198–99, 201n.13
Brendan (St.) 87–89, 94–95, 164, 209n.17
Brewer's Dictionary of Phrase and Fable 161, 217n.17
Brice (Britius) (St.) 116, 176 (f), 212n.9
Brigid (St.) 89–91, 164, 169, 211n.43
Brigitta (St.) 131
Brothers Hospitaller (o) 129
Brown Friars (Franciscans) (o) 12, 141
Brunanburg, battle of 116
Bruno, Giordano (philosopher) 111, 137, 142, 213n.32
Bruno (St.) 137, 141, 176 (f), 214n.7
Budge, E. A. Wallis 84
Budgen, Frank 174, 178, 198, 205n.26
Buechner, Frederick 190
Butler, Alban 88, 184, 189, 193, 195
Byrne, John F. 174

Caesarea 44
Cajetan (St.) 191
Calendars 6–8, 166–69, 178, 198n.15
Camadolesi (o) 137

Canadian Encyclopedia 213n.25
Candlemas (feast) 181
Capuchins (Franciscans) (o) 12, 140, 214n.11
Carlow, Count 176
Carmelites (o) 123, 128–29, 135, 142, 144–45
Carthage 64–65
Carthusians (o) 137, 140, 191, 214n.7
Cassiodorus (church historian) 138
Cathaldus (St.) 86
Catherine of Alexandria (St.) 171 (f), 190
Catherine of Siena (St.) 5, 87, 112, 146, 164, 171
Catherine Ricci (St.) 191
Catholic Encyclopedia 88, 99, 106, 189
Cecilia (St.) 53
Cephalophors 59–60, 63
Chad (St.) 119, 190
Chamson, André and Lucie 1
Charles II (English king) 173
Charon 199
Chartres 191
Cheops (Khufu) (pharaoh) 78
Christ Church (Oxford College) 212n.13
Christian Brothers (o) 134, 151–52, 216n.36
Christina of Stumbela 191
Christina the Astonishing (St.) 193, 220n.18
Christmas 167, 177 (f), 218n.39
Ciaran (St.) 107
Circumcision 35–36, 154, 169
Cistercians (o) 136–37, 139, 191
Clara(-e) (St.) 139
Claudian (Roman poet) 62
Clement (pope) 55
Cletus (pope) 55
Clongowes Wood College 6, 8, 9, 17, 88, 146, 178
Clothilde (St.) 112–13
Columbanus (St.) 86, 95–96, 176 (f), 209n.11
Columbus, Christopher 209n.17
Columella (Roman author) 92
Columkille (Columba) (St.) 87, 89, 91–93, 164, 172 (f)
Compostela (p) 8, 162, 164

Confessors 63–66
Connelly, Marc 84
Conques (p) 176
Constantine (Roman emperor) 50, 63, 122
Constantinople 50, 66, 120, 206n.36, 213n.17
Cordeliers (Corded Friars) (o) 12, 140
Cornelius (pope) 55
Cornelius (Roman centurion) 44
Cosmas (St.) 175 (f)
Council of Birr 96
Croag Patrick (p) 165
Cumpiano, Marion 129
Curé d'Ars. *See* Vianney, Jean-Baptiste (St.)

Curran, Constantine 95, 172
Curtius, Ernst R. 15
Cuthbert (St.) 190
Cyr (Cyricius) (St.) 128
Cyril (St.) 122

Daedalus 4
Dalton, Jack P. 98–99
Dante Aligheri 2, 195
David (St.) 105
Davies, Robertson 190–97, 193
Davog (St.) 164
Deane, Vincent 13, 99, 213n.24
Decius (Roman emperor) 50, 59, 82, 85
Declan (St.) 107
Decollation 25–26, 59–60
Delahaye, Hippolyte 210n.29
De Profundis 42–43, 202n.24
Diarmait (Irish king) 91
Dies natalis 153, 167
Diocletian (Roman emperor) 50, 59
Dionysius (Denis) (St.) 59–60, 205nn.17, 18
Dionysius of Fourna (iconographer) 213n.16
Discalced Friars (Carmelites) (o) 145
Dismas (St.) 28–29
Dixon, James H. 68
Dizier (Desiderius) (St.) 172 (f)
Doctors of the Church 10, 63–66, 108, 120–21, 125, 136
Dominic (St.) 215n.18

Dominicans (o) 5, 131, 132, 134, 138, 140, 142–48, 152, 191, 216n.36
Domitian (Roman emperor) 171
Donatus (St.) 86
Dorcas the Disciple (St.) 38
Douglas, Lord Alfred 42–43
Doyle, Arthur Conan 178
Dujardin, Édouard 200n.21
Dulia, hyperdula, latria 154
Duns Scotus, John (philosopher) 95
Dunstan (St.) 114
Dympna (St.) 5. 113

Eastern Orthodoxy 25, 120–22, 167, 170, 176, 216n.3
Eco, Umberto 157–59, 214n.10
Edict of Toleration 50, 63, 122
Edna (St.) 209n.3
Eglinton, John (pseud.) 188–89
Egypt 14, 63, 77–85
Elias of Cortona 139
Elijah (Elias) 70, 144
Eliot, T. S. 206n.34
Elizabeth (St.) 24–25, 29, 173 (f)
Elizabeth of Hungary (St.) 112
Ellmann, Richard 1, 171, 217n.15
Emeric (St.) 176 (f)
Encyclopaedia Britannica 67, 109–10, 166, 176, 185, 189, 212n.9
Eric (St.) 131
Ermingila (St.) 116
Ethelreda of Northumbria (queen) 115, 117
Ethelred the Unready (king) 116, 176, 212n.9
Ethelstan of Mercia (king) 116
Eudoxia (Byzantine empress) 120
Eulalia (St.) 51, 53
Eusebius of Caesarea (church historian) 63–64
Eve 19, 21, 175 (f), 177
Eve (St.) 175 (f)

Father Charles of Mount Argus (Blessed) 124–25
Feasts 7–8, 166–79
Felicitas (St.) 53–54, 183–84
Felix (St.) 63, 174 (f)

Fiacre (St.) 95, 175 (f), 217n.1
Fictitious saints 12–13, 180–87; Annona 182; Anonymous 12, 180; Baume 183; Collopys 182; Delay 127, 182; Eponymous 12, 180; Giovanni Boccaccio 183; Grouse 6, 13, 174 (f), 181; Homonymous 180; Marie des Paluds 187; Marion Calpensis 181; Miscarriage 127, 182; Mowy 13, 182; Mozos 182; Mumpledum 113; Notre Dame de Siam 183; Notre Dame du Bon Marché 182–83; Notwithstanding 184; Owen Caniculus 180; Pancreas 172 (f); Paronymous 180; Partridge 6, 13, 174 (f); Peregrinus 13; Pivorandbowl 30, 181; Pothinus (Fotinus) 180–81; Pseudonymous 12, 180; Pursy Orelli 181–82; Robo 183; Sophistry 183; Synonymous 180; Thruandthru 184; Tibbs 181
Finnian of Clonard (St.) 91, 93, 209n.3
Finnian of Moville (St.) 177 (f)
Fintan of Rheinau (St.) 177 (f)
Fitzgerald, F. Scott and Zelda 1
Fixed feasts 167, 172–78
Flaubert, Gustave 200n.16, 213n.28
Flood, J. M. 14, 88, 189, 208n.1
Forty Martyrs of Sebasteia 62–63
Foy (Faith) (St.) 91, 176 (f)
Francis Borgia (St.) 197n.8
Franciscans (o) 5, 12–13, 123, 131, 138–42, 145, 152, 191, 214nn.10–14
Francis de Sales (St.) 150–51, 216n.34
Francis of Assisi (St.) 13, 138–42, 193, 215n.18
Francis of Paul (St.) 191
Francis Xavier (St.) 5, 97, 147–48, 155–56, 177 (f), 210n.23
Fratricelli (Franciscans) (o) 139–40
Friars Preachers (Dominicans) (o) 143
Fursa(-ey) (St.) 2, 88, 195, 209n.3

Gabriel the Archangel (St.) 21, 24
Gaudete Sunday 179 (f)
Genesius (St.) 59
Genetic criticisn xii, 14, 67, 72, 207n.49, 207n.4, 212n.5, 218n.26

Genevieve (St.) 55
Gengulphus (Jingo) (St.) 67–69, 72, 184–87, 219n.4
George (St.) 61
George V (English king) 96
Gervase (St.) 61–62
Gherhardini da Borgo San Donnio 140
Gibbon, Edward 60, 74, 82, 189, 203n.1, 208n.22
Gibraltar 132, 181
Giedion-Welcher, Carola 4, 168, 187
Gifford, Don, and Robert J. Seidman xii, 134, 160, 180, 200n.14, 211n.43
Giles (St.) 175 (f)
Glasheen, Adaline xiii, 60
Gleb (St.) 122
Glendalough 14, 88, 97, 98–105, 119, 135, 156, 210n.34
Gogarty, Oliver St. John 34
Golden Legend 24, 34, 52, 59–60, 66, 74, 128, 136, 142, 184, 200n.19, 205nn.24, 25, 208n.21, 216n.1, 220n.18
Good Thief. See Dismas (St.)
Gorman, Herbert 1
Gorman, Marianus (Mael-Marie) 1, 12
Grand Chartreuse (m) 137
Greene, E. A. 88, 134–35, 160, 189
Greene, Graham 190
Green Pastures, The 84
Gregory I (pope) 56–57, 64
Gregory of Mazianzus (St.) 10
Grey Friars (Franciscans) (o) 12, 140–42
Guarani (Paraguan misson) 146, 215
Guardian angels 18, 167
Guthfrithson, Anlaf (Viking-Irish warlord) 114

Hahn, George 58–59
Halloween 176 (f)
Halvard (St.) 131
Hanaway, Jonas 11
Healy, Michael 58
Heigira 7
Helena (St.) 155, 171
Heloise 110–11
Henry II (English king) 97, 119–20
Henry III (English king) 212n.14
Henry VIII (English king) 213n.14

Hermes (Mercury) 20
Herod Agrippa (king) 8
Herod Antipas (king) 25–26
Herodias 26
Hilarion (St.) 75, 76
Historia Calamitatum 110–11
Holman, Sheri 190
Holy and Undivided Trinity (f) 8, 167
Holy Cross 153, 155, 171 (f)
Holy Grail 20, 155, 216
Hrotsvitha of Gandersheim 184–87
Hubert (St.) 128, 195, 213n.27
Humphrey (St.). *See* Onuphrius (St.)
Huysmans, Joris Karl 14, 191–92
Hya (Ia) (St.) 211n.41
Hy Brasil 94–95

Ibar (St.) 107
Ignatius Loyola (St.) 146, 174 (f), 193, 210n.23
Immaculate Conception (feast) 177 (f)
Ingoldsby Legends, The 67, 72, 180
Ingram, Rex 83–84
Innocent III (pope) 141, 146
Irenus (St.) 58
Irish Homestead 5
Isabella of Castile (queen) 12
Isadore the Farmer (St.) 127–28
Ita (St.) 5, 87–88, 94
Ives (St.) 105–6

Jaloux, Edmond 197n.4
James (Jacob) the Persian (St.) 11, 59, 198n.22
James the Great(-er), Apostle (St.) 8–9, 36–37, 161, 162, 173 (f)
James the Less(-er), Apostle (St.) 11, 36, 61, 161
Januarius (Gennaro) (St.) 157, 175 (f)
Jaurretche, Coleen 213n.29
Jeanne des Anges (St.) 157
Jeremiah (prophet) 198n.25
Jerome (St.) 13, 64, 66, 81–2, 84–5, 195
Jerusalem 66, 162
Jesuits (o) 6, 17, 21, 88, 137, 145–50, 152, 174, 177, 188, 191, 195, 214n.28
Joachim (St.) 174 (f)
Joachim of Flora 139–40

Joan of Arc 113
Jonah 17, 92
John Berchmans (St.) 9, 148, 150
John Bosco (St.) 151
John Eudes (St.) 174–75 (f)
John of Damascus (St.) 120–21
John of God (St.) 129
John of Nepomuk (St.) 12, 133
John of the Cross (St.) 128–29
John Paul II (pope) 124, 139
John the Baptist (St.) 24–27, 29, 121, 171 (f), 172 (f), 200n.18
John the Egyptian (St.) 171 (f)
John the Evangelist, Apostle (St.) 22–23, 36, 58, 160–61, 171 (f), 177 (f), 200n.18
Josaphat (St.) 122
Joseph (patriarch) 170
Joseph (St.) 14, 23–24, 29, 155, 167, 170 (f), 200n.14
Joseph of Arimathea (St.) 24, 155
Joyce, John Stanislaus 10
Joyce, Mary Jane (May) 10
Joyce, Nora 58, 177
Joyce, P. W. 164
Joyce, Stanislaus 6, 64, 159, 177, 197, 206, 215n.21
Judas Iscariot the Apostle 94
Jude the Apostle (St.) 161
Julian (St.) 128
Juliana (St.) 51–52
Justin (St.) 58
Justinian (Byzantine emperor) 50, 121

Kenila (St.) 172 (f)
Kevin (St.) 14, 57, 69, 80–81, 85, 86–88, 97, 98–105, 106, 119, 135, 156, 172 (f), 179, 189, 210nn.30–34
Kish Bank 47–48
Knock (p) 1, 165, 169
Knowles, David 197n.5
Knute (St.) 131
Kolbe, Maximilian (St.) 213n.20
Kopper, Edwin A. 91, 132
Kümmernis (St.). *See* Wilgefortis (St.)

Lady Day. *See* Annunciation
Laetare Sunday 178 (f)
Lammas Day (feast) 174 (f)

Landuyt, Inge 94
Larbaud, Valery 106, 195
La Roux, Guillaume 125
Laurence (St.) 59
Laurence O'Toole (St.) 95, 97–98, 107, 119–20, 192, 177 (f)
Lawrence (Laurence) (St.) 174 (f)
Lazarites (o) 191
Lazarus 17, 27, 29
Leander (St.) 170 (f)
Leopold of Austria (St.) 130
Leo XIII (pope) 56
Lernout, Geert 213n.25
Liberata (St.). *See* Wilgefortis (St.)
Lindisfarne 203n.31
Linus (pope) 55
Little Nellie of Holy God 124–25
Lohmann, Dieter 215n.20
Lough Derg (p) 164–65
Lourdes (p) 168 (f)
Lucia (Lucy) (St.) 53–54, 177 (f)
Lucifer 1–19
Luke the Evangelist (St.) 22–23, 160
Lydwine of Schiedan (Blessed) 192, 193

Magee, W. K. *See* Eglinton, John
Maitland, Margaret 70–71
Malachy(-i) (St.) 56, 93–94
Mamertius (St.) 61–62
Mansuetus (St.) 87, 107
Marcus Aurelius (Roman emperor) 62
Margaret Mary Alacoque (St.) 15, 28, 123–24, 213n.21
Margaret of Hungary (St.) 112
Marguerite (St.) 6
Mark Antony 43
Martha of Bethany (St.) 27–29, 74
Martinmas (feast) 168–69
Martin of Tours (St.) 50, 69–70, 168 (f), 173 (f)
Martyrology of Tallaght 3
Mary Magdalene (St.) 27–28, 111, 173 (f), 200n.22
Mary of Bethany (St.) 27–29
Mary of Egypt (St.) 74, 76
Mary the Virgin (St.) 14, 17, 21–25, 74, 90, 121, 136, 142, 144, 154–55, 166–67, 169 (f), 170 (f), 171 (f), 173 (f), 174 (f), 177 (f), 182–83, 192, 199nn.10, 11
Mathurin (St.) 130
Matthew the Evangelist, Apostle (St.) 22–23, 29, 36–37, 160–61
Matthias the Apostle (St.) 9, 36–7, 161
Maundy (Holy) Thursday 218n.27
Maurice (Mortiz) (St.) 63
McCourt, Frank 193
McGinley, Phyllis 73
McHugh, Roland xii, 13, 26, 31, 45, 47, 51, 56, 68, 160, 164, 198n.26, 201n.10, 203n.32, 206n.36, 212n.12
Medard (St.) 172 (f)
Melmoth, Sebastian (pseud.) 43, 48
Mercanton, Jacques 189
Mercedarians (o) 131, 134
Methodius (St.) 122
Meyerbeer, Giacomo 143
Michaelmas (feast) 20, 168–69 (f), 175 (f)
Michael Paleologos (Byzantine emperor) 12
Michael the Archangel (St.) 19–21, 175–76 (f), 199n.8
Milan 54, 62
Millifont Abbey (m) 137
Milton, John 18, 199n.3
Minims (Franciscans) (o) 12, 214nn.1, 4
Minkacsy, Michael 216n.2
Molaise (St.) 164
Mona (St.) 92
Monica (St.) 65
Monnier, Adrienne 1, 173
Monte Cassino (m) 136
Mont St.-Jean 23
Mont St.-Michel (m) 20, 136
Moore, George 203n.33
Moore, Thomas 210n.34
More, Thomas (St.) 212n.14
Moseley, Virginia 199n.1
Moses the Black (St.) 182
Most Precious Blood (feast) 7, 172 (f), 173 (f), 194, 218n.26
Mount Aetna 51–52, 156, 169
Mount Athos (m) 121
Mount Melleray (m) 136
Movable feasts 167, 171, 172, 178–79, 218n.26
Murphy-O'Connor, Jerome 201n.4

Nero (Roman emperor) 8–9, 30, 35, 195
Newman, John H. (cardinal) 86, 88–89, 158, 189, 193, 212n.13, 216n.34, 219n.6
New Testament: Acts of the Apostles 30, 36–39, 202n.26, 203n.29; Apocryphra 24, 38, 200n.12; Epistles 17, 20, 35, 38–39, 40–49, 177, 203nn.29, 33; Gospels 17, 21, 22–23, 25–29, 30–32, 161, 177, 199n.11, 200n.20, 216n.6; Revelation 19, 35, 83, 177
Nicea, Council of 63
Nicholas (St.) 206n.30
Nicholas of Cusa (philosopher) 108, 111
Nicholas of Myra (St.) 50, 67–67, 72, 177 (f)
Noah 170
Norris, Margot 211n.39

Oates, Titus 173
Oblates (o) 125
Observants (Franciscans) (o) 12
O'Hanlon, John (canon) 14, 100–105, 189, 198, 209n.5, 210n.30
O Hehir, Brendan 76, 78
Olaf (St.) 126, 130–31
Olaf the White (Norse warlord) 131, 213
Old Catholics (schismatics) 178
Old Testament 17, 66, 105, 144, 163, 170, 192, 199n.13; Daniel 4; Exodus 204n.5; Genesis 66; Isaiah 160; 1 Kings 70; Numbers 24; Psalms 91–92, 202n.24; 1 Samuel 48; Song of Songs 53
Olga (St.) 122
Oliver Plunket (St.) 172–73 (f)
Olivetans (o) 137
O'Neill, Christine 96–97
Onesimus (St.) 14, 170 (f)
Onomastics (name-play) 1, 5–6, 10, 12–13, 22–23, 35, 28, 30–32, 33, 37–39, 40–49, 76, 78, 84–85, 106–7, 122, 147–48, 183–84, 185, 219n.1
Onuphrius (St.) 14–15, 74, 76–85, 100, 210n.29
Oratorians (o) 137
Osiris 20, 78–79, 84–85, 207n.15
Oswald (St.) 170 (f)
O'Toole (Irish king) 211n.36
Oxford University 19–20

Pancras (St.) 61, 172 (f)
Pange lingua gloriosi (hymn) 109, 212n.3
Paphnutius (St.) 77–78
Parandowski, Jan 64–65, 200n.16
Parnell, Charles Stewart 147, 176
Passionists (o) xi, 10, 124, 151
Patrick (St.) 2, 13–14, 15, 39, 86, 89–90, 97, 107, 114, 159, 164–65, 170 (f), 189, 201n.3, 215n.18
Patron saints 3–6, 129–30
Paul (Saul) (St.) 14, 30–36, 37–49, 201nn.3, 6, 203n.33
Pauline Privilege 45–46
Paul of the Cross (St.) 151
Paul the Hermit (St.) 81–82, 84–85, 93
Pentecost (Whitsun) 172 (f), 178–79 (f), 218n.26
Pepi (pharaoh) 84
Pepin the Short (king) 184
Perpetua (St.) 53, 183–84
Peter Nolasco (St.) 131, 134
Peter's Pence 34, 201n.10
Peter the Apostle (St.) 5, 9, 14, 30–35, 38–89, 94, 106–7, 161, 195, 201nn.2–8, 216n.6
Petroc (St.) 106
Petronilla (St.) 34
Petrus Hibernus (theologian) 108–9
Philomela (St.) 111
Philomena 204n.11
Philemon 41
Phocas (St.) 61
Phocas, Paul 61
Piamonti, Petro 215n.25
Pied Friars (o) 145
Pilgrimages 153, 161–66, 179, 186
Pius IX (pope) 7
Pius XI (pope) 148, 204, 218n.26
Pliny the Elder (Roman author) 138
Plummer, Charles 100
Polycarp (St.) 58
Poor Clares (o) 134, 137, 141, 214n.14
Portiuncula 141–42
Possenti Gabriel (St.) 9–10, 126
Potiphar's Wife 170
Pound, Ezra 187
Premonstratensians (o) 134
Presentation (Purification) 169 (f)

Priapus 175
Prophecies of St. Malachy 93–94, 201n.5
Protase (St.) 61–62

Rabaté, Jean-Michel 202n.28
Rabelais, François 206n.36, 214n.1
Raphael, France 162–63
Raphael the Archangel (St.) 176 (f)
Raymond Lull (St.) 131, 213
Raymond Nonnatus (St.) 131–32
Raymond Peñafort (St.) 131
Reading Gaol 42–43, 48
Redemptionists (o) 191
Regula (St.) 63
Relics 11–12, 153–59, 163, 179, 186
Ricci, Matteo 146
Rice, Edmund Ignatius 151
Richard of Chichester (St.) 190, 212n.14
Roche (Rock, Rocco, Roque) (St.) 132, 201n.8
Rory O'Connor (Irish king) 97
Rose, Danis 198n.17, 204n.12, 207n.49, 212n.5
Rose of Lima (St.) 114
Rose of Viterbo (St.) 114, 191
Rouvière, Jean-Baptiste 125

Sabaria (Szombathley, Hungary) 70
Sacred Heart (feast) 213n.21, 218n.26
Sacred Heart of Jesus 159
Salesians (o) 151
Salome 25–26, 40, 200n.16
Samson (St.) 105
Sapphira 39
Satan 19
Saul (Hebrew king) 48
Scapular 144, 168
Schlossman, Beryl 199n.30
Schmitz, Ettore 126–27
Scholastica (St.) 51–53, 135–36, 169
Scholastic philosophy 108–11
Sedulius the Younger (St.) 87
Senan (St.) 93
Septuagesima Sunday 178 (f)
Servites (o) 169 (f)
Seven Sleepers of Marmoutier 70
Shaw, George Bernard 156
Sheed, Frank 94–95

Sienkiewicz, Henryk 190
Silas the Disciple (St.) 38
Simon Stock (St.) 144
Simon the Apostle (St.) 9, 36, 161
Simon the Magus 39
Simon (Simeon) the Stylite (St.) 73–74, 76
Sisters of Charity (o) 214n.14
Sisters of the Sacred Heart (o) 62
Sixtus (pope) 55
Socrates 141–42
Sons of Thunder 37
Spooner, W. H. 202n.26
St. Agatha's Church 145
St. Grouse's Day 13, 174 (f)
St. John at the Latin Gate (church) 26, 200n.18
St. John Lateran (church) 171
St. John Studion (m) 121–22
St. John's Wood (London) 23
St. Partridge Day 13, 174 (f)
St. Patrick's Purgatory. *See* Lough Derg
Stanislaus Kostka (St.) 6, 148–49
Starling, Boris 217n.17
Stations of the Cross 153, 165
Stein, Gertrude 192–93
Stephen (St.) 4, 88–9, 38, 177 (f)
Stephen of Hungary (king) (St.) 130, 176
Suetonius (Roman historian) 43, 202
Sullivan, John 113, 143
Sulpiciens (o) 191
Swithin (St.) 119, 168–69, 172 (f), 173 (f), 190, 218n.30
Sylvania(-us) 74, 76, 208n.22
Sylvester (St.) 178 (f)
Symbols 15, 30, 32, 34, 76, 153, 159–61, 179

Tacitus (Roman historian) 9
Talbot, Matt (Blessed) 124
Tarsicius (St.) 58–59, 194, 205n.15
Tekawitha, Kateri (Blessed) xii
Térèsa of Avila (St.) 112, 145, 191, 193
Tertullian (theologian) 50, 203
Thaddeus the Apostle (St.) 36, 161
Theban Legion 63
Thebes (Luxor) 81–82, 207n.13
Thecla (St.) 38–39

Theresa of Lisieux 123
Thomas Aquinas (St.) 108–10, 140, 142, 191, 211n.2, 212n.3
Thomas the Apostle (St.) 8, 36–7, 161
Thomson, Virgil 220n.17
Thundering Legion 62–63
Thurston, Herbert 197n.5
Timothy the Disciple (St.) 38
Tobias 200
Tranquilla Convent 144–45
Trappists (o) 136, 191
Tree and Stone 31–32
Tree of Life 216n.5
Trent, Council of 145
Treverius (St.) 191
Trieste 2, 58, 65, 67, 86, 106, 177, 188, 194
Trollope, Anthony 127
Twelve Apostles of Clonard 93

Ultan (St.) 106
Uncumber (St.). *See* Wilgefortis (St.)
University College 8, 88, 111, 146
Urban I (pope) 56
Urbi et orbi (papal blessing) 34–35, 56
Ursula (St.) 55, 62, 159

Valentine (St.) 61, 170 (f)
Valentino, Rudolph 60–61, 170 (f)
Vallombrisans (o) 137
Van Mierlo, Wim 70–71, 94
Van Valckenissen, Mary Margaret 192
Varahran V (Persian king) 11
Vatican 9, 94, 158
Venatius Fortunatus (Latin poet) 212n.3

Vergilius (St.) 86
Veronica's Veil 153–54
Vianney, Jean-Baptiste (St.) 81, 123, 208n.18
Vincent Ferrer (St.) 132–33
Vincentians (o) 134
Visitation (feast) 25, 173 (f)
Vladimir (St.) 122

Weaver, Harriet Shaw 31, 54, 78, 149, 159, 170, 183, 198n.14
Wedmore, Peace of 116
Wenceslaus (St.) 126, 133
Wenselaus IV (king) 12, 133
Werburga (St.) 116–17
White Friars (Carmelites) (o) 142, 144–45
Whitly, Synod of 115, 212n.7
Wilde, Oscar 26, 39–49, 202n.26, 203n.36
Wilde, Speranza 209n.5
Wilfrid (St.) 115–16, 190
Wilgefortis (St.) 54, 190, 193, 204n.10
William of Occam (philosopher) 110
William the Conqueror 118–20
Wiseman, Nicholas P. S. (cardinal) 58
Wit (Candida) (St.) 117–18
Wolstan (St.) 118
Woodward, Kenneth L. xii
Wulhere of Mercia (king) 116

Zechariah (Zachary) 21, 24–25, 29, 200
Zita (St.) 113–14
Zosimus (Dublin beggar-bard) 75
Zozimus the Hermit 74
Zürich 61, 63, 200n.21

R. J. Schork is professor emeritus of classics at the University of Massachusetts, Boston. He is the author of *Sacred Song from the Byzantine Pulpit: Romanos the Melodist* (UPF, 1995), *Latin and Roman Culture in Joyce* (UPF, 1997), and *Greek and Hellenic Culture in Joyce* (UPF, 1998).